RUNNING THE GAUNTLET

RUNNING THE

"Heroes, unassuming but possessed of courage and fortitude beyond the power of words to describe, are these men who pass in and out of our portals. They wear no mark of distinction other than the MN silver button, but their deeds rank with the most courageous in the annals of our Empire and their contribution to victory in this great struggle will live so long as men have minds to remember."
— Navy League Merchant Seamen's Club brochure

GAUNTLET

AN

ORAL

HISTORY

OF

CANADIAN

MERCHANT

SEAMEN

IN

WORLD

WAR II

MIKE PARKER

NIMBUS
PUBLISHING LTD

Nimbus Publishing Limited
PO Box 9301, Station A
Halifax, NS B3K 5N5

Design: Kathy Kaulbach, Halifax
Cover photo: Photograph Collection, PANS
Periscope cover photo: Graham McBride, Maritime Museum of the Atlantic
Printed and bound in Canada

Canadian Cataloguing in Publication Data

Parker, Mike.
Running the gauntlet
Includes bibliographical references.
ISBN 1-55109-068-6
1. Merchant seamen–Canada–Biography. 2. World War, 1939-1945–
Campaigns–Atlantic Ocean. 3. World War, 1939-1945–Personal narratives,
Canadian. 4. Merchant marine–Canada–History–20th century.
I. Title.
D810.T8P37 1994   940.54'5971   C94-950030-5

DEDICATION

This book
is respectfully dedicated
to all
Canadian
merchant seamen
who fought to
keep the lifelines
of the world open.

CONTENTS

ACKNOWLEDGEMENTS

Thanks to the Nova Scotia Department of Tourism and Culture for its financial assistance; Nimbus Publishing; Marvin Moore, Lynne Marie Richards and Graham McBride of the Maritime Museum of the Atlantic; Public Archives of Nova Scotia; National Archives of Canada; Senator Jack Marshall; Kathy Kaulback; Dan Harmer; Ralph Stopps; Gary and Barb MacDonald; Keith and Eleanor Lapp; Roy Spry; Jim Lotz; Paul Brick; Angus Campbell; Aubrey Jeffries; George Evans; Arthur Rockwell; Eugene Wilkie; Paul Fralic; Earle Wagner; Jack Matthews; Bruce Duncan; Ralph Kelly; Roy Thorne; Harry Stear; Percy Lambert; Clarence Purcell; Ray Swinemar; Bernard McCluskey; Doug Bauld; Leandre Boudreau; William Falconer; Henry Kohler; Doug Oxner; John Samson; Clyde Getson; Preston Ross; Donald Mosher; Roland Gaudet; Maxwell Tanner; Joseph Noade; Garfield Chinn; Arthur Curren; Pierre Simard; Eric Publicover; Eugene Creaser; Harold Sperry; Jack Mitton; Doug Bell; Warren Stevens; Edison Yeadon; Gordon Hardy; Charles Macauley; Arthur Lockerbie; Gordon Troke; Adrian Blinn; George Auby; Stan McKenzie; Jim Boutilier; Elbert Coldwell; Michael Ness; Robert Gaudet; Ernest Pike; Roland Pickering; Anthony Ross; Bill Roos; Norman Rees-Potter; Robert Bradstock; Perry Ronayne; and last, but certainly at the top of the list, my wife Helen, whose continual support made this book possible.

Running the Gauntlet is an apt title for a history of Canadian merchant seamen in World War II. One old military punishment forced a prisoner to "run the gauntlet" between two rows of men who beat him with clubs or the steel rods used to clean muskets. Underarmed, or all too frequently, unarmed, Allied merchant vessels and their crews transported troops and vital supplies between North America and Great Britain and theatres of war around the world. On these sea routes they were subject to surprise attack at any time as they ran the gauntlet of Axis submarines and shore-based bombers.

Although they suffered proportionately higher casualties than uniformed members of the armed forces, until very recently merchant seamen who served during the world wars were not treated as "veterans" after these wars, but as civilians. They were not entitled to the special benefits offered active servicemen and women, their contribution to the war effort was not the subject of an official history and their sacrifice was not recalled every November 11. Nor were their interests defended in public and before government by influential veterans' organizations. Thus, after the wars, Canadian merchant seamen had to run another gauntlet, that of government neglect and public ignorance, in their search for fair treatment and recognition.

I have been the chairman of the Subcommittee on Veterans' Affairs of the Standing Senate Committee on Social Affairs, Science and Technology for many years. Some of our responsibilities are to oversee the activities of the Department of Veterans' Affairs and, by hearing from veterans' organizations, to ensure that its policies and programs are sensitive to the needs of veterans and their survivors. Over the past ten or fifteen years the Subcommittee has investigated and reported upon many anomalies in the treatment of Canadian veterans, but it was not until 1989 that we were approached by merchant seamen and asked whether the Subcommittee could hear from their organizations as part of a planned study of veterans' benefits.

The wartime service and postwar treatment of the veterans of the Canadian merchant navy became a major focal point of the Subcommittee's hearings and of its January 1991 report, *It's Almost Too Late*. The Subcommittee recommended that full veterans' benefits be extended to all Canadian merchant seamen who had served in dangerous waters and that these merchant seamen be defined as veterans for the purposes of the War Veterans' Allowance Act. To publicly acknowledge the contributions of merchant seamen in Canadian armed conflicts, the Subcommittee recommended that a "Book of Remembrance" honouring merchant seamen who died in action be placed in the Peace Tower and that suitable monuments to their sacrifices be erected.

Canadians pay too little attention to their own history, and the history of the Canadian merchant marine in the world wars has yet to be written. In the course of the hearings of the Subcommittee, I and the other members of the Subcommittee learned something of this history from the briefs submitted and from the personal testimony of the Canadian Merchant Navy Association and the Canadian Merchant Navy Prisoner of War Association.

In the Introduction to *Running the Gauntlet* and the beginning of each chapter, Mike Parker summarizes the tragic losses of ships and men between 1939 and 1945. Some of the merchant seamen who tell their stories speak with justifiable bitterness about their mistreatment after the war. It was this mistreatment that outraged members of the Subcommittee, as it should all Canadians.

Postwar policy toward the ten thousand veterans of the merchant marine was based on the government's desire to encourage expansion of a peacetime merchant marine. To further this objective, the government decided at the end of the war to deny merchant seamen any benefits which might help them to leave the sea for other employment. While veterans of the armed forces were offered programs which enabled them to attend high school, college and university, merchant mariners were offered only educational assistance that would "further their careers at sea." All merchant seamen were denied the veterans' business and professional loans, and only the war-disabled among them could benefit under the Veterans' Land Act. Even disabled merchant seamen were excluded from preferential treatment in the public service under the Veterans' Preference Act because they were classified as civilians.

The long-term human consequences of government policy after the war can be seen in the relative need of veterans and their surviving spouses for financial assistance. One of the witnesses before the Subcommittee calculated that in 1987-88, only 5.2 percent of uniformed veterans or their surviving spouses required financial assistance, but 29.4 percent of veterans of the merchant marine or their surviving spouses required assistance. He concluded: "Stated bluntly, the generous assistance to veterans permitted 95 percent of them to achieve a self-sustaining capability; the neglect accorded to merchant seamen helped create a public expense for 30 percent of its total enrolment, an expense which is ongoing."

The Subcommittee found the original decision to deny seamen the benefits of uniformed veterans "exploitative and unjust" and the refusal to modify this policy in light of the mass unemployment of merchant mariners after the war "undefensible." By 1948 the Department of Transport, which was responsible for the merchant marine and for the delivery of benefits to merchant mariners, was forced to admit that the Canadian merchant marine could only provide employment for four thousand of the ten thousand wartime merchant seamen. Nevertheless, successive governments did nothing to help the unemployable surplus of merchant seamen to train for other jobs.

Public recognition of the vital role played by Canadian merchant seamen is long overdue. Mr. Parker's book allows some of these men to tell the story of their wartime service in their own words. As you read their stories, you may feel, as I did, that you are actually there, going through the horrors of war yourself.

Treatment equal with that for uniformed veterans has yet to be fully achieved. I hope that the Senate Subcommittee on Veterans' Affairs will continue to revisit these issues and to maintain pressure on the government to eliminate the anomalies in our treatment of veterans.

Canada's merchant seamen served their country with honour and personal sacrifice. They deserve our respect and fair treatment.

Honourable Jack Marshall, CD
Senator

MAP OF CONVOY ROUTES

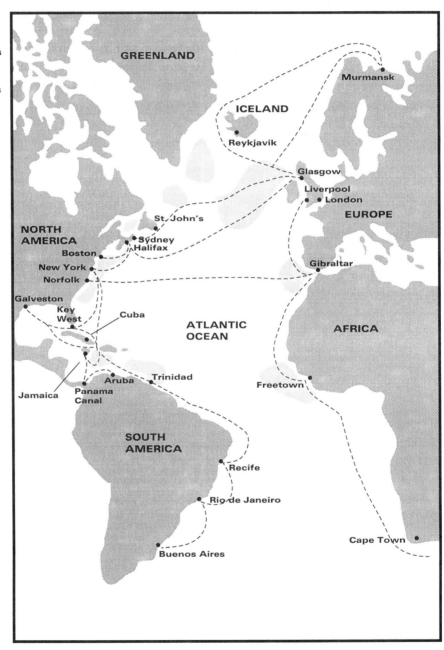

Areas of
Heaviest
U-Boat Attacks

Convoy Routes

GREENLAND

ICELAND

Reykjavik

Murmansk

Glasgow

Liverpool
London

EUROPE

St. John's

NORTH
AMERICA

Sydney
Halifax

Boston

New York

Norfolk

Galveston

Key
West

Cuba

ATLANTIC
OCEAN

Gibraltar

AFRICA

Jamaica

Aruba

Panama
Canal

Trinidad

Freetown

SOUTH
AMERICA

Recife

Rio de Janeiro

Buenos Aires

Cape Town

"My next ship was an old freighter sailing from New York for the British Isles. She was packed with all the high explosives she could hold. We sailed in a large convoy on a Friday. On Wednesday night the cook reminded me that it is a tradition among British merchant seamen that they must have bacon and eggs for breakfast on Thursday. Soon after midnight, therefore, I got my keys and went with the head cook to get the needed stores.

"Being an old-type vessel, the ice-box—a structure about eight feet square, with double walls—was built on the topmost deck so that the cold winds would help preserve the ice and perishable foods. In modern ships, of course, mechanical refrigeration is used. The cook and I were inside this solidly built ice-box when the vessel was hit. It was then that I learned that a noise can be so terrific that you simply do not hear it but instead feel it. You are stunned, deafened. Our ship must have blown up with a tremendous roar, yet I heard nothing. All I know is that the ice-box suddenly heaved beneath our feet; the next moment it was sailing through the air. We crashed into the sea with such force that the ice-box fell apart, and the cook and I found ourselves swimming for it, both badly shaken but otherwise unhurt....

"In a few minutes the rest of the convoy had vanished into the night, but all around us flares were now shedding a weird light upon the scene. Many ships must have been hit, for rafts and lifeboats dotted the sea. An empty raft drifted close and the cook and I clambered aboard. Just before dusk the rescue ship, guided by the flying boat, appeared and picked us up. A few days later we were landed at Halifax and I at once wired my people— resident in Vancouver—that again I was safe. Back came a lengthy wire saying how relieved they were, as they had been officially notified that I was dead; seamen who had seen my ship blow up were positive no member of her crew could possibly have survived. The cook and I did; two out of fifty-five—saved by bacon and eggs!"[1]

Less than 50 percent of merchant crew members survived the sinking of their ships during World War II. Death came quickly, especially in the bone-chilling waters of the winter North Atlantic, often within five minutes; chances of survival then were only one in a hundred. Most of those who did survive kept going back, some to endure other sinkings, others to die. Young Chief Steward Allan Harvie, who recounted the above ill-fated adventure, defied all odds. His vessels were torpedoed on nine occasions and twice he was the sole survivor. It was men like Harvie, and there were many, who led Rear Admiral Leonard Murray, the commander in chief

Canadian North Atlantic, to laud, "The Battle of the Atlantic was not won by any navy or air force, it was won by the courage, fortitude and determination of the British and Allied Merchant Navy."[2]

The Battle of the Atlantic has been described as "the most protracted and bitterly fought campaign ever waged at sea."[3] In six years the loss of ships, materials and lives was greater than the combined naval battles of the previous five centuries. Some have called it the "Battle of the Convoys," others the "Supply War." In March 1941, Winston Churchill dubbed it the "Battle of the Atlantic." He later wrote of its importance: "The Battle of the Atlantic was the dominating factor all through the war. Never for one moment could we forget that everything happening elsewhere, on land, at sea, or in the air, depended ultimately on its outcome, and amid all other cares we viewed its changing fortunes day by day with hope or apprehension."[4]

The Atlantic Ocean stretches from the Arctic to the Antarctic, flanked to the west by the Americas, to the east by Europe and Africa. It encompasses 31.5 million square miles. Across this immense battleground, sailing in all manner and nationality of ships, came the armies and supplies of the Allied war machine. With ever expanding theatres of operation, the supply lines reached beyond the Atlantic boundaries—north to the Barents Sea and Arctic Ocean, south to the Mediterranean, and around the African Horn to the Indian Ocean, the seas of Asia and the Pacific Ocean. It was control of the North Atlantic, however, the shipping lanes between North America and Britain, that held the key to ultimate victory. Statistics show that nearly 75 percent of all merchant tonnage sunk occurred in these waters and those around the U.K. By comparison, only 5 percent was lost in the South Atlantic, 8 percent in the Mediterranean and the Indian Ocean, and 6 percent in the Pacific.[5] "The war had to be waged and waged without cessation in all these theatres. The Allies could withdraw from none of them and neglect none of them.... Yet all their work—even the great campaign against Japan—was secondary and contributory to the final objective, which was the defeat of Germany by an assault mounted from the British Isles....The Atlantic convoy was still the heartbeat of the war."[6]

Convoys—formations of ships travelling under escort—have deterred sea marauders for hundreds of years. The convoy strategy accords with the adage that "there is safety in numbers." This strategy lessens the aggressor's possibilities for attack by narrowing the field of combat from many individual targets to one, while at the same time decreasing the odds of detection. Even a thirty-square-mile convoy, for all its size, is a mere speck in the expanse of the Atlantic. During World War II, merchant ships that sailed independently were sunk four times more often than those that moved in convoy.[7] With adequate tactical support, a convoy can be both a defensive and offensive force. Ignoring the principles of convoy movement proved disastrous for the Allies during both world wars.

In 1578 Englishman William Bourne had first theorized the working mechanics of the submarine. During the American War of Independence

Aerial view of an east-bound convoy, showing vessels taking up their signalled convoy stations from the departure formation outside Halifax approaches, c. 1944.

in 1776, a primitive Yankee submersible nicknamed the "Turtle" put theory to practical application when it attacked a British warship in New York Harbor by trying to attach a keg of gunpowder to its hull. Although the assault was crude and ineffective, it was a first for submarine warfare. Technology developed steadily over the next hundred years, and by the turn of the twentieth century several countries possessed submarines. Yet, the potential of this lethal weapon was still unproven. Entering World War I, Britain and Germany, the major sea combatants, approached its use with different philosophies.

Vanity clouded British reasoning. It was feared that too much emphasis upon the submarine's importance might be seen by other world powers as a sign of weakness. Britannia ruled the waves, its Royal Navy more than capable of sweeping aside any surface-borne enemy threat. Below the surface the submarine might prove useful for reconnaissance patrols or limited coastal defense, but it was viewed as "underhanded, unfair and damned un-English," "the tool of a barbarian." Besides, the rules of war under the Hague Convention clearly stipulated that a warship could not sink an unescorted merchant vessel before issuing a warning and then providing its crew with a safe means of passage to land (and lifeboats alone did not qualify as an adequate means). The confined space of a submarine would prevent these articles from being honoured, thereby restricting its effectiveness. Convoys were thus deemed an unnecessary nuisance by the British, who pursued no means of anti-submarine warfare.

Germany's High Seas Fleet, though powerful in its own right, was clearly no match for the might of the British Grand Fleet. However, its submarines—*unterseebooten*—were superior in range and technology to those of Britain and, by defending its fleet, could possibly balance the scales. When the anticipated battle at sea unfolded into one of cat and mouse rather than outright confrontation, German U-boats took on a more offensive role, first against naval targets, then increasingly against merchant vessels.

Germany pursued a policy of restricted submarine warfare until late 1916, concentrating upon British shipping but at the same time not guaranteeing the safety of neutrals. The nature of submarine warfare made it nearly impossible to be selective and, at any rate, the British were cheating by running up flags of non-belligerents on their merchant ships. Neutral vessels were sunk and damaged, but Germany treaded carefully, fearful of provoking the United States into the war. Germany came close to doing just that in 1915 by sinking the liner *Lusitania* with a loss of twelve hundred lives, more than one hundred American. Despite moral outcries of indignation and tough rhetoric from around the world, nothing materialized from that incident except a hardening of anti-German sentiment.

By 1917 more than thirteen hundred ships had been sunk, yet Britain showed no signs of weakening. Germany's economy was in trouble and the land battle was going poorly. On February 1 of that year, with more than one hundred U-boats in its arsenal, Germany went for the jugular. Unrestricted submarine warfare was declared to starve Britain into surrender and all shipping became fair game. Within three months, eight hundred ships totalling more than 2 million tons went to the bottom. In April alone some four hundred vessels were lost, accounting for nearly 900,000 tons. At this rate it was estimated that Britain could only hold out for six months.

The British Admiralty grudgingly bowed to pressure, swallowed its pride and instituted convoys. Results were dramatic. Losses from independent sailings dropped by more than 80 percent, while only 5 percent of convoyed vessels were sunk. When air cover was used in conjunction with surface escorts, this figure shrunk to a mere one-tenth of 1 percent. When Germany failed to develop new tactics to combat convoys, its fate was sealed.

However, notice had been served. In four years, fifteen thousand men, more than five thousand ships and 11 million tons of shipping had been destroyed.[8] The submarine had brought Britain to the brink of defeat; the nation had survived but just barely. And history would soon repeat itself.

Between wars the victors lapsed into a false sense of security. Germany had lost half her U-boat fleet, and the remaining 170 or so were scrapped. The Treaty of Versailles forbade Germany from ever again building or purchasing submarines. The final assurance against the submarine menace was thought to have come at war's end with the development of asdic, later known as sonar, considered to be the defensive answer. So assured, the navies of Britain, France and the United States rested easy and went about the business of building up their big-ship surface fleets.

Adolph Hitler swept to power in 1933 and, thumbing his nose at the Treaty of Versailles and the world in general, began rearming Germany's military machine. He appointed Karl Donitz to command the U-boat arm of the services. A veteran submariner of World War I, Donitz was the mastermind behind the wolf pack tactics and U-boat surface attacks that would prove to be devastating for Allied shipping during World War II. He believed that Germany had failed against convoys the first time because the U-boats had attacked alone rather than en masse. Give him three hundred from the outset and the result would be different this go-round. He went so far as to publish a treatise on his theory of submarine tactics, an open blueprint for all the world to see. Apparently no one bothered to read or heed its contents.

On August 26, 1939, the British Admiralty issued a prearranged coded message throughout the Empire. One word—FUNNEL—was to signal that all merchant shipping would henceforth be under the directive of the Royal Navy. The Admiralty had resolved not to be caught unawares again. War clouds had been looming for some months and, should hostilities break out, convoys would commence immediately. The storm broke on September 3, 1939, when Great Britain and France declared war on Germany. One week later, Canada issued her own declaration and on September 16, eighteen merchant ships of convoy HX-1 departed from Halifax for the U.K.[9] The battle for the lifelines was beginning again.

Plans for convoys had been in the works as early as 1937. The formidable task of arranging a worldwide network fell to the Admiralty's manager of convoys in World War I. Rear Admiral Eldon Manisty, "whose knowledge of trade matters was probably unequalled anywhere, set off without fanfare on a tour of the world. His leisurely junketings carried him along the great routes of trade and detained him for prolonged periods at the key centres. Shortly after his return to London, those centres began to receive detailed and comprehensive instructions, concerned with the routing, reporting and control of merchant shipping in a time of emergency. The instructions were, in total, a handbook of war; a blueprint for merging the routine supervision of peacetime into the immensely greater and more rigorous process of trade control. By the summer of 1939 the contents of the handbook had been digested."[10]

There was much to digest and it took many months before the entire system worked efficiently. Responsibilities were shared between the Admiralty and the British Ministry of War Transport (the American equivalent being the War Shipping Administration). At the opening shot, merchant captains on British ships around the world opened sealed orders that had been locked away in their ships' safes for a year. These revealed secret call signs, instructions on radio silence and blackout requirements. All movement of trade was controlled from the British Admiralty building in London. From here merchant vessels were herded together, manifest priorities were set, routes were plotted and intricate sailing schedules were tabled. Some ships needed as many as four different convoys to reach their destinations. Naval Control of Shipping offices were responsible for specific ports to facilitate the process. Nine of these were established in Canada. Ottawa played a crucial role as the centre for North American trade control, especially during the first years of the war. Following the American entry in December 1941, a co-operative arrangement between Britain, Canada and the United States was made for the shipping and protection of war supplies and troops.

The task of providing the ways and means of moving trade fell to the Ministry of War Transport. Thousands of ships were needed and many were requisitioned from more than three hundred shipping companies. Everything from tramp steamers to luxury liners were commandeered. As the German blitzkrieg swept through Europe, matters were complicated further as merchant navies-in-exile—from Poland, the Netherlands, Norway, France and Greece—lost home ports and were taken under the Admiralty's wing with all the associated logistical problems. Added to these were neutrals, such as Sweden, who chartered their ships out, and the United States, which for the first two years flagged many of their vessels and crews under Panamanian registry to circumvent the American Neutrality Act. No United States merchant ships were lost to U-boats in the North Atlantic before June 1942, but American ships and seamen under Panamanian flags had gone down as early as June 1940. In fact, most of the 157 Panamanian ships sunk during the war were actually American.[11]

The Ministry of War Transport also oversaw the various agencies whose job it was to arrange cargoes and stow them aboard. Merchant manning pools were established under their auspices to meet the increased demand for crews. Shipbuilding programs were geared up, especially in Canada and the United States, to replace the millions of tons of shipping being lost. Dry dock facilities were needed to repair the more than one thousand Allied merchant vessels that would ultimately be damaged during the course of the war. At any one time the equivalent of two convoys worth of 5000-ton ships were out of action.[12] Millions of dollars in government funding compensated companies for victualling ships, paying crews' wages and lost profits due to wartime service. Wartime insurance claims were underwritten at governments' expense. Financial restitution must have been astronomical— for example, Port Line lost fourteen ships, six of them in the North Atlantic; New Zealand Shipping Company had nineteen go down, ten on the North Atlantic run. No fewer than one-third of British-run ships were foreign-owned.

Within four days of declaring war, the first outbound convoy left Britain for Narvik, Norway, to load ore. Within three weeks, inbound convoys were arriving from Freetown, Gibraltar and Halifax. In its simplest form the strategy was straightforward. With much of Europe soon to be under Nazi control, Britain had to be kept alive for any hope of victory, for it would be the springboard for future Allied assaults. The massive stockpiles required for this task, not to mention to feed the general populace, could only be gotten from North America and had to come by sea. Realizing this, the Germans set out to stop Allied shipping. Both sides drew few lessons from World War I, and so the conflict was fraught with errors.

Winston Churchill wrote, "The U-boat attack was our worst evil. It would have been wise for the Germans to stake all upon it."[13] A check of Allied merchant losses bears this out. German U-boats sank 2,275 vessels in all theatres, compared to 521 sank by mines, 326 by surface raiders, 753 by aircraft and 411 attributed to uncertain causes.[14] Fortunately, at the outset, at least, Hitler did not share Churchill's retrospective appreciation for the U-boat. In fact Hitler was probably Germany's greatest liability throughout the war. He had initially calculated, incorrectly, that Britain would not intervene in his plans to conquer Europe; having achieved that objective he planned to deal with Britian later. Germany's surface navy consisted of only two battle cruisers and three pocket battleships, hardly a threat to the Royal Navy's fourteen capital ships and seven aircraft carriers. Hitler preferred a balanced navy concept and thinking all-out world war was several years away, if it came at all, gave the U-boat arm a low priority. Emphasis was placed instead upon building the reserves of the more prestigious army and air force.

From the outset, Donitz realized the North Atlantic run was critical to the

Allied cause. He calculated that victory at sea and ultimately the war could be won if 800,000 tons of merchant shipping was targeted monthly. But his pleas for an initial fleet of three hundred U-boats to accomplish this task fell on deaf ears and he entered the war with just fifty-six. Even this number is misleading, because ten were inoperable and twenty-four others were only suitable for training exercises and mine laying. Of the remaining twenty-two, only a mere one-third were operational at any given time because one-third were coming and going from stations as relief and one-third were tied up in refit. Reich Marshal Hermann Goering had promised that his Luftwaffe was more than capable of neutralizing commerce. Hitler's underestimation of the importance of North American convoy runs would figure in the final analysis; he listened to Goering, but the Reich marshal never freed up enough planes to impact the battle conclusively.

Hitler's paranoia was another thorn in Donitz's side. He handcuffed the U-boat ace at every turn. Having taken strategically important Norway in early 1940, Hitler was convinced that a British strike to reclaim it was imminent. He insisted upon keeping vital U-boats in reserve to defend this "zone of destiny." And he diverted others to the Mediterranean campaign at a time when they would have been better used in the North Atlantic. Finally, although he tossed out Hague Convention rules early in the war, he gave standing orders to avoid sinking American ships at all costs lest the Americans be provoked into entering the fray as they had done in World War I. Taking on the United States was not in his immediate plans. Thus Donitz's hands were tied.

Roosevelt announced early on that America, although neutral, would give "all aid to Britain short of war." By September 1940, fifty World War I–vintage, four-stacker destroyers had been turned over to Britain in exchange for bases in Newfoundland, Bermuda and the West Indies. In March 1941 Congress passed the Lend-Lease Act. Clandestine support from the U.S. grew and even in July 1941 when the president warned that his country would protect its interests—inserting at least one American merchant ship in convoys as an excuse to deploy escorts—Hitler hedged. After September 1941, United States navy forces were guarding convoys as far east as Iceland. After Pearl Harbor the U-boats were finally turned loose, but valuable time had been lost. Another lesson had been forgotten: submarine warfare cannot be discriminating—barbaric to some, perhaps, but a prerequisite for success.

The Allies themselves were slow studies. They had returned to the more glamorous "big ship navy" mentality. Convoys were of little use without adequate protection. Small, fast-moving escorts, not cumbersome dreadnaughts, were needed but were sorely lacking at the outset. Shipbuilding was geared up, but sufficient numbers of the whaler-design corvette, frigates and sub-killing destroyers were still three years or more away. Merchant ships were armed but most in a token fashion only, more for psychological reasons than practicality. Supply lines lengthened and convoy protection was stretched to the breaking point. Valuable ships were lost at Dunkirk. With a German invasion of Britain imminent and the entry of Japan into the war, escorts were pulled from the North Atlantic run. Others were needed in the Mediterranean for the southern flank battles. For almost the first two years of war, many convoys were left to the mercies of God, good luck and a lone armed merchant cruiser, minesweeper, converted yacht or trawler to see them through.

Asdic gave the navy a measure of defence against submarines, but it had serious flaws. Training manoeuvres had been carried out under ideal conditions. Wartime was another matter. Fluctuations in water temperature and rough weather threw its accuracy askew. It lost targets at close range. Contrary to popular belief, most attacks came not at periscope depth but from the surface. "The U-boat's slow underwater speed made it unsuitable as a full-scale submersible and the Germans used it as a diving torpedo boat. It travelled mostly on the surface, diving only to carry out daylight torpedo attacks or to evade enemy ships or aircraft. The U-boat's main power source was the diesel engines it used on the surface. Because they needed oxygen to operate, the diesels had to be shut off as soon as the boat dived. It then switched to electric motors driven by batteries good for twenty hours at four knots. After that the boat had to surface and use the diesels to recharge its batteries."[15] Unfortunately, asdic could not pick up a surfaced U-boat. Radar was the answer, but it didn't arrive until 1941 and then only on naval ships. The merchant marine went through the war blind.

The navy still looked at convoys as being solely defensive in nature. The view continued that the only way to kill a submarine was to hunt it out, but this was like searching for a needle in a haystack. Much effort was wasted and many merchant ships and seamen's lives were sacrificed pursuing this myopic strategy. It took some time for naval minds to grasp and accept that, offensively speaking, it was better to let the enemy come to you, thus increasing the odds of destroying them or of fending them off with minimal losses in your favour. Air support for convoys was also slow to develop. These principles had been proven in World War I and failure to apply them from the outset caused undue hardships for the merchant navy.

Following Germany's blitz of Poland, the last months of 1939 settled into the "phoney war" on land. "The war at sea, on the contrary, began from the first hour with full intensity."[16] By the end of the first week, thirteen deep-sea merchant ships had been sunk, eleven in the North Atlantic. Until mid-

1940 many merchantmen continued to sail independently, with convoys generally formed up in and around U.K. waters only. Britain required 1 million tons of supplies a week, and at any given time twenty-five hundred merchant ships could be sailing. Within four months of the war's start the combined efforts of U-boats, mines, surface raiders and planes had sunk 215 vessels totalling 748,000 tons of shipping, a rate of loss still considered "acceptable." For the first year, Donitz's plans for wolf packs were hampered by lack of numbers and for the most part U-boats operated individually. Donitz's U-boats were also beset with faulty torpedoes and mechanical defects which took time to correct.

A major break for Donitz came in June 1940 with the fall of France, which provided him with a safe haven on the Atlantic coast from which to operate instead of through the dangerous bottleneck of the heavily guarded North Sea. Still inadequate in numbers, his tiny fleet nevertheless struck out into the Atlantic and began to attack in packs. This was the first of the German "Happy Times." In 1940, 4 million tons of shipping went to the bottom. Convoy SC-7 (from Sydney, Nova Scotia) lost seventeen of thirty-four ships; HX-79 lost twelve. By 1941, three merchant ships were going down for every one built. In comparison, eight U-boats were coming on line to replace every one lost. Another 4 million tons went down that year, and it would get much worse.

The U.S. declaration of war on Germany in December 1941 only made official what had been going on for two years at sea. With all pretenses removed, a second "Happy Time" was in the offing. In January 1942, Donitz dispatched five U-boats to the eastern seaboard of Canada and the United States. What they found was astonishing; the coastline was virtually defenceless. From Newfoundland to the Caribbean they ran amuck. At no time for the next six months were there probably more than twenty-five U-boats on station, but to the helpless merchant seamen it must have seemed like two hundred. By June 1942, one ship was going down every four hours. Only when convoys and air support were rediscovered did the attackers back off.

The outlook remained bleak for the Allies. Donitz merely repositioned his U-boats in mid-Atlantic and now with over one hundred at his disposal in that area alone, turned loose his wolf packs. Long lines of twenty or more U-boats were distributed in grid patterns to intercept convoys. When contact was made, a message went out to Donitz's headquarters in France. Directives were relayed from there for others to converge. When all were in place, the pack moved in for the kill. The results were deadly. Convoy ONS-154, outbound from Britain, lost ten of forty-six ships when attacked by no less than twenty U-boats.

Convoy routes from North America to the United Kingdom took a long northerly sweep past Newfoundland to Iceland and then down, so as to make full use of air bases on Newfoundland, Iceland and Britain. The worst area was the "Greenland Air Gap," a no-man's land of several hundred miles where escorts had no air cover. This killing ground came to be called

Survivors of the *Lady Hawkins*, torpedoed on January 19, 1942. Seventy men lived for five days in an open sixty-foot lifeboat. "Still, voyage after voyage, men who had seen a dozen ships go down about them, men who had been torpedoed once, twice, three times, sailed and sailed again." (Joseph Schull)

the "Black Pit" by the Allies; the Germans knew it as the "Devil's Gorge." At the close of 1942 the year's losses in merchant shipping had reached a crippling 8 million tons.

The North Atlantic run has become synonymous with the battle for the lifelines, but the following example shows just how far-reaching the convoy war had spread. "This Atlantic force of 110 U-boats was by no means the total of German resources. Neither the far northern waters nor the Caribbean were neglected. On one day—March 9 [1943]—five convoys were being simultaneously attacked; two trans-Atlantic convoys, one eastbound and one westbound; a north Russia convoy; a convoy bound from Bahia to Trinidad; and one on passage from the United Kingdom to Gibraltar. The four convoy battles of March involved forces totalling seventy U-boats and thirty-eight Allied escort ships; and resulted in the loss of thirty-seven merchant ships."[17]

March 1943 went out like a lion in the North Atlantic with the Germans sinking over 600,000 tons, 75 percent in convoys. But then the tide turned. The British broke the German secret Enigma codes, thus enabling convoys

Aerial view of the merchant-hulled aircraft carrier (MAC ship) *Empire MacAlpine*. MAC ships generally carried four Fairy Swordfish anti-submarine biplanes. The aircraft were not struck down but were ranged on deck, protected by a rudimentary wind screen.

to be rerouted around wolf packs. This was actually the second time German codes had been broken; the Allies had originally solved them in 1941, but the Germans, unaware of that fact for the duration of the war, unwittingly changed them two years later. The rate of ships built began to outnumber the rate of losses. By the end of 1943, American shipyards had replaced worldwide losses of the previous four years and added 8 million tons. They could build a new ship faster than a damaged one could be repaired. Sufficient numbers of escorts were now available to provide continuous protection across and back. Merchant-hulled aircraft carriers (MACs) first appeared in May 1943 to accompany convoys, thus giving unbroken air cover. Nineteen of these were eventually converted—six from grain carriers and thirteen from tankers—while retaining 80 percent of their carrying capacity. In the 217 convoys escorted by MAC ships—usually working in pairs—no merchant ship was ever sunk.[18] The newer merchant ships were heavily armed. Radar had improved and the multiple bomb-throwing hedgehog proved superior to the depth charge. In addition to MAC ships, very long-range Liberators equipped with powerful search-lights for night hunting closed the mid-ocean air gaps. Hunter-killer groups of frigates and destroyers patrolled the Atlantic; unencumbered by convoy duty, their sole purpose was to rush to trouble spots and hunt U-boats to exhaustion while convoys and escorts moved on. All this spelled doom for the Germans.

In May 1943, Donitz lost thirty-seven U-boats and had another thirty-two damaged. For the first time, sinkings outstripped replacement and the order to retreat was sounded. A counterattack was launched in 1944-45, but by then the U-boat's strength was broken. A deadly new German prototype was in production in 1945 that could have proven disastrous to the Allies, but time ran out. Germany surrendered in early May 1945, followed by Japan four months later. The lifelines of the world had held through six years of war.

It is an accepted fact that May 1943 was the turning point in the U-boat war and after that, as one Canadian merchant veteran stated, "It was all on the down slide for the Germans then." Nevertheless, he was quick to add that, until the bitter end, "the battle for other parts of the world was still going on and you could get torpedoed [not to mention mined, shelled, bombed or strafed] pretty well anywhere in the world." The Battle of the Atlantic lasted for 2,073 days, from the first day of World War II when the liner *Athenia* was torpedoed and lost off the coast of Ireland, until U-881 was hunted down by a United States destroyer east of Newfoundland less than forty-eight hours before Germany's unconditional surrender. In the final analysis, merchant losses were staggering. As just one example, Greece lost 429 of 583 ships. In total, nearly forty-eight hundred Allied vessels were destroyed worldwide, accounting for over 21 million gross tons of shipping. And what of the crews who manned them? Accurate numbers are impossible to ascertain, but the following exemplifies their sacrifices:

In 1938, 192,375 seamen were serving on British merchant ships. Sixty-eight percent were from the U.K., and the remaining 5 percent were mostly other Europeans, 27 percent were Indian or Chinese.[19] By war's end, nearly 30,000 serving aboard British vessels had been killed. Greece lost over

2,000, the United States 6,600. About 1,600 Canadian merchant seamen were killed out of 12,000 who served, making their death toll higher proportionately than Canada's army, navy or air force. Add in the untold numbers of Danes, Swedes, Norwegians, Dutch, Poles, Free French, Australians, Belgians, Yugoslavians, Russians, Estonians, Latvians et al. and the cost was horrific. Churchill wrote of the dead, "Many gallant actions and incredible feats of endurance are recorded but the deeds of those who perished will never be known."[20]

When Canada declared war on September 10, 1939, the country was ill-prepared for the task at hand. Her poorly equipped army, navy and air force consisted of slightly more than ten thousand regular forces personnel. By war's end, more than 1 million, from a male population between the ages of eighteen and forty-five of 2.5 million, had served in uniform. Five army divisions and two armoured brigades went overseas; 222,501 Canadians enlisted in the RCAF and RAF. From a navy of only 11 ships and 1,500 men, the RCN grew to more than 350 warships and 100,000 personnel and escorted over 180 million tons of supplies to the U.K. Their exploits and contributions to final victory have been well documented.

By comparison, the story of our merchant seamen who served on Canadian freighters and tankers or under foreign flags has been virtually ignored. They and their comrades "were another 'few' of whom the many demanded much and to whom much was owed."[21] Without question, had it not been for their dogged perseverance in the face of overwhelming adversity, the wheels of the Allied war machine would have ground to a halt. Far removed from command centres and political arenas, they suffered most from years of neglect, complacency, haggling and tactical blunders. "So long as their ships lined up with the convoys, kept in station, refrained from making smoke or pumping bilges, showed no lights outboard and weren't torpedoed, nobody cared."[22]

As previously mentioned, Canada's merchant seamen suffered the highest death ratio of this country's four fighting services, fully 13 percent. The combined losses of the army, navy and air force were slightly less than 4 percent.[23] What seems inconceivable when hearing of their sacrifices, other than the fact that they went unnoticed and unappreciated for nearly half a century, is that only in 1992 did the Canadian government bestow war veteran status on them, one of the last countries to do so. Equally shameful is the fact that it was not given willingly but only after years of bitter struggle with both of Canada's major political parties.

Lack of a unified voice and little public awareness of what the merchant navy was all about (many still believe they and the navy are one) were in part to blame. However, a greater role was played by the military purists, those in positions to best influence and dictate policy, who felt because merchant seamen were civilians they were in general an undisciplined lot not deserving of veteran status with the other forces. In many cases they were even ostracized by the Canadian Legion for a number of years. Resentment understandably runs deep among merchant veterans. Approximately three thousand remain and it is estimated they are dying at a rate of one every two days. Most see the benefits they are now entitled to—and they are meagre when compared to those the other forces have received—as mere tokenism, a case of appeasement fifty years after the fact.

"The Canadian government always lacked the will to attend to things maritime. They're central; they're worrying about the wheat fields and their Great Lakes and their mines up there and their factories. They don't worry about maritime. More water than anybody in the world except Russia and these guys don't know the first thing about it." This veteran merchant seaman's observation sums up the contentious issue of Canada's merchant marine, or lack of, that simmers today after nearly a century and two world wars. A study in itself and beyond the scope of this book, a few points surrounding this issue must be made to put Canada's wartime contributions into perspective.

At the start of World War I, Canada's experience in building steel ships was minimal, her reputation as a maritime nation based in large measure on the "wooden ships and iron men" of the east coast. This all changed with the losses incurred by the British merchant service in 1917 to German U-boats. Unable to replenish the required numbers at home, orders were placed abroad. By war's end, Canadian industry had produced ninety-four ships, forty-three of them of steel construction. An additional sixty-seven steel-hulled vessels were built for the Canadian Government Merchant Marine (CGMM), which was born out of the necessity to honour her wartime commitments. Another sixty Great Lakers were pressed into active duty. Between August and November 1917, fifty convoys of more than five hundred ships sailed from Halifax. All told, U-boats sunk forty-five Canadian steamships in World War I, taking with them approximately five or six hundred Canadian merchant seamen.[24]

Following the war the CGMM operated with moderate success during the 1920s from both coasts, sailing the world's trade routes. Under the management of Canadian National (CN), the government-owned railway that competed directly with the privately run Canadian Pacific, it became a financial liability during the depression years. Saddled with spiralling debt, the government began to sell off her fleet, and by 1936 the Canadian Government Merchant Marine was no more. Out of the ashes of the CGMM came the Canadian National Steamship (West Indies) Ltd., which ran a

service before and after World War II along the eastern seaboard to the
West Indies (Canadian National Steamship Company Ltd. was a west coast
affiliate). The CNS West Indies' fleet consisted of the passenger-cargo "Lady
Boats" as well as a handful of CGMM freighters that had been taken over
and renamed. A number of CNS ships were lost to enemy action during the
war.

At the opening of hostilities in 1939, Canada was once again in the
position of having to play catch-up. Its so-called merchant navy was similar
in composition to that of the RCN in name only. The merchant navy could
scratch together approximately four hundred ships of all descriptions. The
vast majority were small-tonnage lakers and canal boats working the St.
Lawrence and Great Lakes or coasters plying their trade along the sea-
boards. While many were eventually pressed into service out of sheer
desperation, they were not intended to withstand the rigours of the North
Atlantic. In reality, Canada's deep-sea merchant fleet consisted of only
about thirty-seven vessels, most of them outdated holdovers from the
CGMM days and half a dozen or so Imperial Oil tankers. At the height of
the Battle of the Atlantic, German U-boats could sink this many in one week.

Shipbuilding in Canada was also at a low ebb in 1939 with only two
thousand people employed in the ten yards across the country with the
capacity to produce large, steel-hulled vessels. In 1940, with losses to
Britain's merchant fleet once again growing daily, orders were placed in
both the United States and Canada for replacements based on the British
"North Sands" design of coal- and oil-fired tramp steamers. "British
shipowners, able to rely on domestic sources of cheap and high quality coal,
had been slow to adopt diesel propulsion. In 1939, 26 percent of the United
Kingdom fleet was diesel-engined compared with 62 percent of the Norwegian fleet, which was Britain's main competitor. Although diesel-engined
ships were more expensive to build than coal-fired steamships, they were
cheaper to run and a good deal faster. The fact that such a high proportion
of Britain's merchant fleet was still propelled by slow, coal-burning, steam-
reciprocating-engined ships lowered the speed of wartime convoys, reduced
steaming ranges and inflated the volume of ships needed as well as the
numbers sunk."[25] Those built in the United States for the British carried the
prefix Ocean, while similar Canadian-built ships were preceded by Fort. All
were of similar construction, except the American ships were welded to
speed up production (and a few cracked into pieces because of it), while
Canadians followed the British preference for riveting. Prefabrication
became the norm at many sites, with sections being moved to yards for final
assembly. Canadian-built ships for the British were not sold but "bareboat
chartered" through the crown corporation Wartime Shipping Ltd. to the

British Ministry of War Transport, which in turn arranged for their use with private shipping companies.

By 1942, Canadian shipyards were in full operation on both coasts and up the Great Lakes, turning out both naval and merchant ships. Forty-six of the eighty building berths across the country were devoted to the merchant program and fifty-seven thousand of the eighty-five thousand

Winter scene looking down Eastern Passage, Halifax Harbour, from the iced-up deck of a merchantman. In the background is a laden Liberty ship at anchor, and crossing her bow is the old coal barge *Lucy P. Dow*, a once proud sailing ship now nearing the end of her time.

workers employed worked on merchant vessels.[26] In total, Canadian shipyards launched 456 merchant ships during the war. They were generally two sizes, the 10,000 and 4,700 tonners and 176 were Canadian-owned and operated through the crown corporation Park Steamship Company Limited and named after federal, provincial and municipal parks, for example, the *Point Pleasant Park*. Two hundred and ten merchant vessels served while flying the Canadian Red Ensign,[27] including coasters, lake boats, deep-sea freighters and tankers; sixty-seven were sunk.[28] The early years were the worst for Canadian merchant seamen, who suffered 88 percent of their casualties before 1943.[29]

With the return of British chartered ships at war's end, Canada possessed one of the world's largest merchant marines. Burdened once again with a surplus of inefficient coal-burning ships and with union strife growing, Canada's fleet was disbanded and sold off. "It is a poor epitaph to their gallant, dogged war that the Canadian Merchant Marine died from failure of government policy after it was over. Sixty percent of the nation's trade—its lifeblood in war or peace—must move by sea, yet the Canadian Merchant Marine of those fighting days has never been revived."[30]

Two merchantmen in convoy are silhouetted against the night sky by the spectacular explosion of a torpedoed tanker or ammunition ship.
(U.S. Navy photo)

For wartime services rendered, the reward for most Canadian merchant seamen in the late 1940s was unemployment, as the dream of a postwar merchant marine dissipated for a second time in less than two decades. No fanfare or golden handshakes marked their passing, only baseball bats and gunshots on the waterfront as the infamous Hal Banks was brought in from south of the border to impose the will of the Canadian government and big business to subdue the upstart seamen's union. There were no veteran parades, few war memorials, little if any mention at Remembrance Day services, no land or house grants, education funding or veteran job preferences to honour their wartime contributions as there were for the other services. It seems hardly a fitting tribute for a group one veteran honoured by writing: "These nondescript fellows share a common courage that is one of the wonders of the war. More than the fighter pilots, the commandos, or the dashing torpedo-boat types of our own service, these men truly deserve to be called the Bravest of the Brave."[31]

This book contains fifty accounts of Canadian merchant veterans who served during World War II. They were seamen, A.B.s, stokers, oilers, firemen, engineers, wireless operators, mates, stewards, cooks and galley boys. Most came ashore after the war to other lives, but some remained at sea for a variety of companies, a few becoming masters of their vessels. Their collective voices are representative of the thousands who manned the bridges, decks and engine rooms of tankers and freighters from Murmansk to Rangoon, Halifax to Maracaibo, and countless points between and beyond. They fought through against the Axis powers and the elements. Some were sunk by torpedoes, gunfire, mines or human error. Others were among the "lucky" ones who kept their ships under them for the duration. A few were taken prisoners of war. Their narratives are interwoven with fear, sorrow, resignation, pride, humour, comradeship and sense of duty. In a deadly game of chess played out on the oceans and seas of the world, and under rules beyond their control, they and fellow shipmates were pawns from the opening gambit.

"There cannot ever have been a much harder test of courage than to man a slow merchant ship in a winter convoy—to be stationed on deck with the solitary inefficient gun and see nothing to shoot at but to see the columns of smoke as ship after ship was torpedoed, or to sweat in the stokehold seeing nothing but only feeling the explosions—and all the time to expect to be blown to bits or slowly drowned in the dark and the numbing sea. These men were not compelled by any kind of discipline but their own and nobody can quite explain in retrospect why they went on doing it."[32]

The Fourth Arm

"Merchant seamen virtually form the fourth arm of the fighting services, and despite their reticence to blazen abroad their exploits, we feel that in fairness to them and their next of kin, the Canadian public should be told of their work."
— Hon. J.E. Michaud, Minister of Transport during the war years

In 1939 there were only twelve hundred Canadian merchant seamen, many of them holdovers from the old CGMM days. In six years their numbers would grow tenfold. "All volunteer. You got yourself into trouble with your own mouth by signing up. You said, 'I'll go.' Nobody asked you why, you just went. No experience required."[1] Some came out of retirement; many were too young or physically unfit for the "regular forces"; a few were judged to be the wrong colour. Others simply chose the merchant marine as their way to serve.

Their motto was "we deliver the goods," but in the beginning few Canadian ships were capable of making the delivery. For the first couple of years they made do with what was available, often walking the streets and docks, checking the various shipping offices and foreign consulates in hopes of catching on with any type of flagged ship. Some were choosy but others could care less what they sailed aboard. Wages and living conditions were as varied as the nationality of crews and the personalities of the skippers.

Out of the initial chaos of scrounging ships and men, some semblance of order began to take shape by mid-1941 as the Canadian merchant navy emerged. On May 19, an order-in-council was passed which stated, "The merchant marine, on which our seaborne commerce depends, is under present conditions virtually an arm of our fighting services, and the provision of merchant seamen, their training, care and protection is essential to the proper conduct of war and vitally necessary to the keeping open of the sea lanes on which the successful outcome of the present conflict so largely depends."[2]

A director of merchant seamen was appointed whose responsibilities were varied. Under his auspices, manning pools were established to provide food and lodging for Canadian and foreign seamen and to serve as a source of crews for merchant ships. Four were operated in Canada during the war: they were started in Halifax in September 1941, in Montreal in January 1942, Vancouver in May 1942 and Saint John in July 1942. Training facilities for merchant crews also came under the director. St. Margaret's Sea

Training School in Nova Scotia offered a thirteen-week course for cadet officers, and a six-week course for stokehold and engine room ratings was offered in Prescott, Ontario. Upgrading was provided at various locations for merchant seamen with the necessary experience and qualifications who wished to advance their careers as marine engineers or navigational officers. A twelve-month course for wireless operators provided tuition refunds on condition they serve for two years in a manning pool. Ship's cooks were to be trained in manning pool kitchens, but with only four pools available, numbers would be small and there were hundreds of ships to feed. Most cooks learned at the school of hard knocks as they went.

The welfare of all merchant seamen regardless of nationality also fell under the director's care. This was accomplished by enlisting the aid of many private service organizations. With the aid of government funding, the Navy League of Canada operated nine Allied Merchant Seamen's Clubs and four others specifically for merchant officers to provide social respite as well as meals, lodging and medical care. More than eighty thousand merchant men from thirty countries were housed at the Halifax club alone in one year.[3] By war's end, these thirteen clubs had serviced more than two million men.[4] In addition, a variety of auxiliary groups including the Red Cross, Salvation Army, Knights of Columbus, YMCA, Women's Canadian Club, IODE and women's naval auxiliaries supplied books and magazines, ditty bags of personal items, games and knitted clothing.

An effort was also made to standardize wages among Canadian ships, and by April 1944 a number of minor benefits and perks were promised to entice more Canadian seamen to join the manning pools rather than seek employment aboard foreign ships. This no doubt worked especially in the case of those going to sea for the first time, but many of the old hands who had been at it for some years by then remained independent, preferring freedom of choice to the regimentation of manning pools. Considering the risks incurred, one cannot blame them.

The merchant marine was very much a male-dominated profession with only 2 percent of those working deep sea in 1938 being women, most as stewardesses aboard passenger ships. This percentage declined even further during the war.[5] One exception to the rule was Fern Blodgett Sunde who grew up in Coburg, Ontario. Although one would be hard-pressed to find women who served aboard Canadian ships—not to say there were none— such was not the case with some foreign countries such as Norway. Fern went to night school for eighteen months to train as a wireless operator and through a bureaucratic loophole signed on the Norwegian cargo ship *Mosdale* at Montreal in June 1941. *Mosdale*, a fifteen-knot fruit carrier (the only one of six that started the war to survive) made ninety-eight crossings during the Battle of the Atlantic, more than any other Allied vessel. Fern Blodgett sailed on seventy-eight of them, eventually marrying the captain, Gerner Sunde, in Saint John, New Brunswick, in July 1942.[6]

A level of vigilance and battle readiness was maintained on both coasts throughout the war. However, even though a Japanese submarine torpedoed the Canadian-built (and U.S.-purchased) *Fort Camosun* off the Washington coast in mid-1942 and then proceeded to shell a lighthouse at Estevan Point on Vancouver Island, any threat to Canada from the Pacific was more perceived than real. This is borne out in the case of Imperial Oil tankers which carried no armament on the west coast.[7] Should the Japanese come, the Americans were there. That is not to say the west had no part to play in the supply war. West coast shipyards such as Burrard Dry Dock Co. Ltd. built a large number of Park ships and similar North Sands–style boats for the Americans and the British. Most, however, eventually found their way into the Atlantic via the Panama Canal as did the majority of Canadian merchant seamen.

Chapter 1 is an overview of merchant navy life as seen through the memories and experiences of three war veterans. Merchant seamen were a breed apart from any of the other forces. The conditions under which they toiled dictated that they must be. "Without uniform, unrecognized, back and forth across a hostile sea they sailed...."[8]

Paul Brick

As soon as war broke out, all Canadian shipping and all British shipping came under the Admiralty rules. In certain areas they even took over the running of American ships. The Admiralty had to tell us what cargoes they wanted and where to go. They designated actually when they built a ship, it would be hull sixty-two and people would be jumping in for priorities. They'd say, "Well, that one's going to be called a Fort boat and a company called Cunard will be managing that ship." The next one would come off the line and it would be called a Park boat, "The Canadian Pacific Steamship will be managing that one." Then the Americans come into the war and they didn't know what the hell they were doin'. It was easier to hang their hat on the British, the British were running it anyway. Just make up the convoys, and you're going to South Africa, you're going to the Mediterranean, you're going to Britain and you're going to Murmansk. And you're going to carry a cargo of so and so. The company would proceed to get her loaded, crewed and everything else and put her out in convoy. After that, she was guided by the British Admiralty. There was no great fuss. It was a very complex organization and the British did it very, very well.

We had a standard of wages you couldn't go below. Canada paid a little bit above the British; Australians were not badly paid, about the same as Canadians. Now if the Americans wanted somebody you jumped at it right away. More money, and the American ships, even their naval ships, had far better food than the Canadians. I would say the Americans and the Swedes were the top paid in the world. Swedish were neutrals and they paid double just to get the men because they never went back to Sweden much. The Canadian government for a Swedish charter—they needed bottoms to ship in—they'd pay a hell of a big bonus to the Swedes and the Swedes would pay the crews a big bonus. The Swedes used to travel in our convoys, they were painted white with the Swedish flag painted on the side of the ship; they didn't put wartime paint on. We'd not allow them to put their lights on when they were in our convoys, but if they were travelling independently they kept their lights on as a neutral vessel. Quite a few Swedes were sunk.

Danish, French, Dutch, a lot of Canadians in those [ships]. There were a lot of Canadians in Norwegian ships, an awful lot. We had a place down here in Chester called "Little Norway" where they had a merchant navy manning pool for Norwegians only. The Norwegian government-in-exile [established it]. Then they had "Little Norway" in Toronto Island where their air force was; they didn't have an army here at all. They shipped a lot of their crown jewels and everything to Britain during the war as security and a lot of it came here to Canada. There's quite a few [Norwegians] still here and their descendants.[9]

Once France fell, Britain became a very hungry nation. You would have a mixture of munitions and food for the U.K. If you were going into the Far East once war broke there in '41, you took some food, but mostly munitions, tanks, trucks, bombs and so forth. You'd be taking food, trucks, ammunition, bombs and guns to Murmansk and Archangel. The Malta, North Atlantic and Murmansk convoys were by far the worst. The North Atlantic was a hell of a lookin' place by the end of 1942. Christ Almighty, it looked like a graveyard.

The biggest point on our coast of course was Halifax. Then there was Newport News, Virginia. You went from Halifax to Newport News and formed your convoys up from there through the Mediterranean. Malta convoys all left from Hampton Roads after awhile, the big port next to Newport News. You anchored there and went straight across the mid–South Atlantic. If you were going to South Africa et cetera, you went down to Trinidad and took off from there.

Any of the Allied nations would have made up a twenty or thirty vessel convoy. Some would be up as high as ninety or a hundred.[10] Some would come overloaded, but most came out in ballast to load in Halifax, Montreal, Saint John, St. John's, all the way along the river ports. We had several assembly points here—Halifax, Sydney, St. John's, Newfoundland, and up the [St. Lawrence] River around Father Point. In the winter you didn't get any convoys out of the River and very little out of Sydney, just the steel products.

Could be as much as two or three weeks, maybe four, waiting for a convoy to form. Bored to tears—delays, delays, delays. It was $6 for you to get out to your ship if it was anchored in Bedford Basin. They had small boats and used to pick you up at the Immigration Pier down in the South End [of Halifax]. Generally you made only the one trip and that was being paid for by the company to join a ship, or you made one trip off which was to leave a ship. If the crew had the money they could go back and forth as much as they liked. It was very costly unless the company was paying, and they paid through the nose.

Torpedo net at Halifax Harbour, showing floats and gate vessel *Andrée Dupré*. Two balls hanging from its mast signal that the net is open.

The Naval Control of Shipping, which is still in place [organized convoys].[11] There was an officer and generally two or three ratings with him in every port. I would suggest he was a merchant naval captain or a naval captain with merchant experience. The gate boats came under him. There were torpedo gates here off Halifax. Ships towed the steel mesh fence across the harbour right to the bottom, sixty or seventy feet. They had little floats that kept them up. Two ships, gate vessels, would part it. When they wanted to enter a ship, they gave a pre-arranged signal and, if it wasn't right, there was a naval ship patrolling off there. Lots of ships didn't travel in convoy to go from say Shelburne, Liverpool or Sydney to here. Some were doing coastal trade, some were coming to form part of the convoy. If they could avoid convoy they would, because it was a pain in the arse.

Naval Control of Shipping would do the convoy conferences too. They packed right into the room at Admiralty House or at Stadacona. The captain and wireless officer used to go from each ship. There was always a convoy commodore. He was generally a retired merchant seaman or a retired naval officer and given the title just for one trip only as convoy commodore. He

Convoy conference at Admiralty House, Halifax.

could easily have been an active commodore navy or an active captain merchant navy. There would be several naval officers there. They would be instructing the captains on signalling. There was always the local admiral of the port; he called it to order and so on and so forth. The escort [commander] would be there and several other people. The wireless operators were over on one side being given instructions on signals only. Then they would all come back to the ships. When they took them out to the ship, they were never allowed ashore again.

The captain would have a little black bag that was sealed. The only person that could break the seal on it was the captain. He would have his destination, the names of all the other ships in the convoy, what her cargo was and all the visual signals, flag signals called mersigs, that we were going to use during the passage. Your mersigs book was generally out all day on the chartroom table in case there was a signal flashed. It was a little spiral book that went into a very heavy box with holes cut into it and locked every time you put it there. Everything was in that box on the bridge; each ship had a steel box. The officer of the watch's first duty when the ship was hit was to drop the mersigs box over the side. The wireless operator had his own little sealed canvas bag with a big lead weight on it. In that was his signals he would get over the air. We had three operators [doing eight-hour shifts] right around the clock listening all the time; [they] very, very rarely transmitted.

You generally sailed pretty quickly [after the conference]. Sometimes there'd be a hitch in the system, you could be out there for a week or ten days, but you were stuck, you couldn't get off. They would say to get your steam up for a certain hour—a coal burner you could do it in six to ten hours. You'd stop at about three-quarters steam because you'd be wasting fuel if you didn't. Then you would get the word and we would be right up to full steam. There was a harbour pilot went aboard each ship and that was the signal you could lift up your anchor and go. They let the pilot off out by the Neverfail Shoal buoy. Sometimes they were short of pilots and they let the experienced captains who'd been in and out a lot of times take their own ship out.

So, up anchor at a specific time and we would all come out in a single line through the mouth of the harbour. Then the captain would break his sealed orders. Once we got outside, we would form up in convoy formation—eighteen hundred feet apart to the left and to the right, eighteen hundred feet ahead and astern. It would take you about six hours to form up a convoy, getting everybody into position. The convoy commodore would take the lead and by flags he would be putting people into positions. They designated that before you left. There were signals flying back and forth. Remember, there were no radio signals, no walkie-talkies or any of that; it was all done with flag signals and Morse lamp.

There'd be some coming up from New York, Baltimore, Philadelphia, there may be twenty of them. The convoy commodore, say from New York, brought them there safely and relinquished his charge. Maybe the guy from Halifax was going to be the big cheese this time. Or the guy from Philadelphia was going to do it right across the ocean. He was organized from Philadelphia and the ships from New York, Boston, Baltimore all came out and joined him. Our guys just steamed out and joined his convoy.

You all lined up outside and then headed east. In the meantime the guy

at Sydney was forming his crowd up. They opened up the boom gates there and it was so timed that the convoy from Father's Point was being escorted down, say six ships, and they all had prearranged places. They had attended a convoy conference in Quebec City that was exactly the same that was being held here. The ones in Sydney would have been doing exactly the same thing and each peg fitted into the hole. It was a very complex thing. They all moved into their positions: line nine, vessel six; line ten, vessel four. That took almost a day, still only doing about seven knots.

Merchant ships in Sydney Harbour, Cape Breton. Some would join Halifax-based convoys while others would originate from Sydney. Designated SC convoys, for Sydney-Clyde, they came to be called Slow Convoys as they were many times composed of tramps too slow to maintain a convoy's normal minimum nine-knot pace.

The last in the [outside] right-hand column and the last in the left-hand corner was always referred to as coffin corner. They were generally the first guy to get it. The Germans would come up from the stern, you see. Tankers [and ammunition ships] went pretty well in the middle; they'd be hard to get at. You possibly could get up to ninety, ninety-five ships; they never got much over a hundred. It gave the wolf pack a big target to shoot at—twenty or forty square miles.

You went in off St. John's, Newfoundland, where they were forming up the final one. The major escort party, say six ships, would come out. That's where they were stationed, on the Newfie-Derry run, St. John's, Newfoundland, to Londonderry. The Canadians pretty well stuck to us till we got to Londonderry, then handed it over to the British navy and our guys would escort the other convoy coming back. A lot of the American [escorts] would stop mid-ocean, British would take over and the Americans would go north, pick up a convoy and take it back. Once you were changing escorts about mid-ocean you used to get a little upset because it was more or less, in your own mind, the point of no return. If you'd been torpedoed the day before, you'd have gone back to Canada—if you'd lived. If you were torpedoed the next day, you were going to the U.K. and may be there for months.

You did your own repairs. If it was a case of a permanent breakdown, you had a tug in the convoy. There were rescue ships coming up the stern, generally a small merchantman or a navy vessel, sometimes two or three, depending upon the size of the convoy. They would generally be faster than the other ships. They picked up all the people that were in the water [after being torpedoed]. Some of us stopped, and of course it was at our own peril because once your ship is stopped he's a perfect target for the U-boat.

You had a little blue megaphonic light, a fog light about that size [of a silver dollar] on the stern of the ship; that's what the other ship steered by. The rest of the time you had nothing. Oh, God no, no lights at all! In fog you carried what's called a fog buoy. It was let out on the end of a rope and it had a scoop that shot a six-foot spurt of water up into the air. It just went through a chute like a funnel and, phew, up into the air. That's what you kept a look out for all the time. You'd shout out that you're coming up on the other guy's fog buoy which was six hundred feet astern of the ship. We didn't have [radar] until after the war. The navy ships had it. No merchant ship that I know of had it.

Fog, terrible storms, I think they're all about equal. In fog your whistles were going, you were listening all the time. We iced up a few times, but nothing spectacular; I didn't get mixed up too much in that. I think the worst was your gale-force winds. If you couldn't control your ship all that well that's when it got real dangerous. You'd yaw sixty to a hundred feet either side of your course. The convoy would spread out; you had a lot of collisions. A lot of the masters and mates were very inexperienced and we had to learn. I was very, very fortunate to be with some of the most competent officers that anybody could be with.

Very near ones, oh, I can tell you, very, very close; I'm talkin' six or eight feet. During a storm the ship that was ahead of us pulled out of line and put up a signal that she was broke down. So we altered to go around her and she fell this way with her bow pointed to right angles. We were just going around here when her engines started again. She come right under our stern, oh, you could have thrown a rock at her. That happened quite often. This is where a lot of the masters died young. There was always a near collision in every convoy, nothing ever went smooth.

Dusk and just as the sun was coming up was your most dangerous attack times. Lots of times the submarine would come up in the middle of a convoy, flick up a flare and quickly submerge. He took a terrible risk, but there's always that to do. Then the rest of the wolf pack could see what he was doing—bingo, bingo, bingo—as many as they could. You'd keep steaming. When there was an attack on, you would close up together within about twelve hundred feet, or the order would come to disperse because there was not enough escort to fight them off. Most times you weren't told because they could hold them off pretty well. So you would piss off in different directions, the ships goin' this way and that way. You just aimed for the continent and put every damn ounce of steam on her you could. You take a Park ship, they were built for ten knots. Well, we'd get them up to twelve, twelve and a half, just a pumpin'. You were given a point ahead, maybe 150 miles, where you were to form up again. Everywhere along the line there was a rendezvous point. If you lost a convoy at A, they told you where to get it at B. You knew your rendezvous points all the way across the ocean. There was a lot of thinking went into a convoy.

We would stretch out to our eighteen hundred feet [upon reforming after an attack] and when you got to a certain point in the ocean they began breaking you up. There would be a reappointment of commodores. You broke off and went to Murmansk, Archangel or one of those ports from just south of Cape Farewell in Greenland. You went that far north in a great circle [to avoid submarines and benefit from land-based air cover] and ten, twelve, fourteen ships would be going onto Murmansk [via Iceland]. There'd be the group that was going south to the English Channel, into Falmouth, Southampton, those places. There'd be those that would be breaking off for Ireland, Liverpool and the Clyde. You'd have one escort for every three or four ships.

As soon as you broke off convoy, you knew exactly where you were going. You knew pretty well just by looking at the cargo, you'd have a good feel. God, the place was always ripe with rumour. Right from Montreal, you'd say to yourself, "Well, here, this is Bombay, there's no question about that. Why would they need tropical clothes in Murmansk?" But that was also a ploy of our government, you know. They were very, very smart about it. They would kit out a regiment in England for the tropics. They'd go aboard the troop ship and end up in Iceland with all their heavy weather gear down below. That's how they invaded Spitzbergen way up within the Arctic Circle. There were several other islands they did the same sort of thing and got away with it.

Your whole thinking changed with the cargo. If you were carrying foodstuffs you had a little better feeling. Wheat or general cargo, you had a pretty good chance of getting away. If you were carrying ore, once you were hit you just went plop, straight down. Your chances were nil if she [an ammunition ship] was hit. Take short steps and keep your backside tight, that's the only advice I can give you. These guys that were carrying this casing oil and hydrochloric acid and sulphuric acid–10,000 tons of that– how do you think they felt? Phew! A lot of them as a result of that became heavy drinkers. I must say that the understanding companies sent these people off for treatment and 99 percent of them turned out to be awfully fine people. There were a lot of guys that went through hell, a lot, lot worse than I.

I went to sea in '41. I was coming onto seventeen and-a-half and I knew between then and my nineteenth birthday, and being called up, you had to make your mind up. The only people that were doing any drafting was the army–you had to apply to the navy and air force–and I had no preference for the army whatsoever. Not that I don't have any time for them as a group, you don't go in any wars without an army, it was just not my choice of a way to die. I thought I would get myself some experience in the merchant marine, and if I did have to go into the armed forces I could go into the navy or the air force. I wanted to serve, so I made up my mind, left school [he had been born in Windsor, Ontario], went to Montreal and was able to join a British ship. I wasn't in Canada much after I went to sea.

I had no formal training at first. I felt, if I was going to do this for a lifetime, I would rather be an officer in the ship. I eventually went on to St. Margaret's Sea Training School. You came out of there as a cadet, the most junior rank. We got less than the ordinary seamen; we got paid a pittance because you went back to becoming an apprentice. They started St. Margaret's Sea Training School, a lovely set-up, in Hubbards, Nova Scotia, in late 1941. The old Iona Hotel was where you actually ate and they had two big long barracks and a gymnasium in the back where they taught sea training. They had a mock ship built where you could do rigging and stuff like that. They had rowboats you rowed around in. You did marching; what the hell good that did us, I don't know. My class was 103. It was a three-month course; we were called "Ninety-Day Wonders."

Fifty dollars a month was my maximum for the first two years and found [food and lodging]. I got a pair of pants, a jacket and a hat for a uniform. You went over to Goldberg's Clothiers [on Barrington Street in Halifax] and you had a little piece of paper. He measured you up and the government paid him. Cadets [had a uniform], but not the seamen; seamen didn't get issued with anything at all. I spent three years at sea as a cadet before I became a senior watch-keeping officer. You were in charge of the ship from eight in the morning until noon and from eight at night until midnight. In your eight hours off you did two or three hours work for the ship. By the end of the war I was a senior third mate with what they called a permit, not a certificate. I wrote my second mate's certificate in 1946. It took you twelve years to get your master's foreign-going license. These were in the old days; it's all changed, it's a better system now. Today it's become very, very sophisticated and they've got it so if you really click in properly you can do it in eight or nine years.

Deck boys, ordinary seamen, A.B.s [able-bodied seamen], bosun was the deck department. Also in there you had a lamp trimmer, which was his original job, but he was really a storekeeper. There was a fireman's school in Ontario where they trained greasers, oilers, firemen, wipers, trimmers, which were all about the same rank. Then you had a fellow called the donkey man. He was given that name because he used to stoke the donkey boiler, which was the spare boiler in the ship. You came out as a trimmer, but a trained fireman, and you were also given instruction in oiling and everything else. See, all the ships at the outbreak of war were coal burners; they didn't get converted to oil until about 1943 or '44. You generally had four ordinary seamen, six A.B.s, nine firemen, three trimmers, three oilers, three wipers. It varied on the size and horsepower of the ship. On the smaller ships you would have proportionately less. On those coasters there'd only be about fourteen or fifteen [crew] in those days, and on the foreign-going ones there were about thirty-six to forty. A coaster is a vessel that generally sticks close to working the American-Canadian coasts and up into the [Great] Lakes as opposed to a foreign-going ship which goes anywhere in the world. Coasters are generally small, four- or five-hatch ships. The average [foreign-going vessel] would be about 10,000 tons out of Canada.

On the steward's side you had a scullery man, galley boy, peggy, steward, second cook, cook and chief steward. A scullery man used to peel the potatoes and that sort of thing. A peggy, the lowest form of life, used to wait on tables and served the seamen and firemen. That's deck, engine and steward. Then there was just the officers above that—captain, chief officer, second officer, third officer. You had three radio officers, senior and two juniors. Then you had the chief engineer, second engineer, third, fourth, fifth [engineers] and an electrician who was generally the third engineer. The fifth engineer did all the engineering work on deck, and the other three kept the watches in the engine room.

I was twice in the Montreal manning pool. I was never in the Halifax manning pool, but we would come here and when we were looking for crew we got them from the manning pool. They would allow a foreigner to join the manning pool if they needed them and a lot of them did. I was in the

Allied Merchant Seamen's Club before there was a manning pool. Allied Merchant Seamen's Club [on Hollis Street in Halifax] was separate from the Canadian manning pool and also separate from the YMCA. There were three because there wasn't enough room. The foreign ships come in and wanted say six seamen, they would go to the Allied Seamen's Club. If they couldn't fill it from there, they went to our manning pool. The guy down at the Allied Merchant Seamen's, if he was Indian and belonged to a British company—say British India Line or one of those—he was not on pay. They got an allowance; I don't know what it was. They were torpedoed off here and living in there, waiting for a British ship that wanted a Lascar [native East Indian] crew. When a ship come in wanting an Indian crew, which was often, you were out there, on and gone. You didn't waste much time here.

The Allied Merchant Seamen's Home [Club], the bunks were four high,

Allied Merchant Seamen's Club, Hollis Street, Halifax.

so there'd be sixteen to a room about this size. It could be as high as three hundred in there and she'd be full. There'd be all nationalities. As you went you registered and they tried to put as many Canadians in one room, Brits in the other, Indians in another and whatever in the others. I think it was a dollar a night. You paid for your breakfast. If you wanted lunch I think you paid fifty cents and supper was I think seventy-five cents. The food was adequate. If you were on the system you got little meal tickets you just handed to the girl. Now who actually paid for it I don't know; I think it was subsidized by the federal government.

There were specific rising hours; a chap came along and woke you up at seven in the morning. You had to be up, dressed and clean. Your bed had to be made by yourself. They didn't want you hanging around the bedrooms after eight o'clock. You had fairly big rec rooms where you could set around and play cards, smoke and whatever. Generally all you had to do was walk around, there was nothing else to do. You couldn't move on Barrington Street after ten o'clock in the morning for [all the] service people and merchant seamen. You just walked back and forth. I think you had to report in every twenty-four hours, and the minute a ship came, you were assigned to it right there from the Allied Merchant Seamen's Home or the YMCA and they sent you right down to your ship.

From the manning pool they didn't actually specify an hour you had to be in at night, but when you were in there you were under very, very strong discipline. They had complete control of you over there. Your name was on the board and they'd call out the names [for ships]. Everybody'd be waiting around because you're anxious to get out and on full pay. If you were living in the manning pool you didn't get any war risk bonus.[12] The minute you stepped aboard the ship you got a $44-a-month raise right away. The manning pool, you'd go out for something, come back, and within four or five hours you'd find your name had gone up ten on the board. Then all of a sudden your name would come. You were allowed to turn down your first two ships, but you must take the third, government rule; I think the British and the Americans had the same privilege. The reason for it being, if you were an experienced seaman and you saw the name of the ship, you immediately in your own mind thought you knew where she was going and it would be a place you didn't want to go. A lot of people didn't want to go on the Malta runs and the Murmansk runs but they certainly would like a West Indian run or they would even enjoy a trip to Britain. The reason I say "enjoy a trip" is that when you sailed from Canada to Britain there was beer at both ends—I just use beer as the thing—beer and ladies at both ends of the deal. If you made the trip to West Africa we'll say, there was no beer and not too many suitable ladies.

Most people used to rather be down in the Allied Merchant Seamen's place. First of all it was closer to town and secondly you could get beer there. What they used to do for fifty-two cents, they'd give you a little copper washer one day, a little brass washer the next, each day they'd change. That entitled you to two quarts of beer, a dollar four. You couldn't take them out, and before you got your second bottle of beer you had to give in your first empty. There and the North End Canteen–and I think there was a place up on the Citadel–was the only place we could get beer.

The people here of Halifax that worked in those canteens and so on were marvellous people, just the salt of the earth. All volunteers, they never got a damn nickel for anything. Some of the people would see that you were really on hard times and they would make sure you got the best, all they could give you. Their hearts really went out to us, they thought the world of us. Ashore here in Halifax, let's face it, Halifax wasn't the best place in

Allied Merchant Seamen's Club, Halifax, N.S. "The people here of Halifax that worked in those canteens and so on were marvellous people, just the salt of the earth."

the world to be during the war. People were not very friendly. The only people that really made you feel at home were those that worked in the canteens in public places. There were only three or four restaurants and they went from bad to worse. You had to be anointed by Christ himself to eat in the Nova Scotian Hotel; a line-up four miles long, you'd never get a room there. The Lord Nelson Hotel was for senior merchant seamen– captains and chief engineers. The mates and engineers slept in the Carleton [Hotel] and so on down the line. YMCA or the Allied Merchant Seamen's Home was the bottom of the barrel.

You walked carefully. Several footpads would work you over and take your money quickly. A footpad's a nice fellow–Englishmen call 'em that– they used to pad their feet so they wouldn't be heard walkin' up behind you and pound the piss out of you and take your money. You could get your pants pressed with them right on, get your hat blocked right on top of your head and close your eyes with a couple of fists. Oh yeah, there were quite a few of them and generally our own people. Oh yes, rob each other. That's not confined to merchant seamen, that's navy. If they had civilian clothes, they'd rob you as quick as look at you. Christ, they were as bad as anybody else, they could use the money.

You never got into a Halifax home, nobody ever, nobody. If you did get into a home, it was from somebody who had come here. The Halifax home was closed to you. Matter of fact, I was in and out of Halifax seven or eight years before I got into an actual Halifax home. That's the reason for the terrible riots on V-E Day; they tore the place to pieces. People of Halifax at that time were very, very cold. I guess it was old Halifax.

Montreal was very, very warm. Saint John, New Brunswick, was just beautifully warm, it was a pleasure to go there. St. John's, Newfoundland, was just marvellous, they were great to you, they gave you all they had. Sydney, most of the time you spent there was at anchor, but if you did get ashore you were treated very, very well. There was a Naval Control of Shipping officer there, a marvellous fellow—I can't think of his name—he made sure that you really got looked after.

Halifax at the time was called "Slackers" and anybody who stayed in Halifax was a "slacker." That's a term by the navy, said against the navy. A lot of guys came down here, joined the navy and never got out of Halifax, whole war. A lot of them come to Shelburne, never sailed so much as a dory out of Shelburne. The navy, I think it took nineteen people ashore to keep one man at sea. With us, it took a manager, an assistant manager, an engineering superintendent, a marine superintendent and three girls in an office to keep five hundred men at sea. That's a fact. There were stevedores if you want to count them, they had to load and discharge the ships. We were still an average of half a person sending twenty to sea. There were no slackers. There were a hundred thousand naval personnel and they lost one in forty-seven. We lost one in ten.[13] Doesn't that give you some sort of message? We didn't call them slackers; our guys didn't have time to spell it. We never fought outright with them, just left them alone. If you had a friend in the navy, you'd invite him aboard. We did eat better than they and we had better quarters than they in the end. We got along fairly well; we did our gunnery training with them and they didn't bother us a hell of a lot.

It used to vex us. I came in from Liverpool [England] with about 4,000 tons of Russian ballast in us. We were escorted by a Canadian corvette and went into Digby, Nova Scotia, where we brought out stevedores who hand-unloaded the ballast and dropped it into the harbour. I would say it took about four days. We came over to Saint John, and this corvette was in the shipyards going into refit. The crew were released the day we docked, all going off with their seabags. We went into the dockyard and were out of there in forty-eight hours with a complete underwater clean, painted and everything else—out and loaded. Went over to Manchester, came back down to Swansea, loaded 10,000 tons of coal—we were using a lot of Welsh anthracite here during the war—came back to Saint John, New Brunswick. We're looking at two months anyway. We unloaded the coal and loaded ammunition, guns, tanks, the whole works. We had to go up to the shipyard to get some heavy welding for the tanks; you welded them into troughs on deck. And here was this same corvette alongside, she was still in refit, and the crew just rejoining after two and a half months god-damn leave. Next time I saw her she was in for another refit. What I'm saying is, a corvette as opposed to a merchant ship only had those few guns aboard and an engine not half as complex as what we had. What the hell took all the time?

The backbone of the Royal Canadian Navy at the outbreak of the war were merchant seamen.[14] Most of the merchantmen were RCNR, naval reserves, and they would work for three weeks in the summertime for the navy and the rest of the time the merchant ships. If they were in the reserve [they were ordered to report at the outbreak of war], but an awful lot volunteered too. There would be a man who was a third mate on a merchant ship with a master's certificate in the reserve navy. He knew he wasn't going to get a second mate's or a mate's, chief officer or master's job because the ships weren't coming that fast. So in the navy he would get to be a lieutenant, maybe a lieutenant commander and he would certainly get much more money and supplied with a uniform, medicine, dentistry and everything else. We never got a thing. A lot of ratings—bosuns, carpenters, A.B.s, ordinary seamen—would also be in the naval reserve and when war broke out they went right in. I would say that 60 to 70 percent of the naval ships were manned for the first two years by merchant seamen with naval training. Some of them stayed in the navy; as a matter of fact, a few of them became very top-class naval officers. As the Canadian naval officer got better trained, then he stepped in.

I don't remember when it was they actually froze us in our positions, you couldn't leave. It would be mid-1940, maybe mid-1941. If you left your ship and didn't come back or you left to join another ship they made sure you joined or they immediately conscripted you into the army. They found it terribly difficult to keep track of us and there were a certain amount of desertions, there's no doubt about that. But in proportion to our armed forces it was just minimal.

If you buggered off in a place like Cape Town, they had great plans for you. Say you ran into a well-constructed young lady and you thought you'd use her body for pleasure for a spell, so you just didn't bother going back, you missed the ship. Then the military police very shortly had a handle on you. They let you fill your cup and then they nailed you, put you in jail. You could be there four to six weeks. They didn't treat you all that well, the odd nob across the head if they felt like it, you see. Then they put you on a merchant ship and sent you back to England—that's generally where you went—for a shilling a month; about twenty cents, that was your pay. Nobody ever collected it. You got to England and then you got another four to six weeks to cool off. All this you're not paid for it, so you often wonder if that young lady was worth it. Then you went back to Canada and you were put in the manning pool. You couldn't refuse any ships then, you had to take your first ship, and if you didn't you went in the army. There were some who genuinely did miss the ship, but it was the same boot, same arse.

You had some leave; I think it amounted to about half a day a month. When you went ashore, there was the rum, bum and 'baccy girl. She was there for that purpose, she knew what her job was, she knew it well. Occasionally you got into the romantic situation. Say a little port, I'll just take one out of my head, Lourenço Marques, down in East Africa. Beautiful beaches, lovely hotels, terrific class system, you were going with a real class girl. You'd say to yourself, "Is it worth it? Is it worth me going to jail for? If I get away with it, is it worth hiding until the war is over? Will I ever take this girl home?" You were very, very seriously tempted to jump ship or just miss her—all these thoughts going back to the docks. You generally chose the ship instead of her.

There were some good ports. The West Indian ports we used to call romantic ports, particularly Cuba. You'd get good safe liquor compared to a lot of places like in Egypt; they used to make a drink called "Arrack"—terrible. I think in India the only safe drink was a gin made in India, the rest was just methyl hydrate full and full. If you had Canadian, American or British liquor, that was fine, but the beer out there was terrible, just terrible, so you didn't bother to drink it.

In the early part of the war, if you were going south, which was the West Indies and so forth, you went without convoy, which was very, very dangerous. A lot of people were torpedoed all along the American coast once the U-boats got over there. And the Americans wouldn't black their nation out, so we made a perfect silhouette coming down for the Germans. We implored the Americans to turn their lights down, but they wouldn't until they started losing a few ships. Then they certainly shut their lights down, but they had to be knocked on the head to do it.

You'd stop in Jamaica, Trinidad, British Guiana, Barbados, Antigua; you hit all those ports exporting to Britain or back to Canada. You carried lumber, building materials, you name it, down and brought rum, sugar, molasses back. One of the biggest mines in the world at one time for bauxite was down in British Guiana. That was a regular run from there to Port Alfred, Quebec. They needed the aluminum for aircraft. There were a lot of torpedoings there. The ships were sunk in thirty-five and forty feet of water and their masts and everything else sticking up. Same with the British coast and North African; took them years to clean it up. Cape Town, Port Elizabeth, New London, they were nice ports to go to down in South Africa. A lot of people liked that, but the Germans torpedoed an awful lot of ships down there.

There were ports that you just detested. For instance, the small ports over in Britain, you were being watched very, very closely. Manchester was beautiful, everybody welcomed you. London was being bombed all the time and it stunk. Liverpool was dirty. Ports like Bombay, most of the nights you never went ashore. You had nothing in common. Calcutta, places like that, you might take one or two nights ashore. The Indian run was poor; there was just nothing for you at the other end. The Indian people would have made you feel as much at home as they possibly could, but there was a language barrier. Of course the British were not very popular out there at that time; British aren't popular there now. Once the Americans got out there and began opening up their system a bit, it was good. There were very, very strict rules over there as to who could go where with what. The Americans didn't understand, didn't want to understand, they just bull-dozed everything.

I was one of the ones on the Indian run. I don't know how many trips I made out from Canada to there, four or five: Calcutta, Trincomalee, Vishakhapatnam, Karachi, Ceylon, Colombo, Madras, Pondicherry, up the Chindwin River to Chittagong, all through there; take high octane gas, in cases, up to Trincomalee and discharge it right into the aircraft carrier. Some you'd put ashore; we had a big fighter base out of Colombo—some Canadians, an awful lot of British. If you went into India and West Africa, you couldn't get outside the dock gate without everybody with their hand out. The danger of getting your head knocked off was pretty high. You didn't go ashore much at night, particularly in the early part of the war when there was a great danger of the Allies losing.

The Arabs hated us and still do. You didn't trust him one bit. As merchant seamen we were all right. The Arabs unloaded us okay, went ashore at night, and we put a guard on the gangway.[15] If we were going ashore at night, we always made sure you wore your merchant navy pin or some identification. Then the British troops left you alone, the Indian troops left you alone, the New Zealanders and Australians left you alone; our own Canadian troops welcomed you. But you always went to the proper places where there was a group of whites. You never went into Arab districts at all; you got the hell out of there; they'd steal the eyes right out of you.

During the whole war, I must have been in fifteen or twenty convoys, maybe more than that. Some were very, very short–four or five days–you'd be going, say, from New York to Halifax. When you were going anywhere into the Far East, you would have a short convoy from here to Norfolk, then the big, long convoy across the Mediterranean. The convoy would break up somewhere off Port Said. You'd go through the [Suez] Canal and the convoy wouldn't reform. There were convoys in the Red Sea, but [they] were stopped in 1943 because they pushed the Germans back. You went as far as Aden where you anchored and waited to form up another convoy which took you to Bombay, Calcutta, Karachi. They convoyed all over the Indian coast. Madras to Calcutta was only forty hours, but you were in convoy–five or six ships with an escort. The Japanese were very good at sneak attack stuff. At the mouth of the Ganges River we anchored, waiting to go up to Calcutta, and they were only sixty miles away and could go at us at will. But I must say the British fighter craft were very good there and the Indians were very, very good at ack-ack.

We had one of our ships, the *Fort Stikine*, explode in Bombay. It lifted a 10,000-ton ship right out of the water and put it on the dock. I was there about two weeks after. She had the best on board, gun cotton and dynamite in layers, beautiful. Boom, boom, boom, boom she went; killed five or six thousand, you know. Oh yes, made an awful noise.

Between Gibraltar and Malta we lost an awful lot of big ships and a lot of capital naval ships. God, we lost a lot of people. Everybody on the island of Malta was given the George Cross; they were bombed sometimes seventy times a day.[16] There were a lot of air raids on our convoys. Thank God we were in the middle, we were full of ammunition; fragments and shrapnel, but never enough to stop us from going; bombs going off close enough to shake the hell out of the ship. You'd see some awful dogfights. That's when they came out with glider bombs. They'd drop it from a bomber a good distance away and they'd be able to radio-guide it towards the ship. It wasn't very successful, but they got a few ships.[17]

The whole of the Mediterranean on both sides were German and Italians. Spaniards were worse, bastards; they're the guys that invented the limpet mine. You anchored in Gibraltar and these guys would come along in the two-man submarine and all along your bilges they'd screw limpet mines. As soon as you started up your engines, blew the side right out of your god-damn ship. The Italians were good at that.[18] So what we used to do, they had these little mine layers, about sixty-foot craft, and you used to steam around the harbour with fifty-pound depth charges at night and they didn't know you were doing it. Throw two out, boom, up they'd go. A lot of them just came up in pieces. They did get a few ships, so they earned their pay.

You slept with your life jacket. A lot of people used it for a pillow. You always carried a blanket. Once you were torpedoed you cut a hole in it and put it over you like a cape. You slept at sea in your clothes, and in port you slept in your underwear but with your clothing handy. I slept below in a few of the ships, but mostly I slept on the upper deck. Those guys [below] had two or three flights of stairs to get up and a lot of doorways to go through.

I did one trip to Murmansk; I helped deliver a Canadian icebreaker, the *Montcalm*. That was in 1943 and was a very, very fast, uneventful trip; we were back in six weeks from leaving Liverpool. I did the D-Day landing and the Burma landing. D-Day, we were a mile and a half off the beach. We did three trips, two from Southampton and one from London. A big 10,000-ton freighter, I would suggest we had 7,000 tons of equipment aboard. We had tank landing craft which we put in the water and they got the rest of the Bren gun carriers and scout carriers. Ammunition, we unloaded that like it was going out of style into small boats. The three trips were very, very quick and in six weeks we were on our way through the Mediterranean again because we were desperately needed out in the Far East. The Japanese were very close to taking India–very, very close. If it hadn't been for the British and Indian troops, they'd have taken the whole of India, no trouble at all. Then we would have had one hell of a time getting it back. My part in the destruction of Hirohito or Hitler, you could put a mark on the wall and they wouldn't see it, but I was there and felt I had done my share.

[The years] 1941 and '42 is when it was a really bad time for us both, Americans and ourselves. The Americans didn't have many escort vessels, they were churning them out at the rate of knots, but there was never enough. You'd be lucky to get one armed merchantman in each convoy [in the beginning]. We had several–the *Prince Robert, Prince George, Prince Henry*– I can't think of all the ones we had. These were ships that were manned by both merchantmen and navy people, generally commanded by a naval officer. They generally carried troops, classy ammunition–real sophisti- cated stuff, you know–and they would carry the general staff, the army staff and so on. I would suggest that some of the bigger ones had up to five-inch guns and piles of Oerlikons and Vickers. I never got aboard any of that. The armament was very interesting to me, but I didn't see much of it.

I know what we had at the end of the war [for armament] and I know what we had when I first went to sea. The first one, the Limoges, all we had was the twelve-pounder and four Oerlikons. We had DEMS gunners–defen- sively-equipped merchant ship gunners–aboard. The Americans called them "the Armed Guard." They were naval personnel; you could have a soldier, marine or sailor as a gunner. They were trained ashore and brought to us. The last, going off in 1945, we had nineteen of them aboard. As you came near the end of the war we could throw up some darned good flak. I think we made a very good account of ourselves.

The American Liberty class ship could throw up as much flak as a corvette; they could scare the enemy off very quick. They had a four-inch aft and a twelve-pounder forward. They were more heavily armed [than Canadian merchant ships] because they got into it a little bit later and had time to prepare; we didn't. We were good at firing at aircraft, but we very rarely got shots off at the submarine. We left that up to the destroyers and corvettes because they could put up an awful lot of fight and drive them off. That depth charge is a terrible thing, you know, a hell of a way to die.[19]

At the first, of course, everything was in its birthing stages. Shipowners were trying to find their feet, wages were all scrambly, the stevedores were trying to get themselves organized. Oh yeah, there was a hell of a lot of "friendly" sabotage. The ship itself was in very bad shape. Some of those foreign ships, Greek ships, they had terrible, terrible conditions. If the men thought they could get something for themselves, at least decent food, they would hold the ship up. You can't blame them. In the older ships you got a can of condensed milk. You opened it but only put small holes in it, then you put match sticks in it because the god-damn cockroaches got in. When they baked their own bread on board, you cut it very, very thin, then put it up to the light and poked the rat shit out of it. I'm tellin' you, that's fact, not fiction! Cheese, Jesus Christ Almighty, the mold on that. You didn't get all that much butter. The peanut butter came in five-gallon tins with the oil right on the top and you had to, uuugh, terrible stuff. Jam came in five-gallon tins and all you could say was that it had been introduced to strawberries at a distance. All it was was gelatin with a hell of a lot of sweet in it.

From '41 until late '43 we got terrible food. The British ships got terrible food even after the war. They had ice boxes; once the ice was gone, that was the end of your fresh food, the rest was all salt. It was only after the war that they started building their ships with fridges in them. Americans had it a lot better. Other than that, you couldn't get them to go to sea, could you? No sir, you're not going to get an American to go to sea under those conditions. Now they did go under terrible conditions before the war, they needed the work. And at the outbreak of war there were some terrible ships, oh Jesus, they were old. A lot of the old ships were sunk, thank God they were. They had to do something to attract good men to go to sea. When the rumours got around that the food was good, conditions were better, men came. Between January and June of 1942, it really began to improve. I was always in well-found ships, good feeders; I have no quarrel with that.

In the Canadian merchant marine, I would say, when the new ships started coming, late '41, early '42, the morale started to skyrocket and was at its peak all through the last three years of the war. Willing and able to go anywhere in the world and proud to go. Prior to that, we didn't have very much to offer, did we? But once we got the team going and the chain links in position, gosh, we had high morale. The British kept their morale all through it. Norway, Denmark, Holland, France, their morale was low in this way. Any ship that did get away, these fellows knew that until we got into the invasion and got their homelands back for them, they had nowhere to go but here. Their morale was quite low, I would say, until about 1944 when it started to spring alive again and dreams of getting home were coming to fruition.

You had really good fellowship; there was an awful lot of comradeship. There was no trouble with language or colour. If you were picking people up torpedoed, you didn't ask their religion, what colour they were, you didn't ask anything. Even if they were the enemy, you picked them up, put them on deck and looked after them. Get them washed down, get 'em warm, get 'em a drink, get 'em a cigarette. Politics on board ship, particularly Canadian ships, the older people were rather cynical about it. We paid very little attention to politicians. Very rarely did you even discuss religion. Matter of fact, I was at sea for years with fellows and didn't even know what their religion was or did I care.

Our discipline was twice what their's [the armed forces] was because the captains were very, very powerful. These wartime articles, when you signed those brother, you signed your life away. They could take your livelihood away for good. In the navy you got a rap on the fingers if you were out pissed up somewhere. Sure you got thirty days cell or you got this or the other thing, but once it was over, it was over. With us, the Old Man [captain] would say, "That's going to cost you five days' pay," and that was it. The other thing was, if he wanted to say to the local authorities, "This guy isn't worth a cupful of cold water, I want him put in jail," that's what they would do. They'd say, "There you are, a useless merchant seaman. He's causing trouble on the ship." The captain had the power.

But then we had a sense of freedom, a form of independence. We had the choice of turning down the first two ships—had to take the third. We didn't wear a uniform. We had the respect for the officers, of course, a hell of a lot of respect for them, but we certainly weren't going to bow down. We didn't have to salute or any of that shit, you know. This is one of the things that did not help our cause because we were very quick to tell a fella to go take a flying.... If you went ashore, there was no being back at midnight, none of that crap, as long as you were back to start your day's work, regardless of the state you were in.

But you didn't want to come back with too many hangovers too many days in a row or the mate or chief engineer would see it and you'd have a little chat first, a little heart-to-heart. Then the next time you were logged a day's, two or three days' pay. And the next time you found your arse in a real bit of a rat trap. You were told, "This is your last warning. Do it again and it's cells for you. We're finished, we're just going to pay you off right here in Calcutta or Madras. And although we will pay your way home, there's no question about that, dear boy, plan on a year out of your life getting home because I'll make it so god-damn difficult for you that your hemorrhoids will have hemorrhoids. We're going to keep you here in Madras for investigation for about two months—I'll tell the police. Then we're going to work you up to Calcutta and get you to miss trains. Then all of a sudden, we're going to have mythical dysentery here. We're going to put you in a hospital where you're twelve thousandth on the list. There's nothing that an Indian doctor would love more than to shove a big knuckle finger up your arse about three times a day. Then we're going to take twenty-one days to get you across India along with six hundred people hanging on this one freight car all belching and farting at the same time. Then you're going to get to Bombay. You're going to miss four troop ships. In the meantime we're going to put you in the Seamen's Home down there where there's bound to be a lot of homosexuals. A lot of those Arabs like small boys and you're just about the right size."

The son of a bitch has got nine months out of his life by the time he gets home and he's begging to go back to sea, begging to never drink again, never smoke, copulation is out, never again. This is all bureaucratic mistakes and they're capable of it, make your life so miserable you'd tell people, "Look, here's the three hymns I want sung at my funeral, I'm going to die between now and tomorrow." It was that bad. Now, the army can't treat you that way. You get into a place like Takoradi down on the old Gold Coast [Ghana], you get in jail in there, it's not nice, you know, not nice. They'd dearly love to get at you. So you just behaved yourself, not to your own complete satisfaction at all, but to their satisfaction.

Canadian merchant seamen were noted for their sense of humour, could laugh at themselves. Americans could laugh at themselves. We got shit. "Where the hell were you during the war? I never heard a thing about you. Where's that uniform? Where'd you lose your arm?" But we kept our sense of humour right to today. See, once we left a ship, we went off pay. The navy was on pay 365 days a year. He got free medicine, free dentistry, free uniforms, subsidy, the whole works. We didn't. The minute you [merchant seamen] were torpedoed, your pay stopped. Bingo! You weren't working, were you? You were in your lifeboat. Are you talking about a just society or something? When you got back to port, the quicker you got back to work the better. And if you wanted a little torpedo leave, which I think came to about four days, it took me two days to get home and two days to get back, so you didn't bother with any of that crap, did you? The bullet or torpedo that sunk the ship and sunk the naval officer, the merchant naval officer, the crew member and naval A.B. was the same thing. But the navy, immediately that the husband was killed, or the father or son, the next of kin got their insurance, allowance, the whole works. It was one full year before the next of kin of a merchant seaman, British and Canadian, could be told that he was even missing. And when they did, if the company that he was working for did happen to have torpedo or wartime insurance, the next of kin got pennies.

Those guys that were in prisoner-of-war [camps], their pay stopped the minute they were torpedoed. Some are still paid on the Dieppe formula, an old British rule. I don't think the Americans were as archaic as us. The Dieppe formula is when we lost most of our people to becoming prisoners of war. From there until the end of the war, they totalled up the months from August 1942 until May 1945 and used that as the blanket overall pay they got. Well, some of our merchant seamen were torpedoed in 1940, so they were in the [camps] for sixty months, but they only got thirty months' pay, whatever these guys [received] in Dieppe. Hong Kong people went in '41 and they were living on the Dieppe formula until they kicked up shit. They're starting to come around now. The merchant navy, of course, we're always tail-end Charlie.

One thing has to be remembered: the air force fellow, a hell of a good guy, got a lot of time for him. He had his four hours of flight, came home, had his three squares a day. Certainly, he had that four or five hours where he lived in terror. The Canadian naval fella on convoy work, sure he had one hell of a rough time, rough. Their ships were not that good, neither was their food all that good. But when they got to port they got time off, and when their ships went into refit they had their way paid home, had their dental bills, their clothes, their medical bills, everything, looked after. The army never really did a hell of a lot except the Dieppe raid until early 1943, when they went into Italy, then the D-Day landings. They distinguished itself, there's no doubt about it. But ordinarily the merchant seaman could be at sea and in danger for nine-tenths of your time. We had that terror all the time, night and day, night and day.

I was very lucky and I'm glad, touch wood, that nothing did happen to me. If anything did, it's not visible. I'm not bitter about it anymore, a bit disappointed in the government that they didn't recognize us as veterans. That's the thing to come, but it's almost too late. We're treated shabbily, I can't understand it.

The G.S. [General Service] and the non-conscription issue was the big thing [during the war], there was a lot of talk about that. I never had the privilege to vote [on conscription]; I was old enough to fight for the country but not old enough to vote. There was a thing called a "Zombie," I think that's kind of a derogatory term. You had a little circle black patch with a red G.S. on your arm–General Service–that meant you would go overseas. If you didn't have that on your arm, that meant you were a Zombie. They were perfectly prepared to fight to the last drop of their own blood to protect Canada, but they were not going overseas. A goodly portion of these came from people educated. There were hundreds of them manning the guns out here, they guarded prison camps, all kinds of stuff. They did a hell of a lot of good stuff and, mind you, the army pushed off some crap on them too.... I had no trouble with them, no feelings for them one way or the other. The only guys that bothered me, bothered me badly, were those that got the educational and political deferment. I don't feel too bitter about it now, but I did at the time because I thought it was a rather cheap and dastardly way to avoid a war. Their excuse, and their parents' excuse, was that they had to have somebody educated after the war to look after the peace. You can see how well they did, you can see the kind of mess we're in now. The academics have put us there, great fellows.

I'm rather happy to have been there. I'm very, very pleased that I didn't go into the army, navy or air force. I never took it too seriously, never took life too seriously. You didn't know if it was going to be your last day or not. We certainly respected the enemy, but there was no good crying about it. What the hell, why go around with a long face? If today is the last day, let's live it right up to the hilt, don't save too much for tomorrow.

Charles Macauley

I had always wanted to go to sea. I had polio and my dad, looking ahead, had made arrangements for me to go as midshipman in the Royal Navy. My dad was a lawyer; he wrote and made all the inquiries. They had agreed to take me because I was still capable of doing all these things that were required. However, the Royal Canadian Navy didn't look at it that way, so my mother [his father had died], being a pretty wise woman, when I was just turned seventeen, made arrangements for me to go to sea as an apprentice in the merchant service.

I had to, in those days, go back to Hubbards here in Nova Scotia at the Sea Training School at St. Margaret's.[20] I was there I guess in the latter part of '42 or the very early part of '43. Then I went and joined a ship on the west coast of all places; I went all the way back out. The ship I was on was called the *Mount Douglas Park*, 10,000-ton North Sands cargo type, steam. She was originally a Fort ship, spanking new, for the British. Most of the crew was British, not all but most of it.

The apprentices didn't go through the manning pool, we went directly to the ship. Just the two apprentices on that ship; that was normal for that type of vessel. They called us cadet officers, but I was also indentured to the company; I signed a four-year indentureship. They undertook to train you and pay you very little while it was being done. They'd feed you and board you, but you had to supply your own clothes and so on. We wore a uniform; our parents supplied that. My indentures were exactly the same as my chief officer's word for word—he had served his time in sail—except that I got more money than he did—$8.91 a month and my board. The pay increased marginally but not enough to get excited about really. We got half [war risk bonus] because we were under twenty-one; over twenty-one they got $44 a month. We couldn't get into too much mischief because we didn't have enough money.

I was fortunate in the first two years of my sea time; the men that were on the ship—by and large the biggest majority I worked with on deck and even down below—were old, experienced merchantmen and, if you were willing to learn, they were willing to teach you and I learned a great deal from that. From the older officers too—I learned how to be an officer. We got help—not all ships did, but we did from time to time—if the officers had time they'd give us instruction. Our captain was a very fine old gentleman, a Canadian, taken out of retirement. Captain Steven Clarke was his name and he bought me and the other apprentices our first book on navigation, Volume 1 of *Nichol's Concise Guide*; I still have it.

We were taught under the old system, if you want to call it that. In the beginning every dirty job that came along we got, and I have to go along with that because if you're going to tell men to do things then you've got to have been able to have done them yourself in the practical way. I'm talking about cleaning bilges and cleaning dirty old steam winches and painting them and all that. That was part of the apprentice's job in training. But each year as you progressed in your time you got better jobs and things that would help you more as you went up toward getting the time for your ticket. With me and Roy [Koch], just about the time the war ended, we were getting ready to sit for our tickets. We had, for the want of a better expression, bonus time because we did our time during the war. We didn't have to do the full four years. They would accept I think—now I can't swear this is correct—we only had to do about three and a half years or something and then we could go and sit for second mate's.

When Roy and I joined the *Mount Douglas Park* our chief officer was a little Danish man by the name of Jensen, a very, very fine man, I can't speak highly enough of him. I sailed with him after the war too in a Chinese ship. The first place he sent us was to the top of the TND gear, torpedo net defence gear. That was to find out whether we could work in heights, because he had no special use for what he used to call "flyin' fish sailors" that couldn't get any higher off than the deck. You had to go aloft to please Mr. Jensen.

In the pecking order we were [lower than ordinary seamen] in the beginning in particular, but when you became a more senior apprentice you became more valuable to the ship because you could do more things. Our bosun was an old sailing-ship man and our carpenter was an old sailing-ship carpenter; he was a proper shipwright. Mr. Hansen was Danish and our bosun was a German. First class seamen, boy, I'll tell you; they were good men, but they didn't fool around either. One of the proudest days of my life was when the bosun told me to rerig the cargo gear on the derricks on number two hold when we were underway. It meant that he had confidence in the work I was going to do—my splicing was good, my practical seamanship was good. I nearly popped all the buttons off my shirt. But that's the way it went and this is the way you learned.

We weren't allowed to mix with the crew. We lived amidships. We could be friendly and everything with them, but we couldn't hang out back aft; the Old Man wouldn't stand for that. We were in between; it could be awkward sometimes but not too often. There was discipline and respect, but the respect that was given was earned respect, it wasn't just given because a person was a mate or a master. There's all kinds of respect too. There is that which is required and that which is freely given. By and large you were just one of the crowd and you got along. But you'd run against the odd bonehead once in awhile, but amongst men this can happen because the petty officers and the officers and us apprentices stayed in the ship pretty well all the time, but the crew men would change because in those days if they wanted to spell ashore for a little rest they had to sign off. There was no such thing as leave like they have now; if you wanted it, you went on your own. The better steamship companies used to look after their men that way. They'd bring them ashore for awhile to work in their own sail lofts, something like that, so they could be home with their families for maybe one trip, but this wasn't the general practice.

I was in her [the *Mount Douglas Park*] for over three years. It was a funny arrangement really. Furness Withy seemed to be our agents wherever we went and a lot of Furness officers manned that ship, although officially it was called His Majesty's transport vessel, which it was. It was with Canadian Transport, which was closely connected with Furness Withy. I'll say this for

Furness Withy, they looked after their people, they cared for their people and they made life as reasonable as possible.

Anytime we sailed in the Pacific we were by ourselves. We got routed all over the place. We might start off from some place and arrive there and you couldn't guarantee that you were going to come home. The ship could be ordered to someplace else and someplace else after that and so on, depending what they wanted moved where. We used to sail across the North Atlantic. It was kind of mixed up. We were there [in the Pacific], then we were here, then we were there; we got shifted around a lot. I guess they figured if they lost us it was not going to be any great loss. Wherever they seemed to want transport vessels we went. I guess that was just the way of it.

We went totally unescorted right across the Pacific down to Melbourne, Australia, loaded with ammunition. We got ordered into New Zealand into Christchurch, Lyttelton, because of Japanese activity in the Roaring Forties down there. It's the area that lies between New Zealand and Australia, very strong winds. We stayed there for three or four days until the navy figured it was clear for us to go on our own again and away we went off. We saw a Japanese submarine. It was on the surface and it was a bit of weather, so we had the advantage. They put us on our stations. She was a coal burner, remember. This goes to show you the kind of men that were going to sea in merchant ships. She had three boilers and nine fires. There were three firemen and a trimmer to a watch. All the trimmers went down, this was voluntary, and every one of the nine firemen went down. The trimmers trimmed to the nine firemen, and the old girl I don't think ever went faster in her life. The engineer took the stops off the boilers and stuff and away we went. But if we'd been fished [torpedoed], we'd be comin' down yet. It was just one of those things. There was that quiet—for want of a better word, I guess—bravery that existed there. Nobody ever talked about it, you just did these things. A bunch of old firemen and trimmers, you wouldn't expect it, but they did.

The Americans considered [the Pacific] to be [their war] but the Aussies, it was their war too, don't ever think it wasn't. I must tell you a little thing that happened. We went to Melbourne. Down there at that time the Americans who had been fighting in Guadalcanal used to wear a shoulder patch with Guadalcanal on it and a number, I guess indicating what regiment they belonged to or whatever. The Aussies never wore anything like that but one day all the Aussies came out with a piece of toilet paper around [their arm] and on it they had "Shite Canal"—you know, like sewage, eh—and this was their little quiet way of protesting these kinds of things. The Aussies, I got a lot of respect for them, and the New Zealanders too, for that matter. You say these things and you think somebody's going to say that guy's an anti-American old bastard but this was the case, the Aussies did their job and did it quietly, like most of us do, and the Americans are given a little more to beating the drum. They were beating the drum and the Aussies got fed up with it, so they showed them this particular day, in a quiet way, you know, knock it off mate. They did some very, very brave things, the Aussies, down in that part of the world. Up in north Australia and up in the islands farther north of there they had spotters that went out on those islands and hid from the Japanese for months and broadcast information back to headquarters in Australia about the movement of Japanese troops and ships and all kinds of things. There were a lot of brave men down there.

We were sent over, now I may be wrong in this, just before D-Day; when I say "just before" I'm talkin' about a couple of months. We were sent across the North Atlantic with a load in one of the biggest convoys of its time; there were a hundred ships in that convoy. We loaded on the west coast of North America, came down through the Panama Canal and then in convoys up and we grouped up off Canada. The other apprentice, Roy, was very good with the aldis lamp so he used to be on the mate's watch, four to eight in the morning and evening, because that's where it was used the most. I was on the bridge all day with the flags—a bunting tosser, I think they call them in the navy—putting the international code flags up. We'd been taught how to do that at St. Margaret's.

When the commodore made a hoist, everybody had to make the same hoist. His people had to check and make sure all those dumb old merchantmen got the right message. The gunner that was lookout up on the flying bridge used to help me with that. We roosted up there all during the daylight hours. Lookout and signals, that was it, and that could keep you pretty busy when the convoy was making up and breaking up and stuff like that. There's a code book. The codes that were sent out at this time were secret. All we did was report the hoist that we had made and then the Old Man or the mate or whoever would look it up. There was the international code of signals which was for communication between ships. Some standard ones when you were making emergency turns and so on, then you do it so often you know pretty well what it was, but they still checked it out down below.

Funny thing, that trip going across, one of our wireless operators was fooling around with his machine—they listen, but it gets pretty damn boring—and he picked up a signal that he couldn't recognize, but it was repeated three or four times. So he copied it down and he passed the information out to the bridge and we passed it on to the commodore by flag hoist. What it turned out to be—we found out later, not at that time, of course—it was a homing signal. A sub had spotted us and he was calling his buddies in to have a party. So, being prepared like that, the convoy did some weird and wonderful things, evasive things. It was just one of those things that happened and he was smart enough to recognize that nobody should be sending traffic where we were; we were about half across at that time. It was pure dumb luck that he picked it up and a good thing he did. I think we would have lost quite a number of ships had he not.

In the Panama Canal? Oh yeah, it was a busy, busy place. Oh boy, was there ever [security], all kinds of it. For example, when you were going through the canal, this applied to any ship, you had a canal pilot; that was mandatory. Then you had American seamen on board and they rigged up telephones between the bridge and the engine room. Every engine room movement that went on the telegraphs was checked by voice so that there was no danger of sabotage in the canal. It seems to me that they went back aft where our gunners and staff used to keep watch and they kept watch there with our gunners. There was no trust and I guess it makes sense because there were a lot of funny things happened. That would have been it [if a ship had sunk in the canal] because God knows how long it would have taken 'em to get the thing out of there and in the meantime everything would have had to have gone around South America.

The west coast [of Canada] was on a war footing. They had blackouts, and the entrance to Vancouver Harbour they had gun emplacements and off Victoria there was forts there. All foreign-going vessels were armed. Vancouver was a major deep-sea port. Ships used to load in Prince Rupert, they loaded in Victoria and they used to load in several ports on Vancouver Island. On the coast there was Union Steamship Company and they were a cargo passenger line. Waterhouse was just freighters that used to run up and down the coast. CPR had ships and so did the CN; they ran from Vancouver north to Alaska. The only way you could get around to a lot of the places on the coast was by steamer; they didn't have the planes and the highways they have now.

You've got to remember the Japanese had landed and taken possession of islands in the Aleutians off Alaska, which wasn't too far away from B.C. [British Columbia] and Canada. You know the Alaska highway? Well, Canada was one of the main builders of that highway and that was built to get troops up into the northern part of the continent to forestall the Japanese should they decide to make a landing up in Alaska. So that presence was there and very much felt. Everybody was on the lookout for them. People weren't full of foolish bravado, they behaved the same way out there as people did back here even though there wasn't the same activity out there at that time....

The Canadian government's sweetheart, Mr. Hal Banks—it reached out there too, don't think it didn't—claimed that it [the Canadian Seamen's

Union] was a Communist union. Well, I know myself from being at sea at that time there were some Communists in the union, there's no question about it, I know that, but as far as calling it a Communist union, I don't see how they could. The Canadian government, I guess this sounds terribly disloyal, but I wonder sometimes where these guys come from, I really do. For a country that's got so much water in it and around it, it's got to be the least marine-minded country in the world. God! And the thing is there are so many young people who would really like to go to sea, I think, if there were merchant ships for them to go to sea in. If they go, they've got to go on foreign-flagged ships because there's certainly no Canadian ships.

Arthur Curren

Arthur Curren was not a merchant seaman, but his story of work ashore in Halifax during the war gives a different perspective, that of the shipping agent whose role was vital in preparing merchant ships for sailing. It is reflective of what went on in hundreds of ports around the world.

I worked as a clerk in a steamship agency office called Newfoundland Canada Steamships, which operated a service to Newfoundland but also were general agents for many other lines including Maersk Line, Fjell-Orange Line, the North American Line and so on. There are shipowners all over the world and it's not practical to have a branch office in every port in the world in case his ships go into that port, or he might never, only in his home port, and in every other port he would have an agent.

The master of each ship has a book which is prepared by his company, giving him lists of all the agents in every port in the world. If he shows up in Halifax he'll look up in his book and see what the agent is. It gives the agent's telegraphic address. Every company had a registered name with the cable companies. Instead of writing out a whole long length of a company's name, you just had one registered name; our's was CORTRADE. In those days a wireless message was sent by the cable company to a company in Halifax and they would deliver the message in the form of like a telegram to our office.

When I started to work, our office was in the Tramway building on the corner of Sackville and Barrington streets. Canadian National Steamship, who are long gone out of business, operated the Lady Boats and had quite a large office in Halifax at that time on Salter Street, on the corner across from the Maritime Centre. There was another company called Pickford &

Black, which is a part of Historic Properties now. Furness Withy & Company were large. They had their own pier where the Purdy Towers are now and had a big building on Water Street called Furness House. They also owned ships and were principally a U.K. company. Further up Water Street was a company called T.A.S. DeWolfe & Sons and they were strictly steamship agents. Between Furness Withy and Cunard, those were the two biggest shipping companies when I started to work.

In wartime the government has the authority to do about anything they want to do—requisitioning, moving, whatever. There was still a lot of commercial goods moving in those days as well as war cargoes; people still had to eat and clothe themselves. The companies continued to try to operate as normally as possible, but in many cases the government told the companies what they had to carry, what were essential, as far as overseas cargoes were concerned. Although it was government cargo, in most cases it followed through the commercial agents who arranged the space. There was a Ministry of War Transport office here. We didn't get too much involved; they were in charge of British shipping. They could pull strings and say forget that ship, let him wait, this one has to have priority. They did that sort of thing. They were the ones [who] obviously knew what was most urgently needed on the other side rather than the agent or shipper. They were the expediter, I suppose you might say, of essential goods and I guess if it came down to it they pretty well would have the authority over all ships.

I was only a junior clerk in those days. I started at $28 a month. It was a very interesting job, I'll say that. It was terribly demanding both physically and mentally because you could go 24 hours a day, 7 days a week, 365 days a year, and you couldn't keep up with it. It was a lot of terribly busy, tired people. Every steamship agent was right up to their eyeballs during the war with work. You can imagine the number of ships. You've probably seen pictures of Bedford Basin, well, I can tell you that… I have actually stood and counted 189 ships in the Basin at anchor. And that didn't count the ships that were at docks on the whole waterfront. This was a problem and another reason why we had to work shifts around the clock, to get the cargo into the ship and get her off because the dock was so badly needed for the next cargo. Dock space was limited and we had many more docks in those days than we have now. What is now part of the naval dockyard, there were six docks there alone, all commercial—Pier 2, Pier 3, Pier 4 and each one of those piers had two sides. And of course many of the piers and sheds in the South End have disappeared because of the changing technology of containers and ro-ro vessels which we didn't have in those days. Some cargo was loaded by barges. Down in what we call Fairview Cove, which is about where the Fairview Container Terminal is

now, you'd see out in the water about a dozen barges anchored and they loaded the barges there.

We had to be extremely careful what we said over the telephone. I worked here all during the war and several times I was called on the mat by the authorities because they would monitor your calls; not every one, but they would spot check. You never knew who was listening when. But it's terribly hard to carry on a business without saying something, you know. Anyway it wasn't serious.

First thing we would do when the ship arrived in port, we would contact a naval intelligence office in the dockyard which was called CXO; that was a security office. We would tell them we had a ship so and so just arrived and it was destined for Liverpool, England, or wherever and when was the next convoy? Now the next convoy might be in two days time, three days time, and after that it would be another ten days. He would tell us that. Then we would have to have our own staff meeting quickly and decide whether it was humanly possible at all to get this ship ready for the convoy in three days time or whether that was absolutely impossible. But many times we did the impossible, many, many times, but it meant not only office staff but dock staff and everybody practically workin' around the clock. I worked in the

Aerial view of Bedford Basin with the Narrows, McNabs Island and Halifax Harbour approaches in background. In 1941, British Rear Admiral S.S. Bonham-Carter called Halifax "probably the most important port in the world." By 1943 it was sharing that distinction with New York.

office for five days and four nights without leaving, just [sleeping] in the chair for a little while.

Every ship has to be entered and cleared through customs and immigration. You have to go aboard the ship; the boarding officers were the junior [clerks], that was me. Many times these ships would be in Bedford Basin. If it was fully loaded, she was pretty well down in the water and that wasn't bad, but if you got a ship that was empty or pretty near empty, she was way up. You had a rope ladder hanging down there and the high waves, sometimes it was pretty rough. You'd get on the side of the motorboat and there was a cabin with a rail along the top that you could hold onto. He'd go by with the motorboat and you had to grab the ladder with the other hand and let go of the motorboat, and she was gone. The same thing coming back down off it. It's no fun, I'll tell you that. All kinds of weather. Icy conditions in the wintertime when it was cold and everything was wet; took some awful chances.

Although many ships didn't require to be unloaded or loaded, they still needed ship's stores; could be anything from deck and engine room stores to food. Very often those ships required fuel to get across the ocean from here. We had a lot of coal burners. They may have needed fuel such as oil, diesel–there wasn't too many diesel ships–but there was still a lot burning bunker C, which is a heavy, heavy oil. The master would give us a list of what he needed. He would also supply us with a complete crew list which had to be made out on the Canadian Immigration forms. The customs officer would go aboard the ship and bond the stores such as liquor and cigarettes, usually in the master's cabin but not always. It had to be in a cupboard that they put a red ribbon and some wax on.

When we got back on land again we had to go to the custom house. In those days it was next to the old post office on Bedford Row; it's gone now. We would enter the ship in customs and go to Immigration which was upstairs in Pier 21 and put in our forms. Then we'd go back to our office and get on the telephone and order the provisions through one of the provisioning houses. Howards Limited on Barrington Street was one of the big shippers of food for ships. We would make arrangements if they needed fuel or water. Between Pier 4 and the dockyard there was a couple of coal piers and also at Pier 9. We had several water boats here to bring fresh water to the ship. If they were coming to a dock they merely ran a hose to the nearest connector and ships were supplied with water, no problem. These are all the tasks of an agent. He takes care of all the requirements of the ship. If any of the crew had to have medical attention it was up to the agent to make those arrangements. The agent didn't do all these things but had to have the knowledge of where those things were available and get the goods or services that were required to the ship.

This had to be done as quickly as possible in order to make the earliest possible convoy date. Otherwise the ship would sit in Bedford Basin for another eight or ten days and that wasn't helping anybody. It was terribly demanding because every agent was like we were, calling the suppliers for this and for that and they [the suppliers] were up to their eyeballs in trying to keep up with it too. You were calling them back because your ship was going tomorrow morning, it was nine o'clock the night before, and the stores weren't aboard yet. You had to arrange launches—motorboats—to take these goods from the Halifax dock up to the ship and get them aboard in the dark. Today, my office has cellular phones and walkie-talkies; we didn't have those then. Once we left the office and got up to a ship in Bedford Basin we were out of contact with the office until we got back to the mainland again to get to a telephone. They've got so many conveniences today that we didn't have which made life really difficult to get by with.

We had to have replacement crews. There was a manning pool up in the north end of the shipyards where you could call and get crew members and officers. Captain Thomas was shipping master—he was under the federal government—and all the crews had to be signed on in front of him. Practically all the major countries had consulates here or agents. I think most of the consulates kept him informed of what people were available and where they were. You had to present the names and he would put them on the official crew list of the ship. The man's wages would be shown.

When we came to sail a ship we had a list of places to go that went all the way from the south end of Hollis Street up to Pier 9 where the ladies were entertaining crew members. While they were told to be back on board at a certain time, well, they weren't always back on board. Men being men, when they got ashore they were looking for a lot of things beside food. We searched them out until we found them so the ship could go. This was just another one of the little kinks that the agents had to do to assist the departure of ships in convoy. We got pretty good at it after awhile because we knew all the dives and hangouts and we usually found them all. Many times I've gone to this place [Allied Merchant Seamen's Club], not that that was a dive or a hangout, but they did have entertainment there at times and they had bars and places to eat and so on. That was a legitimate place, but there were a lot of pretty shady spots.

There were a lot of ships operated by good companies and good countries. We had lots that would come into Halifax and the crew would refuse to sail on the ship and that would cause the local Department of Transport to come in and get involved. They would find out how bad the ship was and then they wouldn't allow it to go. But it was really the crew that started it by saying they weren't going to sail till something was done with it. They realized how bad the ship was. We had to deal with it. Those were the few cases I can recall that we had the consuls down on board the ship trying to sort the thing out.

You see there are always some companies that are prepared to take advantage of situations and they were taking advantage of the war to cut corners on food, repairs and make money. Probably figured if she makes this trip she won't make the next one anyway, so why spend a lot of money on her. But these people were human beings and they had to go to sea on these things. Some were just a bucket of bolts. Many problems we had, they hadn't been paid two months, three months—no pay. You'd get people that hardly speak English. We'd get the shipping master to come down and we'd get the particular consul of that country to come down. Not that he had the authority, but he could use his office to contact his principal over in the parent country and have him try to put some pressure on the company to transfer some money over so the captain could pay some of his crew. Most of these crews, when they sign on the ship, whatever their wages are, they allocate [so much] to go to their wife in Madrid or wherever she is. She writes to her husband and he finally gets a letter saying she hasn't got any money for the last two months; they get pretty upset. The man gets to be in terrible shape. I sympathize with him because they're away from home, they don't seem to have any authority and their family is not receiving any money and here they are out risking their lives to sail the ship. We got in some awful pathetic cases.

Each agent in port had his bailiwick, his own ships, to take care of. We had twenty-eight, thirty ships, just our office. Try to keep all those straight. At that time we had about twenty-five [personnel]. In addition to the physical part of loading ships, the part of getting money was an important point too. We had to go to the shipowners and get an advance because we couldn't afford to handle all these ships and put out money without having some advance from the owners. We would send an estimate and if the estimate was $20,000 the shipowners in most cases would probably send us fifteen and say upon receiving your final disbursement we'll send the balance, which was fine in a way, but it also meant we were owed a lot of money at times. The estimate might have been twenty and run to thirty. By the time we got the invoices all in for the suppliers in the port, the ship's gone.... The more ships you handled the more accounts there were, the more invoices had to be paid, and in many cases we would get instructions from the owners saying the invoices had to be signed by the master, otherwise they wouldn't honour them and that was a real headache. It meant we had to insist from the suppliers whether it be for water supplied or provisions or fuel or repair works, somebody had to make up an invoice to cover that and over to us as an agent so we can have the master sign it before he sails. It was just another thing we had to be chasing all the time.

Pilferage was a major concern to shipping during the war, there's no question about that. It's a completely different scene today when you have everything locked up in containers. Everything was shipped as loose cargo. You could go down to one of these piers and see everything there from pickles to boots. When I first went to work, there was by far a great number of wooden boxes, but that seemed to change very quickly to cardboard cartons. Whether the war had anything to do with that I don't know. Of course a lot of them got damaged and torn, and a lot of them were torn intentionally and the goods spewed out onto the docks and into the ships. It was more tempting to steal and easier to steal, it was right there. It was not only a major problem from the point of pilferage on the docks, but it made a lot of work. We had a whole claims department just processing claims because people would put in claims for a cargo they didn't receive and somebody had to pay for it down the line somewhere. If people signed for it and couldn't produce a receipt at the other end to cover it, you were held responsible and had to pay for the lost goods whether it was the ship or railway company or whoever.

You had to have booking sheets for every ship. You knew what the capacity of the ship was in cubic measurement and dead-weight tonnage. You didn't want to get twice the cargo what the ship could handle and yet you didn't want the ship going out half full, so you had to keep a very accurate check on what cargo was coming and what you were accepting for that ship. That had to be all done before the cargo ever left the shipping point. It's like any system, if you get it working properly it's not as complicated as it sounds.

The space had to be booked on these ships and then [cargo] had to be shipped from point of origin wherever it may be, in Canada or the United States, to the seaboard for loading on whatever vessel was nominated for it. That was all done through agents in Toronto or Montreal or Chicago who booked space with us, the agents in Halifax. We had to follow it from the time it was shipped. We had to get the car numbers from the shipper and trace the cars to the railway to make sure they were going to be here on time and not pushed off on some siding up in New Brunswick or somewhere and forgotten about for awhile. Keep them moving to get here at a certain time so it would be in when the ship arrived.

Cargo has to be stored in the ship according to the type of cargo it is. You can't put light cargo in and then put heavy cargo on top of it. The people in the main office had to make up car allotment slips with the shippers and the goods and the car numbers. Then your man on the dock had to order these cars in through the railway's local office in Halifax as he wanted them.

He wanted certain cars first, get those unloaded on the dock or even into the ship before he brought other cars in. Not only stowed properly according to the type of cargo, but the ship might be going to three different ports and naturally it has to be stowed so that the first port the ship calls you can get at that port's cargo. On the dock they had to make up stowage plans. You have a big sheet of paper

Stevedores load a hold with TNT.

about three feet wide and about a foot and a half high. The ship is drawn out on that piece of paper with the various holds and number of decks the ship would have in it. The people on the dock have to show in there what cargo they have stowed where. Every ship would have their own. It was complicated. Everybody worked day and night. We would get as much cargo into the piers as we could physically get from the railway cars so as to have it ready. But pier space was at a premium, so many times the cargo would still be in railcars when a ship was coming in the harbour.

There were steamship checkers, railway checkers. There were groups of people who unloaded the railway cars. The people who unloaded for the railway were not the same people who loaded the ship. There'd be several hundred, more than that including the stevedores; there might be a couple thousand, yes. An awful lot of people came on the docks from all along the coast of Nova Scotia from Cape Breton to Yarmouth and supplemented the people who were on the docks prior to that. Certainly people did a lot more than they thought they could do. It just had to be done and people did it, that's all.

The shipowner had a part to play. He had to keep his ships operating and keep them repaired so they could continue to sail. Then you had your crews, officers and masters, they certainly had their part to play. Then the people ashore had their part because the ships had to be loaded and they had to be discharged on the other side. The railways had a big part to play because the cargo had to be moved to seaboard, and many people in the railway worked long hours in very difficult times to get the cargo here when it was needed. People in the Customs, people in the Immigration, it was all a big team.

It was an exciting time to be connected with the port. If you were told ahead of time that this is what had to be done, you wouldn't believe, you would say it can't be done. But it's amazing what can be done. Most individuals are capable of doing a lot more than what they do. I'm talkin' physically and mentally. As a person they surprise themselves in what they're capable of doing if they really want to do it. And as a group of people or as a port or even as a country you can do a lot more than you think you can do and it comes out in wartime and in a case of disasters.

CHAPTER 2

Operation Drumbeat

Angreifen! Ran! Versenken! (Attack! Advance! Sink!)
— U-boat motto

In 1917 Germany had sent U-boats to the North American eastern seaboard, where they preyed for a time on freighters and fishing vessels. It should have come as no surprise then, but it did, when similar tactics were used in World War II. When Donitz launched Operation Paukenschlag [Drumbeat] in January 1942, the entire coastline south to the Caribbean became wide open to attack. Its murderous effects were such that in June 1942, U.S. Army Chief of Staff General George C. Marshall lamented, "The losses by submarines off our Atlantic seaboard and in the Caribbean now threaten our entire war effort."[1]

By October 1941 Donitz had already begun to send his U-boats ever further afield into the western Atlantic to intercept shipping off Newfoundland. By year's end his fleet consisted of 250 U-boats, with its strength growing by fifteen more each passing month. One hundred of these were operational at a time, and this number was to double within a year. Of the nine varieties of U-boats built, the Type VII's were the favoured, numbering more than 660 by war's end. They had a range of 6,500 nautical miles, a surface speed of 16 knots and carried 14 torpedoes. Newer models included the Type IX's (11,000 miles, 17 knots, 19 torpedoes) and the Type X's (14,450 miles, 16.4 knots, 66 mines, 13 torpedoes). There were also Type XIV's—Milch Cow tankers—1,600-ton supply submarines capable of covering 12,000 miles. These supply vessels carried spare ammunition, torpedoes, fresh food, medical supplies and replacement crews for the sick and injured; more important, they could hold an additional 720 tons of diesel fuel, thereby increasing the range and station-keeping time of patrolling U-boats. In January 1942 Donitz was poised to bring the "war over there" to the home front. It is a sobering thought to ponder what might have been had Hitler not been caught unaware by Japan's attack on Pearl Harbor and the two Axis powers had instead launched simultaneous attacks on both coasts.

The sinking of the British freighter *Cyclops* 160 miles south of Halifax was the opening move in Operation Drumbeat. It was another of the German "Happy Times," known in some quarters as the "American Hunting Season." As mentioned earlier, it had begun with only five U-boats, the most Donitz could initially persuade Hitler to free up, but soon twenty or twenty-five would make the twenty-two-day, three thousand-mile trek. The areas of heaviest concentration were the shipping lanes from New York to Cape Hatteras and down to the Florida Keys. If convoys were the lifelines of the war, then oil was the lifeblood, and so the U-boats went after the sitting-duck tankers plying their trade to and from South America. Within the first two months, sixty tankers were sunk or damaged. Submerged by day to avoid detection, the U-boats surfaced at night like vampires to hunt and found no shortage of prey. One German commander reported that ten times the number of U-boats would have had no difficulty finding targets. When torpedoes were spent, they used deck guns. So brazen and unmolested were they that running lights were burned at night to avoid collisions amongst themselves.

The carnage could have been avoided. Churchill wrote, "It is surprising indeed that during two years of the advance of total war towards the American continent more provision had not been made against this deadly onslaught.... With all the information they had about protective measures we had adopted, both before and during the struggle, it is remarkable that no plans had been made for coastal convoys and for multiplying small craft. Neither had the coastal air defence been developed.... Thus it happened that in these crucial months an effective American defence system was only achieved with painful, halting steps."[2] Although the blame must be shared among many, the man most often credited with this oversight was commander in chief of the U.S. Fleet Admiral Ernest J. King, an advocate of big-ship navies. In fairness, the Americans were fighting a two-ocean war with a decimated fleet. Admiral King, however, had no use for the British Admiralty and steadfastly pursued the outmoded concept of roaming aimlessly in search of U-boats, a tactic which provided no kills in five months. Direct intervention by Roosevelt was finally necessary to have convoys organized and an escort-building program started.

Not only were defences lacking but so was common sense. For a time the U.S. government bowed to public pressure and refused to turn out coastal lights at night. This, in large measure, was because it was the height of tourist season in states such as Florida. "The American shore seemed a fairyland of glowing lights and street signs compared with blacked-out Europe. Automobile headlights moved up and down the coast, a coast clearly marked by dozens of bobbing, well-lit marker buoys."[3] This provided a perfect backdrop for the U-boat snipers. From Boston to Key West, two hundred ships went down within ten miles of land.

The Canadians were having problems as well. The RCN was still trying to recover from years of government neglect because of the country's dependency upon Britain for defence. As industry worked around the clock to build much-needed escorts, and boys from the hinterland struggled to gain their sea legs, U-boats moved into the unguarded St. Lawrence River. Between May and October 1942 they torpedoed twenty-three ships, killing seven hundred people, a national embarrassment for the Canadian government that resulted in the closure of the river to all but essential traffic for several months.

Operation Drumbeat was a relatively short-lived offensive, lasting but six months. By July, 1942 with the network of coastal convoys and escort protection growing daily, the U-boats (with the exception of a couple that continued to terrorize the St. Lawrence) pulled away to safer hunting grounds in the mid and South Atlantic to carry on the battle. In their wake, they left five hundred ships, 2.5 million tons, littering the Atlantic seaboard, virtually in sight of land. Hundreds of merchant seamen, many of them Canadian, lay with them.

Earle Wagner

It stems back from family tradition. My father was a fisherman out of Lunenburg and LaHave; as a boy eleven years of age, his father took him to sea. On my mother's side there was quite a tradition of seafaring activity with her brothers and father. I had an uncle who was a captain in the merchant navy, Captain Earle Mulock; he had his foreign-going master's certificate. He was a successful individual and I think in my eyes he set that little bit of a standard that stood out to me. So it was one of those things, that's what you were brought up to and you related to it because you saw other people doing it.

The war broke out just a few months after I finished school. I was fifteen. When I was sixteen I went to go in the Royal Canadian Navy as a boy seaman and they wouldn't take me, didn't need me. So a few months later when I turned seventeen I went in the merchant navy. It was usually sixteen you could get in, but people lied about their age and got in fourteen and fifteen. Things weren't too strict. If you looked able and willing and had reasonably good health, they took you.

I joined a ship out of Halifax called the *Reginolite,* which was part of the Imperial Oil fleet, as ordinary seaman, February 12, 1941. We were primarily in the North Atlantic to Caribbean area carrying crude oil from Colombia and Venezuela up to eastern Canadian ports. From 1941 up to even the spring of 1942 we were running individually, but when the U-boat menace struck the eastern Atlantic seaboard, then they rerouted us so that we had a limited amount of time at sea. We went by convoy from Halifax over to maybe Boston area, Cape Cod, then you took the interland seaways down through Cape Cod, Long Island Sound and right down the East River into New York. Then from there you'd take a convoy or you'd go singly out on the coast in daylight hours early in the morning so you'd get down into Delaware Bay. You'd go inland waters then, go up and through the Chesapeake-Delaware Canal out into Chesapeake Bay and come out to sea again. The canals were deep enough that they could handle most of those ships. Then you skim along the coast in daylight hours and anchor somewhere at night; your most vulnerable time was during darkness. Weaving in that way from sea buoy to sea buoy along the coast, you could go individually. You'd be in shallow enough water that submarines couldn't operate and you had surveillance of aircraft overhead.

You worked your way down the coast to Key West and anchored for several days. You formed up convoy and from there you went across the Caribbean area down probably to Cuba. Lots of times when you got down to Cuba they'd let you go on your own because they were scattered, some would go to the Panama Canal, some would go to Venezuela, Colombia and the British West Indies. But then as it got on a little later in 1942, if you were leaving Halifax, for instance, you'd take a direct convoy right down to the Caribbean or go over to Boston and take convoys out of New York and go down that way. I've taken full convoy in '44 right down to Cuba and from there we were dispersed on our own.

[The year] 1942 was really the worst year, there's no doubt about it. In the spring, about April or early May, in one day off the American coast somewheres around Chesapeake Bay down to Cape Hatteras, we went through eighteen ships during the daylight hours that were sunk or in the process of sinking. A lot of them were tankers in shallow water. They were layin' on the bottom, bows or funnels would be out, masts would be up. Or the ship would be floating, abandoned, burning, may have a list on it. You knew it had been fished—torpedoed—but no signs of life except planes buzzing around. But you see, being a boy of eighteen years of age, at times like that you always think it's not going to be you, it's going to be the other fella. You knew it was dangerous. They weren't gas-freeing the ships; they were impregnated

"In the spring, about April or early May, in one day off the American coast somewheres around Chesapeake Bay down to Cape Hatteras, we went through eighteen ships during the daylight hours that were sunk or in the process of sinking." Pictured here is a 10,000-ton Park ship in her death throes. During the height of the Battle of the Atlantic in 1942, the Allies lost one ship of 10,000 tons every ten hours for thirty-one days.

with old crude oil. It was just like a bomb. All you had to do was set a little spark and it would have blown up.

I was lucky, or we were lucky, we never got torpedoed, because we were going through where it all happened. I remember one day coming up through the Mona Straits where Cuba and Hispaniola are, we just got north of that and we steamed for a whole hour–just reeking of oil. You knew the ship had gone down but there was no sign of it or sign of the submarine. We didn't see any survivors. We were steaming about ten knots, so it was at least ten miles of oil. I remember it seemed like one hell of a long time to go through the oil before we got out of it.

You take it in your stride as a young fella. You have to think about when you leave home as a young boy, you go into a complete new environment. You leave your family and friends, all the things that are dear to you. You're cooped up in a little cabin, blacked out at nighttime. The tropics are pretty stinkin' hot below decks. There's a fair rate of food; I worked for a reasonable company. It's just according to what kind of captain you're with; some can be a real strict disciplinarian, next unto God as far as their authority is concerned. For any misdemeanor they can fine you two days pay or four days pay, even cut your rations. You sign articles of agreement that allows you so many dry peas and so many dry beans per day and so much liquid and so much lime juice. It's a hard fare. That was the articles of agreement, you signed a contract to serve in a certain capacity as, let's say, a seaman for such a period of time, one year, for $45 a month. They could hold you to that. You couldn't go below that; most of them were above that ration. That was to overcome the greedy shipmasters and the greedy chief stewards they had on a lot of the British ships. The companies paid the captain and the chief steward a certain sum of money to victual the ship. The least amount of food that they could provide, the more money the captain and the chief steward could divvy up between 'em. The company I worked for was more advanced than that and, North America, those old ties of colonialism had been dropped by that time and they were providing food more liberal than they would on British ships.

I got $45 a month and they put a 35 percent war bonus on top of that. Comparisons of wages between the Royal Canadian Navy and the Canadian merchant navy overall, invariably it wound up they were all making more than we were. That can be proven out.[4] But the myth was that we were overpaid. They thought we were mercenaries, that we could go wherever the biggest money was. That was one of the things the navy always threw at us. Whenever we got in port sometimes it could end up in a drunken brawl. They were wearing uniforms and we were just around in civvies, and sometimes it was just according to what you could afford. If a guy spent all his money on booze, cigarettes and women, he didn't have much for clothes. This is one thing, that adversarial feeling between navy and merchant navy. It was a good turn in my career that they rejected me from the Royal Canadian Navy. I spent forty-eight years in the marine profession as a result of that.

The primary target was us in the merchant navy. They weren't after those little frigates, mine sweepers and corvettes. They were after the loaded tanker or loaded cargo ship or a troop ship.

There were those people like myself who were rejected, too young to get in the service. I was called up later on, but I was in the merchant navy so they didn't take me anyway. There were some people too old or they were impaired because of some physical defects and some mental defects too. You had your oddballs, you get them in any service, but you never screened them out because you were looking for bodies. Basically that was it, you fill a position. "What can you do?" "Oh, I can do this." They'd want to see your discharge book. "Well I lost my discharge book on the last ship I was on, I was torpedoed." Nobody checked it out too much.

To give you some things, you have to think about what's convoy work. Convoy work is very nice in the tropics during daylight, and even at nighttime it's nice and clear. You can pretty well see where your ships are in line ahead. If you're following in the wake of another ship at nighttime, you see the florescence in the water. That looks pretty good. You could see another dark shape off to the starboard, and off to the port you'd see another dark shape. Or you could see the bow wave and that's how you position your ship. Now that's all right. You had no radar.

But just imagine when it got thick of fog, you didn't know where the other ones were, you heard lots of whistles blowin'. You're tryin' to follow a little fog buoy that was trailin' the stern of 'em. It didn't take long before you lost that. What do you do in the nighttime there was nothing there? You hoped that ship was ahead of you, you hoped the other one was over here, you didn't know where in the hell they were. And if there was alteration of courses, one ship broke down or somebody made a mistake in steering, it was extremely hazardous. Then throw that in with all the meteorological phenomenon that you can put into that—hail, rain, snow, a howling gale in the North Atlantic. You didn't know where the hell you were, even probably within fifty or a hundred miles, after sailing several days in the North Atlantic because you weren't able to take sights; you didn't see the sun for days upon days. It was extremely hazardous just from a navigational point of view.

Then you had these wolf packs of submarines that were tracking you day by day ready to pick you off or smart enough to sail right through the middle of a convoy and plug off the ships. You throw in your overflights by German long-range planes and surface raiders, the Battle of the North Atlantic was extremely hazardous, statistics show that. There is no other service in that period of time that suffered proportionately such major losses in property or in life as the Allied merchant navies.

Can you imagine a ship being torpedoed in the North Atlantic in the wintertime, somebody scramblin' to save his life in a gale? All pandemonium breaks loose. The lights go out, generators stop and confusion reigns. You heard a big explosion and were probably thrown out of your bunk. You're tryin' to get out, if you're still alive, to get enough clothes on. You try to get your life jacket on. Then you get outside, your ship could be on fire; if you're on a tanker, everything's full of oil everywhere you step. You try to get into a lifeboat or a life raft that's probably not there. You're goin' to save yourself, you jump overboard. You're covered with oil, the place could be ablaze with oil and, Christ, you could burn up. And when do you get picked up? Maybe days later or never. It could be a hellish nightmare really. When you think, you get a bullet through the head you're dead, but that's quick.

Jack Matthews

Jack Matthews (left) with Captain George Vincent Thomas. "He'd shoot you just as quick as look at you, but a good seaman and smart."

A lot of our masters in Imperial [Oil] ships during the war were Englishmen, Scotsmen and Welshmen. It wasn't until a little later on that the Canadian fellers started gettin' their foreign-going tickets. You sign on under the master, he's God, there's no other name, God personified; you didn't talk back to them. They were God, master, doctor, lawyer, teacher, you name it. I been with some hard skippers. George Vincent Thomas, there was a hard bastard; he was a Welshman. He'd shoot you just as quick as look at you, but a good seaman and smart.

Old Captain Treeweek, Cecil Treeweek, was an ex-RN man from the First World War and he thought he was Lord Nelson for Jesus' sake. Oh, nasty! Only a little bastard about four or five foot high. I'm tellin' you, he gave me the life of hell. I had my third mate's home trade ticket and of course he had a master's foreign-going ticket from the old country. Mine was just a street car ticket as far as he was concerned.

During the war, gum was some hard to get. The Red Cross sent us a little thing with a couple packages of Chiclets in it. I'm out on the wing of the bridge and I'm chewin' gum. I felt this breathin' in my face. "Ah, Mr. Matthews, you chewing gum?" "Yes, Captain, I am." "Blasted filthy American habit," he says. "I'd rather see a man chewing tobacco than chewing gum." I didn't even have the flavour out of the thing. "Spit it out!" he says, and I spit it out. That was continuous, everybody. It was all right if you were English, the sun shone out of your asshole.

Then not long after that, I was about the only one that could take sights, he [Treeweek] come up this day. The second mate was supposed to be navigating officer, but stars, that was something up in the sky to look at. He had some kind of inland ticket from the Great Lakes. For every hour we'd put a little arrow on the chart with the latitude and longitude so that if we got torpedoed we could hand the position right to the wireless operator. Holy geez, he come storm burnin' out of the wheelhouse. "Mr. Matthews. Mr. Matthews, what's this blasted mark on the chart?" I was lookin' at the chart and I couldn't see nothin' out of the ordinary. Everybody else did the same thing. "Look! What's that on there?" "Oh, I put it there." Phew! "You get out of this chartroom and don't come back in here again as long as I'm here!" Geez, I wasn't allowed to take a sight, I couldn't take an azimuth, I couldn't even go in the wheelhouse. I said, "This is the procedure that we've done before you came here." "Well, you're not doing it any more!" he says. I thought it was a good idea, you know, by the time you try to get a position if you're torpedoed, shit, you'd never get it to the wireless operator in time. That was everyday there was somethin'.

Another little episode I'm goin' to mention is with this bloody old Captain Treeweek. We come around from the west coast on the *Brentwood Bay Park*, a beautiful ship. The west coast skipper got off and they put this god-damn Treeweek on. I was only second mate on her and I was put gunnery officer on the twelve-pound gun forward, and scared shitless of it. We only had a couple days training with these navy fellas. Your ammunition, it's not like a navy ship, it's all around you—explosives, cordite and everything there. He'd have fire drill in the morning and gunnery drill during the afternoon, you never got no sleep. So the signal goes for gunnery practice. We were forward on the twelve-pounder and they were at all the stations. It was our job forward to fire a smoke float—a smoke shell—and the Oerlikons used that as a target.

They had this beautiful starboard Oerlikon with two mess boys on it. They used to put a piece of waste in the barrel with a celluloid cap over it to keep the weather off. When you got to gunnery stations you took that out first. These poor little bastards didn't clear the damn gun and when they started firing, the barrel splits wide open. Here were the shells comin' right over forward—yellow tracers, white ones, red ones. This Treeweek is up there. "Mr. Matthews, get another shell away."

"Can't do it, Captain, I can't do it. The gun's out of control on the...."

"Don't talk back to me!" he says. "I'll have you court-martialed when we get to Trinidad!"

"We can't stand up, Captain. There's white shells and red shells...."

"I'll have you court-martialed!"

I says, "You're goin' to have to have me court-martialed."

I'm only twenty years old, you know, never away from home too much before that. That kid's froze to the gun and the barrel's white. Of course, old asshole up there saw it then, the thing's just about melted. Finally it jammed, that's the only reason it stopped. It cut the rigging on the boom holding up the forward torpedo nets. That come crashin' down; just missed the boys on the gun. It looked like we'd come out of the Battle of the Atlantic.

We got into Trinidad, sure enough, buddy boy, he had the navy officer out, a commander from the base. So Treeweek gives his story first. I could see me breakin' big rocks into little rocks for the rest of my life, disobeying orders in a time of war, Holy Christ! So the fella listened to him. "Now, Captain," says a big broad English accent, "we better hear this young man's version of this." So I told him exactly what happened. He turned to Captain Treeweek and he says, "Captain, you want to be thankful the first shell that come out of that gun wasn't the explosive one [or] none of you would have been here." End of story.

But did he ride my arse from there to Halifax, a whole month comin' up. I called Dad from Baltimore. My whole family was seafaring men, and Dad, Captain William Lloyd Matthews, was an old sailing master in steam and sail. I says, "Dad, I can't take this anymore, I'm goin' to get off this thing." Dad wasn't too pleased. He says, "You get off on account of that Limey bastard, don't you bother comin' home! You go back and tell that feller just what you think of him!" My old lower lip was just a quiverin', [but] I got it out of me. The next day there was a bottle of rum, a bottle of whiskey and two cartons of cigarettes under my pillow, and I never smoked and drank then. But he never got any easier on me all the way north. That's the kind of men they were: God. The navy gunner would have a birthday, he would get the chief steward to make them a damn birthday cake. Us, oh boy, it was unbelievable. But this is the stuff you had to put up with. Thank Jesus he was taken off when we got north.

I always wanted to go to sea, even as I was goin' to school, that's what I pretty well made up my mind to. There were no better than Canadian, and Nova Scotia, seamen. You won't get them any better in the world because one time we had the largest merchant navy fleet in the world [third or fourth in the late 1800s]. They weren't big ships, but they were three-masters, four-masters, and them men sailed all over the world with very little education, but first-class seamen. And up on the Great Lakes, that's where the biggest part of your Canadian seamen came from and they were good too. Same as your navy men, most were from the Prairies.

I'm not a navy man. It's a different life altogether; it's like night and day. I get right upset when I hear that [merchant seamen were undisciplined]. There was more discipline in many merchant ships than the navy will ever have. And we didn't have a hundred and fifty or two hundred men to do things. You had a crew then, which was a big crew, of about fifty men on the 10,000-ton ships. They [the naval seamen] were always superior to you. We tolerated one another, that's about all. I don't think we better talk too much about that.

I was on [the *Petrolite*] over twenty-four months without a bloody vacation. You might have got a little time in dry dock, but you were still on the ship. You hear about these fellas in the navy go away for a month and you'd think the world is goin' to come to an end. We were gettin' $52 a month plus 10 percent war bonus and that was supposed to be big wages. And we had to pay for our own duffel coats, oilskins and everything else. We all used to go to Maurice Goldberg's [on Barrington Street in Halifax]; in fact he used to lend people money and surely he never got it back 'cause a lot of the poor buggers were lost.

We used to go to these canteens and that, and a big sign, "Welcome Army, Navy, Air Force and Merchant Seamen," but once you arrived there in civvies, you'd think you had leprosy or some bloody thing. Now in the States, I must say, the USO looked after the merchant seamen, not only theirs, all Allied seamen; you were most welcome. They'd have tickets for you to go to Radio City and visit the Empire State Building; there was always nice stuff like that to look forward to—navy men especially but also the merchantmen. They had special clubs for the [merchant] officers, same as in Halifax there was the Merchant Navy Officer's Club, but then they also had places for the ratings to go and they had dances for you.

St. John's, Newfoundland, was a wonderful place; the Newfies treated you like gold. See, Britain and Newfie, those islands depended upon merchant ships; no other way they could get their goods there. I remember seeing big signs "This Island Depends On You Merchantmen" in Newfie and Great Britain. You should have seen the ships in [St. John's]. We used to go ashore in little bum boats and you used to take a shortcut through the chain locker of this big Dutchman, in one side and out the other. The whole bow was blown, just his anchors hanging down out of the chain locker. Newfoundland boys would take us through just about anything.

I started with Imperial Oil and I went from ordinary seaman right to master of the biggest ship they had—*Imperial Ottawa*—forty years, eight months, ten days, four hours and thirty-two minutes. Imperial Oil was a good company, the very best. They were noted for good food and good conditions. We had the *Vancolite, Reginolite, Trontolite, Calgarolite, Montrolite, Petrolite* [and *Victolite and Canadolite*] and there were about fifteen coastal ships running to Newfoundland. They had a big [Great] Lake fleet which they had to bring out here to help replace the ships that were being sunk. Imperial Oil also had fifteen ships under Panamanian flag that we manned and there were a hell of a lot of men in that. These were old things they hauled out after the First World War and put Canadian crews on.[5]

In 1940 I joined the *Petrolite*. I signed on in Halifax and we went from here to Saint John, New Brunswick, then down to Baton Rouge, Louisiana, over to Aruba in the Dutch West Indies, then through the Panama Canal and ran from Talara, Peru, down to Valparaiso [Chile] for about five months. We would load in Aruba for Halifax and when we got here we used to spend about three months running over to St. John's, Newfoundland. There was a big navy base in St. John's during the war. That was one hell of a run between the weather and the submarines, it was hard ol' goin'. This was a hot spot between Halifax and Newfoundland that was deadly [part of the infamous Triangle Run]. They sunk ships off of the entrance to Halifax Harbour. *Nipiwan Park* was [torpedoed] about twenty-two miles east of Halifax. We had two big ships burning right out here off Chebucto Head by the pilot station. They got the fire out and they beached them on McNabs Island. One of them was one of the old East Indian ships; they had Chinese and Indian crews. Them poor bastards, they tried to climb up the masts and were burnt to a crisp right on the masts.

They preferred the tankers in the middle of the convoy because there was such a shortage of oil. That was the lifeline of the bloody war, wasn't it, to keep the tanks, planes and every damned thing going. But when they started these wolf packs, no place was safe, they were so organized. They were right into the lightships here in Halifax. We had an east lightship for the approach and the south lightship, right off the mouth of the harbour. In fact, my dad in the last years of the war landed up on the lightship and he used to tell them that the bastards were laying right underneath him. When the couple [of German U-boats] surrendered off of Halifax on V-E Day or shortly after, they told them that's where they were layin'.

Every night a convoy was attacked, but we were fortunate. I was never torpedoed, had some damn close calls though. The night the *Christie Painie*, an American tanker, was sunk, we could feel the heat from her, we were that close. She was lost just north of Aruba. We just had to keep goin', you're not allowed to stop, you'd be the next one to go. It's sad 'cause when I was running down to Venezuela, every night there were ships being sunk and you couldn't stop. A lot of them caught fire, but this old bunker C, that's what we burnt for fuel, once that hits the cold water it's like tar. The [smell of] oil was so thick when you're on watch you'd be half sick when you come off.

Going south to Venezuela was deadly because the Germans had all those passages in the West Indies closed right off—Mona Passage, Anegada Passage, Sombrero Passage—you got to go through these passages to get to Venezuela [and] they had it sewed up. In the latter years the only way you could get through, you had to go down through the straits of Florida, through the straits of Yucatan and over to the [Panama] Canal and get escorts from there. Lucky? The Old Fellow was right with us all the time.

I was on one of the first ships into the American base at Argentia [Newfoundland]. The night that we went we took a convoy to Sydney, got new escorts and went to Argentia. There was a brand-new American tanker goin' in with pretty well the first load to Argentia; we were continuing on to St. John's. He broke off the convoy about midnight 'cause I was on the twelve to four watch and it happened. He wasn't twenty minutes away from us and she went up, a brand new tanker. That would have been 1942. Off Cape Hatteras, we were running steady down there. A couple of times we saw people in the water. They wouldn't have got out because the crude oil and bunker C on the water, all they could do was lift their arms with old black shit on them.

But this was every night, every time you went out you never knew if you were comin' back. I never took my life jacket off, I slept with it. I was lucky if I did get an hour or two sleep at night, most of us. The rest didn't ever sleep, they'd go play poker all damn night. One watch would come off and sit at the feller's seat that they took off. You didn't dwell on that [being torpedoed] because you'd be down in the old looney bin pounding your head against the wall if you'd been thinkin' somethin' like that all the time.

You talk about comradeship, my God, it was there. There was never a bad crew, never. I never sailed with such a good bunch of men in my life and never will again, the best in the world. Never ran into any animosity at all and I don't know how, now that you talk about it, because we had bugger all to do. We had nothin'. You weren't allowed to have a radio, you weren't allowed to have a camera, there was nothin'. What a lot of us did, we were studying for our tickets and we'd get together and help one another that way. That killed a lot of time and helped us at the same time 'cause we weren't making any money. You had to get permission from the company to go to navigation school in Halifax, but you didn't get paid. Once you got your sea time you'd get off as fast as you can to try to keep ahead of the fellas. You'd come ashore, you didn't have unemployment insurance to keep you in the damn schools, you had to save every penny you could to go to navigation school for about five months. I was lucky that I was able to go back with [Imperial Oil] every time. I got right up to second mate foreign-going during the war, but I was sailing as chief officer with a Mate Home Trade ticket.

You had nothin' for the first three years or so to fight back with. Even with

"You had to zigzag in case there were submarines around, instead of a direct line, when they'd just have to come up and wait to blast you."

the twelve-pound gun on the stern, what could you do with it? Now these Park ships were beautiful. They had a twelve-pounder forward, a four-inch gun aft, and Oerlikons—they were a Swedish gun, a beautiful gun. We had two on the masthouse forward, two on the wings of the bridge and two back aft. Plus torpedo booms which were quite effective; they saved a lot of ships. I went on an old one called the *Imperoyal*, she was running continuously to St. John's, Newfoundland, [with] navy fuel and stuff like that. They put an old twelve-pound gun on the stern of her and we went out on trials and fired a few rounds. They had navy gunners with us to show us what to do. The first shell they let go, it knocked the gun off her mounting, tore the screen doors and broke pretty nearly all the dishes in the galley. What a mess.

They sent a shell through our rigging on the *Imperoyal* just off Argentia. We had an old mate by the name of Aaron Curley. We were on the twelve to four watch. I was at the wheel. God-damn near shit myself that night. We didn't see anything until the flash of the gun. God, it went right between the bridge and the foremast. That was a submarine on the surface, but we never seen the thing at all. They're so low in the water and we're so damn low; a tanker, you only had a couple feet freeboard. That was hair-raising; heard the whizz as she went by. Ol' Aaron said, "Johnny boy, what was that? What was that?" I said, "Geez Capt, I don't know what it was, but it was awful close." There was a lot of activity that night. There were a couple of collisions after that. Ships get excited and forget you got another line of ships on the other side of you and [pull] hard over.

Just to keep on your station and not hit one another was, I don't know, God must have been there with you all the time. You had to zigzag in case there were submarines around, instead of a direct line, when they'd just have to come up and wait to blast you. We used to have a clock and it had a little alarm on it. Every twenty minutes or so you'd veer off forty degrees or forty-five degrees, and then another twenty minutes you'd alter course the other way. The commodore gave orders what sequence it would be. We used to use the aldis lamp but no more than you had to. They had a blue glass over it so it wasn't too prominent. Such a sequence of light meant alteration to starboard, or another for port. It was in your sailing orders. They changed the sequence every couple of hours because if there was a submarine he could take the time and know that you're doing it systematically. Then he could be there waitin' for you on your next swing. It was a continuous thing and dangerous because you had Norwegians, Swedes, Greeks, half of them didn't speak English and we didn't speak their language, so it was marvellous how you got along.

You were so close together, if you had steering gear trouble you were right into the next ship. There was nothin' you could do about it. Then when you'd get these alterations, some of them would get mixed up—some would be goin' to port and some to starboard—and then there was chaos and many, many accidents, bad accidents. We almost hit the old *Watuka* one night. I was so close to him I cut his log line which they tow astern to tell how fast you're going approximately. I was second mate at the time and Captain Lawson Thomas had to go to the convoy meeting in St. John's when we got there. He was a real cool customer from Owen Sound. He came back and said, "John, you were pretty close to that ship ahead the other night were you?" "No, Captain, Jesus no." He says, "You're a bloody liar. Here's the bill for a log line you cut off of the *Watuka*." I didn't think we were that close to him, but we were. We could hear them talkin', haulin' the bloody thing, tryin' to get it clear of us, but I didn't think we were that close to them. She was torpedoed and lost not too long after that [see Gordon Troke interview].

I was on a diesel ship this time, the *Norwood Park*. You'd have a coal burner ahead of you. You'd get up [to them] and they'd throw in a shovel of coal to get the fires goin' good, but till it took hold takes quite awhile. But then they'd get goin' like hell and you'd lose them, you couldn't see very far, you know. Then the next thing you're up to ten revs and you're right on top of the bugger. This is goin' on all the time. I went to starboard and cut across the bow of another ship. Why we weren't cut in two, I'll never know. Lawson Thomas was always back aft playing poker, it went on all night, nobody slept. By the time he got up on the bridge, my old knees were just shakin'. I can't see a friggin' ship anywhere, I lost the convoy completely. He said, "Ah, John, where's the other ships?" "Captain, I don't know. I pretty near ran that fella next to me and I was very close to the ship ahead of us." All night, all you had was a pair of binoculars at your eyes continuously. Daylight broke and we can't see no ships or no escorts, there's nothin' around. We made it to St. John's. But he was cool. He could have bawled the shit out of me, but he didn't. "Oh, didn't hurt anything," he says, "that's the main thing." I said, "It wasn't my good judgment, Captain."

The natural elements were worse than the menace from submarines. The weather on this coast is unbelievable and to be in convoy it's nerve-wracking. You had to be on the button every second. Some of these old English tramps and Greek, I don't know how they got around. The only navigation they had was an old magnetic compass, sextant and a chronometer, that's all. Very few ships had gyrocompasses on them then. There wasn't radar on merchant ships till after the war. Collision? Can you imagine about fourteen, fifteen ships in a convoy in black thick of fog and everybody's blowin' their whistle? Lord Jesus, you don't know exactly what's goin' on. You got a ship ahead of you, one on each side of you and one astern, and everybody's blowin' their whistle. You used to tow a little thing behind that used to send up a flume of water. Well, when you got that close you better start slowin' down. And remember, I'm only twenty years old, the ink wasn't even dry on my bloody ticket then. And old Thomas back there as cool as a cucumber.

We came out of Sydney one night makin' up convoy over to St. John's. That was one of the hardest ones in the world between the submarines and the bad weather. I was only eighteen then. I was at the wheel and Gilbert Mossman was on the wing of the bridge. Thomas was skipper on that one too, the old *Imperoyal*. Geez, it was rough. Mossman had just left the starboard wing of the bridge and went over to check the side light on the port wing of the bridge. You had your navigation lights on very low, that's all you had. You had to report the lights every half hour or hour as burning: "Lights are bright, sir." He just got on the port wing of the bridge and there was a crash of sea come down, and it took the starboard wing of the bridge right off and the starboard lifeboat. He had been out there just minutes before that. I was on ships where a couple of fellas went overboard on one wave and the next one threw them back on deck. God was with us all the time out there, I think. I never thought of this until you started talkin' now; I don't know how we did stay apart in them damn convoys.

Another bad thing on this coast in the summertime was the icebergs goin' to Newfoundland. I pretty near hit one of them one night too. I didn't see a damn thing till this big mountain of ice loomed up in front of us. See, nine-tenths of that is underwater and here I am lookin' up almost straight at it. I was at the wheel that night too. The Captain and we both saw the thing at the same time and how we missed it I'll never know. We were just lucky she, that was the old *Imperoyal*, was a small ship and could swing around fast. Underneath you don't know how far out they go. It was just a dark night. If it had been fog we'd have hit the thing for sure.

Ice in the spring of the year was bad stuff. The first time that I ever ran into ice was with Captain Crouse. He never warned us about it and I'd never seen this ice in the Gulf before. We were on our way to Corner Brook. He was layin' on the settee. I saw this, I thought we were goin' aground. All you could see was white, looked like sand; didn't know it was ice. BANG! Crashed right into this thing. It was quite heavy ice. Old Crouse jumped up off the settee. "Jesus, John, what was that?" I says, "Damn it, Captain, I know now what it is, but I didn't know, and I never had a chance to call you. It's ice." "Well," he says, "keep her goin' and get well into it and we'll stay here for the night. The submarines can't get us in here." So that was fine by me, I thought that was pretty good thinkin'. It's a wonder we didn't hole her 'cause them ships weren't built for ice.

It's bloody terrible the way we've been treated. I'm heartbroken over it. Armed forces got money to go to college after the war, they got land grants, furniture grants; we got nothin'. We had the third largest merchant navy in the world during the Second World War, and during the First World War, and then after the war's over they sell them to the Greeks, Italians and God knows who else. There were over two hundred Park ships built and I forget how many there was of the smaller class. They did a marvellous job; them ships were some well-built for war-built ships. I can't express, I'm so upset and disappointed. I don't care who I'm talkin' to, I'll tell 'em, our own members of Parliament are just as much to blame as anybody. The government should have been there throwin' the torch for us. Without the merchant fleet you couldn't get your supplies across the ocean. The troops were all carried by troopships. There were no big airplanes like they have today that can get people across there. I'm seventy years old. Thank God I worked for a good company and had a job all the time, but a lot of the people that were on ships, the companies folded and they didn't have a job. The mistake we made, we should have gone to management of these companies who were there at the time, not some kid who is manager today who doesn't know there was a god-damn war on anyway and doesn't care.

Bruce Duncan

I was on watch one night and first thing: BOOM! BOOM! I looked over and didn't see nothing. "Jesus, something hit." "Yeah." The next morning, went up, put the binoculars out and they said, "Two gone." People don't realize, to be in a convoy, you have to visualize, it's twenty-four hours a day waitin' for a guy to take a shot at you. If you let it get on your mind, if you were by yourself on that ship, which you were a hell of a lot especially in the engine room, you thought, "If a god-damn torpedo comes through here, I'm all by myself." Then you go up in your room and that was all blacked out, there was nothing open, no radio, it's like a prison. You lay there in the heat, boy, I tell you, it's pressure after awhile.

I was one of the lucky ones. I was on one ship, *Nipiwan Park*, got off of her and she was hit. I was on for a dogwatch; I relieved a guy. I got off, took my bags and right onto another ship. And that ship [the *Nipiwan Park*] got hit outside of here. Two of my friends lost their lives on that. Think about this. If you went over to the shipping master and he said, yeah, sign on, you could be two hours outside and you'd be twenty miles out wouldn't you? That's where the submarines were layin' waiting for the convoys and that. If you were never to sea before, within two hours you were in a war zone.

I was on the *Trontolite*. We lost one of the lifeboats over and they wouldn't let us out of the harbour until they put a wooden boat on. I was sittin' watchin' the guys paint it with fireproof paint. I said, "Where we're goin' we don't need lifeboats, we need parachutes," because she was carrying casing head. If that went, it'd be like the *Victolite*, not a soul got off. What happened in a lot of cases these ships [tankers] went out and they weren't gas-free. When you pump a cargo out you got to put ventilators on it to get the gas out. They're big canvas ventilators, like a big sock. They'd drop it into the tank and you'd switch it around to pick up whichever way the wind was blowing. I imagine they'd keep those things up two or three days. If you ever hit them when they were gas-free you couldn't sink them unless you hit them in the engine room. I think 90 percent of the time these tankers weren't gas-free because we never had the time, you were waiting to catch a convoy. We were sittin' on a bomb.

The thing is, if you were aboard of a destroyer—I'm not takin' nothin' from 'em—but you're listening and you got a gun. We're just sittin' ducks waitin' for 'em to hit us. A lot of guys took life jackets in the bunk with them, a lot of guys didn't. No, I figured if I was goin' to go.... See, if you're on a tanker and get a flash fire, the thing would hold you up in the water and you're goin' to get burnt. If you're goin' to die, you're goin' to die, why be tortured?

Merchant seamen are an entirely different breed. They weren't all healthy people. I sailed with guys, one had no knee cap, completely gone, he had just a club foot. I tried to get in the air force and I was colour-blind, so they see me maybe in a galley someplace peelin' potatoes and it wasn't for me. I was like a lot of other merchant seamen, I don't think I could stand that, saluting and all this stuff and being pushed down the bottom, so I went on the tankers. Myself and four other brothers were at one time or another on the tankers during the war.

We got $60 a month. That was the goin' rate at the time. We got a bonus on tankers, it was danger money. You wouldn't get it goin' on the Great Lakes. A lot of them sailed anywhere the money's at. If you were on an American ship, they paid 100 percent war bonus. It makes great sense to me if somebody said to me, you get a $100 to go on a tanker and you get $65 to go on something else, I'll take the $100. That's where the money was at. This lieutenant commander (RCN) had a write-up in the paper called "Canadian Merchant Seamen Mercenaries." "Mercenary" I always figured was the enemy. Well, none of us was on Japanese ships, or German or Italian. The only ones we sailed on were on our side.[6]

The merchant navy we took as a civilian job, but we manned all the guns, on watch or off watch, when the time come. These DEMS guys were great fellers. When they first come on, they were army, then the navy took over. They looked after the four-inch gun. They stood up there and had a pretty soft job. Some of our crew members went down to St. Margaret's Bay and trained to be gunners. When the gunnery officer would say "Action stations," everybody had a place to go, cooks, everybody. In your gun crew you could very well have two mess boys passing the shells up because on one ship, the *Cyprus Hills Park*, we had ten guns but only eight gunners. When they would sound the alarm, everybody on board that ship had a position to go to.

On the *Cyprus Hills Park* we had what we call torpedo nets. They'd be steel, about a foot mesh and they'd catch a torpedo before it hit the ship. This boom would be just like a big fishin' rod, two would come out on each side, and there'd be a net come out over the engine room and up over the bridge. I bet you, them things, they'd be out about forty feet. The only part that

would be showin' would be the stern and the bow. My job was to go up
there, put the headphones on, and I'd sit up there and wait. First thing they
would say, "Action stations, drop booms," and I'd drop the booms over with
a big steam winch. You'd pay out, let it [the net] go, your back one, and I would
just run her in. That boom was up pretty high. All it looked like was a ship goin'

**A burning Liberty ship in Halifax.
Note torpedo nets tied back at the
stern of the ship. "They'd be steel,
about a foot mesh, and they'd catch a
torpedo before it hit the ship.... The
only thing I ever seen them catch, we
picked a few sharks up."**

by with these two big nets up like that. When the nets
were stored they were stored upwards, tied back. We
never picked a torpedo up with them. The only thing I
ever seen them catch, we picked a few sharks up.

   The *Cyprus Hills, Willowdale, Brentwood, Point Pelee,
Clearwater* that I know of were freighter-built, but they
converted them for oil tankers because they ran out,
we were losing so many tankers. They displaced that
cargo hold with tanks and steam pumps. They only carried sixty thousand
barrels. If you were at sea and looked at it you'd say that was a freighter;
to the person that knew the ships, he'd say, no, that's a tanker but freighter
style. All those Park ships like that, I was on the *Point Pelee Park* and she burnt

coal for propulsion—nine firemen aboard—but carried oil. To be a tanker carrying oil and burning coal was strange.

The only source of oil in those days was down in Venezuela and Colombia in South America, and Texas and California in the United States. There was no Middle East oil, and Canadian western crude never came until '46, '47. Our run was Halifax, Venezuela, back up to New York or Portland. We come to Halifax very seldom. They put a pipeline in Portland, Maine, during the war to Montreal. The rationale behind that is because there were so many ships hit, and if you came to Montreal refineries, you'd have to go up the St. Lawrence—that's three extra days. If we come to Halifax, they'd refine it here.

You went where they told you to go. We were on wartime articles, we couldn't get off. We had discipline; on the *Cyprus Hills Park* I was twenty-four hours off in four months. They brought in that act, you were froze on your ship, you couldn't get off. The thing is, if we didn't do our job they blackballed you, your discharge books were marked.

We'd pump out in Halifax, take ballast, water, and go to a South American port. We could come in to Aruba, get refined products and [bring] it over to Panama, drop it off there in navy bunkers, come back, then they'd say, "You're goin' to North Africa now with a load of diesel." Clean all our tanks, put a load of diesel aboard, then they said, "You're not goin' there now, you're goin' back to Panama." What I'm tryin' to say is that you never knew where you were goin', you could go anywhere. If your cards come up, you went, that's it. You're on, you couldn't get off.

I was on the *Point Pelee Park* and we got rammed off New York by an American tanker. Aw, Jesus, did a lot of damage to her. Brought her back in Halifax shipyards to fix. Under normal circumstances you might think I'd get home, I lived in Dartmouth. That was not the case. A taxi come down, took you to Imperial Oil and put you on another ship. We were right down to nobody, you know. If they run short-handed out of harbour, DEMS gunners took the job on and split the wage. On the *Reginolite* the second cook aboard was a navy gunner for the longest while because we couldn't get a cook. He did the cookin' and his watch was picked up by the gunners and they split the [cook's] wage four ways. Cook's wages weren't bad.

It was quite an honour to sail with Imperial Oil because they paid fair'y good wages, food was good and everything was clean. On those ships you'd have what they called Imperial Oil crews, company crews. If you sailed for a company, that was your company, you didn't go from one company to another. The manning pools, those guys, they'd go anywhere. The last going-off we had manning pool crews 'cause we couldn't get the men, we were running out. Imperial Oil lost half their ships. They had eight seagoing tankers, I think, and they lost the *Calgarolite, Victolite* and the *Montrolite*; the *Canadolite* was captured off of Africa.

I relieved a guy for three weeks and made two trips up to Newfoundland and back. Those poor buggers on those coasters. Jesus, they were terrible. They were under the water more than they were out. Hard way to make a livin' on those. When you're on a big ship, you don't have that to contend with.

We never got a clothing allowance or nothing like that. If you came aboard ship with a big heavy coat and I was coming on watch, I borrowed your coat 'cause we never had enough clothes to go around. If you were in the engine room your working clothes—dungarees and boiler suits, cover-alls—usually that was left when you paid off. Another person picked them up and wore them. Merchant seamen never had uniforms. All they had was a pin and an identification. If you came ashore in a military place with a civilian uniform on, you might as well take an ass-about-face and come around because you never got no treatment. When the ship come in, we went to the first tavern or stayed aboard. Where could you go? You couldn't go to a dance where there was military. The only [place] we were ever treated with the same respect as military was in Panama. Service personnel got ditty bags of different stuff—playing cards, toothpaste, a few magazines, nice socks, mitts; I never. You talk about discrimination.

Hours, you have no idea the amount of hours we worked to keep them things going because they were old. A lot of those ships were built in the early twenties. They were modern in their time but were ready to be condemned before the war came. No spare parts; you had to make a lot of your own parts and that. There were no shipyard workers to repair those engines, you know, 'cause there was a shortage of personnel in the shipyards. Those engines were repaired by the crew, the black gang, the fellers in the engine room done those. In convoy your speeds are back and forth. You may go slow speed and that means a lot of carbon. Fast, slow, fast, slow, drop her back two revs, up her two revs. Before the war, when you set those engines at sea you don't look at them, they just go one speed. You had trouble but not like it was during the war. You wouldn't get the parts you may want to get and you wouldn't get the shipyard workers to come do the work, you had to do your own. A lot of people think, they don't visualize that there's men aboard them ships, they're not remote control.

I'll give you the hours now I worked. Go to work eight o'clock in the morning. The guys coming off watch would shut one engine down and we'd have two pistons to pull. At every station where we're goin' to work, the engineer on watch or the junior engineer would lay out the tools. When they shut that engine down, it'd be just like a madman, a bunch of people runnin'.

No whistlin', no hollerin', because you're not allowed; you may be caught in the machinery and somebody hollers, Jesus, you run and look. Very seldom you ever hear anybody holler down there; enough noise as it is.

A piston in your car is that round. These were seventy-four inches, just the skirt and the crown, not the rod; a three-foot bore. One head, one piston—not like your car that has one head, four pistons. And them heads are big. You'd haul that out—no electric cranes either, all hand—and drop a new piston in. The only clothes you'd have on was a pair of pants, work boots, work socks and underwear. Change your pants two or three times; they'd be soggy from the sweat. The feller workin' about you, you'd have to tell him to move or you could move, 'cause it would be just skin and bone and he'd be sweating so much on top of you. I worked from eight o'clock in the morning until six o'clock next morning and this was quite often.

Six o'clock you'd come up. Now you're black, eh? No nice warm showers. Down between, what we used to call the flats, in between the props where the tail shaft come through, [you would get] a bucket of diesel oil and wash your frame down with that. Go up and take two buckets of water back, hot and cold, from the galley and wash yourself down. They used to issue us with Rinse-O. Take an hour to clean up, go in and get your breakfast about seven o'clock. Then you turn in, eight o'clock, and it was hot, I'm talkin' hot. Twelve o'clock, call you to get up, get your dinner and go to work again, build a piston, so you always had two new ones all ready to go. Not one penny of overtime. This would be sometimes six days a week.

Jim Boutilier

I wasn't old enough to get in any of the other three forces, I was only fifteen years old. So the only thing I could get was to go on one of the ships and I went on the tankers. They'd take anyone in those days, glad to get them, on the tankers especially. I stayed there pretty well all during the war. You started as a seaman, and I was sailing as second mate [by war's end]. I was on several: the *Royalite*, the *Reginolite*, then the *Montrolite*, the *Petrolite*, *Imperoyal*, the *Norwood Park*. It wasn't a matter of leaving or quitting these ships to go on leave; there was times down here to Imperial Oil or different places, the ship would be ready to sail and maybe a few in the crew wouldn't show up and you'd be asked if you'd mind going on the other ship. I always volunteered.

It happened [the *Montrolite* was torpedoed] at quarter to eight in the night, just about the time I was ready to come off watch. It was raining and sort of rough and we weren't expecting anything that night, but things happen when you least expect it. The fourth of February 1942. About three days we would have made Halifax, coming from South America, full load of crude oil. I was up at the wheel at the time, steering the ship; I was only seventeen years old. Well, a bit of hell broke loose, I can tell you that. I never saw a flash or experienced anything like it since. I was one of the closest ones to it. The torpedo hit right about the midships, between the midships and the

"When the first torpedo hit, well, the main deck and everything was awash, she was pretty well down then. We were dead in the water and we knew that we were going to get another one."

pump room and tore one awful gash into her. Yeah, they did get a message off, but we were sailing on our own, no convoys. That was the bad part of it, we never had any protection or anything, not in those days. We took some chances; we were slaughtered, there was a lot of ships sunk.

It was sort of a blinding flash. For a few minutes I didn't know anything. It just knocked me right away from the wheel over in the flag locker at the side of the wheelhouse. I scrambled to my feet. The way I look at it, I must have been out for a few minutes because when I came out on the boat deck, one of the boats had been launched and was gone. So then we saw one of the lifeboats from aft—we had a following wind at sea from the stern—and the boat was launched and was drifting up alongside the ship towards the bow, so I jumped and they pulled me into the boat. The rest of them took to the after boats.

She was a big ship. When the first torpedo hit, well, the main deck and everything was awash, she was pretty well down then. We were dead in the water and we knew that we were going to get another one, so the best thing to do was get out of the way, abandon ship. About fifteen or twenty minutes later, they hit her on the other side with another torpedo, but we were all clear of it by then. It hit we figure between the fuel tanks and cargo tanks. You take, with diesel oil mixing with the Venezuelan crude–it was a good grade of light crude–boy, she just went, everything went. She caught fire and all you could see was the flames and the smoke. The first thing, she was gone.

There was supposed to be three boats that got away. There was twenty in our lifeboat and I heard there was only three in the one they launched from midships. That would have left twenty-five in the other boat, and that would have been really loaded right to the gunwales. We were in some pretty bad weather. Forty-eight, and there was only twenty of us picked up in one lifeboat. All the officers were lost; the fourth engineer and the electrician were the only two [saved]. We don't know what happened to the other two [lifeboats]. Course, when we landed here there was a lot of their relatives and next of kin and they started inquirin' about the others. Well, you don't just tell somebody it was a miracle that we were picked up and they may never be found. So there was different stories circulated, said they think they were picked up and headed for another port and all this and that stuff.

We were in the lifeboat about three days, rough weather all the time. We managed to keep her afloat; if she'd have swamped, there wouldn't have been a chance at all. It was just like a nightmare. We had everything, even sleet. You take where we were sunk, it was pretty well around the edge of the Gulf Stream, but [we were] being driven north in a gale for three days. We had to use our sail for a sea anchor; tie it to a rope and put it over. Tried to keep the lifeboat up into the wind and sea, but there was times we had to take to the oars. But you had to have a rest too, you couldn't do it all the time. We bailed steady all the time, just a couple of buckets, whatever we could [find], and spell one another off. We tried everything we could [to keep] from filling with water. At one point we had to take the sea anchor in, and take the sail and try to lash it around the boat because we were tired of bailing.

I don't think they put on too much of a search to look for anybody. It was an old British merchantman who got astray from a convoy [that found us]. It was really rough, around noon, and the ship's carpenter happened to be out on deck up around the midships and he reported to the bridge that he saw something over there. They couldn't see us from the bridge. He reported it two or three times–"There it is again"– and pointed it out. First thing, God, we were here and they were right abeam of us, pretty near going by. He altered the course about ninety degrees and came towards us. That was a sight. They put a scramble net over and we had enough energy to get up it. We were getting pretty weak, I'll tell you, but managed to get enough reserve strength for that. They were good to us, we shared bunks with them and they fed us good. Course, we had no clothing or anything either; all I had was a pair of denims and a singlet and comin' in here in February. One of them gave me a jacket and something else.

I was [hurt] in a way, but I didn't say too much about it. You're young, you're careless, and all I was interested in [when] we landed here was gettin' home. I had some sore ribs and some bruises on the side of my head. A lot of the other fellas were from different parts away from here and they stayed over in the Seamen's Club on Hollis Street, but for me it was my home. They said you'll be on pay up to three months—survivor's leave they called it—provided you're unemployed. It was around $65 a month they would have paid us. God, three days later, the phone was ringing trying to get you back on a ship. I think today how foolish we were, or I was. I just kept goin'. There was others like me. There's somethin' else I should mention that was pretty mean of Imperial Oil. The day we were torpedoed and took to the lifeboats, we got our pay [but] they cut our war bonus off; drifting around the ocean and no bonus.

After the torpedoing of the *Montrolite*, I applied for the air force. I still got the letter in there yet. They just up and as much as told me that I was more valuable on the tankers than I was in the air force and they appreciated my offer of service.

The only regrets I ever had was the rotten deal that we did get. All the privileges and goodies that they give to the servicemen after they were discharged.... I got a job in the dockyard and stayed there for twenty-odd years. When a competition would come up for a job, you worked on the point system. If you were in the navy—you had to be in the service—you got so many points to start right away. Well, how about my experience in the merchant navy? "Oh no, that don't count." But some of those fellows over there in the dockyard never left the dockyard, they worked in the fleet mail office all during the war or something like that. They were drawing pensions and getting points and everything and they went for a competition and we got nothing. They owe us a lot, but we'll never get it.

Paul Fralic

I've said it many times and I'll say it again, war is a young man's job. I sailed with men in their fifties that had ashore a family and some of those men just broke up. Here I am, a young buckaroo, seventeen, eighteen years old, and seeing a man cry. You thought he was nuts, but he had something to cry about. Where that really hit home was down off Miami. We were coming up the coast this evening, it was suppertime, when the American navy moved in with depth charges and they really hammered whatever they were after. This one particular guy, he went to pieces, just broke up.

A couple of nights we had to stand by all night. We had escorts and they would put us on the alert. One of the guys ready to change shifts was scared to death. We couldn't find him to change watch. Where'd he get to? Where'd he get to? We finally found him sleepin' in the lifeboat. He wanted to make sure he was the first off.

One morning we were heading south and we were down around Cape Canaveral and there was a Swedish cargo ship just got it. I'll never forget it. The men were rowing ashore and they were singing. Here again, this was youth, it didn't upset us that much; pleased that the guys got away. We took it more or less, come day, go day, never thought about you're going to be the next one to go down.

We weren't supposed to keep a diary, but I did. In two days going down the American coast we counted eighty-three ships: there wasn't enough water to sink them; there was a funnel up or there were just two masts or a bow up. Eighty-three in two days I counted!

Doug Oxner

I loved goin' to sea. It's been bred into Lunenburgers for centuries. Tradition; father, grandfather, great grandfather, all went to sea and it's just quite normal, I guess. The year before [the war] I got myself a marine radio ticket in Halifax and it was quite easy to get a job once the war broke out. I got it fairly quickly. I had been in the militia for quite a few years, and as a signalman I knew the Morse code perfectly well. It was an eight-and-a-half, nine-month course and I got through just a little over seven. Money was very, very scarce, so you were thankful you finished ahead of time. I was on a French trawler for a little while. The next one was a big Swedish freighter, the *Radmanso*. The reason I got on, the Sparks—the international name for a radio operator—ended up in hospital and I jumped at the chance.

The first trip was over to Scotland on a slow convoy and it took us twenty-some days to get there. It was kind of secretive for goin' aboard because they were neutral. When we got unloaded over in Edinburgh, I wanted to go to Sweden. Naturally I didn't see Sweden. The skipper said, "No, you'd be interned. I'd have to turn you in or I'd be in big trouble." I was a combatant in a neutral country. I shouldn't 'ave been there in the first place, but they grabbed the first guy they could get because the convoy was sailin' in a day or two. The deal was, it was a one-way trip; I get paid off and they find me passage home. In those days, say a customs officer got $85, $90 a month, that was about average. The pay wasn't great, but it went a long way. I got paid damn near three hundred bucks, an enormous amount. Well, I was lousy rich, but of course after a depression like that I owed most of it home. My family was in debt. Father owned about a fifty- or sixty-foot fishing boat; cashed his life insurance to get it. There wasn't enough to carry marine insurance, which was very expensive, and the thing sunk.

I was on the [Imperial Oil] *Sarnolite* two years, three months and eighteen days. I remember one time in '42, that's when the subs got here, and it got so damn hot that we didn't think we'd live any more than three months; especially on tankers, they loved the tankers. We were in a small convoy from Montreal probably headed for Goose Bay 'cause we had gasoline and Goose Bay was then opening up for the air force. Five or six assorted merchant ships and one or two naval boats. We were just off the Gaspé when it let loose with torpedoes. Within fifteen or twenty minutes it was only us, a small Norwegian ship and one of the naval boats left [out of] seven or eight that started.

One time we were goin' up [the St. Lawrence River], I can't remember if we were in convoy or not. It was just about sunset and the first thing on shore—flame, bang!—a torpedo missed us and hit the shore. This huge sheet of flame and these people runnin' like the devil was after 'em. You talk about a racket. It was right calm like it is this morning. One of the mates watched it, "My God, look at those Frenchmen runnin'!" And I think it was me, I says, "Yeah, we don't have any place to run, do we?" But anyway, no more; we weren't in good range or somethin', I guess.

You always slept with a life jacket. I had a little pint of rum with a big sign on it, "For Lifeboat Use Only! Do Not Touch!" and maybe a couple of other little things tied onto my life jacket. If you're in a lifeboat half frozen, a pint of rum goes a long, long way. I know one time off Cape Race, I was kind of beer sick and seasick, just about half, and it was blowin' a livin' gale. I was in bed. The first thing a big crash. Naturally you'd wake up. Here the water was sloppin' around in my room, along with books and suitcases and an assortment of things. What happened, the mate was on the bridge and he looked up to see this big white comber comin'. It whacked us and cleaned off two lifeboats and catwalks ripped up. I remember sayin', "My God, what a night to die!" I figured she fell apart. That was one damn stormy night, I'll tell ya. It wasn't funny at that time.

The closest one was right off Chebucto Head [near Halifax] one Christmas Day. It was a big convoy, probably forty ships or more. The first thing, a big bang and our ship shook like that. Naturally I thought we were hit. It was snow flurries then and they'd come and go and we didn't know who was hit. Maybe two or three minutes later the snow cleared and it was a navy boat, a corvette, only a few hundred yards away. A big loss of life too. It wasn't long before everybody went hellbent for election for Halifax Harbour again.

Naturally, around Christmas, the New Year, it gets dark very quickly. In the middle of the afternoon we were ordered to proceed again to Saint John, New Brunswick, by ourselves. Well, we could see what it was. When we got out to the mouth of the harbour by the gate there was navy boats around and airplanes circling. You know what we were: B-A-I-T. They thought maybe a sub would come up and go after us and then they'd get them with the airplanes.[7] I remember the skipper gave a bottle of rum to the officers' mess and a bottle of rum to the crew's mess. "Don't ill use it, but everybody have a big slug." We didn't exactly think we'd see tomorrow and that was on Christmas Day, mind you. At that time we knew we wasn't goin' to live forever. You get that worked into your system that you say, well hell. It's like the army on an attack; you know that not everybody's goin' to come out of that, so you kind of settle your mind into it. But like I say, that was close. That bait, that was hard to stomach. It was fun, wasn't it? What a lovely war.

Henry Kohler

I wasn't a very good student because I was interested in going to sea. It was sort of a foregone conclusion for me; I guess it's almost hereditary. Grandfathers on both sides of my family were shipmasters and my father was a shipmaster. They were all foreign-going shipmasters, we were never in the fishing industry. I had been to sea a lot with my family on sailing vessels on world voyages just as a very small child. My father was German and only came to Lunenburg in 1908, but my mother's people came here in 1753. However, my father became a citizen very shortly afterwards and he sailed under the British flag and the Canadian flag in the two world wars. He was awarded the Order of the British Empire for work in the evacuation of France. It's very interesting to me, after I was a captain very shortly after the war, I was in German ports where I had a lot of cousins and I used to visit with them. I remember two had been submarine commanders and, you know, putting our thoughts together and dates and so on, they were in subs that were shooting at the convoys I was in.

I was serving my time then [in 1939] as a young sailor in the West Indies, South American trade in steamships. The first one I served in at the outbreak of the war or shortly after was the *John Cabot*, a steamship out of St. John's, Newfoundland. South-bound would be general cargoes, could be anything, a lot of salt fish; and north-bound would be sugar, molasses, rum and that sort of thing. She was also involved in the trans-Atlantic trade. We had a three-inch naval gun of a vintage of about 1915. She was too slow to sail in convoys, she'd fall out of them. Many ships did. Many, many couldn't keep up even in slow convoys, particularly if you got any weather. If they were nine-knot ships and were in heavy weather and head winds, they'd drop back to four or five knots pretty quick. Not necessarily the age [of the ship] but the lack of power. So, normally you were just left on your own. Somewhat [unsettling], but then again there were many times travelling alone on your own you weren't as much a desirable a target as a whole convoy to a submarine.

There were routes used which wouldn't even be considered in normal times. We used to squeeze some pretty big ships through some of these very small and shallow-draft inland waterways along the U.S. coast. In that way they could keep them in off of the coast. There were tremendous [numbers] of ships lost on the east coast by enemy action, tremendous numbers; all types, tankers and cargo ships as well.

After two years in those ships in the West Indies and South American trade, I went in the Imperial Oil deep-sea tankers. I had forty-five or fifty years at sea and that was in all oceans of the world. Don't let anybody tell you this ocean or that ocean in the world are the worst, because we got it all right on this coast, every bit of it. On the North Atlantic in the wintertime, on the Canadian Atlantic coast, it's a hell of an ocean. I spent just as bad a time tryin' to get to St. John's, Newfoundland, from New York as you'd spend gettin' anywhere. In smaller ships [and] some larger ships, it's not at all unusual to be overcome and lose your entire ship and it's still happening right today. Many times I think the true seaman, and I like to see myself in that image, you just feel that's the way of life and accept it and try to do what you can to survive and live with it. Many, many, many, it's very common, people can just go to pieces. And that didn't matter if it was a mess boy right up to a captain, I've seen all of it. Some can be quite successful to the time when they get the real acid test and go to pieces. That's in all walks of life.

In times of peace you try to work with the weather. Even though you do get it bad and you may get badly beaten up and may have very difficult times, you still try to work with it. Then [in wartime] you were forced to work against it, whatever it might be. If it was against you, that was tough, you just had to fight on. That was very hazardous, of course, and the real reason for a great deal of damage at sea. I can remember being at sea on Christmas Day and it was just terrible in the North Atlantic. It was snowing and blowing a gale. We had a hell of a time, losing our deck cargo and all that sort of thing. So, anyway, we were still looking forward to a pretty good Christmas dinner, we could see it being prepared in the galley. Normally you got a couple bottles of beer or something like that. About eleven o'clock in the morning, the ship took one tremendous sea over here–tremendous–completely washed out the galley star lights, filled the galley, cleaned it out completely, just about killed the cooks and that were in there. We ended up for our Christmas dinner we had an apple and a bottle of beer. I remember it well.

I guess, on a very serious and deep thought, I'm not an agnostic, I'm not an atheist by any stretch of the imagination. I'm not a religious fanatic either. But I feel very deeply, whatever your denomination may be or religion may be, there's an overall being. Now, I don't know what that it is. I'm also a true believer that when your number rolls up, it's all over. I don't think there's any great book how that's going to happen to you, but I got a feeling if Mike Parker's number rolls up tomorrow there's not a thing you can do about it.

"In times of peace you try to work with the weather.... Then [in wartime] you were forced to work against it, whatever it might be. If it was against you, that was tough, you just had to fight on."

I was always very fortunate, or very lucky I should say, and I used to say jokingly, but I guess I meant it, to some of my friends on ships, "You go on the same ship with me, you'll be all right." I never was in the water; close, really close, but never was in the water. I can remember, certainly in convoys, when we actually saw torpedoes pass under our bow and get the ship in the next column. Oh yes, that's not too uncommon. I can also remember very well passing through the debris of ships that were five miles ahead of us. One particular incident in Halifax, we were in, I think, the *Vancolite* and Imperial Oil gave us the opportunity to transfer to the *Victolite* and go to sea. The *Vancolite* was goin' a few days later. One of my friends said, "Well, I'm goin' on the *Victolite*." I said, "No, I'm goin' to stay right here." He went on the *Victolite* and she was lost with all hands.

I think of the most hazardous things that happened occasionally in routing, for whatever reasons, you might get two large convoys that would get mixed together in the middle of the night going in different directions, with no lights. That was really hazardous. I was involved in one very serious collision. It was a black, black night with everything blacked out. I was on an Imperial Oil ship loaded with crude from South America and we had a collision with an American gasoline tanker. That was a bad one and happened just like that. The crude that we were carrying at that time was a very gassy crude and the other [being] a gasoline tanker, normally what's going to happen in a case like that is immediate explosions and fire, or fire and explosions, whichever comes first in a situation such as that. We didn't lose either ship and neither one exploded, but boy when they collided there was fire going. I was third mate. As I remember, I wasn't there on the bridge at the time this happened. I had finished my watch at midnight and was having a cup of tea and a sandwich, maybe at 12:30, one o'clock in the morning, when suddenly we had this severe collision. Of course, we people that were down below [thought a torpedo had hit]. It was severe enough that we felt this vessel was going to sink, but she didn't. That happened not too far from New York because both ships, although very seriously damaged, arrived in New York a couple of days later. I can remember we had lost an anchor, and the anchor and chain was inside of the other ship. We only learned that when we got in port. I don't know what the reason was [for the collision]; in those days, in wartime, things were not investigated very carefully. If you didn't lose a ship, the ship was cleaned up, repaired and out to sea and not too much talk about it. You were operating without lights and that was good and bad, whichever way you wanted to look at it; sometimes it was very good and sometimes very hazardous.

Thick fog and a dark night you had a lot of problems. I think it was as big a hazard, particularly in the early stages of the war, going in convoy, as the submarines were, because merchant ship captains are not trained in fleet manoeuvres. Navy men are trained in this. But I'll tell you, after awhile, people got pretty damned good at it. I wasn't old enough to be a captain during the war, although I was a very young one after, but they had a pretty tough ride. Oh yeah, they had a tough time of it.

Many naval men looked down their nose at the merchantmen. Now the smart navy man, there's a lot of 'em, they appreciated the things that the merchant service had, they understood that they were specialists in that particular business. In the navy they were especially trained in a certain area, in a certain discipline, and they're good. But if they had to do the generalized work that happens in the merchant navy, they couldn't do it, no more than we could go on their ships and do their work. It's that simple. I think it's necessary to have a proper appreciation and understanding of each other's, what shall I say, positive points and negative points. It didn't happen all the time.

I sailed on an awful lot of convoys as a young officer when we had American navy commodores of the convoy. Generally they were far easier to have on board of a ship, far easier to deal with, had more appreciation for what we had to do, than the British or Canadian-trained navy officer. They had no tolerance or understanding for the problems of our work. The average young Canadian officer, if he had training in England, he was just as bad as the Limeys. A lot who didn't were trained here and adopted their thinking. That didn't sell very well in the merchant service. We didn't like that much.

A lot of these young men who came out of universities and Central Canada developed into exceptionally good men. They were intelligent and they were well educated [but] totally green as far as the seamanship and being at sea and sea life. But when the navy expanded so quickly and they took in a lot of merchant navy captains and merchant service captains and officers, these were the men who operated the ships and they had the ability to do it. But the young men did learn quickly, as is well recorded in naval history.

I can't see that there were any great animosities. Seamen are a rather unique group of people in the world. There's a brotherhood in my opinion, totally unwritten, a brotherhood among seamen all over the world. There's some real basic understandings in all languages that nobody teaches, but it's there.

In many cases there were many young men who were in the merchant service and they were in there for the first six months or year of the war and then they went and joined the navy and served well. I would think they were just as well off in either service. There was always a certain people who would say, well those in the merchant service were better paid and so on. Not really. We didn't have any benefits, you know. And we didn't get a hell of a lot of money either, although I think at that time it might have been more cash in hand at the end of a month than the naval man got, but not a hell of a lot of difference.

There's no question, in the first week of the outbreak of war, I would have been in the navy, but I had the physical disability of a stiff hip, so I had no choice there. I have few regrets serving in the merchant service. There were some who were bitter about it until this past year or so, quite bitter about the fact that they'd never been recognized [as veterans] and also that they didn't get any benefits and there are some who need benefits. While in my case, I was fortunate enough I made a good living and I'm not worried, I can live nicely, there are some who can't and maybe now they will get some benefits that will help them live a little better in our country. There are so few who are left. There's no question in my mind that our contribution in the merchant navy was just as valuable as those people who served in the navy. The broad-minded people believe that, the narrow-minded people don't.

Eric Publicover

When I first went to sea I was a mess boy with my dad. In '40 or '41 I went to relieve a guy one winter for Imperial Oil on the old *Talaralite*. My father Eldridge was chief steward and cook onto her; he was always a cook. He went there [Imperial Oil] back in the twenties. And I'm tellin' you, just because he was my father, he didn't favour me any way. If I didn't do what I was supposed to do, I bloody well got told and you had to do it right. I learned a lot from my dad, different things. That was my first trip on an ocean-going ship. Well, then the company made some kind of arrangement with the War Admiralty after they lost all those people down the States. There were four brothers lost in one ship.[8] They said we're goin' to cut that out, we're goin' to try and keep the families separated. Now you want to go to sea, you can't go on the same ship that your father's on or that your brother's on, so I tried it on my own.

Them days you had a manning pool in Halifax. You go to the manning pool and twenty-four hours there'd be ten guys up there tryin' to get you out. My God, they'd come in and hound you: "Want a cook, want a cook, want a cook." I don't know how many different ships I could have went out on. You were lucky to get a cook, my dear man, aboard ship during the war because they were so scarce. The thing was there was so many god-damn ships, all of a sudden they wanted all these [cooks]. Some ships they had some awful guys for cooks.

We had a cook on the *Liverpool Loyalist*; he had a job to boil an egg to make it look right. That's the feller used to serve you beans about four times a week if you could stand them. And boy, they'd be like glue. Beans was only three or four cents a pound, you know, in them days. Five pounds of beans would feed a hell of a lot of men. Oh, that feller was a wiener cook. The first Sunday I was onto her they had a roast beef, I'll never get over that. I said, now my God, I wonder what blacksmith had that in his forge for about three days before he ever brought it out. Now you could chew on that for a week and you'd never be able to swallow it, it was roasted to death. I've never seen a chunk of meat so paralyzed in all my life as what that was. A big old tall fella he was, always hah, hah, laugh if you said anything to him. You couldn't get him mad. We had some lousy god-damn cooks, but when I got cookin' myself, I said I'd never feed a man like that.

I never cooked outside of the tankers. Imperial Oil was one of the best outfits you could go to sea with as far as food was. Oh yes, everybody got the same food. That was one thing I wouldn't do, I wouldn't cook anything for a seaman that I wouldn't cook for the Old Man or vice versa. If it was good enough for the seamen, it was good enough for the Old Man, that's what I used to say. I always had pretty good luck with my cookin'. I'll tell you one thing, it doesn't matter where you are, if you're cookin' on a ship or if you're cookin' in a hotel or if you're cookin' home for yourself, tidiness is one of the greatest things for cookin'. I've seen some old guys come in there with a dirty old shirt on, [never] wear white clothes and I used to say, "My God Almighty, I can't understand how you allow anybody...." When I cooked, I always wore my whites.

Some days it was pretty drastic. I made a rule—my dad always used to do it and I said I could do the same thing—it don't take me any longer to make a poached egg as it does a scrambled egg, so I used to serve eggs any style. But you take, say you got to do a dozen eggs at a time on top of the stove, sunny side up. You crack your eggs and all of a sudden the ship takes a list. Now it takes what, two or three seconds before the heat's goin' to hit that egg before it'll stay in one place? If you've got too much grease onto it, the next thing you know they're goin' to be on the deck, aren't they? You didn't have a fryin' pan like we know a fryin' pan in our home, it didn't have sides onto it, eh. Your griddle pan was just a flat thing with about that much of a ridge on it. A good many I lost before I found the trick. When they started goin', you got to have your slicer to turn 'em over the other way. You had racks about that high all around your stove. It was made that you could put a rack in here or a rack there or there, section it off. Whatever size pot you had, you section that one off so it wouldn't move back and forth. But when the ship rolled that pot still rolled with the ship, eh, and if you put it too full it would roll out on top of your stove, so you made sure when you made your soup that you had at least three or four inches room for your ingredients.

On a real rough day if she's goin' this way, you don't mind it—head to, what we call, into the sea—but when you're goin' side to the sea, when she starts rollin' from port to starboard, that's the worst one. That's when you lose everything off your damn table and everything goes haywire. If she hits a bad roll and you're sittin' at the mess table havin' your dinner and you got a bowl of soup in front of you, if you don't grab that, it's goin' to be on your lap or on the table. I've seen that happen a good many times that you had your meal in front of you and all of a sudden it started goin' just like somebody had a magnet on the other side haulin' it away from you; you'd think the thing was alive.

A ship cook is really a different animal than anybody else. You got so many different elements that you got to work against. Your stove in a lumber camp don't move, it's steady, but on a ship it's bouncin' up and down; it's bolted down but the ship is goin'. It had to be pretty god-damn rough that you couldn't make nothin'. You could always boil an egg. I seen it you could hardly keep a pot on the stove, but you could always make a pot of soup. It was miserable but you got used to it. You got banged up here and banged there, you had lots of black spots on you; you got chucked around. We always had coarse salt, sprinkle that something like kitty litter, 'cause the deck on those ships in the galley was all tile—for cleanliness—and slippery as hell. You hose that deck down every night. I was never on a ship, outside of some of those old bastards, never had a bug, and ships are bad for cockroaches. I used to use that Pine Sol and black creolin, take the steam hose and put the boilin' water to it.

I used to bake pies on the ship but not too often. Oh, pies was somethin' hellish to make on a ship. Pie with a crust is all right but don't try to make a pie, like a pumpkin or a custard pie, somethin' that's goin' to roll with the ship. Don't try that. Bread wasn't too bad. You could make your sponge and get ready to make twenty-five or thirty loaves in the night. Now this is the old navy bread pans I'm talkin' about; they'd be pretty near two feet long and about six inches wide. It's when it comes out of the oven, that's what used to get me. You got to store it on top of your counter to let it cool down before you store it away. Leave the galley about two o'clock in the god-damn morning and come up the next morning for your bread, half of it [gone]. Ah geez, them DEMS gunners and the night crew used to get in there 'cause I never used to lock the galley. Not in the wartime, you never locked the galley. Anybody that was on duty had to have something to eat. I always put so much in the night locker. After they was off duty, after they had their three meals a day, we figured that was enough for them. They'd go in and see that nice smelly bread settin' there, that's when they'd have a feast. I never used to growl too much, only when they used to waste it. When I'd go in and see bread layin' on the deck that they didn't look after properly and put away, Christ, yes, cut 'em off for a couple of days. I said, "The hell with you fellas. I'll go back on the god-damn old baker stuff again." You generally took at least, oh, fifty, sixty dozen loaves of each, like twenty-four cartons of white bread, ten cartons of whole wheat, ten cartons of brown. Now twenty-four loaves to a carton I think in those days it used to be. We used to keep bread for pretty near a month, I guess.

I used to get some awful messes in port. Guys go ashore and have a few drinks and then they come back and they'd be fryin' eggs or fryin' bacon. One night I had a bunch of chickens all ready, I had it all quartered and marinated and fixed up nice, you know. I was goin' to have southern fried chicken for Sunday dinner. Sunday meal was always somethin' special, I used to do a little extra for 'em. I was ashore myself. Somebody got one of the big fryin' pans out and I come back the next mornin', half the Jesus chicken was fried up!

Standard procedure aboard ship, if you made a mess for yourself or have a feed, you clean up your mess, don't make the cook clean it up 'cause he's got to come in in the morning and make breakfast or dinner for the whole bunch. I'll do you a favour if you do me a favour. I'll put the stuff out for you that you can have a lunch, but I want you to clean up. I had some of those smart-ass guys from Ontario and places like that that thought they knew it all, but they soon found out who was boss. You don't fool around with the old cook. You tell him once. If he don't do it, you don't get it next time; I'll cut you off right quick.

You watch that certain guy. Say you had clam chowder or a seafood chowder. I'd say, "Who's that for?" "Oh, that's for the god-damn smart aleck gunner."

"Here, I'll fix his ass." Take the salt shaker. "Now go in and give it to him."

"What the Jesus happened, Cook? You dip the god-damn ocean dry?"

"What? Nothin' happened."

"Well, how come my soup is so Jesus salty?"

"Yeah, that'll just learn you a lesson. The next time, don't fool with the old cook."

I never went to the Old Man for nothin', I kept away. The only time I ever went to the Old Man was if I wanted my cut of the rum. We used to get forty-five-gallon wooden kegs every trip to Montreal, that good old Montreal stuff. Ratings weren't allowed, just the officers. We wouldn't be out of Father Point twenty-four hours, one of the deck hands come back, say "Steward, the Old Man wants to see you." We never had phones aft at that time, only on the bridge and in the engine room. So I'd don a jacket or whatever happened to be in the galley hanging around and run up the catwalk. "After you finish your work, Cook, come on up. I got a job for you." Well, you knew right away what he was goin' to do. Everybody used to have their own little jug. You had your jug all whipped in marlin, rope, so when you hung it in your locker, when it got rough it wouldn't break. Oh, it was nice to have a little shot like that if anything was around like a submarine. That was always a bad time in the nighttime when everybody had to scramble to their stations. Boy, when you got back down in your room, a little toddy always.... I always had a jug in my locker all the time, not that I drank that much, but it was always there if I wanted it. Now I guess that's why I like the old black rum so much today. You can't beat the old navy rum.

I ended up on a god-damn old coal boat, that was my last ship durin' the war. It's a dirty old ship, like Stompin' Tom says, you're a dirty old man on the coal boat; but by God, look, everybody seemed to be happy, had a good crew. I don't think the Jerrys would bother sinking one of those old things 'cause the torpedo would cost more than what the ship was worth.... The old *Liverpool Loyalist*, my cousin and I were runnin' back and forth down to Newfoundland a whole lot one season on what they call the Newfie run, carryin' supplies for the Canadian armed forces in Newfoundland. The *Liverpool Loyalist* was owned by a British outfit that run the Markland Shipping Company. We carried everything, all kinds of supplies—foods of all descriptions, clothing, Red Cross stuff, a lot of booze, mostly booze. The steel was so bad in 'em, well a good many nights I slept with my oilskins on so I wouldn't get wet in my bunk. We was back in what they call the tiller flat, way back in the ass-end of the ship, and when it rained, the rivets was so bad into it that the water used to run down alongside the rivets and right into your bunk. I often wonder how we ever won the war, you know, some of the equipment we had and some of the things they put on the ocean.

Harold Sperry

I started as a messman, then I went second cook and baker. One time it was rough and on those [Imperial Oil] tankers when you got into a storm, a heavy sea, she'd go down like this and when she come back up, she'd bend and then slap like that in the stern, and the galley, of course, was in the back. The chief cook, I remember he was cookin' soup. It picked the soup—she went like that, and the soup went right up and came down on the floor. And it all runs down to scuppers all around the floor. It was pretty near dinnertime she did this. He said, "Run quick and get a towel." So we plugged the scuppers up and he gets the old soup ladle down and dips her all back in. I said, "You're not goin' to serve that to the captain?" "Why not?" he said. "They won't know the difference." He dipped her back in, mixed her up, added a bit more stuff to her and served her up. I'll never forget that. He was a dirty old fella anyway, it didn't make no difference to him what happened. So anyway, the soup went over better that time than any he had. I think back, they were good ol' times.

I went through a lot of it on the coast on the *Talaralite* [an Imperial Oil tanker]. We carried airplane gas down to Argentia, Newfoundland. I could tell you some stories about that. Our skipper was an old feller and he liked to drink quite a bit. He'd get brave when he was out in convoy. If it didn't suit him, the speed the convoy was goin' [in theory, convoys were supposed to maintain the speed of the slowest ship], he'd run away from 'em. I saw him one night, he said, "Give me that gun." We had sort of a Bren gun. They didn't want him to use it. He got into the porthole and started firin' at the corvettes. He was pretty well drunk up. It's a wonder they didn't sink us because we were a menace.

Then we'd go down to Newfoundland somewhere and he'd have to go over to St. John's to a [convoy] conference. We used to get some kick out of him. He had his uniform, all the stripes and everything. All the convoy skippers, they'd get their orders how the convoy was goin' to go. The only way to get him to stay in the convoy was to make him commander [convoy commodore]. If they didn't, you knew we were goin' to get in trouble. They'd put him in charge and he'd come back all puffed out, boys, I'm tellin' ya. A feller from Ontario; we had a lot of those [Great] Lake fellas down on the coast. There was U-boats out around us.… I'll never, never know why we ever made it. We weren't supposed to get it, I guess. When you think back of all the stuff a fella got away with in those days....

Donald Mosher

On a Saturday morning I went down to the shipping office to pay off as chief officer on the *Maid of Sterling*. What you used to do in those days, leave your name, address and telephone in case somebody wanted you. They were always lookin' for merchant navy fellas, they'd grab you off the street during the war, especially if you had a ticket. I got home to my friends around quarter to twelve. I used to stay on Henry Street in the South End when I was in Halifax. First thing the telephone rang and it was a Captain Ogilvie from Liverpool, Nova Scotia, and he offered me a job as second mate on the *Western Head*, which was coming up at that time from the West Indies. You know, steamship companies had to be ahead of themselves during the war because merchant navy officers were hard to get. Maritime Navigation Company, but she was registered in Nassau [because] you don't pay income tax. You can live in Canada, you can be Canadian, but if you got your ship registered in these countries you don't have to pay income tax. He told me the salary, which was better than the Canadian National [Steamships] and a few of the companies paid.

I went up Monday and stayed four or five days in Liverpool till the ship got into Montreal, then I went up and joined her. She was only small, about 6,000 ton, what you call a tramp. We went all over the place with that ship, down to three or four ports in Brazil, British Guiana, Panama Canal, Montreal, St. John's, Newfoundland. I never did like running around the Canadian coast—lot of thick fog, bad weather and so forth. Goin' to foreign countries, yes, I loved it. I'm used to the West Indies where there's nice sandy beaches and things like that. I liked that ship, she travelled around a lot; you never knew where you were goin'.

We had two coloured fellas on board from San Domingo had stowed away on the ship about two or three months before that. In those days the Canadian government was pretty strict with the immigration, a little different from what it is now. When we got to Montreal, the boss who owned the ship was responsible for these two fellas, so he had to put them in jail. We were in Montreal for about a week. Then he had to get them back to San Domingo. Well, how the heck do you get 'em there during the war? No planes runnin' to San Domingo. So he signed them on the ship as mess boys and they turned out to be two good men. One fella used to be a barber. The night we got torpedoed, I said to him around 5:30, "John, would you give me a haircut?" He said, "Mr. Mosher, I got to work till about 6:30. I'll get my work done, then I'll give you a haircut." So around 6:30 I went out on deck in a chair and he give me a haircut.

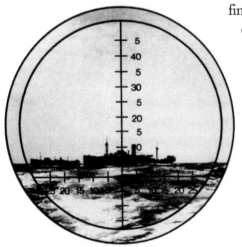

A doomed merchantman enters a U-boat's cross-hairs.

We were on our own. We had left Kingston, Jamaica, finished loadin' raw sugar for Montreal. About two days out, we were off Guantanamo Bay when we got torpedoed. After I got the haircut, I took a shower and went to bed. It was so darned hot, I just had a pair of shorts on, layin' in bed, two portholes open in my room and the screen door open. It was dark, because down in the West Indies it gets dark at six o'clock, there's no twilight. There was a bit of a moon. About 7:20, 7:25, I heard a torpedo hit in the stokehold. All you could hear was dishes go. The officers' mess was right above the stokehold.

I made a jump and I was all ready for being torpedoed; had a lifebelt on my settee in my room, a light and whistle onto it. I decided not to take it and I'll tell you why. Seems like a funny thing but it wasn't. In those days lifebelts were made out of cork. I never learnt in my life to dive head first—I was afraid to—I always went feet first. I figured when I jump over the side of the ship, it's goin' to be twenty, thirty feet high, and if that thing comes up, that cork hits me in the chin, it's liable to knock me out. So for that reason I didn't take it.

The lights went out right away. When I went out of my room it was pitch dark. There was a little alleyway that ran out on deck and the cook was there. I couldn't see him, but I knew him by his voice. He said to me, "Mr. Mosher, I can't get the door open," a wooden door for the main deck. So I said, "Stand aside a little bit, I'll try." I put the flat of my foot against the door and opened it. The two of us got out on deck. I said to the cook, he was an older man than me, from Parrsboro, "Get your lifebelt on right away and get over the side." With that I climbed over the starboard side—she had a port list—and I walked back to the superstructure.

The wireless operator, who was a young fella about seventeen, eighteen years of age from New Brunswick, had his head out, "Donald, can you get an emergency aerial up?" I said, "Never mind the emergency aerial. We're half sunk now." Well, we were half sunk before the torpedo hit us, we had a full load of raw sugar. Seventy-five percent of the ship was under water anyway when we left Jamaica, so it didn't take much to sink her. I was standing in the waterway holdin' onto the railings along there. "Sparky, get your lifebelt on, I'm goin'!" He hauled his head back in and I haven't seen him since.

In the meantime, while I'm talkin' to Sparks, we got the second torpedo back around number four hatch. I'll tell you what. The Germans were no different from the rest of us. They liked to get home and see their wives and their girlfriends and all this stuff. If they could use two torpedoes instead of one, they had an excuse for getting home that much faster when their torpedoes were out. So he gave us two; one would have done it.

What I had in mind when I jumped over the side was to get the heck away from the ship. She was sinkin' and the water was boilin' and sucking, [could] haul you under water. As soon as I came to the surface, I only swam twenty-five feet and I looked back and she was gone. It took about a minute and a half for the ship to sink from the time we took the first torpedo. A minute and a half is a long time when you got to save your life. I was young and I could travel.

I saw something floating and it was the top of the wheelhouse—the top was wood—and I started swimmin' for that to get on it. I looked to my right and I thought I saw somethin' in the dark, so I altered course and swam up to it and it was this life raft. We had four life rafts and one broke loose, thank God. The Lord God Almighty does some wonderful things. The two coloured fellas pulled me aboard; there was five aboard already, and myself. The next morning a seaplane came out of Guantanamo....

We lost twenty-four of the boys; there were six of us saved. I was the only officer on the ship saved. The captain, Joe Faulkner, was from Falmouth, Nova Scotia. He shouldn't have been goin' to sea 'cause he was damn near as old as what I am now [75]. He had retired from the Canadian Government Merchant Marine, and because the war broke out, I guess he thought he'd do his little bit towards the war. The man was too old to be goin' through that.

Elbert Coldwell

When I was through high school, I started going to sea; this was in 1941. I went with the gypsum company out of Wentworth, the Gypsum Packet Company just outside of Windsor [Nova Scotia]. I went on the second one of their ships early in December [1941] and I was on that until it was sunk in March 1942. That was the *Gypsum Prince*. I think they had four initially. They were running to the east coast of the States, that was their original run, but I think the Ministry of War Transport took, I believe it was, the *Queen* over and, if I'm not mistaken, she was sunk off Iceland on her way overseas in a convoy. The *Prince* was sunk off the States and the *Empress* was sunk down in the West Indies. The *Queen* and the *Empress* were both torpedoed. So only one survived the war, the *King*.

I was A.B. We were on our way to Philadelphia with a load of gypsum and we had just picked up the pilot for maybe a half hour or so off Cape May; you have to go up the Delaware River. It's my understanding that an English tanker had come down the river the night before and because of the weather and submarines and so on, he decided that he'd stay at anchor inside a breakwater until just around daylight. I think it was a lend–lease tanker that the Americans had given to the English. He hove anchor and was on his way out and he hit us on our port side at about a forty-five-degree angle and roughly just about at the bulkhead between the two holds. It was a beautiful morning, the sun was coming up over the horizon and I don't know what happened. She just backed away; they didn't even [try to help]. Even if she had kept a little bit of weigh on her engines to keep the hole plugged until we could get the boats off, why, it would have been beneficial for us, but she didn't, she backed away from us.

I understand at the time that it was roughly three minutes and she [the *Gypsum Prince*] was down and out of sight. I think they carried somewhere around 8,000 tons, those ships. I was sleepin'. I didn't hear the other ship when it struck us and I didn't hear our abandon ship signal. There was an old chap—to me he was an old chap—and he came running down the alleyway and he said, "Come on, boys. She's goin' and she's goin' damn quick!" I got out of my bunk. Because it was in the winter, the fourth day of March, you used to take a shirt and two sweaters off as one piece and two pairs of dungarees off as one piece so I slipped those on before I went to my locker. I had a combination lock on it. I unlocked that, put that in my pocket and an old dollar pocket watch, a Big Ben, and my wallet. The life jacket was hangin' by my bunk, it was tied on with sail twine; never thought about the life jacket.

We went out in the alleyway and you sort of walked partly on the deck and partly on the bulkhead because she was goin' over. Our companionway going from our quarters up to the starboard side of the ship was at quite an angle and it was with difficulty we got up there and up on deck. The lifeboat on our side was jammed, so the life raft was parallel with the water and you couldn't get that to slide out of its cradle. There was this other young fellow, he and I went back aft and picked up a wooden grating we used to coil rope on and threw it over. We jumped overboard and swam for the grating. She was going over and I guess the galley stove was lettin' go as we went because there was smoke and fire comin' out of the skylight in the galley. You know, I think now of some of the things that we did, we didn't even stop to see whether the engine was still going, we went. Fortunately, the engines had been stopped [because] we went directly over the stern.

We swam to this grating and then we happened to see this life raft and they pulled us aboard. Course, these things were so big and cumbersome that you couldn't manoeuvre them. They had paddles, but they were just platforms, there was no shape to them. They couldn't get to us; we had to swim to them. We found out afterwards that this was the raft from the port side. The bosun let it go and it slipped down out of the cradle in the water and came right back up to the ship's side. He stepped over the rail onto the raft, held it there and five others got on without ever getting their feet wet.

It was a hodgepodge [crew]. We had Norwegians, Canadians, English, a Spaniard, an Estonian, the chief engineer was a Scotsman. I won't say there was any chaos. I think the ones that were up on the boat deck and were unable to launch that boat went over to the other boat and realized they had the same difficulty with that one. I guess some did jump overboard and some got down on the raft. I think as she was going down someone had cut the falls on one of the boats and she did float clear, but she had turned turtle and there were a couple of guys up on the bottom of her.

The captain had some sort of exposure suit on and he was in the water. They were holding onto him and their hands started to freeze. They told him that they couldn't hold onto him much longer. It's my understanding that he said, "Well, I've got a pretty good chance of being picked up, let me go." So they let him go. No. [He drowned.] We lost six—the captain, the mate, wireless operator, the cook and two A.B.s. I think there were twenty-four on her.

I was pretty cold. It was below freezing, although it was a nice sunny morning. Our clothes and hair started to freeze. We put our hands in under our armpits. Some of them on there that didn't get wet rubbed our feet because we had nothing on our feet to keep our feet from freezing. I suppose it may have been an hour before we were picked up by the American coast guard and they landed us in Lewes, Delaware. There was a little American coaster came down and it stopped and put a lifeboat off. The lifeboat was just about to us when the coast guard came. This was only a few months after the Americans had come into the war and they had taken so many recruits in the coast guard and so on that they were having training exercises day and night to train these young chaps. Apparently they got the alarm there was a ship sinking and they couldn't see anything because she was down out of sight. When they got out far enough, they could see wreckage in the water. There was one guy, I think he was an Estonian chap, he was in a vegetable box that was upside down. You laugh at some of the things— where you were and what you do.

I think one chap was in the hospital for just a couple of days; he had a bad cold or somethin'. The American Red Cross came down to the coast guard station. The clothing that the eighteen of us saved you could put in an orange crate, so you know what we looked like. The Red Cross fitted us out with clothing and it was all second-hand; most of it was worn out, it should have been going to the garbage heap. The company sent a Greyhound bus down that evening to bring us to New York. We paraded out and boarded this bus and we looked like delegates to a hobo convention the way we were dressed. We spent, I guess, ten days to two weeks in New York making statements to the lawyer's office and so on. I think it eventually did go to court. If I'm not mistaken the company gave us, I believe it was, a month's pay, which amounted to around $60 plus $100 for our clothing and an amount of money that we could use to get home with, so we didn't come out of it wealthy. I think they blew her up afterward because I understand there was a buoy marking the spot where she went down and she was a menace.

I came from New York to Saint John, New Brunswick, by bus and crossed to Digby on the *Princess Helene*, and I guess from Digby to Wolfville by bus. I was home a couple of weeks and I went on her sister ship, the *Gypsum King*. We made a trip to the States with gypsum and then we went down to St. Thomas in the West Indies for a load of bauxite, which they used to make aluminum out of, and we brought that up to Portland, Maine. This was in the summer of '42. I think bauxite was a cargo that the Germans delighted in depriving the Canadians and Americans of, because it was used in planes.

So we left St. Thomas to come north and we were zigzagging all over the place to foil anything that may have been after us. I think we landed in Cape Fear and they were just starting the coastal convoys then on the American coast. We were leaving to form up in a convoy and I don't know if they discovered submarines outside, but we all went back in again, then a couple of hours later we sailed again. If I'm not mistaken, there were thirteen ships in the convoy. It was about three o'clock in the afternoon, I guess, when we got underway and that evening all hell broke loose. We had no gun or anything. We had blimps over, dropping markers, and we had planes dropping markers and we had ships firin' their guns, it was priceless. I don't know how many ships they sank in the convoy. I know there were three— the one alongside of us, the one ahead of us and the one ahead of it—we saw those. Then around midnight a tanker got it and that was the most beautiful fireworks you ever saw in your life. We were gettin' up off Cape Hatteras. Anyway, we got up off Norfolk and you'd take the pilot and go up the Chesapeake Bay, then you'd go across the Chesapeake-Delaware Canal, come down the Delaware River and you'd be outside from Cape May up to New York, then you go in East River and Long Island Sound. We'd go through Cape Cod Canal and that time we went to Portland and discharged....

Early in '43 ... I got a job on the *Lady Rodney*. I was on her maybe three months as A.B. She was carryin' troops to Newfoundland. Then I left her and went on the [*Lady*] *Nelson*. I was on the *Nelson* for about a year and a half. We were carryin' sick and wounded. We'd leave Halifax empty and go to North Africa and Italy and we'd pick up a load of patients and bring them up to England, drop them off and then pick up another load in England and bring them back to Halifax. We'd been on her close to a year, I guess, and you know you didn't have much time off on her. So we came in Halifax for refit and someone went to the bosun and complained about having a toothache. The bosun said, "Well, take the afternoon off and go up and see the dentist and get your tooth hauled." Well, he didn't have a toothache and he got the afternoon off, so we all used this, not all at one time, but every day there was someone up to the dentist. It was making its rounds the second time when we finished refit.

The chap that we had as chief mate, he's dead now, he was good. We sailed and went down to the Mediterranean and came out and we were heading up to England. Our mess room was forward and the food used to come up in dixies, these pots stacked one inside of the other, and a cover and two handles. So every blessed night for supper we had stew. It was stew, stew, stew, stew, stew. The mess boy came forward this night with the dixies, brought 'em in the mess room, took the cover off, and it was stew again. Well, this is enough of this. We took the dixies and we headed for the mate's room, the twelve seamen. We knocked on his door and he said, "Come in." We went in and planked this down on his desk. He said, "What can I do for you fellas?"

We said, "Mr. Sealy, we've had stew every night since we left Halifax and we're getting sick and tired of it."

He scratched his head and he said, "I don't know what I can do for you fellows."

We said, "How's that?"

"Well, the rate you had your teeth out in Halifax," he said, "I don't know what you could eat besides stew."

Roland Pickering

Roland Pickering

Halifax, April 10, 1942 — A second, and greater, "Halifax Explosion" was averted here early this morning when the munitions-laden British steamship *Trongate*, on fire since ten o'clock last night, was sunk at 3:25 A.M. in seventy-six feet of water by gunfire from the RCN minesweeper *Chedabucto*. All the crew escaped safely ashore.
—from H.B. Jefferson's files, Public Archives of Nova Scotia[9]

The *Trongate*...it's a famous story, but they certainly didn't tell it too often.... The people should know a little more about that, I think. The ship come over from London and loaded ammunition. We was ready to sail and pulled out into the stream at six o'clock in the morning. The watches was all set and I was down aft in my bunk. A young feller come down and he said, "Better get out. The ship's afire." So I grabbed a few of my papers and some clothes and put them on.

When I got along the deck the fella told me there, he said, "Too late. It's all over." But when I got lookin' around, I could see it wasn't over by any means. They thought they had the fire out, I guess, but there was no reason for them to think that. You could see the tarpaulins on the hatches was raisin' and lowerin' and smoke comin' out of the ventilators; it wasn't hard to tell there was somethin' wrong. Just then the ol' chief officer and the captain got out and the chief officer said to get the hoses and get the water goin' and put it down the ventilators but you couldn't do nothin'. The fire was so well along that a bit of water wouldn't do it much damage.

They phoned the fire department from Halifax and every fireboat in Halifax was there in a few minutes. She was just inside of George's Island. They was goin' to hoist the anchor and take her outside the harbour, then they decided it wasn't safe, that she might blow up before they got her out. So they decided they'd sink her right there where she's at. They opened up the sea valves and she wasn't goin' down fast enough, so they pulled a big destroyer [minesweeper] up and put twenty-some rounds into her.

They took us off her. Now this particular ship had a crew of negroes in the engine room and they wasn't very concerned about a fire, so they went down and they put on all their good clothes. They dressed all up, white shirts and ties, and then took everything they could take with their valises. When it come time to take us off, they stepped up off with all their clothes, but we was all soakin' wet and our good clothes was still all down in our quarters. They couldn't take us ashore because we was all cleared for sea. The only way they could was as shipwrecked mariners, that's sea law, so we had to stay out in Halifax basin half froze to death till three o'clock [next] mornin' before she sunk. She was all afire and goin' to sink anyway; they could have took us in, but nobody wanted to do what wasn't right, you see, break the law.

So then they took us all up to the merchant seamen's manning pool and, my gosh, the old feller that was runnin' the place, he was goin' to fire us all out. He was goin' to have us arrested for comin' in there that hour of the mornin' and all this stuff, no arrangements made. Well, by and by, the captain stepped in and he just had on his underwear and a pair of knee boots and an overcoat. He had the ship's articles and everything. He threw that over on the counter and he told the old feller to make room for these men. I suppose there was forty, and all a pretty rough crowd too. I was the only Canadian on her. There was a lot of Liverpool Irishmen; if you ever heard tell of them [they were] pretty rough customers.[10] It wasn't long before we got action [were allowed in].

We was up the whole week on an investigation tryin' to figure out what caused the ship to burn. It could have been a lot of different things happen, but you never know. When it was all over they told us our ship was sunk by marine peril. That didn't mean that we were entitled to our clothes. There was only one man on that ship entitled to his clothes and that was the ship's carpenter. That's the British seaman's rule at that time. I had what I had on; I don't know what the rest got. We got that all over with, then a few days after they took us down to the shippin' office in Halifax to sign off. I think I got a hundred and fifty bucks out of it extra.

When she went down, the blaze was goin' right over the top of the masts. And that light ammunition was explodin' and shootin' into the sky just the same as tracer bullets, so she wasn't too far from the main thing goin' up. If that thing had a went up, there wouldn't have been much left of Halifax, that's sure. When she went down she had a list on her, but her yardarms, her cross arms on the mast, were still above water. They left her there, I would say, for about two years and they went down and they took that ship all apart, dismantled her, and took the cargo out of her. So that's the story of the SS *Trongate*.[11]

Ernest Pike

There was once when I was on the *Lady Rodney* and we were trooping to St. John's, Newfoundland. We always had the same call letters: Three George Chief, and the senior escort was Three George Boss. This time we were sailing a zigzag course and we got a call: "Three George Chief, this is Three George Boss. Course so and so; speed so and so." I was at the wheel at the time; I was quartermaster. The captain said, "Give her a double ring, Mr. Mate," and he grabbed the telegraphs and he gave her a double ring. That meant open up the links, give her everything she had. Now it could have been two or three minutes after, it might not have been that long, when we got this call back saying, "Three George Chief, this is Three George Boss. Disregard that last order." The Old Man said, "Silence!" He wouldn't allow them to speak over the set at all. What it was, the submarine got our call letters and he wanted to put us on a certain course and speed, so he was just settin' us right up for the kill. The Old Man knew there was something wrong, he knew right away that the accent wasn't right and the way he was given the course and that it wasn't right. The captain, when he got into St. John's, Newfoundland, I guess when he went to the Admiralty, he did get some credit, I don't know what it was, but he saved all of those troops and all of our lives.

The *Bick Island* was a freighter. She had been an Italian ship and they tried to ship out of Quebec at the beginning of the war. Somehow she got grounded on Bick Island and they named her *Bick Island*. Well, then she was runnin' across all the time to U.K. ports. I went on her, [but] I never sailed onto her. We loaded ammunition in Bedford Basin and she used to carry

3,500 tons; that was the maximum any one ship was supposed to carry in a convoy. As soon as we got that loaded, we were ready to sail the next day when someone from the CNSS [Canadian National Steamship] office or somethin' come and asked for some of us able seamen to go to the *Chomedy*. The *Chomedy* was on the Far East run and she was in Halifax then. They were short of qualified people and the *Chomedy* had taken a number of people out of the [St. Margaret's] seamen's school, ordinary seamen, but they never went to sea. Rollie Pickering–that was the first time we got shipmates–him and I were in watch together and we had an ordinary seaman with us. Then there'd be a couple more A.B.s have an ordinary seaman with them.

To be an able seaman on any of those ships, even wartime, when you went aboard of a ship and you were able seaman, the bosun–the deck foreman–the first thing that he would do is give you some wire runners to splice and you'd have to prove yourself. For instance when I went on the *Chomedy* he took me up under the fo'c'sle head and he said, "Here. Renew the two runners there on number one winches. There's your wire there." I said, "Okay. What kind of splice do you want into it?" "Oh, put a Liverpool in." So he went away, he had more crew to work back aft and different places, then after awhile he come along. He just looked at what I was doin', never said nothin', and he sat down on a can of paint there. He cut off a wire runner, just a piece of waste, [took] a marlin spike and in no time he was shovin' a splice in. Threw it down on the deck and went and come back, I was still at mine. Oh, he was a real rigger.

I put my two splices in, he looked at it and he said, "All right, that's good enough. Now come with me. Pick up a coil of six-thread rope and come up on the boat deck." So I went up on the boat deck and he said, "Renew the grab lines along that boat. We might need them if we get torpedoed." So when I spliced that, it was all right, and then I had to go and make some cargo slings and trays. You'd have short splices and long splices into 'em. He said, "Okay, that's fine." But you had to be an able seaman. He wanted to find out who he had aboard, you know. It's no good to send someone to do something, there could be an accident if a wire wasn't spliced properly or a rope or something like that. His name was Charlie Veinot from down around Lunenburg; he was a great seaman.

She [the *Bick Island*] never got across that time. I knew a lot of fellows onto her. About five o'clock in the morning they just heard a report, a noise, and they looked over. There was just a cloud, a mushroom of smoke rollin' out over the sky, and that was the *Bick Island*. She wouldn't have a chance, get a torpedo with that stuff aboard. Yeah, could have [been me], but I was always lucky. I seen the other fellows gettin' torpedoed and sunk, but I never was.

Gordon Hardy

On September 5, 1942, the *Lord Strathcona* and *Saganga* were torpedoed and sunk off Wabana, Newfoundland. Nearly two months later, the *Rose Castle* and PLM-27 went down in the same vicinity after being torpedoed. The following two accounts, first Gordon Hardy, then Pierre Simard, tell first-hand of these four sinkings.

The *Lord Strathcona* and *Rose Castle* were almost twins; I think they were built in the First World War. [They sailed] from Belle Isle to Sydney with iron ore for the steel plant. My father was on the ship then, the *Lord Strathcona*, and my brother Clarence had been on the *Lord Strathcona* earlier [in1941], then he joined the *Grayburn*. He went overseas and was torpedoed and

SS *Lord Strathcona*, torpedoed on September 5, 1942.

drowned. This is where the connections came for me to know about these ships. There was no work and nothin' to do at that time. I was too young to get in the service, so I went to Sydney and joined the *Lord Strathcona*. I was on her up until the fifth of September '42. That's when she was torpedoed at eleven o'clock in the day off of Belle Isle, Newfoundland.

I was ashore that day. I hadn't been home for a year or so, so I didn't get back in time to go on board, so she sailed without me. I went to Sydney and waited for her and she never came back. There were no lives lost on her; she had forty-six of a crew and they all survived. They torpedoed the *Saganga* first. There was twenty-eight, I think, lost on her. The third mate [on the *Lord Strathcona*] gave orders to abandon ship when he seen this because she was settin' there a target anyhow waitin' just off the island to go in to be loaded [with] iron ore. As soon as they got in the lifeboats from the *Lord Strathcona,* they put two torpedoes in her.

They also fired at the *Rose Castle.* She was in at the pier loadin'. He missed and it caused $30,000 of damage to the pier; they blew the side off the dock. The people thought the island was attacked. It was the exact same on that island, in that area, as England was during the war. Everything was blacked-out in the nighttime and the cars had little tiny lights with the metal over the headlights so it wouldn't shine any distance.

There was a lot of people when this one [*Rose Castle*] had the torpedo fired at her in at the dock and seen what happened to these two, a lot of the crew wouldn't go back on her. When they got in Sydney, a lot of them abandoned ship, even the captain. The first mate, MacDonald, from the *Lord Strathcona* ended up captain on this one [*Rose Castle*]. As soon as there was an opening I joined her [on September 17, 1942]. We had a lot of our own crew from the *Lord Strathcona* on the *Rose Castle,* but they weren't as lucky this time. We were torpedoed sometime after midnight in November [2, 1942]; same place off Belle Isle.

We were attacked one night, only about two or three weeks before they finally got us. We got out of the convoy and off course in a big storm. You couldn't do anything with her, the storm was so bad, and she was flyin' light. We had a torpedo fired at us somewheres between here and Newfoundland, well out in the Gulf. The only thing we can figure, either it was a dud or when the seas struck her and her bow went up, that it went through under her bow. Everybody went to the boat deck and stood by the lifeboats all night. We sent out an SOS and an American destroyer bound for St. John's to refuel picked up our message and came the next morning and escorted us into Argentia. We were there for a couple of days till we got escort to take us around to Belle Isle. My father got chilled [standing by the lifeboats all night] and we put him in the marine hospital in Sydney and that's the trip they got us, the next trip. He'd never came out of it, especially if he was in the stokehold.

I was in bed asleep when the first torpedo hit. I knew we were torpedoed, so I jumped out of bed and ran out from my room. The third engineer and the second engineer were standin' on deck. They must have been on duty. They had a flashlight and they said, "Where are you goin'?"

I said, "I'm goin' over the side."

"Don't jump in that cold water. It'll kill you."

I said, "I can't help it. We'll get another torpedo yet." That one struck up forward of the bridge, number four hatch. So I got up on the railing and jumped overboard. I just about struck the water and the second one came in through the engine room on the opposite side. That finished her. She went down, they estimate, in less than a minute. The record says thirty seconds, but I'd say probably fifty. We were just like a rock anyhow, we were loaded heavy. I'd say thirty-five went down in her; eleven survived. Some of the records say six, but I would say eleven.

I was swimmin' before I struck the water, you know what I mean, almost into motion 'cause I figured she'd roll over on me. When that torpedo hit her, I could see this big black thing—I was just about alongside of her—and the suction did take me down. When I broke water I was filled up with water and that took a lot out of me, slowed me down for swimmin'. It all happened so quick you don't have much time. If I hadn't have jumped overboard I mighten of survived the second torpedo. There were guys that tried to get out of the engine room that never made it. One guy made it to the deck and we got him on a life raft later on. His buddy didn't make it all the way up; when the torpedo hit, he fell back down in the engine room, I suppose.

A fella by the name of George Hardy from Newfoundland and the second mate, Jack Savery, were on duty and seen the torpedo comin'. They were on the bridge. There was an alarm system you pressed to let you know that you were attacked. They didn't get a chance to press the button; the torpedo was all the button you needed. They tripped a life raft in the rigging and then they jumped overboard and got on that. After I'd been in the water for, I don't know, a couple of hours or more, I suppose, I started to get numb and I was almost helpless. I was tryin' to swim towards the island. It just happened that they run across me or found me. I don't know how come. I never had my light—a light that's on your shoulder—I never had it turned on. I don't know why because I was tryin' to be as cool as I could. Talk about a small world. The guy on the life raft [George Hardy] shook hands and said, "Welcome, we're first cousins." I never met him in my life. He was on her all the time, he was one of the original crew, and he knew I was on there, but I didn't know he was.

You couldn't see anything; dark as pitch. It was just the same as if you had your eyes shut as far as seein' much. Oh, we could hear them hollerin' to the Virgin Mary and to God and everything in the water. We seen this light comin' and we could see this thing movin'. It was the third engineer that was standin' on deck that I'd spoke to before I jumped overboard. He had a flashlight and he was swimmin', beatin' his way towards the life raft.

The way the life raft was built, they were just square, made out of like gasoline drums and in the centre of them was a place the water would come up through. It was so cold and I never had clothes enough on. My hands, if you handed me a thousand-dollar bill, they wouldn't [hold it], and my legs and my knees, I had to get back down in that water because it was warmer than the wind. And that in November. I got in that hollow 'cause the water was warmer or no worse than the cold air.

The little Q-boat I call them, or "fairmile" or whatever—they're smaller than a corvette—that's what picked us off the life raft before daylight. On our life raft was Jack Savery and George Hardy—the seaman and the second mate—myself, a guy by the name of Jimmy Percy and Jimmy McDonald, the third engineer. The wireless operator survived and one of the gunners; he was from Ontario. To be truthful, I think that's the only life raft that ever got out, the one we were on, so they must have got them [the remaining survivors] out of the water. We met on land the next day.

They got me on the little corvette or Q-boat and wrapped a blanket around me and put me in the bunk. I didn't stay in it too long. We had a guy they found on the sounding barrel from Bombay, India; he was one of the firemen. They put him in this little bed alongside of me. Tried to get us warm, but there wasn't much life in him, so they give him somethin'. I don't know if it was whiskey or rum or what it was. He stiffened right out and his eyes turned over. I'll tell you, I wasn't long gettin' out of that. I can remember his name: Ali. Now that's all I knew him by. That's about the third time he'd been torpedoed.

There were three of them on the ship from Bombay, India, in the stokehold. They wouldn't eat pork. They'd come up to me at midships and I'd always know what's for dinner. He'd [Ali would] say, "Harrrdy, what's for dinner today?" and I'd say, "Pork." "God-damn pork," he'd say, then he'd go across the flyin' bridge to the chief steward and he'd want a can of bully beef. "What do you want bully beef for today?"

"God-damn pork for dinner."

"No. No pork. Who told you that?"

He said, "Harrrdy."

I could tell him every time and still he'd go for the bully beef. You know, badness, yeah.

They landed us in a place called Lance Cove in Belle Isle, then they took us up to the village. There was an army stationed there and they come down with army trucks with steel boxes, fifteen hundred weights they call them. Get in the back of them was as cold as what I went through in the water. Anybody that was mobile enough, the people were there gathered around to take them to their homes. They couldn't do enough for you. From the two torpedoings in September they were used to the whole thing. They had a hospital there, a big home it was one time. This fella came to me and he said, "Are you well enough to go?" I said yes. I still had this old gray blanket over me and I was in my bare feet. You know what that'd be like, walkin' and stubbin' my toes. I got to his place and they put me in bed and covered me up good. They gave me breakfast in bed. It was a Jewish family by the name of Nathan Cohen; he had a dry goods store on the island. His store was downstairs and the living quarters was up on the second floor.

U-578 Commander Frederick Wissman (centre) flanked by his officers. U-578 sank *Rose Castle* and PLM-27 off Belle Isle, Newfoundland, on November 2, 1942.

Everything was kept so secret. I was there a couple of days and I took for granted they let people know home that there was survivors and who survived. The word they got, I'll tell you how they got it. Like I told you, my father got chilled on the boat deck in that storm, he got pneumonia, and they had to put him in the marine hospital in Sydney. So we sailed then. The marine doctor that was in the hospital come in in the morning and said, "Mr. Hardy, you don't have to worry about goin' back on your old ship anymore." He said, "How come?" "She went down last night with all hands." He screeched and jumped up and he said, "I got a son on her!" That's how he got the news.

We had no money and we were in a different country 'cause Canada and Newfoundland wasn't joined. So the second mate went to St. John's—he was the only officer survived—and he got $20 for each one of us through the Canadian government or some arrangement and he give us that. I met one of the fellas and he said, "Did you phone home?" I said, "No, I had no money. The company would notify them anyhow." He said, "Nobody knew there was any survivors. They figure there's none." So I phoned. My father, they gave him the news in the hospital and he got out right away. It was about six days that they didn't know. It was quite hard on my mother. We already had one son gone and later on my other brother was killed in Italy. There was five sons and my father in the war at one time.

Pierre Simard[12]

I was supposed to go to university, but all the things that were going on during the war fascinated me and I decided to go on a merchant ship of any kind. I just couldn't stay in school, I had to go. I went to Montreal to the Norwegian consulate and they said, "We have a ship leaving very shortly from Quebec City to overseas." My father thought I was on my way to school but I had other ideas. After we left, I wrote a letter.

So I joined this old broken-down coal-burning ship—SS *Skotland*—in September '41, the worst ship I could have joined. I joined as a seaman to begin with and then they ran short of trimmers. You do a lot of shovelling and you have to be in good shape. I was perhaps not in good shape to begin with, but I certainly was a few months later. Small, about 4,000 tons, she was built and served as a coastal vessel around the Scandinavian countries. A coastal vessel is made differently than an ocean-going vessel, but this was war and they didn't give a damn what you were, away you went. She was very old—forty-two years old—and of course in a storm great stresses are applied to the ship, so rivets popped and water came in and we used the pumps. It was very rough. You had to be young to go through that, young and stupid; the two go together.

We were carrying timber. We went to various places all around the British Isles, then we went to Philadelphia to load timber. We did a couple of those trips to the States to overseas. When we left the States one time, we were torpedoed three days out of Philadelphia. We were the first ship, I believe, to be torpedoed so close to the American coast. We were torpedoed on the seventeenth of May, I believe it was, National Norwegian Day. We were alone. The crew was only made up of twenty-five people and we were invited to the captain's cabin for a drink. We had a drink and we went back to our jobs. Somebody thought they'd seen a submarine, but this happened all the time because it could be a log, could be anything. At the time of the torpedoing we were at the gun platform at the afterdeck. It was Norwegian National Day, as I said, and we were there to celebrate. We fired two or three rounds at nothing.

The U-boat thought he could sink us with gunfire, so he pumped quite a few shells at us and into us. We had only one old American gun, I don't remember what it was, but it was breechloading. We had one Norwegian gunner, the only naval person on board. We were firing back—we had been trained more or less—and we did such a good job of coming close that he thought "The hell with this" and pumped two torpedoes into us. It was a hell of an explosion, two of them. Course we had timber on board and splinters went all over the place. I remember that I was on the gun platform and I went straight into the air. I was not hit; nothing was broken, just twisted. We lost three or four and those people just disappeared. I think two of them were in the boiler room and that is a bad place to be at any time.

It took the ship awhile to sink. We had only one lifeboat, the other one was destroyed. We had a bit of a time to lower it to the water because she was leaning fifteen to twenty degrees to starboard. We were just about to shove off when the captain's steward, a wonderful old man with one glass eye, suddenly came out saying, "Hey, wait for me!" He had a case of whiskey with him. This was lowered into the boat and he came down. He had gone into the captain's cabin and saved the photographs of the captain's family, the last that had been taken before he escaped from Norway.

We shoved off and then we had nothing to do but look after the people who were wounded. A lot of people were seriously wounded from shrapnel, large pieces of wood that exploded at the time of the torpedoing. The engineer officer was in bad shape; he had a piece of wood sticking out of his back, in his kidneys. We sawed off the piece of wood sticking out of his back and left what was in there in. Some had splinters in their faces and legs. It was very unpleasant because they were in pain and we had no morphine or anything like this. We had whiskey and we had biscuits and we just waited. My leg was the size of a telephone pole; my back was all twisted.

We were very fortunate, the sea was calm the whole time and it wasn't too cold. The next day we were spotted by an aircraft. Two days after that, a fisherman came alongside and picked us up. That was a bit of a job because by that time those who were badly wounded were in really bad shape. It took us another day and a half to get to Boston. When we got there the U.S. naval ambulances were waiting for us. We went to the USN hospital in Chelsea across the Charles River where we were extremely well treated.

Of course we made great news in the newspapers 'cause it was the first torpedoing of a ship so close. Somehow the papers said the crew was made up of Norwegian, Scandinavian, one British, so on and so forth and one Free French—that was me. Where they got this from, I don't know. But a few days later a whole delegation arrived in the hospital with flowers and fruit and all kinds of goodies. They were the French people living in Boston from the consulate. I saw the nurse pointing to my bed. Well, they were a little disappointed. They were very good, they kept coming to see me—even after they found out I was Free French from Quebec City. I eventually got out and I was invited by the same people to go spend a few days with them.

The Norwegian gunner and I used to get along together very well. One day we were feeling very good, we were in wheelchairs out by the fence and we thought that we would love to go downtown. So we passed the sentry, who didn't pay much attention to two civilians, and rattled down a big hill. I never went so fast in all my life as I did in that wheelchair! We went to a bar but about ten minutes later the Shore Patrol came along. We were taken back and paraded before the captain, who said with a grin on his face, "Do you people realize that if you were navy I'd throw you in irons?" He chuckled and said, "Your leave is stopped until you get better." About three weeks later we were in better shape; by now we were on crutches. We escaped again and that time they didn't find us for three days. One day at about six o'clock A.M., the FBI came and found us in our hotel. We heard "knock, knock" and the doors flew open and they rushed in with guns. Our leave was stopped again.

Eventually we all went our separate ways and I went home to Quebec City for a little while. My father said, "Well, you've had a lesson now. Surely you're going to settle down." I had no such plan. I came to Halifax and went to the Free French consul. I joined the PLM-27 which was part of a large fleet of merchant ships the French had. The Paris-Lyons-Marseilles was the name of the line. Most of those ships were torpedoed. It was people from the French colonies manning the ship. You had Senegalese, Indochinese, North Africans.

We travelled to a few ports, most of them overseas, then we came back to Canada and went to Wabana, Newfoundland, to get iron ore and bring it back to Sydney. In September 1942 at noon we were in Wabana and two ships right in the bay were torpedoed. Around the second of November we were again anchored off Wabana fully laden. There were two ships there, the *Rose Castle*, a Canadian ship, and ourselves. Around one o'clock in the morning there was a hell of an explosion. *Rose Castle*, which was a short distance from us, blew up, and we did. Two torpedoes in each ship. All the windows in the village of Wabana were shattered and needless to say this gave a hell of a shock to the people living there—in the middle of the night all hell breaks loose.

I was sound asleep. First thing I knew, the ship just jumped up almost out of the water. That wakes you up. If it doesn't wake you up, that's where you're going to stay. I was on the upper deck. Those who couldn't make it to the upper deck went down because it was no time at all. We just went down in maybe two minutes. You can imagine. We were laden with iron ore, so we went down like a ton of bricks. It's amazing, it's all luck. You happen to be in the right place at the right time, you made it. Somebody else

PLM-27, owned by the Paris-Lyons-Marseilles line, was torpedoed by U-578 on the night of November 2, 1942. "That wakes you up. If it doesn't wake you up, that's where you're going to stay."

could have been in the same situation in the next cabin but couldn't open the door because the ship was twisted and went down with the ship. About ten or fifteen [were lost] out of forty-five men, I believe. The *Rose Castle* also lost a lot of people.

I had nothing broken except in this case my legs again took the brunt and I couldn't walk. Same as the first time; I must have bloody good bones. We had to walk, or you went down. We swam all the way in; not very far, about three-quarters of a mile. It was a nice night, but of course at that time of the year it was bloody cold. After the first torpedoing I got the message that you wear lifebelts at all times. Those who didn't have any lifebelts didn't have a chance.

On board was an old seaman. We used to call him Papa Henri. He was an old alky; he'd been captain, mate and finally ordinary seaman. He was in his forties; I guess that's why we called him papa. We used to have wine at all meals on the French ship, just very common wine, and an apple, if we had apples. Old Papa Henri used to say, "*Mon petit Pierre, je te donne ma pomme si tu me donnes ton Pinard.*" "My little Pierre, I will give you my apple if you give me your Pinard," a name for cheap wine. So to begin with I gave him my wine, but after awhile I tasted it and found out I liked it and he used to say, "I'll give you deux pommes!" He was amongst those swimming ashore. I heard him call my name and I tried to swim to find him but he went down. It's pretty sad but, mind you, I'm over that now.

In this case again, these people took us in and covered us with blankets. They looked after us beautifully. I remember when I hit the beach it was rocky and I tried to walk and I just couldn't. We must have been in the cold water for about half an hour. We were partially carried up to various houses and I remember I was placed on the floor next to a potbellied stove in a miner's small house. Many of us had something like lockjaw; we were frozen solid just about. They said, "What should we give them?" Somebody mentioned, "Give them Screech." Well, I thought to myself, God bless your hearts. They had to pour it down our throat because we just couldn't relax. After a little while, I was okay, felt good, and I slept for nearly twenty-four hours; we all did. It takes a lot out of people to be torpedoed. Just the explosion itself is like someone hit you with a sledgehammer.

Some of us spent several days there and then we were taken to St. John's. Military people or merchant seamen, they give them this awful blue suit, a jacket and a pair of trousers, a survivor suit, if you wish, that most areas around this part of the world had for people in the hospital. We managed to meet some gals and we had a fairly good time. They recovered some of the bodies and we had a service in some chapel in Newfoundland and they were buried there. But the French always recover their dead—like the Americans—and they were repatriated after the war. I was taken back to Quebec City, my home, and finished my schooling, then joined the navy in 1943; I ended up a captain. I learned my lesson, I thought "To hell with this, this is dangerous." I was very fortunate. It's all luck—where you are, where you stand, what type of explosion. It's up to Him. Just last year I went back to Wabana and I took a walk on the beach. I mentioned this [torpedoing] to some fisherman. "Of course, I remember well. You bastards blew up everything that we had in the house."

We had some merchant seamen, captains and officers, who were much older as a general rule. And many of them had family in Norway or France and they had plenty to think about. They didn't see those people until the end of the war and, when they went back home, things were sometimes very sad. But that's war; war is horrible. We didn't see ourselves as patriots or brave people. It was war and away you went. It's quite an experience. You have to be young to go through this—young, strong and stupid. When you're a young man you're a bloody idiot. These were terrible experiences, but this happened to thousands of ships. One of the most critical problems the Allies had during the war is the number of merchant ships being torpedoed, because this was the lifeline to England and everywhere. Without food, without materiel, they wouldn't have made it. It's just as simple and terrible as that. They came very close to not making it, very close.

Gordon Troke

I was just a young lad in the early part of the war. I went down [to the docks] and this friend of mine was on her [the *Watuka*] and there was a job goin' and I got on—coal burnin', steam job. I was a fireman. She run coal out of Louisbourg and Sydney. She was built in Pictou and she run for years here [for] Dominion Coal in Sydney. She was well known around the coast. We were runnin' to Halifax and New Brunswick and then we had a couple of runs down to the States—New Jersey, we brought coal back for Halifax. A lot of runs to Newfoundland. We were runnin' from Louisbourg the time she was lost.

We left Louisbourg in the afternoon in a convoy and we were thirty-five miles out of Halifax the next mornin' [March 22, 1944] at six o'clock when the submarine bumped us off. The others scattered and got into Halifax. We used to tow a log [line] to tell how fast you were goin'. Foster Billard went to read the log with a little penlight and he just got to the bridge when she hit. They picked the light up, the German sub, I guess. We were hit in the stern with one of these acoustic torpedoes; followed the propeller up and broke her off there.

I was in bed, sleeping up forward. All the crew were forward, the deck hands and the firemen; the officers were midship. When she hit, everything went black and she stood on end and went down in just a few minutes. Deep loaded. It's pretty hard to judge, but I'd say maybe five minutes. We run out and she was iced up and we couldn't get our rafts clear. But the boats in wartime are slung out over the side, so they got one boat off. We just jumped over the side into the boat. Of course the boat was rotten and filled with water and we were all in the water then. I would say the longest would be three-quarters of an hour. There was a little corvette called the *Anticosti* came and picked us up. My father was third officer on her [the *Watuka*] and we were all floatin' around the side of the corvette. Captain Bennie Pope from *Manido* was unconscious. He had a life jacket on, so my father put a rope around him and around my arm and I was holdin' him till we got them aboard.

There were several unconscious, the cold I guess; see, it was below zero. The third engineer had his leg punctured and it never healed till the day he died. He was able to work but it was always open, the sore. I think they hooked him with a boat hook or a gaff, tryin' to get him. We lost one man, a fella from down here in Tarbot, a Murray MacDonald; he went with her. I was talkin' to him when I run out. I had no clothes on, just my underwear. He was standin' there by the door. Now what happened, I don't know, whether the suction pulled him down. When she stood on end and started goin' down, the whistle started to blow–see, the pressure of the water on the whistle cord–she blew her heart out, then she disappeared.

We picked a young fellow up here in Louisbourg the day before we sailed, a young mess boy from Glace Bay. I think his name was Munroe, about fourteen, fifteen years old. The commander of the *Anticosti* could hear him cryin'; I guess, he was screamin', you know he was frightened and he [the commander] held his depth charges. They were standin' by, had them ready to let them go and I guess that's what saved our lives. He would have killed us all if he had of.

We landed in Halifax and they took us to the Navy League and dressed us up with clothes. The following day they brought us home to Sydney, then I went right back to sea again.

Doug Bauld

There was no work in the thirties and things were tough. When war started to loom up, they wanted people for the services, so I went over with some of my schoolmates. They interviewed them first and they got in. When my turn came, it's because I was black, they said, "We're not takin' no blacks in right now, but when we want you, we'll send for you." A lot of blacks couldn't get in the navy or army or whatever. Course, after that some got in. That's how I come to be in [the merchant navy]. They did [eventually call me up] but I didn't go because they didn't want me then, why should I go now?

I worked on construction work and things like that, then I happened to know the shippin' master in Halifax on Granville Street, Mr. Drake, so he told me three or four ships were lookin' for men to go on firin' boilers. There was one ship with the Cunard Lines that didn't come in, so the Colony Steamship wanted some men. So that's how I come to get on that. White fireman, black fireman, they didn't discriminate. As far as the men you worked with, you got along with them very good. I believe they had four

A group of merchant survivors arrive in St. John's, Newfoundland, aboard a corvette, September 1942. "A lot of people don't know what dangers the merchant ships went through or the crews that were on them."

or five freight ships, all coal burners. They ran up the St. Lawrence River, right up through the Great Lakes to Cleveland, St. Catherines, Detroit, down south to Cuba, Mexico, Newfoundland, St. Pierre–Miquelon, all around. Harbour Grace, St. John's and Marystown were the three places we went in Newfoundland. That was our regular route.

In St. Pierre–Miquelon they had a hotel and bar there and we got in with the fella pretty good. He liked American [news]papers, so when we come down from the States, we used to bring 'em. He was very, very good to us.

Every time we went in he'd give us a drink on the house. The last trip we were in there he put a party on for us. Every place we sailed in we had good hospitality. Through the American merchant seamen we were invited in homes in Mexico. All my experience going to sea I was treated very royally.

The one I was on was named the *Colony Trader*. Me and a cousin of mine both went as firemen. We joined the ship in Montreal; went up [from Halifax] by train. She was old; had a couple of old guns but it didn't mean nothin'. We were carryin' anything—fertilizer, big barrels of corn beef, flour, sugar, whatever—to Newfoundland and St. Pierre–Miquelon. We done that all summer, then the winter we came to Halifax and sailed from there to Souris, Prince Edward Island, and loaded up with potatoes, takin' them to Havana, Cuba. Then we sailed out of Havana all winter to Mexico, British Honduras, Jamaica. We were alone, loaded up and went on our way.

We were in one [storm] from Souris, Prince Edward Island, to Cuba. It smashed the whole side of the ship. We ended up goin' to Brooklyn, New York, to dry dock and stayed in there for a good month and had our work done, then we went on our way to Cuba. That was scary because we had to go from forward to midship to get our food, even to go for your watch, and the waves are just goin' over. You couldn't move because if one of those waves hit you, you're gone. After we did get up, we had to stay midship, we couldn't go back to our quarters. That was practically two days. You get used to the rollin' and pitchin'. It's not too bad dippin', but when you're doin' both, rollin' and dippin', you don't know if she's goin' to capsize. It depends how your cargo is. If your cargo shifts, she could shift to one side and you're gone. There's a way the stevedores load the cargo on, it's got to be well balanced so that it's not all goin' to shift over onto one side. You're out there, you don't see land, you don't see nothin'. You have to be really in one to realize what it's all about.

You were young then. You weren't thinkin' how dangerous it could be but, after, you realize how much danger you were in. You were worried but not that bad; this won't happen to me. When you got in port, once you got the papers, you'd read about what ships went down. Thank God you passed that area before. Even going up the St. Lawrence was dangerous, ships went down there too. Subs were all up in around the river 'cause they knew supplies were comin' down through from the Great Lakes.

A lot of people don't know what dangers the merchant ships went through or the crews that were on them. Newfoundland was an English colony; it had to be merchant ships to bring supplies in there. St. Pierre–Miquelon was the same way. You're supplyin' a French colony and you're supplyin' a British colony; if the merchant ships didn't bring it, you'd be starvin'. People don't realize how many subs were out around here. The merchant navy ever since 1914 was never recognized until 1992. I don't think it's right. Nobody realized what a merchant seaman had done. We were just nobody.

Ralph Kelly

I went as a mess boy on the old *Vineland*, a general cargo ship, 5,000 tons, for the Mersey Paper Company. This was a neutral ship under the Panamanian registry [carrying] newsprint to Australia and New Zealand. In 1942 she was taken over by the Canadian government, then we had to run from the States or wherever down to the West Indies. We joined that ship in Portland in 1942. We were headin' for St. Thomas in the Virgin Islands to pick up bauxite to bring back to Portland.

We went down along the American coast without convoy, without lights. The further we got south, the more you knew you were goin' to get it, you could sense it. Down around the Diamond Shoals off the Carolinas, you could see where the submarines had chased ships right up onto the shoals and they were sinking. They were afire, there were a lot of bodies around. We seen bodies pretty near every day. Then we said, "Well, it's goin' to be our turn."

This one particular afternoon it was a nice day, calm as could be. That was the day of the sinking [April 20], Hitler's birthday. The submarine must have been laying in the sun so you couldn't see nothin', that's when it got us. I was lookin' over the side, back to the gun crew, and that's where it hit, between the gun crew and myself, right back by number four hatch. I was about fifty feet from where it hit. There was no hesitation then, you knew what it was and you went for the lifeboat. They fired the first one, which hit us, the second one missed and the third one hit right amidship. While we were gettin' ready to put the lifeboats over the side, we seen the second torpedo go by us. Then when we got in the water in the lifeboats, the third one hit.

One man was killed; he was in the lifeboat with me. Up on the top deck was oil which was used for the galley stove and that just come right down over the top of us. We were just as black, we were coated in it. He said, "Let's jump," and I said, "No, wait a minute." He said, "We better jump." Everybody else jumped. The chief cook—him and I were the last two in the lifeboat. He said, "No, let's stay," so we stayed. This other young fella jumped out. What happened to him, they think either the gang plank or the funnel from the ship hit him. We got away from her altogether after that, then started pickin' up the other survivors. The sub fired twelve rounds into the ship's bow for target practice. From the time she was hit until the time she went down they estimated it at about twelve minutes, so that's pretty fast.

The [Germans] give us cigarettes, asked the captain where he was goin' to and what he was goin' to carry, if we needed medical aid and told us the nearest course to land. One course was ninety miles and the other was a thousand, so you could take your pick. They were reasonably good, didn't bother us. He just went in and out of the lifeboats like that, takin' pictures of us. They left on the surface.

I can't remember how long it was from the time we were sunk until we got back on land. But I know, either the second or third day, it was around sometime in the evening, we seen this ship off in the distance. We said, "Well, we're goin' to be picked up." As this ship kept comin' towards us, we said, "We're goin' to get picked up for sure." It turned and went the other way; it was a German supply ship. We were the next thing to being POWs. I guess they didn't want us, had enough troubles of their own. After that, I don't know how many days it was—I'd say between five and seven days I guess—just driftin' around.

Fishermen picked us up, native people in the Turks Island[s]. That night we got ashore, they scrubbed us and scrubbed us, tryin' to get the oil out. Even when I got home sometime in June, I was still oil-soaked yet. For some reason or other they wouldn't let us stay there. This fishin' boat took us from there to Grand Turk and that's where we stayed for a couple of weeks. They give us clothes that they didn't think they'd need at that time. They sold us all their cigarettes they could possibly spare because they were on rations too, you might as well say, 'cause a ship only come around about every six or eight weeks. A Dutch liner used to go between the islands supplying them with food, so we managed to get on that and get taken down to Curaçao, a Dutch colony. Pretty near got hit there by a torpedo goin' between Grand Turk and Curaçao. When we got to Curaçao they took us into a store and outfitted us with everything we needed—shaving equipment, suits, socks, underwear, you name it. And they give us money to spend.

We were there three or four days and we were put on a ship loaded with ammunition back to Halifax. It was a German ship, but it was taken over by the Dutch as a prize of war. Fourteen days comin' back to Halifax; everybody was scared stiff. We were taken to a merchant navy club on Hollis Street, Mission to Seamen, and we stayed there overnight and the next day we came back here again. From there I went to the navy in the fall of '42. Being in the navy I was satisfied because we got three submarines, so that paid well for that sinking.

Eugene Wilkie

My father John Wilkie and my grandfather David Wilkie were both sea captains. I had an uncle Malcolm Wilkie, he was a shipmaster too, and when I was a kid about six, seven, eight years old, whenever they happened to be home together and I heard them talkin' about their trips and everything, I guess probably that was one of the things that influenced me more than anything else. Always grew up with the idea [of going to sea], never thought of anything else really.

I was a little stupid. I should have stayed in school a little bit longer; it would have made it easier for me when I went for my certificates. But there was an old friend of my father's, Captain Dawson Geldert from Lunenburg, and he had a four-masted schooner, *James E. Newsom*. She would have been roughly two hundred feet. There weren't many of them left at that time; the Americans had a few. He was out here visiting my father and when he was leaving he said to me, "You should be goin' with me son. I'm goin' down to the Turks Island." So I got after my father: "What about it?" "Nope. You stay in school." My mother was the same. I said, "Listen, it's no use for me stayin' in school. All my friends around my age [fifteen] have gone, I won't do any studyin'." I was trying to use every angle that I could to get out of it. In the end it worked out that my father said, "Well, if your mind's made up, you can go." My mother still wasn't very happy about it, but I went anyway.

The first of it wasn't no bed of roses for a young feller. I used to get seasick and anybody that knows about that knows that it's one of the worst things that can happen to you. When I was called for my watch the first night, apparently I didn't respond the way they thought I should and the next thing I knew I had a bucket of water over me, and this was in the winter.

The captain was part owner of the ship and things were a little bit tight then, but he had bought up some lumber and hay and stuff on his own, so we discharged that down at Turks Island[s]–just north of Cuba, not too far from San Salvador. Then we loaded salt and brought it back here to Halifax, I believe. That was in 1940. We went to New York, loaded coal and brought it back to Halifax, then we left for Barbados. We had no cargo goin' down. We got there finally after about thirty-seven days; used to always take quite a little time, she was strictly sail. When we anchored and got straightened away, we found out that they didn't have any cargo of molasses ready, so we stayed there for thirteen weeks waiting for a spring crop. In the mornings we worked on the ship and in the afternoons we went in on the beach and swam. This was in the harbor at Bridgetown, Barbados.

Captain Geldert took the ship down there and, while he was down,

Aruba had been shelled by German submarines. At that time it was a very large oil refinery. Apparently this skipper didn't like the look of things too well and he had a chance to sell the ship, so he sold her. He was managing owner and Swicker & Company in Lunenburg owned the rest of it. He sold her to a merchant in Barbados by the name of H.O. Emptage & Company and he wanted a Canadian crew on it and he wanted a Canadian master. The fella that was mate, Herbert Stevens, had sailed with my father previous to that quite a few times and he knew that my father at that particular time was home, so they contacted him and he came down—they flew him down—to take the ship.

We left there, I think it must have been around just after the middle of

Schooner *James E. Newsom*, sunk by submarine shellfire on May 1, 1942, on voyage from Bridgetown, Barbados, to St. John's, Newfoundland. Crew consisted of master John R. Wilkie, mate Herbert Stevens, bosun Allan Cross, cook Robert Mosher, and A.B.s Arthur Rhodenizer, Arnold Lohnes, Wilfred Langille, John Allan, and Eugene Wilkie.

April 1942, and started northbound for St. John's, Newfoundland, with a full cargo of molasses in puncheons, barrels and tierces. They engaged another fellow in my place on account of having my wrist broke. The doctor had told me, "Now, every day just take that and soak it in some sea water, it's the best thing in the world for it," so I was doing that. On this first of May, I think I must have been down in the cabin; I had moved in a spare room in the after cabin and had given my bunk to the new fella. My father was down there too. It was about 11:30 in the morning and he was just going up to take a noon latitude sight.

Just about that time, the man at the wheel yelled out, "Captain, there's a submarine comin' up astern." So we went up and, sure enough, she was just comin' along deck level to the water. She'd probably been trailin' us for awhile and surfaced. We didn't think too much of it, we thought probably an American, and we watched it for a few minutes. The first thing we heard a WANG-O!, and she let go with a shell. My father said, "They want us to heave to." He said to the man at the wheel, "Let her come up in the wind," so he did. Then she kept firin' and we had to get off as quick as we could. They were gettin' fairly close then.

My father said, "You better go forward and call out the watch." I went up and said, "You better get out, there's a submarine comin'." "Oh, get out of this." "Well," I said, "there is." One fellow got out and looked back and when he saw it, they weren't long gettin' out, I'll tell ya. From that time on we headed for the lifeboat which was swung across the stern on these old schooners and got off as quick as we could. The cook had like a galley forward where he used to do his cookin' and he was comin' back aft with some fresh bread in a basket so he threw that in the boat. The thing was we weren't very ready for this because the boat had just been painted out not long before that and most everything was out of it. We had to grab it all in a hurry. We got a few cans of sardines, we had the bread, and that was about it, I guess, in the way of food. Our main concern was just to get off.

When we had finally unhooked the boat and dropped back astern, it was one of those days, a long oily swell, but it was long enough that the boat floated good, there was no problem. When the ship had come up in the wind, the submarine was heading right for her then and he was hammering shells into the hull. We figured at the time they put thirty-six shells in her, no torpedoes, just the shells. I'd have liked to had a camera because some of the halyards had been cut off the sails and they were hanging down partways and, when she went down, she just stood up on her nose like that, and went down. But when she did, everything that was wood and most of it [was], anything that was loose floated off. There was cabin drawers, everything was floatin' around.

It's funny how things go through your mind. I had heard about submarines machine-gunning crews, you know, and I was keepin' an eye on this and I thought to myself, if they do start, I'm goin' over the side.[13] Survival's the main thing, I suppose. So anyway they sort of sat there the way they were for a few minutes, then she started to swing around towards us. By this time we had drifted back astern quite aways of the ship. Once he was headed right for us, then my thoughts were, well, he's goin' to cut the boat in two. He got down, oh, I would say, about seventy-five feet; the master of the submarine had a uniform cap and there were two or three other fellas there with him. They were all young, I mean he wasn't over twenty-four or twenty-five, the rest were around that age too. He had spoke to one, and one fella went down below and came up and he had three tins about that high and about that round. He [the U-boat captain] didn't try to find out what the ship's name was, what her cargo was, it almost seemed if he knew that. He spoke fairly good English. He asked my father, "Do you have any food?" "We have some." "Do you have any fuel for your motor?" The reason he said that is because there was a practically full drum of gasoline that had floated off the ship when she was sunk. This fella came down on deck. By this time her deck was washing again, they had submerged her down to deck level. There was quite a bit of water goin' over it, [so] he used a rope tied around him. This fella threw these three cans over to us which turned out to be bread. The first one that we opened up had about that much [two inches of] mold on the top and it was very, very coarse. They were taking pictures of the whole thing while this was happening and there were two or three of the men on the tower with binoculars sweeping the horizon the whole time. She swung off again and we watched her out of sight on the surface.

Then we started to kind of take stock of ourselves and find out how we stood. It had a motor and sail. They didn't carry a regulation-type lifeboat, it had a square stern instead of being pointed on both ends, and it was roughly twenty-six feet, it wasn't a very large boat. There was nine of us in it: master, mate, second mate, cook, four sailors and the extra man. We got this drum of gasoline in, got some in the tank, set it all up, and tried to start the motor and found out that the battery was dead. So we threw the drum of gasoline over the side and then we unscrewed the motor off the base and threw it over the side to lighten the boat up. I think the worst thing of the whole works was the shortage of water. The water we had put in the boat had been in the keg for probably a year or more and it was all stringy, but we used it anyway.

My father had taken his sextant with him, so he could get a noon sight on latitude even if he couldn't get a longitude, and he figured we were approximately 250 miles northeast of Bermuda. So with that in mind he set a course. We did some rowing and tried the sail some. We didn't see anything for the first three days. On the fourth day we saw a ship on the horizon, but it just passed by. On the sixth day, about ten o'clock in the morning, we heard a plane and after awhile we saw it. It wasn't too far away from us, but I guess enough that they couldn't see us. We had some of the sardine tin covers off and we were trying to flash the sun on it. After awhile it went out of sight and about twenty minutes later we heard it again. It was coming back, almost headed for us, and there was a second one which was well down below it towards the surface of the sea. We found out later they used to send those planes out every morning to scout around for survivors; that was the time when they were sinkin' an awful large number of ships around Bermuda.

We watched it and tried to flash it. I don't know whether they saw that or not—we were goin' to ask him afterwards but we never did find out—but finally the lower one come right for us and he landed in the water. It was one of those amphibians with the two floats on the ends of the wings. He got over as close as he could to us and asked how long we'd been in the boat and we told him six days. He gave us whatever supplies he had and said he had to take off, but he'd have a boat out for us, so we didn't do any rowin' from then on. My father said to him, "Where is Bermuda in relation to us?" He said, "You're twenty-one miles off, headed right for the sea buoy." Pretty good [navigation]. Well, me father had spent a lot of time in southern waters and I think he was kind of used to the currents and that sort of thing.

We kind of just sat around and first thing we saw this boat comin' towards us. It was an American Coast Guard, about a ninety-footer, that they'd sent down from the Great Lakes for the purpose of pickin' up survivors until they could get something else, but they had so many of them comin' in that they kept her down there for that. When we went to get up out of the boat to go aboard you're pretty stiff sittin' there, you know, for six days. They treated us good; they had a meal set up. If I remember right it was just soup, but the main thing we were after was water. They warned us not to drink too much, but every chance we got we'd get some.

They took us into Hamilton, Bermuda. When we got in we went to the British sailor's home there; they put my father in a hotel. They gave us I think it was something like five pound to get whatever clothes we needed. Now five pound didn't buy too many clothes. I think the only reason it went as far as it did was that they had some sort of a deal made with these people that supplied the clothes. From then on we sort of sat around, oh, I guess, six or seven days. Every time the American Coast Guard boat came in, we'd see some of them and they kept us in cigarettes and all that sort of thing.

At the end of six days ashore, the mate had been up with my father and he came and said, "Look, as far as I know we're goin' to go down to St.

Georges this evening"—which is the other end of the island—"but don't pass that onto anybody else." So we got in the launch that evening and headed out and here was two tankers. One was the *City Service Fuel*, an old American one, that had been put in service because the war came along and she could only do about nine knots. Four or five of the crew went on that one and the rest of us went on this new Norwegian ship called the *Britain Sea*. They were a typical Norwegian bunch. The captain was a big, raw boney fella, didn't care for anything, nothing worried him.

They were both loaded, on their way back to Halifax. The only thing they could scare up for protection for us was one old four-stacker, one of these old American four-funnelers which was goin' up to Halifax for dry dock. So we started and after the first night out the fog set down thick. This Norwegian captain said, "Not goin' to hang around for these," and he put her up. I think she could do about sixteen knots and he put her on full speed. The night before that, we had heard the wireless chattering away, and the next morning when we ate, the captain told us that they'd sunk someone not too far from us on the way up.

We got in Halifax I guess about twelve or so hours ahead of the other one. It was on a Sunday and there was nobody around to come aboard in the way of immigration or anything. This kind of annoyed my father. When they finally did get to us I think it was someone from the navy and they said, "Captain, we trust you're not going to let this out, this tale of the ship." He [my father] was pretty sore. He said, "Well, I don't feel too good after spendin' a whole day on board ship in the home port." I've got the note of protest that my father made out after we arrived back here which tells the story of the ship being sunk and all that. If a ship went out here, say for instance she had a deck load of lumber and it was swept overboard, the next port you got in you'd have to note a protest in order to claim against the loss. But anyway, we finally got clear and came home. I had said at the time when I was in the lifeboat, if I ever reach dry land, that'll be it. I was home I think just one week and went back to sea on an old three-masted schooner.

John (Stan) McKenzie

There was a lot of those big sailin' schooners got sunk, sure. I know a guy who was part owner in one of the boats I was on after the war. He was on one of them old square riggers comin' back from somewheres in the West Indies with a load of molasses and a submarine sunk 'em. They only had a small lifeboat and they were upset and everything else. They were ten days before they got picked up and they all died but two. One fella, his son died in his arms.

That's all I ever done, goin' to sea in an old sailin' schooner; I was in it when the war started. The first one I went in was the *Audrey Bartlett* and the next one was the *Catherine Burke*. Then from there I went to join an English ship, the *Corner Brook*, 10,000-ton freighter runnin' from Newfoundland to England. Then after that, the *Kittys Brook* was an English ship too. She was old. Bowaters owned her, the same company. They owned a paper mill in Newfoundland and they owned the ships.

I joined the *Kittys Brook* in St. John's, Newfoundland. We left New York [alone] with a load of mostly machinery and we were goin' to take it to Argentia, Newfoundland, for the base that the Americans were buildin' there. Some said we were goin' to Halifax to meet up with a convoy, but I don't know 'cause nobody told us anything. You sailed under sealed orders and the captain didn't know really until he got outside. He knew where he was goin', but he didn't know what course he was goin' to take. We were eighty-three miles east southwest from Lockeport on the Nova Scotia coast, it must have been close to Sable Island somewhere, and the Germans just drove a torpedo in us. It was the ninth of May 1942 between nine and ten o'clock in the night and it was dark, man, was it ever dark, and it was spittin' snow. There was no wind; if there was, there wouldn't have been anybody saved. So I put in from Friday night around ten o'clock till Sunday morning around nine o'clock in a lifeboat with just a pair of shorts on.

THE MERCHANT SERVICE IS *Silent* TOO !

DON'T TALK ABOUT CARGOES OR SHIP SAILINGS

"Nobody told us anything. You sailed under sealed orders and the captain didn't know really until he got outside."

She didn't take too long [to sink]. I thought the captain said seven minutes; I know she wasn't very long. When the torpedo hit, everything went black. I was in bunk with just my shorts on. A lot of us took for the raft, we had a big raft in the stern. We was on it maybe half a minute and I said, "This raft is not going to clear, I'm gettin' out of here." It had to float off because there was oil drums in it and it was goin' to go down with the ship. So I took for the lifeboat.

I had no life jacket on. The only life jackets we had was up on the boat deck in a big box. I never thought about anything like that. We never thought we were goin' to get torpedoed. When I got up there it was so dark you couldn't see if there was a boat down there or not, so I grabbed the man rope—that's the rope on the stave between the two davits to slide down on—and I went down for the boat. There was no boat there, it was gone, and I went overboard [in the water]. Everything was full of bunker oil, I was full of it. So I went hand over hand up to the top of the ship to the boat deck again and I went over on the other side. The only thing that was left there was a little jolly boat, the other boat was gone. We had to get that down, and I forget how many of us got aboard of her; she was full, I can tell you that, all she could bear.

The captain was in the boat with us. We got clear and when we pushed off from the ship I heard the captain say to the chief mate, [who] was sittin' on the raft with two or three more fellas, "We got room enough if you want to come." He said, "No, we'll be all right." Well, that's the last we seen of him. The raft went down and whatever was on her went, clear of one man; he come back and we went and picked him up. There was only two lifeboats—we let the little jolly boat go 'cause she was no good to us—and we stayed together close enough to talk to each other all the time. The old lifeboats was just as old as the ship, about forty years old, and they leaked like a basket. We had some biscuits and a little water and some condensed milk. When you got hungry and sucked on a can of that, now, I'll tell you, it wasn't too pleasant.

We rowed eighty-three miles, right in under the light in Lockeport. We never seen nothin' from Friday till Sunday, never seen a ship. There was two little fishin' boats there haulin' trawl, so one fella put a buoy on his trawl, come up and took us out of the boat and took us up the harbour. The other fella towed the other lifeboat up. They took us into the cold storage there in the engine room [in the fish plant] at the wharf and they give us a drink of brandy. We washed ourselves. One of the A.B.s had a pair of dungarees over his pants and he took 'em off and I put 'em on. Another fella threw down an old sweater and I put that on with a piece of rope tied around me. And somebody give me a pair of boots. We went up to the restaurant and had breakfast, then they took us to the hotel and we had a bath and went to bed. Somebody there give me a pair of pants, real big heavy work pants, and a pair of work boots.

From there when they woke us up that afternoon they put us on a bus and took us down to the dockyard in Halifax. They examined us and thirteen of us were put in Camp Hill Hospital for exposure. My feet were swelled up; they stuck needles into it and you couldn't feel it. We were there five days and I got fed up and I walked out, I wouldn't stay there no longer. So I went to the Merchant Seamen's Club and stayed there three or four nights. We went back home [to Newfoundland] for two weeks and I went back to sea again. I never went to bed anymore with my clothes off, I can tell you that. I said, if Jerry ever gets me again, I won't be naked.

Nine [were lost] out of the thirty-two. That's too many men to lose out of a small crew like that. Course, lots of them lost them all. We lost three I think it was their first trip at sea, two real young fellas about seventeen years old. We had one fella, the block struck him there and took the top off of his foot, that's the only fella I know got hurt. There was another fella, we just took him out of the hospital in New York, he had an appendix operation, he survived all right. Oh, there was a lot of hardships to it, there was a lot of fun to it. When you got ashore you forgot all about it.

Aubrey Jeffries

Imperial Oil had an ad in the Toronto paper asking for crews for oil tankers and they listed, amongst other things, engineers.... I had training in the U.K. before then, I spent my teen years in the U.K., and whilst I was there I was apprenticed. I had a great uncle who was the works manager for a manufacturer of steam turbine engines, steam engines and diesels, those kinds of heavy equipment. I spent four years, an indentured apprenticeship. I was kind of excited about this, I was goin' to sea and I was goin' to be a junior engineer on an oil tanker.

I went to Philadelphia and joined my ship called the *Victolite*; she was in dry dock there. The vibration of the plates underneath my feet and the motion of the ship and the feel of those engines, the power, you could just feel it right through your soul. I just thrilled at that. We had ten engineers on board—five seniors and five juniors—and I was on the bottom of the totem pole. She could do nine knots in fair weather. She was one of the larger tankers, standard I guess for her time, but one in a larger group. She carried 125,000 barrels, summer loading. On the Plimsoll marks there's several loadings. There's the winter North Atlantic (WNA) marks, and then there's the summer; it really relates to how much overloading can the vessel stand during summertime compared to wintertime. Winter North Atlantic is pretty severe weather and things are standing on their beam ends no matter how big they are. Even the *Queen Mary* will stagger in those seas; you got seas like Everest comin' at you for God's sake!

I sailed on the *Victolite* for eighteen voyages between Halifax in the winter and Montreal in the summer. Most of my voyages were to Cartagena [Columbia]. That was in the summer of 1940. Zero convoys; we started off on our own and we came back on our own. We had no cover, no protection, we just sailed. We had many, many adventures in engine breakdowns. We would have pistons cracking at sea, and to pull a piston on one of those things took you about twenty-four hours right straight through plus we'd do our watches. We normally had two watches a day to do. You'd just drop your tools and the guy comin' off watch picks it up. That was the norm.

To start with, watchkeepers don't have a hell of a lot of sleep anyway. We were workin' four hours on and eight hours off, seven days a week. And you do that forever. When you're in port you do that unless you're in dry dock, if you're lucky enough to be in dry dock—we used to hope they'd find something they can't do rapidly. Imperial Oil was awfully cost-conscious and they'd try to limit our dry dock into about two or three weeks. It ended up usually four, which was pretty good. Those tankers, normally you dry docked in the States. Newport News was a popular place. I wasn't there, but I was in Staten Island shipyards for a dry docking. We did work that we can't do when we were at sea. If you break the integrity of the vessel [at sea], of course she's goin' to sink, so you can't do that work. All the underwater valves have to be taken out—intake valves and shut-offs and discharge valves where everything goes out of the ship, like cooling water and sewage and bilges. They would give us our stuff to do, but the heavy big stuff they brought in crews where they'd put maybe twenty men on one of the engines.

When I was on the *Victolite* an incident happened. That was March 26, 1941. We were coming in from Cartagena with a load of crude oil. It was a rotten, rough, tough miserable day out there, big wet flakes comin' down. There was smoke on the horizon and we got up to it. The *Otter*, a converted yacht the Canadian navy had, was out here [in the approaches to Halifax]. We sighted this thing and the captain pulled towards it. There was another ship by it, a big Polish freighter, massive thing. With aldis lamps they talked together and it turns out the *Otter*'s on fire—about twenty-five, thirty miles off shore. And there was a Dutch submarine there.... By marine law an oil tanker can't approach a fire within at least a nautical mile, so we had to stand off a mile. The *Otter* was full on fire. There were men jumping over the side, which we clearly could see, with life jackets on. Looks like they couldn't get their boats down because they were on fire. The Polish freighter signalled to us to get in a certain position; if they could get some seaward protection, windward protection, they were prepared to put over a boat, so we said okay. They got in fairly close as they could, put over a boat, and we were the windbreak. She burned there and she sank and the crew all died, every single one. The Dutch submarine was going around picking up bodies—picking the guys up out of the water and lettin' 'em go, pickin' 'em up and lettin' 'em go, dead. The Polish freighter, they were picking guys up, bodies, they were all dead. They froze and drowned. It's wintertime, temperatures out there are thirty-two degrees; if you're in more than two minutes it don't matter, you're dead already.

There was a certain amount of migration of crews in the [Imperial Oil] fleet, but by and large the ships stayed pretty much together. Oh yes, there was good comaraderie amongst all the crews. The boys knew each other because the relief guy come on–the second off one ship would come relieve a chief on our ship for a month. The crews were very much family-oriented, it got to that in the sense that there was a bonding went on which was very meaningful. We'd go ashore in a group after hours; in dry docking time we

Imperial Esso tanker *Victolite* was sunk by U-564 on February 11, 1942, northeast of Bermuda while on passage from Halifax to Las Piedras in ballast. Time restraints did not allow proper gas-freeing of tankers and because of this all forty-seven of her crew were lost when the ship exploded.

were free to do what we wanted to. I remember one time we had a weekend [off]–Saturday and Sunday– weekends are great. We used to sleep all night. Holy God, I couldn't believe it.

After eighteen voyages a strange thing happened. We needed a junior engineer and we were short leaving Halifax. The Royal Navy sent over a sub-lieutenant to fill the position, so of course we took him. He was off the *Revenge*; the *Renown* and *Revenge* were both doing convoy duty out of Halifax to the U.K. This kid, Johnnie McGough, was assigned to my watch. I was fourth engineer. During the voyage–he was on two trips with us–he convinced me that this man-killing bloody tanker was inhuman. People don't have to work like that. "Half these guys," he says, "are goin' to end up in hospital. The hospitals around the world are full of people workin' out of these bloody things." I said, "Is that right?" "Yeah. Look, they'll kill a man. You can't keep it up forever." The hours they have to work, not to mention the gaseous environment, the old 1927 diesels weren't perfected engines, believe me. They were all experimental practically. After all, they were only invented in 1905. Anyways, he said, "What you need to do is be on a cargo ship, steam-driven. You don't want to spend the whole war on these. If a freighter gets torpedoed, you might have time to get off. But this thing, it goes up." They didn't gas-free the ships; we were a floatin' bomb. We knew that, of course. We would have loved to gas-free, but it takes a week. There's twenty tanks in them.

Yes, we thought about it all the time. We used to figure ways if this thing gets fished, how the hell do we get out of it? We're four storeys down, you know. Some people had miraculously survived these wrecks. We come to understand when ships were torpedoed, from survivors who joined our crew, the first thing that happens, all the ladders and gratings fall in. How the hell do you get out? The steam pipes break off and the cooling water pipes, and the ocean comin' in and the thing standing on its beam ends one way or another perhaps. We used to figure this ship was kind of easy because they have horizontal ribs, the main frame of the ship is horizontal with vertical scantlings. Cargo ships are vertical beamed, then you have scantlings filling in horizontally. This thing we figured, if she was laying on her side, we could crawl up the ribs. Now how do we get from the ribs across the fiddley, the ceiling? We used to figure and devise ways if this one and if that, we'd find ways we could try and survive.

I had a way to get out through the tiller flats where the steering engine is. A steam engine drives the rudder back in there and your refrigeration plant. A rectangular hole I could crawl through, I tried it. One guy, Tommy Spofferd, was junior to me on the ship. A Halifax guy, a great fat guy, couldn't get through that. I don't know what happened to Spofferd. The ship was torpedoed and sank the day after I got off it.

I got a leave at the end of 1941; I'd been on the ship for fifteen months. Norm Smith became convinced that the tankers weren't a great idea for him either. "If you're goin' to get off, Jeff, I'm goin' to get off." So we got off and we went to Norman's Restaurant that night, the best restaurant in the city [of Halifax] then; it was very popular. A number of experiences in my life have been unreal, most unusual, and that was one of them—McGough coming into my life. He got off with us. I went into the washroom. The guy in the next stall to me looked over and says, "Aubrey Jeffries, my God! I thought you were dead. The ship is lost and all hands." He couldn't believe it, he turned right white. I said, "What do you mean? What's all this about?" "She went out and got torpedoed. We got a message at the dockyard says, '*Victolite* under attack.' Period, nothing else. There was nothing left; she just blew." Well, old Spofferd didn't have to worry about how the hell he got out of there. They were all gone, all of them died, good friends. All my friends were lost. We were stunned by it, absolutely stunned.

At that time everybody was short of crews, of course. We went over to Canadian National Steamships [CNS] to get some steam experience in freighters. Johnnie went on his way and I went into Canadian National with my two friends.... They had a ship at dock called *Chomedy*. *Chomedy* was recently back from Rangoon; superstructure was half full of holes, funnel and bridge was shot up, and they were puttin' patches on it, welding, and so on. She was just about loaded and the crew had left, they paid off, good-bye. They'd had it. They got shot up and didn't feel very good about goin' back for more of the same.

The guy I relieved had joined the bloody navy. He said, "It's safer in the god-damn navy than this thing. Do you know what the cargo is?" "No, what?" "Munitions. Do you know where it's goin'?" "No." "It's goin' to Rangoon." The nearest big place to it in India is Calcutta. Well, you do what you have to do, so we signed on the bloody thing. We had choices, didn't have to sign on. Could have hung around and got somethin' equally as bad or worse, so what the hell's the difference? Besides, CN was pretty good, and from a career point of view I thought I was goin' to stay at sea forever. A third engineer looked pretty good to me; I was fourth on the *Victolite*. Tankers paid more than other ships. A tanker paid a junior engineer $110 a month. In CNS, they paid $90 a month. As fourth engineer on the *Victolite*, I think it was a $125 and I was going to get paid $115 [as third on the *Chomedy*]. Second [engineer] got $145 on all CNS ships, chief engineer got $180. Anyway, that was neither here nor there. I was going to get steam experience and I was going to be on a freighter, all pluses in my mind then.

This voyage took ten months to come back. On the way from here to there we had several events. The first instance, before we went out of Halifax, things started to be not quite nice, difficult shall we say. None of the crew had been on this ship before, so in order to get sailors and oilers and firemen, A.B.s, they were all sent down from the manning pool. Under the regulations of the day, people who were in the manning pool for merchant seamen were not obligated to go on the first ship they were sent down to. The first crew came in, they looked over and saw the welding going on on the funnel and bridge. "Where'd they get that?" "Out East." "How far east?" "A long way east." You can't say where the ships are going, except we had a deck load of steam locomotives, four of them [marked] Rangoon Railway. "Is it goin' there?" "Yeah." "Takin' them?" "Yeah." Well sir, that thing was way overloaded. She had these big steam locomotives on the deck; the foredeck ahead of those were casks of acidic acid, and on the afterdeck, big boxes. Inside, there was mobile machine shops for the army. Down in the holds was munitions. The crews didn't like that and away they went back to the manning pool. "Thanks but no thanks, boys."

They had a second chance. They came and looked it over, looked at the quarters. "Got to live in there?" This ship was built in 1919, 1917, something like that, during the First World War, called the *Canadian Constructor*. The old CGMM [Canadian Government Merchant Marine], all the ships were

called "Canadian" vessels and they renamed them and made the Canadian National West Indies Company. Anyway, the second crew went back. Now the regulations called for: third time, game over, you take it no matter what it is. The boys were always kind of leery of the second because very often you get assigned to a Greek ship. Well, that's no place for a Canadian, believe me, because they don't eat the same kind of food that you do and their standards of hygiene are different from ours. It wouldn't be very good for the boys not to want to go with us and they didn't have any more chances. So they went back, refused to go. They said, "Well boys, I'm sorry about that, but you can't refuse; you're goin'." The navy shore patrol got a bus, put them all on it one by one and they sat there with a bayonet at the door. Nobody got off. They drove them down to the

SS *Chomedy* in prewar colours of the Canadian National Steamships. She began as the *Canadian Skirmisher*, 8,600 dead-weight tons, in the CGMM. Taken over by CNS, along with the *Cornwallis* and *Colborne*, the three vessels came to be known as the "Vagabond Ships," spending some of their time running wartime cargoes to India.

dock and put them all aboard. They stood a man at the gangway, at the bow and at the stern, all armed. One guy went over a bow line in the night. He was up to the rat catcher and he couldn't get past, so they caught him. So we went away with a press-gang crew, unhappy as hell.

They had trouble getting a chief [engineer], so they got a fellow out of the U.K., a chief engineer by the name John D., a very heavy man, a very old man, well into his sixties, white hair, a kindly gentleman. I presume he had been quite a good engineer in his day, but he didn't believe in goin' down below because it was too much for his heart. He said to me, "You're the third engineer, Master Jeffries, and I'll be expecting you to report especially to me at the end of each watch." He had very specific ideas on what to do and how to do it. He said, "You have nay steam experience." "Well, they had steam generators on the *Victolite*." "That's a help, but you'll have to be cognizant of certain things of which I will describe to you." So he did all that.

I had a fireman from Owen Sound and we weren't out past Sambro Light and that guy was seasick. Dear God. Smith's oiler had been torpedoed, a guy named Joe Dudman from Sarnia. Joe had been over in the evacuation of Dunkirk on a cross-channel steamer as an oiler. He was the tunnel oiler. Ship's engine is in the middle and you got a long shaft called the tunnel. It's a steel tunnel you walk through that envelopes the propellor shaft with couplings, bearings all along. You got to watch the tunnel bearings all the time. On the end of the tunnel are watertight doors so if the ship is in danger of foundering you close the watertight doors wherever you got them. Joe was in there and they were gettin' all kinds of stuff from every direction coming from airplanes and torpedoes and shore fire while they were getting these evacuees out. They locked him in the tunnel. I don't know how long he was there, but when he came out he was a mental case. This guy lost his mind down there. And we had him. Joe was nervous, he wouldn't go in the tunnel, he just refused. Joe had been hit in the head with something and they put him in the hospital in the U.K. and put a silver plate there. He never went in the tunnel as long as he oiled on my ship. He wouldn't go, he refused. He said, "I don't care if you make me walk the plank, I ain't goin'; you go. I can't go in there." Joe Dudman.

The guy I had as my oiler, Eric, he made a sketch for me, beautiful, should have been a graphic artist. He was a U.K. oiler from London. The reason he was in the merchant navy was he belonged to the British Nazi Party and at the first of the war they interned all the British Nazi Party members and put them in a camp someplace with a lot of other undesirables. Poor old Eric thought it was terrible; he said the politics of the Third Reich was right. All these Jews and black people and stuff, he didn't think much of that—keep the white race white. One of those guys, white supremacy I suppose, but he was not in any way militant. He was a super guy really, he just had this strange political point of view. They wouldn't take him in the British army, so to get out of the camp he said, "I don't mind working for the war effort but not in the military." So they said fine, go on the merchant ships, so he did, got torpedoed, ended up in Halifax and got on our ship. So we had him. Things were not going very well.

On our way down we had two serious problems with the ship. First of all we had a crack across our main intakes. Cast iron pipes just cracked from something and the sea was coming in. I devised a frame, made a concrete block and poured in there. We had to do the best we could, and we got that done. Then one night, about evening time–torpedo time–the main steam supply line blew out. A total shut-down job. I told Captain Burns my problem. The steam was screamin', didn't need to tell anybody. I told him that I had to stop the ship, there was no way I could isolate this system. I was new on the ship myself and I had to trace this line from wherever to wherever, every inch, to find a stop valve in it. So we stopped the ship and he said, "But for God's sake...." I said, "Captain, we'll do the best we can." Me and these two guys went in and shut her down, killed the fires in all the boilers. There's three boilers, nine fires. But the uptakes caught and sparks goin' out, advertising just at dusk exactly where we were. Dead in the water and the bloody smoke stack lookin' like a Roman candle shootin' fire. The captain and the mates comin' down, "Geez, stop that god-damn sparks comin' out of her!" "What sparks? There's no fires on." "There's fire comin' out of there. My God, they can see us for fifty miles!"

Montrolite just got torpedoed yesterday in our area. There was half a dozen sinkings, then, there. It's a big ocean, you can't see anybody, but by God, I'll tell ya, when they're fifty miles away or forty, and you got a Roman candle, you're advertising your whereabouts. The residual soot in the flues off the furnace up through caught fire. There was no way we could stop it, just suffered it out. Captain had everybody standing by the boats ready to go over the side. It took us about four hours, but it died out after awhile. The heat, you drop the bloody wrench and the bolts and the nuts are red hot. You burn your fingers and drop the washers, go down two grates and get them. We're uptight. We thought we were goin' to get torpedoed any minute, fully expected it. Sittin' ducks with what we had on board of that god-damn thing. Anyway, we got that thing put back together and away we went.

Before we got to Trinidad, our first fueling stop, it turned out John D. was a gone alcoholic; we didn't know that. It was getting pretty obvious. Everybody had a bottle in his room. Some of the ships we couldn't drink at all. Tankers, they wouldn't let you have a bottle on board and very rigid smoking regulations too. On the freighters it was different, depending upon the skipper to a large degree. Some skippers were dry and some were wet. If you sailed with a dry skipper you were in for real problems, and if you sailed with a wet skipper you had a problem on the other side. Some could handle it and some couldn't, it just depends. I sailed I suppose with a dozen skippers, because sometimes you get relief skippers. Some of those guys were pretty wild; that's why they were relief skippers.

Jamaica rum, terrible on a man. Three dagger rum, two dagger and one dagger, that was the variety. We always figured there were two fights at least in every bottle. The number one dagger was the lowest grade of rum; it cost say seventy-five cents a quart. The next one was like ninety cents a quart and then the three dagger would be maybe a dollar ten a quart. Jamaica rum is highly aromatic. You open a cork, you could smell it on the fo'c'sle head almost immediately. Barbados rum is the best rum in town.

I went to get my off-watch shot; bottle was gone. I went next door. "Smitty, did you borrow my bottle?"

"No."

"It's gone."

"Maybe Wally got it."

"Wally, did you borrow my bottle?"

"No."

"Where the hell is it? It was right there. Better watch out then."

"Oh well, maybe the mate came down and got it. It'll show up."

Next time, Smith comes in, says, "You didn't borrow my bottle did you?" "No." Turns out the old chief, he knew we were on watch of course, he goes in and gets the bottle. We never locked our rooms. He cleaned all the officers out. The next thing went missing–we used to have Bay Rum for aftershave lotion–the Bay Rum went missing.

On my duties while reporting to the chief, he was getting stranger and stranger. It was pretty obvious then. The little steward, the engineers' mess boy, I said, "John, you been in chief's room? He wasn't up for lunch."

"Yeah," he said, "I had to take him in a sandwich."

"What was he doin'?"

"He was just in his bed."

"Is he sick?"

"I don't know."

So I went down and went in. "Chief, are you sick or somethin'?"

"No, I thought I needed a little more rest."

"Are you sure you're all right?"

"Oh, absolutely fine."

When I next went up, his door was locked, couldn't get in.... The skipper come down and called for the second engineer. Well, this second engineer was another strange bird. Didn't seem to know too much about the running of the ship, how much oil you use for example per watch, which is a very significant thing. You're stored for so much. Seconds know all these things, they do the storing. It got to be I was doing the second's job 'cause everybody was coming to me for instructions.

Certain times it got pretty bad. I had to go up to the captain. I said, "Captain Burns, somethin' about this second engineer doesn't ring true. Have you seen his license?" "No." I said, "You better have an interview with him, see where the hell he's from, what kind of ships was he in. He's very vague." It turns out the man was an oiler off another ship faking as an engineer. That's a very serious offense; you just don't go around doing those things. Like saying he's a surgeon and he's an ambulance driver.

So anyway when we got to Trinidad the first thing we had to do was bury John D. because he had died in his sleep. After the fourth day at sea, this guy was getting pretty high—it's a hundred degrees pretty near down there in the tropics, you know. We had to get the inquest over. We went to a sad funeral and buried poor old John. So we had no chief, and second was in jail in Trinidad. Besides that, two or three of the crew had mutinied. They got the word out, the ship's voodooed, hoodooed, whatever you call it, there was a Jonah on board. In the old sailing days, if a ship had a Jonah on it, she was goin' to founder, certain death for the crew. There was a Jonah on board the ship, they figured they knew who it was, the crew did, all figured it out. One of them took a poke at Smitty, the fourth engineer, and we got that guy subdued. He was for jail. Two or three of the sailors, similar kinds of things; certain others refused to come back so they went in the Trinidad jail, a terrible place to be. So we had to get a crew off the dock in Trinidad to fill the holes. Well, they were some kind of guys. We had a Greek who had been torpedoed, Johnny the Greek, couldn't speak English but he knew how to fire a boiler.

Our next stop was Cape Town; we saw one ship all the way out. The *Queen Elizabeth* come past us one day and she was just a-roarin'. The big ships always ran unescorted because they didn't need any protection because of their speed.[14] We were chuggin' along at eight knots. She did thirty knots all the time; even a torpedo can't catch her. A big thing way out there, it looked like an island comin' at you. The word goes on the ship, "Ship ahoy. A big bastard!" When you first see it you don't know if it's a surface raider or not. The lookouts were all up there tryin' to get a fix on what the hell it is, but we could tell by the size of her it's anything but. She come up and hove to quite close to us, give us a big signal, flag dipping and all, the troops were all wavin'. Away they went, off into the distance, and in about ten minutes she's gone and we were ridin' her swells. Oh, I tell you, it was a sight to see, quite thrilling.

We had fuel for thirty days and the best we could do under favourable conditions was thirty-two days. From Trinidad to Cape Town is one hell of a long haul. We had the engines squeezed into the most economical settings, very carefully using our fuel up daily by slowing down. Engineers have to calculate these things. We made her. The trip to Cape Town was absolutely a nightmare all the way from the day I joined the bloody thing until I got there. In order to go down on the watch in one of those engine rooms in wartime is an act of heroism every time you do that. You screw your guts up and force yourself to go down those ladders, believe me. It is not a nice thing to have to do. You don't know where the enemy is. In the army you know where the hell he is, at least you can see the son of a bitch. We can't see anything, blind to it all. We only knew when we get the water and the wall comin' in on you.

We didn't have to worry [about reaching Rangoon] because the Japanese took it. They came down the Irrawaddy River with their army, beat up everybody on the way down, blockaded the port; nobody could get in. We got wireless on this; somebody was thinkin' about us back home, I don't know who. They told us to go to Singapore, so we altered [course], but having digested Rangoon they moved over to Singapore and captured that. At the same time thereabouts, give or take a month or whatever, the Japanese kamikazes put the British Pacific fleet on the bottom of the ocean by flying their bombers down the smokestacks of several big capital ships. That was the end of our protection for anybody out there.

We're sculling around out there with this bloody cargo and they said go to Calcutta. Then Calcutta got blockaded and they sent us around up to Karachi. There were so many ships in there because of this. Calcutta was the major place for commerce and all the ships there were rerouted to Karachi and Bombay. There were three or four ships tied up to each other at the dock spaces and we got next to a U.S.A. ship. The second off that ship became quite a good friend of ours. He had just come back from Calcutta and said it was unmerciful. They had one hell of a time gettin' out; he didn't know how they escaped with their skin.

The Ganges comes down into Calcutta and there's a delta goes out for a long way to sea and you have to sail your ship in channels. The Japanese had put their ships on each side and they had target practice with everybody comin' on out, all the merchant ships. They were just pickin' them off. After the ships were sunk and the crews were in their boats, they went around with small boats with machine guns takin' everybody out with them. And the survivors on the decks of the sinking vessels were all machine-gunned. It was a harrowing, terrible, terrible, terrible massacre going on. These guys got out somehow.

When the docks are filled, everybody waits outside till they can get dock space. We were there, it must have been two weeks, maybe three, just riding at anchor, all on board keeping our regular watches. Just sitting there, steam up. It was monsoon summer rains, twenty-four hours a day solid rain, straight down. Almost everything turns to mildew very quick. You go to bed and your mattress can't even dry out from the last time you were in the bunk. In your shoes, you're squashing in your own sweat. The engine room temperatures, my friend, were a hundred and forty degrees. You'd lose so much water you'd lose all the salt out of your body. You're down in the engine room and you're puttin' your hand up to tighten something and you can't get your arm down, you pull it down, because the communications, the electronics in your body goes to rat shit. Put your leg up and the cramps, no salt. It's a terrible experience. We used to eat salt tablets. Some guys can't take them, give you a lot of stomach problems, just throw up. I'm one of those kind of people. It was quite a depressing experience. We suffered badly in those conditions.

We had to get the boilers cleaned while we were over there because it was cheap. I've forgotten the ridiculously low price; somethin' like a hundred dollars to clean a boiler. All boilers at sea would scale. Now these are huge round boilers, old fire tube boilers. The boilers were cleaned by children, seven and up; the oldest might have been ten or eleven, the leader. No clothes on—a little bit of a rag around their private parts. Each kid has a candle with a little piece of wire twisted around it so they could hook it in over a tube or whatever. They had a chippin' hammer and they'd go inside. The manholes were open and the boiler was cooled out, well as cool as you could get it down there. I suppose inside it'd be a hundred and fifty, like it was in the engine room. They'd go in there and they're small, they can crawl in the spaces between the tubes and the combustion chamber, the boiler's contour and so on; clean her up nice. They worked in there from seven in the morning till noon. Most of them hung around the ship, sleepin' on the boiler top or whatever, and they ate something. Then they worked until five o'clock, six at night every day. We had three boilers on the ship and I think they were there for about probably a week. There were maybe about a dozen kids; worse than the chimney sweeps. A shoreside contractor these are people that work for a ship repair contractor, these guys, it was something else. Sirang, the head guy—an old seaman who had fallen off the mast of a tall ship and broke his back—went around on his hands and knees; his legs were paralyzed. The children got eight cents a day. If we had our boilers cleaned in Montreal, Quebec City, [it would] cost $1,200 each.

Everybody got their boilers clean if you were in port long enough, and you usually were with cargo vessels, especially wartime; we were dockside for a very long time with the difficulties of logistics they were having with the changing circumstances of wartime.

We discharged our cargo in Karachi and loaded some stuff—hemp or something—and went down and loaded 500 tons of jute in Bombay. The ship carried about 8,000 tons of cargo and we had 7,500 tons of chrome ore in number two and three holds; filled the rest up with tea [from] Ceylon. Now, they [the Germans] were looking for this chrome ore because chrome was a highly desirable metal, very rare; there's none in North America. You can't build a big gun barrel, you can't build an aircraft engine without it.

It was a neutral port where we picked this up, in Mommagoa [Marmugao]. The enclave in India is Portuguese-owned and the name of the enclave is Goa, which is a separate country from India. They have chrome mines there. Because it was a neutral port, at the outbreak of war the ships from the Axis—Italian, German—that were in the area made into there for sanctuary and they were interned. Well, they could have gone out anytime except the British had a destroyer out there waitin' on them and it stayed there for the whole damn war. At night we'd go ashore and go in the taverns and there were the German and Italian sailors and engineers. We drank with them and talked to them.

We had took the position that, as merchant seamen, we weren't belligerent with these people; they are just the same kind of guys we are. They are stuck in there for the war and we're stuck where we are for the war, so what the hell? They were friendly guys, they didn't have cigarettes, they were havin' a hard time—been there for two or three years. They were sellin' their cargoes piece by piece to keep alive. Every vessel had a political officer on it and they would punish the guys for talkin' to us. Our captains didn't like that [Canadians talking to the enemy].

It was all right until Norm Smith takes a collection of cigarettes off the ship. All the guys kicked in a few packs 'cause our stock and trade was cigarettes at sea. We always had our bottom drawer full of cigarettes. We'd take our two or three packs ashore and trade them off for whatever. The bars, that's what we used for money; everywhere else you could use it for money. No use having Canadian dollars in a place like Goa. What the hell's that? You can't spend that or anything else. British pounds you could spend, that's about all. So Norman takes these ashore and gave them to the mate of one of the German ships.

Next thing we know, we get a motorboat out; a captain's gig comes over from the German ship with a real pusser crowd aboard bringing back this package to the captain. Captain Burns was livid. Holy Jesus, what's all this? He didn't know anything about it. The [German] captain said it was impossible for him to accept gifts from the enemy and so on and so forth, very formal. Well, the next thing we had was the British consul down on board and the roof fell in. Smitty was in shit up to here for giving aid and comfort [to the enemy] and that's punishable by Indian jail. He come awful close.

The *Ehrenfels*, as it turned out, was a communications centre between Berlin and Tokyo. They had all kinds of apparatus: big aerials on her, radio stuff. She was sunk not long after I was there. A group came up from Calcutta, a bunch of British guys, non-military, and sank the son of a bitch. They had submarines off there waiting, getting instructions from the *Ehrenfels* and the *Ehrenfels* was getting all this information out of the bars from us guys. They could see us loading chrome ore; several ships were loading this stuff there.

On our way down the east coast of India, the continental shelf is very shallow, sandy, goes way out for miles, so you can be quite away from shore and still not in very deep water. Captain Burns sailed as close as he could to the shoreline all the way down till we got over the straits into Ceylon and Colombo. We figured that's what saved us, because we knew they were going to be out there lookin' for us. And the way we knew is the German sailors told us. They said they got subs out there waitin' for anybody goin' out and this ship [the *Ehrenfels*] is sendin' messages. Seamen to seamen, it's a fraternity. Everywhere you go, you see another seaman you talk to him. The locals won't talk to you because nobody likes sailors very much. They always steal the women and get drunk and get in fights. That's true, they do, it's the nature of the work we do, it's the lifestyle. It evolves from circumstances in which you find yourself. In prisons they have fights too.

We narrowly missed torpedoing. We were off the horn of Brazil coming up from Cape Town towards Trinidad. We were going to Pernambuco [Recife] for fuel. Early, about six o'clock one morning, the lookout saw the torpedo coming. He saw the periscope first; if he hadn't it would have been game over. The mate maneuvered the ship such that the torpedo went right alongside. We were ready for them, had our guns crew on watch as well as our guys. They had stationed a group of submarines out there and got an awful lot of ships, like eight or ten, about the time we were coming past. The alarms were soundin' and we were all there watchin' for the second one; everybody was ready for going over the side. We waited and Johnson [the chief engineer] says, "Open her out for all you got." We were conserving fuel because we only got thirty days' fuel and we got a thirty-one day voyage or something like that. How you use your fuel was of vital importance. To make it simple we have ways of which we can adjust the stroke of the valve, the steam emission valves to the various cylinders so that we can carry steam further down the stroke to provide more horsepower and consequently more speed. So he said, "Link her up as far as she'll go," so I did. I think we must have had her up to nine, nine and a half [knots] maybe even. We were pushin' hard.

He down-periscoped as soon as he fired and we never saw him again. We went all day, then we thought for sure he'd get us at sunset 'cause he could see we had guns on board. We could easy take on a sub, we would be happy to take him on, on the surface, but we can't do anything with him when submerged. That night, I'll tell you, goin' down to take over those watches was somethin' hellish. Tremblin', weak knees, just forcin' yourself to do what you had to do. We waited, waited for the dawn, the next night, and all through the day. After two or three days we felt comfortable. Obviously he had not taken up the chase. It must have been his last torpedo.

There was a U.S.A. navy base [at Pernambuco]; had a nice time there. Our instructions, first they said to go to Trinidad. They told us where the sinkings were, where the possible submarine locations could be, known then, and they were goin' to give us cover when we got to certain places. They routed us from there till we got into somebody else's territory. The next thing we know an airplane comes over, zooms down on us, looked us over. The second pass, he's got a guy in the back seat with an aldis lamp telling our guys who he was and what to do. He said, "All communications by lamp. Enemy in the area. We're providing air cover for you during daylight hours. Proceed to Cape Haitian. Be there six o'clock P.M., no later than. Await further instructions. We'll be back."

We were there three or four days. Got our instructions, up the hook and away we went. Air cover all day; they were circlin' around us lookin' down in the blue water; they could see anything down there. In the nighttime they put us in a little place. We went in there through a narrow way and we were scared to death. It was enclosed by high hills and cliffs and in the cliffs were great caves, beautiful submarine pens, natural made. When the nightfall come, if somebody was comin' out of there, we'd be sittin' there, bingo, sittin' ducks. We were shit scared. It was a moonlight night. Strangest thing, there's a town in there, absolutely no people, no traffic noises, nothin'– abandoned. But in the night, fires on the ring of hills all the way around. Campfires or signal fires, we didn't know what the hell they were. It was eerie. We only stayed the one night. Thank God we got out of there. In the morning that Mustang come down whackin' his wings, "How are you today, boys? Follow me." So out we go and he took us over to Guantanamo, a big American naval base—aircraft carriers, cruisers, admirals' gigs and everything.

Smitty had to fuel from the tanks into the day tanks. He did this always on the morning watch. Smitty's up here gauging the tanks up in between decks and he hollers down, "Shut the pumps off, Joe"–Joe Dudman, same old oiler. Joe says, "Okay, Fourth." So he goes around to where the transfer pumps were to shut it off. But poor old Joe, always a maniac–he lost his mind in the tunnel–forgot what he was sent for time he walked around the end. Smitty goes in his accommodations room next to mine, having his night lunch which they always put in our room for us. While he's sittin' there he smells oil. Of course he says, "I just fueled and you can always smell fuel oil." But the next thing he knows it's comin' over his doorstep because we all live in between decks. He went out and steps into six inches of oil. He yells down to Joe. "Oh God, I...." Bunker C. Down the chief's office, outside of his, it

The *Dalwarnic,* "the hardest crock you ever saw to put a man to sea in.... We were a four-knot ship and we couldn't keep up with a four-knot convoy."

was dry yet, hadn't got that high. Smitty comes in and wakes me up. "Jeff, wake up. Got a hell of a mess. Don't get out of your bunk. There's oil all over the deck." It run out the scuppers into Guantanamo Bay and all the beautiful light-grey warships–it spread out all over the harbour, and they're risin' and fallin', paintin' 'em black. Biggest mess you ever did see. They fined us ten thousand bucks and sent us way off to the other side–get out there.

We got a convoy to New York from there and there were some sinkings; I think two or three ships were lost. We got up to New York and a Canadian corvette brought us to Halifax. So that was the voyage–*Chomedy*–that trip went on forever. We got back eventually; a lot of adventures.

I joined the *Dalwarnic* on January 18, 1943. The hardest crock you ever saw to put a man to sea in. She was built in 1919 and she had come down here from the Great Lakes. She was a package freighter and she and two or three others were called the CAT Lines, ships of the Canadian Atlantic Transit Lines, a Canadian National Steamship subsidiary company. The whole year we spent in the Gulf, running all the time to Newfoundland. We hauled general cargo sometimes, and sometimes we hauled coal. Coming back from Newfoundland, at Lewisporte we would load paper and take that to various and sundry places—sometimes to Halifax, to Montreal, to Three Rivers. Other times we would load fluorspar coming back, a flux for making aluminum.

Normally we sailed Sydney to Lewisporte. If we were going out of Louisbourg we went with a little contingent of four ships. Oh my God, they were some crock; ships built in 1890 with generators in them. The engine room had oil lamps to see the gauge glass, stuff like that. It used to take us about four days, five sometimes, to run over if we had a good run, depending how many knots we got out of the old crock of.... We were a four-knot ship and we couldn't keep up with a four-knot convoy. Leaving Sydney Harbour, those old trampers, old clunkers, were gone over the horizon; we're stopped tryin' to get steam up. I remember we went to Montreal one trip and the current at the Jacques Cartier bridge is four knots; we were there an hour. Unbelievable.

We were the straggler always. This vessel had a serious problem. The uptakes in the boilers were all rotted out. Now, why the company ever sent the ship to sea like that I don't know. They put us in a six-knot convoy, which was a joke even if the ship was healthy. By the time we hit the Sambro light vessel, they were out of sight, so we trundled on, trundled on, about four knots. We got to Newfoundland; nobody torpedoed us, I don't know why not. The name of the game was not to make the boilers smoke, we worked at that diligently, but this thing, we had to poke so much coal through it to get it to go at all, it was just a plume. She smoked like a Roman candle, you could see that thing on the horizon. We just hoped for bad weather and we got it lots of days. Goin' on that run there's lots of bad weather, lots of fog, oh great stuff.

We were in convoy, four ships, not more than twelve hours out of St. John's, two of them got torpedoed. A rotten day again; it's always rotten days most of the time in the winter especially. The iron ore carrier from Wabana sank like a stone behind us. She wasn't afloat a minute and thirty seconds.

The only coal-burner I was on was the *Dalwarnic*. A coal trimmer on any vessel had the hardest job in the war. I said it was an act of heroism to go down in those engine rooms; well, this guy has to get the Victoria Cross to go in those holds where the coal was, with one light bulb there. If you ever meet a man that's been a coal trimmer, ask if he ever got a medal because every one should have for that. People don't realize being in those black holes, there's no way out. He worked hard and he worked in solitude up in there.

January '44 I joined the *Cornwallis*, a sister ship to the *Chomedy*. Those ships were built in 1917, '18, '19 for the most part and they were really pretty much fatigued things by then. She was loaded with armaments. She had a four-inch [gun] on the stern, a three-inch on the bow, Oerlikons, a battery of rocket launchers between number three and four hatch. We used to have kite-flying stuff so we could fly these stringers; kamikaze bombers would tear their wings off when they come down to fly in your smokestack. She had a lot of small arms, anti-aircraft stuff besides; she was really rigged. She carried about 8,000 tons, mostly sugar and molasses north from the [Caribbean] islands, and general cargo going south.

One trip we had to go to Trinidad and we outfitted the decks with stalls for the horses. We carried these animals and the jockeys and the trainers with us to various islands we'd stop in going north–Dominique, Barbados, Antigua. These horses were on a racing circuit they used to do annually and we went to the races. It was a great experience; we talked to the jockeys, who's going to win today, you know. You don't bet on the horses, you bet on the jockey because he's the guy fixes the thing with whoever, how they do these various schemes. So we made a little on the side there. It was kind of a unique thing.

I was not unhappy to be transferred off her. Shortly after that the *Cornwallis* went away and got torpedoed on the way home. That's her second torpedoing by the way 'cause she had been torpedoed in St. Lucian; not me on it. The *Cornwallis* had been sunk in St. Lucian tied to the dock along with the *Lady Nelson*. The same night they got four or five ships there– some foreign ships and those two Canadian National ships. I was supposed to be the seventh engineer on the *Lady Nelson* that day, then the *Chomedy* thing came up and they transferred me off. The seventh engineer was killed. I have a very, very charmed life. I escaped more lives than a cat; I'm supposed to be here.

The fellow who relieved me on the *Cornwallis*, Jimmy McLaughlin, was a third engineer off one of the other ships. I had known Jimmy over the years, I don't know how, but you get to know people who sail on other vessels. Jimmy says, "I'm goin' for my seconds. You just went through an exam, can I have a list of the questions they asked?" That's what we used to do, anybody goin', get me the questions. They won't ask you the identical ones, but I said, "Sure, Jim." Matter of fact I gave him not only the questions, I gave him the answers I'd provided, my rough one. He said, "Gee, I appreciate that, thanks a lot. When I get done, I'll send them back." So Jimmy went away and he lost his life in her. She was torpedoed in the Gulf of Maine and there were two white men survived—the bosun and a seaman from Dartmouth—and there were four black men out of the galley—a cook, a second cook, captain's steward and mess boy.

We know the circumstances of the torpedoing because the bosun and the sailor told people who picked them up. The boats were swung out, they always were for the most part at sea. As soon as we got away from the docks and squared up, out the boats. She was torpedoed at six o'clock in the morning just before dawn—half light, flat, calm, frigid sea. The crew were in the boats, but she sank so fast they didn't have time to cast them off the davits. The ship rolled when she sank and dragged the boats down in the water, took all the people with them. But the bosun always thought if he ever got torpedoed, and this was exactly my thinking, to hell with the boats, drop the rafts from her. Now the rafts, all you had to do was knock a pin and away she went, and you jump in after it. The bosun jumped in, gained the raft and he then went around pickin' guys up. He picked up the sailor, he picked up the four black guys and they sat on the raft. Our crews were normally about forty-five, so forty went down.

I was transferred to the *Cathcart* and was on her when the European war ended. The authorities had earlier indicated that, merchant seamen, the war ain't over yet and nobody could be buggerin' off for awhile, because they had to fight the Japanese still. In fact, in order to get any wartime recognition—monetary recognition like the troops did—we had to sign contracts or documents that would commit us to go to sea until after the Japanese war was over, so we did that. But the war ended. I went on the *Lady Neslon*. I had been relieved from my position on the *Cathcart*, I think as part of the management strategy for staffing the ships after the war. They moved me as second off of that one—1945, just at the end of the war—to the *Lady Nelson* which was operating as a hospital ship under Canadian army charter. The captain was the operative head of the vessel, but the ship to all intents was owned and operated, consumed, by the army. The commander of the ship was army. Our Canadian army medical corps was the crew on board for the medical thing. The ship's crew did what ships crews just do normally, operate the ship. I was fourth engineer. We went where the army said we had to go, took on what they said and so on. We had special articles to sign which effectively put us in the service for the time on that vessel. You're like a branch of the military rather than operating as a commercial thing.

On the ship we had sixteen wards, I think fifty in a ward. We had three operating rooms with six army surgeons and either twenty-four or thirty-six Canadian army nursing sisters. We had literally dozens of male nurses or orderlies who looked after the wards. Thirteen of the wards were mental wards. We had amputees, burns—air force and tank guys badly burned, we had a lot of those coming back—a few guys blind. But mostly guys psychiatric, been damaged forever. We had guys come on couldn't stop cryin'; we had guys couldn't stop babblin'; we had guys come on gone morose, tuned out of life, in the depths of depression, fear or whatever the hell it was. We had a lot of navy guys, an awful lot of sailors. We didn't carry any merchant guys; they would go through the civic hospitals in the U.K.

We made I think two voyages when we stopped in Halifax and converted half the ship to carrying war brides. They made a bit better accommodations for them. I think we brought somethin' like 150 brides back first trip. We had a couple of births on board; the medical guys took care of all that. They were supposed to not be pregnant within some length of time, but what they had done in order to get here was bind themselves up so they looked pretty good, you know, and there were two births. When we got back to Halifax they discharged all the war brides. A lot of them were consigned to various cities across the country where the army sent them on trains. There were some of the war brides who for one reason or another had to return, didn't get off. Either they had been abandoned, they didn't have anybody to go to, or else they didn't like what they saw. I think we took twenty-four back.

They had army trains come in for the army guys, damaged personnel. Hospital trains—sleepers with red crosses on them—and all the guys were billeted on them and they took them off to wherever. A big hospital in Montreal, took a lot of 'em there. I suppose some went to Toronto—wherever they had veterans hospitals. So they went away with them.

You know, we were still bringing military people as well, on the way going over there. We had Red Cross people who were just going overseas for the first time, like the war was still on, and in a sense it still was. They had stopped shooting, hopefully. There wasn't any guarantees on these things by the way. We ran with lights on and everything. We were not very comfortable with the truce at sea. We simply didn't know if it was going to hold or not. And then of course there was always the danger of mines, which was another matter. We had heard there was reports of certain groups of submarine commanders who decided, to hell with that, they were going to carry the war on. All these things were made known to us and we had to be prepared.

Then on that hospital ship, rather interesting enough, we were the second ship to go to Germany at the end of the war and we took German prisoners of war from Canadian camps. They all came down on military hospital trains to Halifax and we loaded them on board, a big crew of them, several hundred.

I was transferred off the *Lady Nelson* in April [or] May 1946 and appointed as second engineer on the first of a new line of ships they were building, the first postwar ships. Designs had been going on during the war getting ready for after. They were express freighters—nineteen knots, diesel, twenty-five passengers. They made three: the *Canadian Cruiser*, *Canadian Challenger* and *Canadian Constructor*. The second mate that came on this new ship at the end of the war—the *Canadian Cruiser*—he was a Bermudian, served his time in the Canadian navy; he was a lieutenant, a deck officer. He and I were sittin' up on the boat deck one evening chatting. He says, "Well, now that it's all over Second, what do you think about your own experience?"

I said, "Well, what do you mean, what do I think about it?"

"Well, aren't you sorry now you never went in the navy?"

"What in the hell would I want to do that for?"

He says, "Well, that's where the real action was."

I said, "What? I saw enough real action. I got shot at. I gave them all the opportunity they needed to kill me, same as they did to you, I guess. So my answer, my friend, to your question is, I'm proud of what I did, I'm glad I did it and I'd do it again."

I feel cross about that and a certain disappointment that that's the impression people have of us [of being an undisciplined lot]. The impression is rather widespread. The point is that was grossly unfair and grossly misunderstood. Our guys are just as dead as their guys except we had more proportionately than any of them. They had advantages we never, never had. For example, they got leave, dental care, clothes, they got taken on courses, they had barracks time. They went to the front and came back after two weeks and rested someplace, then went out for another go at them. Most of them spent four years in bloody England before they ever saw any war. Of all the veterans in the field who were really on the front lines, we were every day at sea, that's where it was. It started at Sambro [off Halifax]; we lost ships at Sambro, we lost them at the pilot's station at Father Point in Quebec and everywhere in between there, and wherever else in the world we were we lost people. But, you know, the guys sittin' in Aldershot in England and Sussex and the Downs, they didn't hear nothin'; they heard airplanes flyin' someplace to bomb. And of all the guys that went to Normandy, for every one that was in the boat goin' to Normandy and stayed in there fighting, actual fighting, there was ten backing them up someplace—half of them in Canada, the other half in the United Kingdom or the back bases. Sure, I know we brought guys back who suffered badly.

I'm glad I stayed in the merchant naval services rather than to have gone into the military service. I don't think I'd have enjoyed military life; my personality doesn't adapt me well to that. I do well at what I have to do, but in the military you can't do what you want to do, you have to do what somebody tells you to do and that would have put me in a position where I would have been rendered less than useful. I think what I'm trying to say is that my contribution to the war effort was any number of times more than it would have been had I gone into the military. That makes me feel satisfied. I'm grateful for it.

The war was a great experience for me and did a lot for me. I think I gave back as much as I got—I'd like to think that I did—in dedication, duty. Suffered a lot of fear of course and I learned a lot of things. I learned how to do things well and stay at them. You can't give up at sea when you got somethin' wrong; you work till you die. Well, I can do that. A lot of people don't know what that means, they don't understand that. I

A group of merchant seamen about to be rescued. Surviving the winter North Atlantic in a cramped, open lifeboat, often for a week or more, with only a minimum of water and possibly hardtack or biscuits, could test the mettle of even the hardiest.

think a lot of servicemen have gone through those kind of exercises where survival counted—do or die kind of thing, literally—and I'm glad I experienced that. I'm glad we're now recognized [as war veterans], but that hasn't made much difference. I was always proud of what I did.

CHAPTER 3

Lifeline of the World

"Had those embattled, rust-streaked ships not kept sailing through the terrible years of loneliness, misery, and loss after loss, the war itself would have been lost; all the vast effort, the blood, the technology and skill thrown against the U-boats would have been to no avail."
—Tony German, *The Sea is at Our Gates*

The numbers speak for themselves. By war's end, the industrial might of the United States had produced 296,429 aircraft, 102,351 tanks and self-propelled guns, 372,431 artillery pieces, 47 million tons of artillery shells and 44 billion rounds of small arms ammunition. The worth of war materials alone was $183 billion.[1] Canada's contribution was no less impressive for a country of only 11 million people. In addition to the millions of tons of food staples and raw products, industry churned out 900,000 rifles, 794,000 military vehicles, 6,500 tanks, 24,000 light machine guns and 16,000 aircraft.[2] More than 180 million tons of cargo were ferried on the backs of merchant seamen from North America to the United Kingdom, and more than 25,000 merchant ship voyages were required to accomplish this formidable task. Of the scores of convoys that sailed on the North Atlantic run, only one, SC-52, was turned back.

A convoy's manifests could be as varied as the nationality of the ships that made it up. In July 1944, for example, one convoy carried a cargo of a million tons—85,000 tons of grain, 85,000 of sugar, 38,000 of molasses, 50,000 of other foodstuffs, 35,000 of lumber, 37,000 of iron and steel, 310,000 of oil, 80,000 of tanks and military vehicles, and 250,000 of other military supplies.[3] It has been said that one Canadian merchant ship could transport enough food to feed 225,000 people for one week.[4] With the bombing of London, Liverpool became Britain's most important convoy port from the middle of 1940 until war's end. The Mersey River, with 144 docking berths, received 1,285 convoys, at an average of four a week, with a similar number sailing out.[5] Ninety thousand tons of war materials passed through Liverpool and other ports at Glasgow, the Clyde, Londonderry and the Bristol Channel on a daily basis to feed the Allied armies.

From 1941 to 1945, forty-one convoys sailed to Archangel and Murmansk in relief of beleaguered Russia, carrying $18 billion in aid from the United States, Great Britain and Canada. Among the millions of tons of supplies were an estimated 12,206 aircraft, 12,755 tanks, 51,503 jeeps, 1,181 locomotives, 11,155 flatcars, 135,638 rifles and machine guns, 473 million shells, 2.67 million tons of fuel and 15 million pairs of boots. More than 1,500 merchant ships were convoyed to and from Russia; 105 were sunk and 869 perished.[6]

In 1942, Operation Torch, code name for the invasion of North Africa, involved five hundred American and British ships sailing simultaneously from the United States and United Kingdom. For the initial assault, merchant ships carried 107,000 troops, 11,000 tons of food and 10 million gallons of gasoline.[7] In 1943, during Operation Husky, the invasion of Sicily, 3,300 ships were required, landing 80,000 troops, 7,000 vehicles, 300 trucks, 600 tanks and 900 artillery pieces in the initial forty-eight hours alone.[8]

Operation Bolero was the ultra-secret two-year stockpiling of Great Britain for the D-Day landings. From April 1942 to April 1944, merchant vessels transported 1.5 million servicemen and 5 million tons of supplies and equipment for the invasion. Included among 320,000 individual miscellaneous items were 8,000 airplanes, 1,000 locomotives, 20,000 rail cars, 450,000 tons of ammunition and 50,000 vehicles. More than 5,000 ships were used in the actual Overlord operation.[9]

Allied merchant fleets shuttled hundreds of thousands of troops and millions of tons of war materials, food, fuel and various day-to-day necessities, in addition to prisoners of war, casualties and evacuees from around the world, during the war. They maintained the lifeline of the military and the civilian populace. Canadian merchant seamen saw action in all theatres and sailed under virtually all Allied flags. "The morale of the merchant seamen...stood for the rock on which the convoy system was securely based."[10]

Warren Stevens

In early November 1940, Convoy HX-84, eastbound from Halifax for the United Kingdom, was attacked in the northwest Atlantic by the German pocket battleship *Admiral Scheer*. In one of the most heroic and infamous battles of the war, the convoy's lone escort, *Jervis Bay*, an armed merchant cruiser, fought for twenty-two minutes before succumbing to insurmountable odds. Her stand, while brief, allowed the convoy to scatter with a loss of only five out of thirty-seven merchant ships. Thirteen Canadians survived the sinking of the *Jervis Bay*, and eighty-six-year-old Warren Stevens was one of those. Although serving in a naval capacity aboard ship, he was one of only about six Canadian survivors alive in the 1990s who could provide a first-hand account.

I enlisted in August 1940 in the Royal Canadian Navy. My first draft to sea was the *Jervis Bay* on convoy escort duty. She was a merchant ship, a 14,000-ton Australian passenger and freight boat. She was taken over by the navy when the war started, an armed merchant cruiser—seven six-inch guns and one anti-aircraft gun. I'll tell you what they were, they were old obsolete field guns converted over and mounted on pivots on the deck. The extreme range on land was eight miles, and six and a half when we had them. The merchant crew was still on, but they were all in uniform; they had to sign on for the duration. Then she had so many RN ratings besides and twenty-six Canadians on loan to the RN for a year.

There was supposed to be another armed merchant cruiser with us. She brought a contingent up from Bermuda and joined us three days outside of Halifax. On the way up they tried out their guns and started her leaking so bad they had to get right back to Bermuda and get on dry dock. The other ships joined with us and then she went back, so that left us alone with the convoy. We sailed the 28 of October and the 6 of November we ran into a German pocket battleship, the *Admiral Scheer*, off the southern tip of Greenland. That was her first raid out. We were supposed to have met the escort there from the other side, but one of the ships, a Greek freighter, broke down and held us up long enough that we had to change course. When we got to where the escort should have been, she wasn't there, that pocket battleship was.

The only warning we had, they [the Germans] had a man that was broadcasting every day from I don't know where; they called him Lord Haw Haw.[11] We were only out of Halifax a day I think when it was announced the *Jervis Bay* was sunk with all her convoy. A couple of days after, we get the same broadcast from the same man, just propaganda. We were in three lanes, and when the action started, the three lead ships started dumpin' smoke bombs overboard and the convoy scattered behind the smoke screen. She picked the biggest ship in the convoy first and fired a salvo at her. I don't remember now which one, she was a passenger ship carryin' nurses, medical equipment and all that stuff. One shell hit her in the stern and set her on fire, but they got that right out and she kept right on her way.

Of course, we were the escort ship, so right away the captain [Fogarty Fegen, RN] called for full speed and aimed straight for her and started firin' with our guns. That would take his attention off the other ships. Our extreme range was six miles and a half, his was twenty-eight, so you can imagine what chance we had. She [the *Admiral Scheer*] opened fire at eighteen miles and the closest she came was between nine and ten miles. By the time she got that close up to us, we didn't have a gun to fire, we were just a blasted-out hulk. That battleship never missed. They had eleven-inch guns and they were some accurate with them.

The first salvo that hit us cut our main steering wheel off in under the bridge. The next one went in the engine room and put our main steam line out of action. So we just laid there a helpless hulk broadside to her, ready for her to pepper away at. I didn't see this myself, but the fellas on deck said that when those armour-piercing shells would hit, they'd hit just above the waterline on the one side and go out underwater on the other. They could see the streaks of them goin' in the water after they went through the ship. See, a ship, all she's got is her iron plating, no armour plating or anything like that on her, just the same as she was built.

I was stoker on board and I was down in the shaft tunnel, me and two other fellas, chippin' paint at the time. When action stations sounded, we beat it right up, and it's a good thing we got out when we did because the first thing we took was a torpedo back in the shaft tunnel where we'd been.... She took a list over to starboard and settled down by the stern. The bulkheads is all that saved her from goin' down because they stopped the water from goin' ahead into the engine room compartment and all our cargo space. Her cargo space was filled with empty oil drums that was supposed to have kept her afloat from a torpedo. There was two destroyers with her and I think we got the torpedo from the destroyer.

I had to go to the second engine room floor on standby in case anyone was injured in the stokehold. One shell exploded in the room next to us. She was an old ship and the paint on her walls was so thick that when that shell exploded in there the paint bursted off and was flyin' around like bumble-bees. One of the men I had worked with, he was feeding ammunition up on the hatch for one of the guns and nobody was taking it away. So he come up to see what was wrong, just in time to see a shell hit that gun, and the gun shield took one of the gunners right across here, cut him right in two.

It started at quarter to five in the evening and I went over the side I guess about six o'clock. When we got orders to abandon ship, I went down to the cargo deck where they unloaded. At that time they were shelling us with these napalm shells. When they would hit, they would explode and that fluid, whatever it is, I don't know, would run down over the iron steps goin' from one deck to another and the iron would just melt and bubble right up. I went up on deck. The officers were all gone, they were all shot. The only one I saw after was one of the engineer officers. The captain, when the salvo went in under and cut off the main steering gear, a piece of shrapnel hit his arm and it was almost severed. He left the bridge and went back to the after steering house to control the ship from there. Just got to that when a shell hit and wiped out all the deck officers, there wasn't one of them left.

She was afire. Everybody was getting away. They got one big carley float away. I don't know how many men was on it; two of them perished from the cold. If this had happened the day before there wouldn't have been a survivor; oh, it was a bitter cold day and snowin', a regular blizzard. One lifeboat got away, but it had two shell holes in it and it filled with water. There was twenty-three men in that; two of those men perished. We had another carley float like the first one up on deck [but] no way of gettin' it overboard. There wasn't enough of us to raise it up and get it over the rail. No arrangements of any kind made to get it overboard unless you had steam so you could hoist it off with the davits.

I went over the side down one of the lifeboat falls, the only lifeboat that got away. Had I known enough and would have crawled in the other lifeboat—you couldn't get it off the deck, the deck was so warped that you couldn't swing the davits and one of the lifeboats falls was shot off—the lifeboat floated off and drifted away when she sunk. All the rest of us could have got in that lifeboat and stayed there. I was hanging alongside the ship trying to push away from it. I puttered around from one piece of wreckage to another to try to find something big enough to float me and I couldn't. I had two of those old cork life jackets that was put on that ship when she was built and I was only in the water a few minutes when I had to take 'em off; they were so heavy they'd have sunk me.

As soon as they put us out of commission that our guns ceased, they went right after the rest of the convoy. I saw four other ships go up in flames while I was down alongside the ship. That's all they got out of the convoy. A Swedish freighter only steamed away for an hour and stopped and laid there until everything quieted down. Then she came back and picked up the survivors. Her captain got all the credit and he was drunk in his bunk, he didn't know what was goin' on. The chief mate had to take over and bring the ship back.[12]

I hung there for awhile and somebody on deck threw a five-by-five hatch cover overboard. Three men come down and got on that. They were all a lot bigger than me and it wouldn't float one, let alone three. I had been there quite awhile in the water. They asked me how much she settled. I said, "I got a mark there and it hasn't changed since I come." I was in the water I guess over an hour then. When they saw that she wasn't settling any, they went back up on board and I got on the hatch cover. There was the head of a lifeboat rudder floatin' around. I got a hold of that and put it on the hatch cover and I sat on that; that kept me up so I was only about two inches of my rear end sittin' in the water.

I was a born-again Christian before I got on that job. While I was hangin' alongside of that ship I asked the Lord if he would spare my life to get home to look after my family. I had the assurance right there. Before that I couldn't keep my teeth from chattering, I couldn't grip them tight enough. That stopped immediately and I felt no more cold. I had a lifeboat oar and I was tryin' to push myself along the ship to get away from her 'cause I knew if I was alongside and she went down I'd go right down with her, the suction would take me down. I couldn't get away. I'd shove myself as far as I could with that oar and I'd come right back against her. She was all afire. The fire got close enough to the hatch where they were passin' the ammunition up for the guns, the pile of cordite they had up there caught fire and lit everything up. I pushed as hard as I could and my momentum was just barely stopped, I would say, when there was an explosion down inside of her somewhere, a dull explosion, and she just rolled over on her starboard side, slid away from me that way, stern-first and down. There was twenty or thirty men left on her; they went down with her. The other big hatch cover that got away, there was eight men on that. They said they could have reached out and touched the tops of her masts when she went down by them. She was just goin' on a slant like that and there was no suction from it. Those men what was on that big hatch cover, only one of them got off it alive; they all perished [from] exposure.

A ship [the *Stureholm*] come up to me, I judged, about twelve o'clock at night. She had picked up the men on the big carley float that had got away and the ones out of the lifeboat. She drifted then that she was close enough to me that I hollered for help. They heard me, but I had fished a navy duffel coat out of the water and I had the hood up. Well, all they had was flashlights, they didn't dare show any other light, and they looked and they couldn't see me. They went by and I said, "That's the last of that, I'll have to wait until the escort from the other side comes around in the morning."

I sat there I don't know how long and after awhile I looked and I thought there's somethin' black there that's blacker than the rest of the horizon around. I said to myself, "Could that possibly be a ship?" I called and they heard me. It was the same ship that passed me before and couldn't see me. She turned and came right for me and I thought first she was goin' to run right over me. I threw the hood back and they could flash the lights on me. They just sheered and come close enough to throw me a heaving line. I got that, tied it around under my arms and they hauled me on board.

I wasn't picked up until quarter to five next morning. I had no use of my legs, none whatever. I could stand, but I couldn't bend my knees or anything. At eleven o'clock I felt the first sign of circulation comin' back in my legs. We were eight days, from where we were hit, gettin' back to Halifax. When I got in the hospital the navy doctor said, two more hours [in the water] and I'd have lost both my legs, the circulation would never have come back in them. All I went in for was to get a dressing on my hand. This hand, in slidin' down the lifeboat cable to get in the water, rope burn took all the skin off the palm. I was only in long enough to get a bandage put on it.

When we got back into Halifax, we were put on special duty, all the survivors, on what they call the NCSO, Naval Control Service. We searched all ships comin' into Halifax to go in convoy; we checked them for fire hazards and sabotage. I was on that job for twenty-five months and then I was drafted off....

The nearest we can tell there was 268 [crew members] all told and there was only sixty-five survivors. Official account from the RN only gave somethin' less than two hundred, but they only counted the RN ratings that was on board. They didn't count the regular crew that signed on that ship for the duration, or the Canadians.

Michael Ness

Anything that could sail at all they put into action. I remember I made inquiries about a whip [the *Wilhelmina*], she was a passenger ship that had been converted over for operations by the Americans. Of course at that time the Lend–Lease was in operation and we got a lot of help from the United States, otherwise we'd have been up against it completely. She was under the British flag and a British crew aboard her. The officers of the ship were all from Scotland or England or Ireland, but the crew we picked up off Newfoundland. I started off as fourth engineer and was promoted to third on the ship. We travelled by train [to San Francisco]. They were still doing renovations to the ship and after she was ready for sea, of course we familiarized ourselves with the ship and we sailed. I think our first trip was to Vancouver and loaded supplies on there, came back, loaded supplies in the United States, and left there through the Panama Canal.

We had problems and we arrived in Jamaica and we were held up quite awhile. We were running alone as far as there. After, we headed for Halifax and joined a convoy. If I can remember right, we had a mixed cargo, ingots of copper and alloy metals and I think we might have had some munitions on it. The convoy ahead of us at that time was the *Jervis Bay* convoy. In fact, we would have probably joined that convoy, but we had electrical problems aboard ship, one of our generators. At that time degaussing of the ship was very important, for the polarization of the ship for mines,[13] and one generator broke down; we had to have two operating.

Mines were very active in Britain; they were dropping them on the coast by plane and that.

We didn't have very much in those days [for escorts]; protection was limited to so far off the American coast and so far off Ireland. Guns were scarce too. We didn't have any, not on that ship. It was a very large convoy and there were several ships sunk. The second of December 1940, I was third engineer and I come off watch at four o'clock–twelve to four daytime was the third engineer's watch–and I come up on deck lookin' around. Someone else was nearby and we were talkin'. I looked back [at the trailing ship], I almost think it was the *Clan Sterling*, and while I was watching, she just sort of disintegrated. The wind and everything was freshening up and the weather was getting dirty. We had had the impression that in real dirty weather the Germans just couldn't torpedo you. You know, we were protected by the weather, that's what we thought.

Just after eight o'clock I turned in, when first thing I knew the ship seemed to come right out of the water. It was an awful boom; we were torpedoed. It had a sensation that you don't forget very easily. Over a period of time it wears off, of course, but it's an unpleasant sensation. Water was everywhere. It was up around my feet in the cabin. I can remember, getting up. Now most of the crew turned in in those days with their clothes on. It's something I never enjoyed, so I had undressed. The only thing I could get a hold of was an old pair of pants nearby and my uniform jacket. I don't know if I got into shoes or not, but anyhow I didn't have much time to do anything.

The boat I was to assist at was the port boat and when I got [there] the ship started listing to starboard and the boat was swung in. It [the torpedo] hit, I would say, just aft of the bridge, from what I can remember of it now. The chief officer, he was there and he said, "Let's get this boat clear." Some of the crew were in the boat by this time, quite a few of them were in the boat in fact, and she was hung up, sort of catching on the ship's side and wouldn't run free. We got her clear anyhow and Mr. Davis [the mate] said to me– the British ships are formal you know–"Mr. Ness, you better go for the starboard boat." I said, "What about you, Mr. Davis?" He said, "Don't worry about me. I may not make it. Don't worry about me." That's the– he wasn't the only one [who didn't make it]; the wireless operator and all the mates except the captain was lost, and the second engineer and a couple of oilers, if I can remember right.

I went to the starboard side and they were lowering the boat away at that time. I got in the boat, but I had to jump for it. Fortunately I landed among all the other men. The only other officer in that boat was the chief engineer. We tried to get clear of the ship, that was the important thing, 'cause she was going down fast. In fact before we got even clear, she had gone under the surface. The skipper said she went down in less than nine minutes. We had the good fortune to pick the captain and the bosun up later on. The only way they got off, there was a life raft on deck and they held on and the life raft floated and they remained with it.

We were all alone on the ocean. It didn't look very promising, you know, especially with the dirty seas running and everything, the boat was flopping around like a cork. Trying to sail one of those boats or even to row them was just impossible. That's kind of the worst experience of all, but as I say in those days we were young and you didn't even think of the worst happening to you. No one was very cheerful. Tried to get them to sing or something, to get a little life into the crew, but nobody wanted to, they all were dead quiet. I thought, well, by morning we'll probably get a bearing where we are and we can get a little more cheer into the crew and do something, you know, get a little bit more comfortable, but fortunately we were picked up before daylight.

I think it was a British destroyer picked us up. Daylight was breaking. They said at the time they just got a faint radio signal that we'd been torpedoed and they hung around the area for a bit. That's the only indication they had that we were gone. But there was a lot of other ships sunk before that, so they were pickin' up all kinds of messages. They threw scramble nets over for us. They had to keep moving because they didn't want to become a sittin' duck for the U-boat. When they got alongside as many as possible would scramble up and eventually we all got aboard.

We were a couple days aboard the rescue ship. I remember one morning we were out on deck and there were quite a few ships around us. In the distance we saw what we thought was Sutherland Flying Boats. However, shortly thereafter, more planes appeared, but this time it was the German planes and they bombed the ship. In fact, they machine-gunned us and we were firin' back at them. I can remember as clear as I can see you, this [Me] 109, or whatever the German aircraft was at that time, backing her over on her sides comin' around the ship and him grinning out at us. I can see him yet.

We were landed in Londonderry and I think the next day I got a telegram offering me another ship and I said yes, I acknowledged that I'd take the ship. You took what was coming and you didn't think anything. I personally, and I think I can speak for all the other crew members, never give a thought to the enemy action or being blown up.

Angus Campbell

When Canada declared war I was first mate on the *Zenda*, owned by the Interprovincial Steamship Company. F.K. Warren in Halifax here was head of it. We were coming down the Lachine Canal and at the end of the voyage I went up for my master's home trade certificate in Yarmouth. I sold my sextant to the second mate of the ship for the same price I paid for it, thirty dollars. I was going to buy a modern sextant in Halifax, but I couldn't, every nautical store was sold out; so many retired fellas goin' back to sea. I spent a week in Halifax looking and I finally got another second-hand one, same as I sold for thirty dollars; paid fifty for it and spent thirty dollars making it serviceable.

I went home to spend Christmas, and Christmas Eve I got orders to return to Halifax. I had an application into Imperial Oil before I left Halifax and they ordered me to be in Halifax next day, Christmas Day, to be second mate on the *Petrolite*, one of the small tankers they had. I joined her and spent the winter down on the coast of Peru. At that time Imperial Oil owned the oil wells at Talara and they had a refinery down there. We were trading from Talara to Callao, that's the port of Lima, Peru, the capital. We stayed there until April and were ordered to Aruba. We discharged kerosene in Aruba and loaded kerosene for Halifax.

The captain had a coasting ticket, but he never sailed anywhere but on the Lakes and he knew nothing about navigation. He didn't know anything about celestial navigation because all they learned up on the Lakes was pilotage. It's surprising the number of men that traded to the West Indies that could only find latitude; couldn't work a longitude sight, but they'd head south and keep to the easterd until they got the latitude. When I joined the ship the first question he asked me, "Are you a navigator?" I said, "What do you mean?" "Can you navigate?" I said, "Yes, I can navigate."

Our first cargo we loaded from the Halifax refinery up to Bedford Basin to supply Irving. Then we came back and that's when I learned about the master; he was an alcoholic. He went ashore and came back tight as the.... We had to go inside number four dock. It was blowing hard and I thought, we're heading for a disaster tonight 'cause it was a tricky place to get a ship in, especially when it's blowing off the dock. He could only stand up by holding the wheel, but he put that ship in behind that dock like an expert. No matter how drunk the man was, he could handle a ship. The lakemen out in the canals were used to handling ships in narrow waters.

When we came back to Halifax we were ordered in April to go back to Aruba. The captain went ashore [in Aruba], got himself loaded up, came

back and never told me what the orders were. He asked me the distance to
Halifax to see if we needed to fill our forepeak with fuel. We had ample fuel
in our bunker tanks to make it to Halifax direct. So he asked me what route.
You either come up east of Hispaniola or west of it. The Crooked Island
Passage you come west of Hispaniola, and the other passage east of it is the
Mona Pass. I told him the best way was to go over to the Crooked Island
Passage; it was a bit longer but we'd make better time. Submarines were
getting over here at that time, so he got orders to come back by naval route
through the Mona Passage but never told me about them. He just asked me
if we could make Halifax without filling our forepeak. He waited till we got
sixty miles north. We had to head along the Bahamas until we got up off
Florida, then follow the American coast up to Halifax. Well, we didn't have
enough fuel for that. I said, "Captain, what are you goin' to do? We got to
make up our mind." He said, "Are you sure we won't have fuel enough?"
I said, "No. We can go in an American port and get fuel." He considered
a minute. He says, "No, we're goin' to go direct, but if we get a torpedo I'll
lose my certificate." I said, "If that's all you lose, you'll be damned lucky."
So we came direct to Halifax.

The ship was goin' up the Lakes again, so I told him I wanted a transfer.
He went ashore and came back with a bottle of rum and he and the mate
kept me awake all night trying to persuade me to go up the Lakes. I said,
"There's a war on. I'm goin' foreign or on the coast." Well, he said, the
submarines wouldn't get him up the Lakes. I said, "I'm not worried about
that." I told him to see Captain Finley who was port captain with Imperial
Oil. He never told Finley and so Finley came aboard a couple days later and
I told him, "Did the captain tell you I was not going up to the Lakes with
him?"

"No. Why not?"

"There's a war on. I don't want to go up behind the Lachine Canal."

"What do you want?"

"A coastal ship or a foreign."

He said, "I wish I had a dozen more like ya. The *James McGee* is over the
next dock. Join her as second mate."

She was a Standard Oil tanker. The Americans passed what they called
the Neutrality Act which forbid any American ship or American crews to
trade with a country [at war]. They wanted to keep out of the war. 'Course
they had all kinds of ships under the Panamanian flag, but this banned
[American] crews as well. So Standard Oil turned fourteen of their tankers
over to Imperial Oil to man and operate. She [the *James McGee*] was an
American ship, but she was under the Panamanian flag. They were
circumventing all the laws.

First we went to Newport News in dry dock and from there to La Guaira, Venezuela, to load for Le Havre, France, and came back north to Halifax for convoy. While we were in Newport News we asked to get the ship armed by the navy. Couldn't do it. Panama wasn't at war; we were a neutral ship. You could buy any kind of guns cheap down there, so I went ashore in Newport News and bought a .38 calibre revolver. The mate wanted it, so I sold it to him, and I went ashore again and got a .45. When we came to Halifax for convoy the mate decided we needed a longer range gun than a revolver so he sent me ashore and I bought a Lee Enfield rifle and a hundred rounds of ammunition. So that was our main armament when we sailed. We left Halifax capable of taking on the *Bismark* with a Lee Enfield rifle.

We went across with forty-eight ships with the armed merchant cruiser *Maloja* [as escort] with six-inch breechloading guns on her. We had devilish weather going across. Before we got to Start Point [on the] west coast of England, the Germans got to Le Havre, so they sent us to Brest. Two British tankers went with us. We were five days in Brest and the Germans were closing in, but we're still landing Canadian troops there to go meet the Germans. They sent us down to Quiberon Bay down the Bay of Biscay, further south of France. We sandbagged the whole bridge and wheelhouse while we were in Brest in case we got strafed from the air. We were there two days when Jerry dive bombers got over there. Just before daylight in the morning, the British destroyer *Wolverine* came alongside of us, hailed us with a loud hailer and told us to weigh anchor at ten o'clock and proceed in convoy to Milford Haven in the Irish Sea. There were sixty-three ships went out and one destroyer, even the French trawlers on the boom defence. We're the only one he lost.

We steamed due west the first day to get off the coast clear of planes and then headed up for the Channel. Two days later we were coming up off Lundy Island, the entrance to the Bristol Channel. He broke convoy there and told the smaller ships to proceed to Milford Haven. There were fourteen of us ordered to follow him up the channel. We went by Swansea and the captain was telling what a wonderful place Wales was. "Campbell, you see a Welsh girl, you'll never look at a Canadian girl again." I was standing outside of the wheelhouse leaning on the rail conning the ship–keeping the ship on station. Every ten minutes I had to change the revolution to the engine room to keep her station. We had a buzzer to the engine room; if you want to go up so many revs you give a long ring, if you want to go down revs you give two long rings and the number of buzzes afterwards you want to go down. He [the captain] and second mate had made a dodger, a canvas screen over the bridge tied up to the awning spares to blow the wind over your head. So between times I was out leaning on the railing of the bridge under the dodger listening to the captain.

The mate came up five minutes to four [to relieve] and he come into the chart room. Captain Thomas turned around, "We're safe in Wales now, Jerry won't get us here." The words were hardly out of his mouth and the ship went up like that; she [the bow] raised about forty-five degrees. I just gripped the rail and I was out horizontal like a sheet in a gale of wind on a line flapping. I pulled myself up the dodger to look ahead; everything was black ahead of me. I turned and glanced towards the wheelhouse and I seen the oil flowing in the wheelhouse windows. The next whip of the ship threw me halfway up the ladder on the side of the wheelhouse to the landing on top—monkey island we called it. I was running up the ladder when the oil hit me and just flattened me on the ladder. Every step of the ladder bruised my flesh. When I got on my feet, I continued up and got on monkey island. We had a lookout up there and he was hanging on the tripod holding the gyro repeat compass, otherwise he'd have been blown clear. One leg of this tripod was pulled out of the deck.

I thought we were torpedoed. I said, "Did you see the torpedo track?" He said, "No sir, whatever hit us came right from the bottom." These magnetic mines had fifteen hundred pounds of amatol, the highest explosive made at that time. The day before, they [the Germans] dropped them from a plane in the channel. All the ships ahead of us were degaussed; they went right over the mine and it didn't explode. The HH *Rogers*, another Panamanian ship, was ahead of us; she got degaussed in Brest. The bottom of the ship was pressed right up to the deck. You can't compress liquid so the deck left her completely from her foremast to her bridge about two hundred feet. The only plate that was left was on the starboard side of the stringer plate. The rest had gone over our heads.

I looked over the monkey island. The two anchors were goin' on the run; both brakes was parted. We were pretty close order and the first thing I thought of was to stop the anchors because when [they] took hold we'd sheer and the ship comin' behind us couldn't stop. I never stopped for the bridge at all, I just slid down the ladders, they were well greased in crude oil. I slid to the main deck and run forward along the only plate that was left on the starboard side. I got up but couldn't stop the anchors; the brakes was parted and the cast was shattered. I run back to the forerigging because I figured the chains would part because we were doing ten knots over the ground and eight knots in the water and a four-knot flood tide of us.

When I got back to the forerigging, I looked up for the lookout in the crow's nest and he was climbing down. He was a young Belgian chap. The force bent the ship just like that, the whole hull. Her foremast was leaning towards the aftermast. The lookout was blown out of the crow's nest. The damned thing was only about thirty-six inches across the top and he come back in. The ship was steaming at eight knots, and the mast went back, the ship bent and he came back in the crow's nest. He was forty feet above the deck. The top mast was twenty feet above the crow's nest and he was above the top mast. He said he could see about halfway down the funnel, he was that high above the crow's nest. When he came down he wasn't hurt, only the bones of the instep broke. I said, "Are you hurt?" "No." "Well," I said, "go stand by your lifeboat station."

I stayed there to see what the anchor...the chain didn't part. You could see the bow go down [from] the pressure. The chains were shackled down in the keelson in the bottom of the ship and they run to the bitter end. When I went back to the bridge, the starboard aft lifeboat was in the water with practically a whole crew in it. We lowered the boat; there was only the third mate, the mate, the wireless operator, steward and the captain on the boat.

An A.B. at the wheel got a knee cap fractured against the wheel with the shock. The standby man, Jim Baggs, was standing twenty-four feet above the main deck when she was hit. He was catapulted over the awning spars. According to the trajectory he must have gone about fifty feet above where he was standing and landed about a hundred and fifty feet aft on the main deck, skidded along the deck up against the pipeline and dislocated his shoulder.

The destroyer come back and picked us up and made us throw all our clothes overboard. They gave us survival gear and we all got a shot of rum. The fella in the crow's nest was happy as a lark, didn't have any pain at all. The ship went down, hit the bottom and she was standing at a forty-five degree angle. At low water there'd be about forty feet. They landed us at Barry, Wales, about thirty miles below Cardiff. We were there about a week and we got passage back from Glasgow on the *Petori*, a Polish liner. The twentieth of June 1940 we lost the ship; we came back in July to Halifax.

Imperial Oil had no employment. The Americans took back the rest of the tankers, put us on the beach, because there was no more trade to France. The navy was looking for navigators so I joined the first of August 1940. I had two weeks training, a bit of parade-ground bashing, rifles on our shoulders and a little drill on the six-inch naval rifle. When I joined I was a sub-lieutenant and I came out as a skipper lieutenant. In the navy you could fight back. I joined for revenge, to see if I could get a heavier gun than a Lee Enfield.

Percey Lambert

I was born in Halifax. My father was from Grand Bank, Newfoundland, and in 1924 or '25 he took myself and my sister back to Newfoundland on a schooner, the *Christine Eleanor*, 'cause his mother was dying. So I went to school there and grew up there until I was eighteen. I was seventeen when the war broke out and I tried to get in that first year. Originally I wanted to get in the navy but I was underweight, I was pretty small. You had to be 112 pounds. That's the only thing I know because I was healthy as a bull moose and I still am. So any rate, I bothered no more until July of '40. I worked around a bit and I was gettin' tired of it. This one was sayin' let's join the merchant navy, so I joined up, myself and another fellow I went to school with, Bill Barnes. I started out in the British merchant navy. A fishing firm was there [in Grand Bank] and they signed up people and sent you to St. John's. So we went down on a boat around the coast to St. John's and we got a passport and got fingerprinted. They wanted seamen and I wanted money. Including bonuses, we were getting $85 a month. It was rough. You were just a glorified janitor, that's all a seamen is, and let anybody tell you the difference, they're crazy. That's my honest opinion.

I went from there in the fall of '40 out to San Francisco by train and joined an English ship called the *Ocean Voice*. The ship was built brand-new for the Lend–Lease program for the British. A freighter ship, I think there were ten of them built–*Ocean Voice*, *Ocean Vanguard*, *Ocean Viking*–all Ocean boats. We had to wait for the ship, must have been a month or more.

We loaded in San Francisco and we came through the Panama Canal. We had general cargo in the hold and two airplane fuselages on each side of the deck. We come up the Atlantic seaboard and got in a big storm in the Gulf Stream. Oh, that was rough. English captains are good seamen; they're egotistical snobs, but they were good seamen. I was at the wheel; I was steering schooners when I was sixteen. He said to the mate, "We better try and get this ship around and run 'er with the wind." We were heading into it trying to come up the seaboard and it was blowing and we had lots of thunder and lightning. All of a sudden–I'll never forget it as long as I live– this U.S. destroyer–it was in the night–he started flashing the light. The captain said, "Tell that so and so to switch that light off or we'll be sunk." We ran the ship for a day until the storm was over, then we went into Norfolk, Virginia, for repairs. We had a few leaks here and there, nothin' much, but they had to get some work done.

We got fixed up and then we come up to Halifax alone and anchored off in Bedford Basin waiting for convoy to go across to England. I think we were there about two and a half weeks. We never got ashore at all. They knew we wouldn't come back; English ships weren't the best. You never got linen, just got a blanket and a pillowcase, no sheet. Every seven days you got a can of condensed milk and a can of jam you had to keep for yourself. That's the way you worked. Seamen weren't too well treated, bottom of the heap. The only thing we got, coming through the Panama Canal they gave us quinine for malaria fever. In Trinidad they had a public gardens like Halifax. They had a sign, "Dogs & Sailors Not Allowed." Sailors didn't have a very good reputation before the war.

We sailed out of here and went across to Scotland; fifteen days from here to England. It was quite a convoy, sixty-odd; we picked them up from New York. We had corvettes, I think there were four—one up front, one on each wing and one bringing up the rear. I got off that ship and stayed ashore for about two weeks. We paid a shilling a night to stay in the Salvation Army. England was full of different nationalities—Polish, Czechs—you name it, they had them there. It was quite an experience the first time I got there.

I was interested in coming to Canada. I went to the manning pool and asked for one to Canada and they said, "Well, we don't know where this one is going, but we'll put you on it anyway." This fellow that I left Newfoundland with, we got into an argument, a bit of a discussion. I didn't want to go where he wanted to go and he didn't want to go where I wanted to go. I don't think either one of us knew, but I said, "To hell with you, you go your route, I'll go mine." I've never forgotten this. A week later he was gone to the bottom; the ship he went on went out and went down.

"The English had a system of dropping an oil barrel overboard, a forty-five-gallon drum, and all of a sudden they'd call for battle stations. The aim was to blow the oil drum out of the water."

They sent me on a gunnery course when I joined this second ship, the *Marquesar*. I learnt the Oerlikon, the 4.7 and different things. From there I thought we were comin' out to Canada and we ended up in Freetown, West Africa. She was a big English fridge ship, about 16,000 tons, twin-screw. You could get cold water anytime you wanted—that was nice—and lime juice. The Limeys liked their lime juice. We went to Freetown in convoy. This ship got hit and just like that she was gone. I don't know what she was carryin'; there was no big fire. There was only about ten or twelve ships, but in Freetown there was an awful lot of ships waiting for convoy. We had several gun drills on the way down. The English had a system of dropping an oil barrel overboard, a forty-five-gallon drum, and all of a sudden they'd call for battle stations. The aim was to blow the oil drum out of the water.

From Freetown we went to a place called Punta Arenas, down the Straits of Magellan. We were on our own, zigzagging back and forth every six minutes. I think we were about thirty, thirty-five days—boring. We went into this place and loaded with a full cargo of mutton, then we come up to Buenos Aires by ourselves. We were there about a week, ten days, picked up a little more general cargo, went ashore and had a few drinks. Then we came across to West Africa once more—Freetown again—picked up convoy and went back to England, all in one piece, never had a thing. I was batting a thousand up to then. We went to Manchester and unloaded the mutton. The next ship, I got torpedoed on.

I hung around England and drank a little—young man you know—chased some of the ladies around, then I got on this one where you see "sunk enemy action" [in my pay book], the *Loch Katrine*. I signed on her coming out to New York. She was Royal Mail, Pacific Steam out of London. She was a lovely ship, diesel-electric, 16,000-ton, twin-screw. She had quite a few passengers.

We were on the tip of the Grand Banks, about ten o'clock at night, I just done two hours watch. And I was in the galley settin' my watch back because of the time change. It's an awful bang when a torpedo hits a ship; you go about twenty feet in the air, or I did. It's hard to describe the noise, it's such a racket. Right in the engine room. Everything went black, everything went out. I knew the minute you got it 'cause I'd seen one get hit goin' down to West Africa and she went down like a light. I jumped and I knew right where to go for boat stations. We had an oiler, he wasn't black but mulatto; he's the only one I know for sure that got killed.

I started to put the lifeboats in the water. I said to hell with this, I'm going on the next one. Instead of going down the ladder, I jumped and grabbed the halyards or falls and went down. We hauled some people out of the water and that's when I found out my hands were burnt. I reached down to haul a fellow out and salt water hit my fingers. I burnt my fingers, I imagine, lowering them [the lifeboats] in the water with the rope and then grabbing the falls and going down. You know, you're nervous, you want to get in there too. Panic is an awful thing. I never knew panic till I seen that. I was never one like that. People just dove in. If you haven't seen panic, you don't know it, how people react. Even in the dark you could see it.

We rowed around till about two o'clock in the morning. They say she didn't sink till the morning. We got picked up about three o'clock in the morning on a Canadian corvette, the HMCS *Agassi*; she was in the convoy duty. It took us three days to get into Halifax. They took us all down to the Seamen's Club on Hollis Street and give us some dry clothes and fed us. The next day I took off; my grandmother lived on Henry Street. I had to go back down; they called a meeting of all the survivors in the seamen's hostel. There was quite a few of us, must have been sixty-five anyway. The captain got up and he said, "We are sending you seamen back to England, DBS"– distressed British seamen. I stood up. "Yes, Lambert," he said, "what can I do for you?"

I said, "I don't wish to go back to England, sir."

He said, "You'll go back to the place from whence you came."

"Sir, I was born in this town here, right in the city of Halifax."

And old Drake I think his name was, the shipping officer down on Hollis Street where you signed on, he said, "If this lad is from Halifax, sir, this is his home. He can stay here." So I stayed.

They gave us $50 for a clothing allowance. We had to go up to Barrington Street, Maurice Goldberg's. We didn't even have a choice of what we wanted, we had to take what Maurice Goldberg's gave us. I took a blue serge suit in August. Who wears blue serge? Young people don't wear that; I had to take it. That was the only thing that fit me. That's how the merchant navy was treated: Take it or leave it.

I decided I'd go to the Canadian navy, so I went down to the dockyard. A feller said to me, "What can I do for you?"

"I'd like to join the navy, sir."

He said, "Here's an application. Fill it out." So I put down able-bodied seaman.

So he said, "You've got to prove to us that you are an able-bodied seaman."

I said, "I don't have to prove it to you. My ship was just torpedoed. I came in on the HMCS *Agassi.*"

"No," he said, "not good enough." So I went back to Hollis Street to the shipping office.

I went in. Right away he [Drake] knew me 'cause he remembered me from the meeting. He said, "What can I do for you, Lambert?" "I'd like my discharge papers for that ship I just got torpedoed on." Right away this fellow Dowling looked around at me. "What the hell are you doing here, Lambert?" "I just got torpedoed, sir, and I'm joining the navy." He was the captain of the *Prince Albert Park*, a freighter, 10,000-ton. He was somebody in the navy in the First World War, an older man. He said, "Sailing tonight, *Prince Albert Park*; first Park boat built in Canada." I said, "Oh, I don't think.... No." He wouldn't take no for an answer, so I sailed that night out through the Halifax Harbour, August of '42.

That was an experience in itself. Here I was, see, I'm full of vim and vigour, just got torpedoed. I got the bull by the horns. They got to look up to me. For six months it was horrible. If you jumped and made a noise, if somebody slammed a door, I jumped. We were headin' to West Africa. We were out two days and we had to go to Bermuda, the boilers went on her; the first Canadian Park boat built in Canada. We were in Bermuda for a month and a half, I think. That's another story. Life at sea is good, you know, I had a lot of fun. I didn't do anything out of the way, just drink and act the fool and carry on.

We left there and went across on our own, right back to Freetown, West Africa. I love that place but never got ashore there. We had a mixture of cargo. We left Freetown and went to Lagos [Nigeria] where we discharged cargo. One of the Empress boats, a big liner, the *Empress of Halifax* I think it was, got sunk and we were a day or two looking for survivors. They thought we might see some but we didn't. We went to Port Elizabeth and discharged. I got malaria fever in Lagos and went in hospital for a day or two. Then we went to Durban [South Africa] and I got sick again and almost got married. I was in the hospital and got to know her [my nurse] quite well. She wanted to come to Canada, but I was young, twenty, you know. We were there quite awhile. I brushed her off, as the saying is, and we went up to Port Elizabeth, then we come back to Durban and loaded manganese ore, then down to Cape Town and Cape Town to Guantanamo Bay. We waited there for a week or two to come across, then we left and came across to a place called Bahia, Brazil, on our own.

I had an interesting experience coming across. I was on the bow and it was dark as pitch, I'll never forget it. The porpoise were running up the bow of the ship; they're great to watch at sea. I turned around—I'm not a devoted Christian or anything—I seen this fellow standing there. I went to touch him, couldn't, he was gone. I done this two or three times; every time I couldn't catch him. I went back when I got off of watch and I said, "I believe something happened at home." This feller said to me, "What do you mean?"

"I seen a forerunner tonight."

"Don't talk so crazy. Nobody sees them."

I said, "I never did believe it, but I do now."

I'll leave it there and come around to it. So we come across to Brazil and were there for a week, took a convoy up to Trinidad; Trinidad to Barbados. When I got to Barbados we were anchored off, loadin' molasses in between decks to bring to Saint John, New Brunswick. I seen this Newfoundland schooner; they always went down to Barbados. There were always little jump boats come out to the ship to take you ashore. So I said to the fella,

"You see that schooner there, you know her name?"

"Yes," he said.

"What is it?"

"*Helen Forsey*."

"Take me over?"

"Five dollars."

"Good enough." I went over. I knew she was from Grand Bank—two-masted schooner. Harry Thomas was the skipper, a Norwegian; I went to school with his son in Grand Bank. He looked at me and said, "You had any mail from home?"

I said, "Not for two or three years. Why?"

He said, "Your brother got burned to death in Knights of Columbus hostel in St. John's. They had a big fire there."

That was my forerunner. You can't make somethin' like that up. I've never forgotten it, I was taken back so much. I couldn't help but think about it, why should I meet this *Helen Forsey* in Barbados? Strange.

Leandre Boudreau

I was in the army training in Fredericton, New Brunswick, before I went in the merchant navy. They used to train you for one month and then send you home and you'd be called in a month or so to go in the real army then. Oh I done so much walkin' that, oh Lord, it was too much for me. I said to myself, you better catch me quick because I'm goin', I'm not foolin' around with you fellas. I wouldn't like to be stranded in the army all the time or the air force or navy. You were more like in prison, aren't you? In the merchant navy it was more my life.

I was on the Indian run a lot. It was very hot in the Red Sea. Some of them guys were not exactly tough, you know. You never knew what you can do until you try and we had to do a lot of extra work to cover for them fellers because they were sick, the heat got them. Guys were passin' out. A coal burner down below, I'll tell you, to walk on the steel deck you had to have a good pair of shoes or it would have burned your feet. Sweat? The only time [you didn't] was at night after the sun went down, then you'd get a cool breeze.

We got out of there and come into the port of Aden and then we crossed to Bombay. We unloaded and they wanted to transport some tanks, guns and all kinds of stuff for the American army up to Calcutta. It was dangerous around there. That's where the Japanese were posted with suicide squads.

You could hear them comin', divin' down. They missed our's, but some of them they didn't miss.

I took a Norwegian oil tanker, the *Hing Gian*, the first ship I had. This ship had just come out of Germany before the war broke out. I was an oiler because it was a diesel ship. She was a big bugger, one of the biggest oil tankers in them days. It was carrying benzene gas. We started from Halifax in convoy headed for Bristol, England. That was in '40, I guess. When we got about eight hundred miles from north of Ireland, we had to break convoy because it was too dangerous because of the submarines. There were three or four ships that had to stay back about ten miles. With benzene gas, it was very explosive stuff for airplanes; if they hit a ship like that it would have blown the whole convoy up. The captain told us that we wouldn't be with the convoy anymore, we'd be on our own and to keep your life jacket close to you everywhere you go. When you don't know something, it doesn't bother you, you had never been in that kind of trouble, but when you know, that's a different thing. If I was goin' in there right now that I know all about that stuff, it would be a different thing, but when you were young you don't care about stuff like that.

We lost some ships in that convoy. Closer to England they were bangin' them, but the other ones were goin' more down south to pass between England and France and Spain. I never seen the other ones after we left the convoy. There were some destroyers around and aeroplanes from England in case there were some survivors, because they can't do nothin' about a torpedo, an aeroplane can't stop it. We got to the north part of Ireland and sailed down the coast into Bristol. We didn't take the same direction comin' back to North America, we took more a southern pattern because we were gettin' the stuff in Port Arthur, Texas. They claim we were chased by a submarine once around the coast of Norfolk, Virginia. There were aeroplanes in the air all the time and they'd send you a message that there was a submarine around. We weren't loaded at the time, but they don't care because if they can blow the ship, you're not goin' to get back with another [load].

We came back to Halifax to take convoy. Four o'clock in the afternoon I was in some tavern on Barrington Street or Hollis Street, I forget now. This Norwegian come over and he said somebody told him that I was on a Norwegian ship. I said yeah. He said, "You're goin' back across?" "As far as I know." He said, "Do you want to change jobs with me? If you don't want to go back across I'd like to go home." I felt sorry for him, to see his wife and children and parents. It was nothing to me. I could get another ship right away as far as that goes. Port of Halifax, holy geez, there were all kinds of ships to get. They had a shippin' office on Water Street. There was a guy used to stand outdoors. "Who wants a ship?" You fellas seamen? You fellas seamen? You want a job?" A lot of ships had to leave without the right amount of crew because there were so many ships goin' down. At first it was almost like a dream to go away.

I said, "If you want the job, you can have it. I'll go aboard the ship with you and bring you to the captain. He's Norwegian. You fellers can talk it over." So we left the tavern, hired a boat and went to the ship and told the captain. "If it's all right with you, Mr. Boudreau; you bring another man, that's all I care," he said. He paid me off, everything he owed me. I took my clothes and suitcase, the fella stayed there and I went back with the boat and went back to the tavern. I had a place to live in Dartmouth and I was there that night listening to the radio. It was around nine, ten o'clock. They said that ship was sunk, blown to hell, everybody aboard. Benzene gas, there's no hope for you; nobody survived that ship. That was my first experience.

Anonymous (name withheld by request)

I always wanted to go to sea. I discovered that I could go to night school and learn to be a wireless operator, so I did and got myself a job at sea in '31. When the war started I was down on the west coast of South America on one of the Imperial Oil tankers, *Talaralite*. The way the thing worked in those days, there was only one employer for the wireless operators, the Canadian Marconi Company. They would make a contract with the ship owner to supply the equipment and the operators and for so much the Marconi Company would take care of all the communications. All the ship would have to provide would be the room for the equipment and the accommodations for the operators. Our work was a complete mystery to everybody else on the ship, so they kept away. All the operators were officers. We ate with the officers and had accommodations with them. As far as the ship was concerned, we had nothing to do with it. We were responsible only to the captain. As a matter of fact, one of the mates tried to boss me around and I kicked him out of the room. There were three of us there, twenty-four hours a day, four on, eight off. I got a big salary, $80 a month, and that was in charge of the other two fellas, so you see we weren't overpaid.

We come back from [South America] and she went into the Lakes. They didn't want me up there so I took another one, the *Petrolite*, and went right back to South America for awhile. There was no refueling system in St. John's [Newfoundland] so when they brought us north they used our ship as a bunker boat in the harbour. Do you remember hearing about those destroyers that the Americans turned over? Well, they were crummy things, tin pots mostly, and they couldn't carry enough oil to get across the Atlantic. They could make it from St. John's just barely to Iceland. They'd fill up in Halifax and then they'd come down there and we'd top them off and from there they could get across. We fueled a lot of them.

After that was over, we went back south again. On the west coast, Talara [Peru] was the Imperial Oil's refinery. We traded up and down as far as Valparaiso, Chile, and all around the Caribbean. We used to go through the Panama Canal so often we were practically commuters. After that we came back and she went into the Lakes. They didn't want me there either, didn't carry operators on the Lakes, and I got another ship, the *Colborne*. She had been a combination cargo and passenger ship to the West Indies, but the time I was on her she was just cargo. We went out to the Far East—took automobiles, pipe, whiskey, [brought back] mostly rubber and tea. We went in September and got back to Halifax in March. We left Montreal and went to I think it was Kingston, Jamaica. From there we went to Cape Town and Colombo, Madras, Calcutta, Pinang, Singapore, back to Colombo, Cape Town, Trinidad and Halifax.

The only time we'd break radio silence is if we were attacked. Everything was blacked out. We used to sneak along in the dark and hope nothing would happen. They had special messages we had to copy at certain times; it was all Morse code. And you had to listen for distress calls from other ships. We were hearing them all the time, usually around daylight in the morning. Every morning I'd have a list of ships to give the captain that had been sunk, some of them in our area only a few miles away. We never got close. The idea was of course to keep away because it was a favourite trick of the Germans, if the survivors got in the lifeboat, they'd submerge and hang around. Then when somebody come to pick them up, they'd sink 'em. In the First World War there were three cruisers sunk that way. One of them was torpedoed and the other two went to pick them up and they sunk them too. There was a special signal to tell you if it was a submarine, aircraft or a warship [that attacked]. They had special codes; they were changed from time to time. See, a ship would be captured sometimes and the Germans would get the code, so as soon as that happens your codes would all be changed.

We were chased by warships. I don't know what they were, they didn't identify themselves. We had to identify ourselves and when they decided we were friendly, they'd buzz off. They'd be standin' off maybe a quarter of a mile with guns aimed at us. A friendly warship would have your list of secret call signs. They would ask you your call sign and if they could recognize it, you were all right. If they didn't, you got the....

We were attacked once. The Japanese caught us out in Malaya and really gave us a plasterin'. We come home with fifty-six bomb holes in that ship, the *Colborne*. We were in a place called Pinang, a narrow harbour not much wider than the Halifax Narrows. There's only one dock there for an ocean-going ship. Most of the ships anchor out in the harbour and load from barges. We went in there, must have been on a Friday or Saturday, tied up at the dock and unloaded our cargo. We had to leave Sunday night at midnight, so went out and anchored in the harbour. Another ship come in and took our place and she was loaded with bombs, mines and high explosives. The next day was Monday, which was Sunday here, and at breakfast we heard about Pearl Harbor.

After breakfast we went out on deck and we had a little bit of an exhibition there ourselves. There was an airport about as far away from here as out to the top of the hill and the Japanese were shooting that up. They caught everybody in bed. Those planes come down and they'd run along the runway and their machine guns going. You'd see the flash every time they fired. There were only three planes got off. Two of them were old World War I biplanes; they lasted about five minutes and they were shot down. The third was an unarmed bomber and he got away down to Singapore. When the Japanese were through, that airport was all ablaze.

We didn't get it until I guess it must have been Thursday. We were loading from barges all day Monday. Tuesday they came over and raided the city again. Fortunately they didn't attack the docks, the Japanese wanted to use them. I remember that ship that was at the dock got his anti-aircraft guns going, but I don't think he hit anything. They didn't bomb him which was lucky for everybody, or I guess the city would have been blown if that ship would have gone up.

They come over [again] on Wednesday and then on Thursday they went right up and down the line. They made four runs over us, twenty-seven bombers, and those bombs were falling all around us. We didn't get any direct hits fortunately, but the barges that were tied up alongside loaded with rubber, these bombs blew them to bits. The bomb had to hit about as close to the ship as I am from you [six feet], that close. And when they exploded, of course, the shrapnel went right through the side of the ship. She was punctured with holes all over the place, just small holes big enough to put your finger in. After it was all over we went along the deck and picked up handfuls of bomb fragments. But she was pretty tricky, they made four runs over us.

I know what I was doin'; I was layin' flat on the deck in the safest place I could find. The wheelhouse section had concrete shielding on top of it because that's one place they would machine gun and we were underneath the wheelhouse. I was asleep in the bunk and I remember I woke up, somebody yelled, "They're comin', they're goin' to use machine guns!" Well, I looked up at the deck and it was only about that thick of wood. I thought, those big machine guns, the bullets will come right through. So I got out of there and the safest place I could figure was underneath this concrete shelter place. There were rooms on each side and a sort of alleyway between the two. I got in the alleyway and lay flat on my face on the deck. It was silly, come to think of it, but I had one of these pith helmets, they wear them in the tropics and I put that over my face to protect it. It was about as good as a piece of paper.

Anyway, I was layin' there and some of the others, I don't know if they got the same idea I did, but they all piled in on top of me. There was about a dozen men layin' on top of me; I was crushed. These bombs come down and the ship used to jump every time, like that, when they'd land. As I say they made four runs over us and we didn't know what was goin' on. After they started, they got the anchor up and we got out of there, outside of the harbour. Everybody else was out by that time too.

Checked and nobody was hurt, but we were leakin' badly. Fortunately the holes were all on one side, so since we didn't have much cargo we trimmed her and laid her over on her side so we got the holes out of the water. Then we went back into the harbor again. Malaya is a long narrow peninsula, it's only thirty miles wide at the narrowest point. Sumatra is over here on the side and the Japanese had taken that place, so if we had gone north we'd have had to go between the Japanese. So we went back in to see if we could get a chart for the channel below us. We got a chart, but they told us not to trust it because there was a minefield all the way from there down to Singapore. We decided we had to go, so we travelled through the minefield with the ship leanin' over on her side like that all the way. That was the only way we could get out. We were expectin' any minute to hit one, but fortunately we didn't.

We left around two o'clock on a Friday morning and the city was evacuated by the British army on Saturday morning. They left on two ferryboats and headed down towards Singapore. One of the ferryboats broke down and they all piled aboard the other one and arrived safely. We got in Singapore, had the holes patched, took on a load of women and children and left. We put them ashore in Cape Town, all except for two men and a woman we brought to Halifax.

That was the only time we actually got close enough that, as they say, we could see the whites of their eyes. It was just by luck that they missed that ship. I wouldn't be here if they hadn't, because if that ship hadn't been capable of sailin', we'd been prisoners of war and you know what happened to them. In my physical condition I couldn't have come through it. But that's a long time ago.

Bernard McCluskey

I was thirteen years old when the war broke out. We had a lot of boys from Charlottetown join the army and navy and what have you. I had a brother, Tom, he joined the navy when he was sixteen; lied a little about his age. I had an awful urge to get away. Every day I'd go down to the train watchin' the boys leavin'. Even at that age I didn't care too much about the services, but I went up anyways to try and join the navy. They put the run on me, said come back in four or five years time. So anyway, we had a few small boats in Charlottetown that was runnin'. There was one called the *Brent*, sort of a supply ship, a buoy boat. I joined that for a little while, then I joined the *Saurel*, an icebreaker, and we went down off Newfoundland supplyin' the lighthouses—St. John's, Corner Brook, Port-aux-Basques, Cape Anguille, Port Saunders. My job there was mess boy. They'd take you in them days if you were able to walk, no trouble at all.

Then I started goin' deep sea. I started off with the Foundation Maritimes, they had some deep-sea, ocean-goin' tugs. If there were ships broke down in the Atlantic anywhere within four or five hundred miles, we'd go out, hook onto 'em and tow 'em in. There used to be quite a few accidents in convoys. We took one American Liberty ship in that was torpedoed on the bow; she was all tore apart. I done that for awhile and that wasn't good enough for me. I was in the manning pool and I joined a Norwegian freighter around '41 called the *Spurt*. Them days if a ship come in that needed some men, it didn't matter what flag it was under, you went aboard.

We carried quite a bit of ammunition. One old [Norwegian] fella could speak a bit of broken English. I asked him, "Where's the life jackets at here?" He kind of laughed and said, "If this thing is hit, you'll need a parachute." Used to hit London quite a bit and Liverpool, England, and Glasgow, Scotland. When you hit London you seen more action than you did at sea. There was bombin' day and night. And the docks—they wanted in the worst way to stop the supplies. They were bombin' hell out of the place, everything was afire. It was somethin' like you'd see in a movie. There was sometimes, accordin' to the amount of ammunition we had aboard and depending how heavy the air raids were, they'd put us in air raid shelters. This is where I learned a great respect for the Englishmen, what tough people they are. I was in some of them air raid shelters where they were just like horse barns. They were partitioned off like horse stalls and that's where you kept your family. Some of them people were down there for three and four years. Real, real hard, tough people.

I was in London the first night the doodle bombs came over. They were

A heavily damaged Liberty ship. "If there were ships broke down in the Atlantic anywhere within four or five hundred miles we'd go out, hook onto 'em, and tow 'em in. There used to be quite a few accidents in convoys".

flying bombs, V-1s. I'm in this pub, I'm only a kid, and I meet this little girl. So I'm walkin' home with this girl. When a flyin' bomb got over you, it would cut out, then it would spit up again and then cut out again. The second time, watch out, she was comin' down. After a few days of that you knew what was

happenin'. When it got over my head I knew I was all right, it had to go a bit farther before it dropped. This little one took to cryin'. I said, "What the hell are you cryin' about? What's wrong with you?" "Oh my God," she says, "you Canadians are so brave." My knees was just knockin', I was just shakin'. Little things like that I can remember so well.

I seen tankers hit. It was just like an atomic bomb goin' off, just a big pile of fire hittin' the air. I remember one time leaving Saint John, New Brunswick, we had a 10,000-ton ship and she had about 9,000 tons of ammunition. A friend of mine joined the ship. We sailed and I never saw him till about a year after. I asked him, "What happened Charlie? You missed the boat." Charlie said, "There was too much ammunition there for me."

I always sailed down below; I didn't like the deck too well. I fired for quite awhile and I was oiler for quite awhile. I was in one convoy, we left St. John's, Newfoundland, to go over, and eight ships were torpedoed. I was on the *Rideau Park*, a 10,000-ton freighter. It used to bother me a little when you were down below, especially a 10,000-ton, you're down probably fifty feet below the waterline. You'd hear a ship gettin' torpedoed, the vibration would come through the water so bad that it'd knock dust off the pipes. You'd be in a cloud for awhile and not knowin' one minute if you're next.

I'll tell you one little story when we were runnin' convoy; this was 1943. I was on the four to eight [in the morning] watch and we went in the mess; we had our tea and stuff waitin' to go below. It was a foolish thing in them days; you wouldn't go below one minute before your time, you'd hang around the cold deck waitin'. We were standin' on the stern of the ship and I said, "Look!" The ship behind us was probably a couple hundred yards [back]. I swore a little bit. "Look! Look at the periscope! Jesus, it's a submarine!" I told one of them fellas, go to the bridge and report it. I didn't know at that time, but this is what they used to do—they'd get under a merchant ship, then the navy couldn't pick them up on their asdic gear. It was an awful feeling goin' below knowing that bugger was underneath ya. That morning at six o'clock we heard a hell of a blast up ahead. The navy sank a sub. So I don't know if it was the same one or not, but I was kind of glad to see it goin'.

My brother Tom was on a corvette called the *Prince Rupert* and they were escortin' us over one trip in '43. There was times you could see the navy guys walkin' up and down the ship, they were so handy to us. I knew the number of his corvette. I got the wireless operator to signal over to say hello. Well, he said when he got that message he near died because he said he couldn't sleep no more after knowin' I was in the convoy. He had no idea I was there until he got the message.

I was torpedoed on the *Bristol City*. Every morning about four o'clock one of us would go up and make a pot of tea and take it down to the stokehold. This morning it was my turn to go up and I didn't feel like goin'. Course they'd grab lumps of coal and fire 'em at ya. "Get up, you lazy this and that." Anyway, I got up and just put my foot over the mess room door back aft and she took one right in the engine room. That was the end of that. All the engine room was gone. I was supposed to be gone; being on the four to eight watch, I had to be gone. That's why they got word home I was missin' at sea, wrote off.

We didn't have anything on, just old bricks. What they would do with the merchant ships when you'd go into England and unload, you had to have so much ballast on to come back and this is what they'd load you up with, old bricks and stuff of the houses that were bombed out. There were probably five or six ships torpedoed that morning. I got my life jacket and went over the stern and I was picked up with a bunch of Hindus. There were probably fifteen or eighteen and I was the only one that spoke English. I was more scared of the people I was in the lifeboat with; I didn't understand them. They were there with turbans on and all kinds of gear. Those people had their religion and they were both bowin' and mumblin' and goin' on. There was a bit of hard crackers and very little water. Really, I didn't get my share; they were lookin' after themselves; but I got a little, enough to keep goin'.

This happened off England. After seven days we were picked up by an English corvette. We were taken in and brought to the hospital. They put us on another ship and sent me back to Canada. I came home and mother near fell down. I didn't even know they got word that I was supposed to be missin'. I was probably sixteen. There was times I was sittin' there wishin' I was home in school where I should have been but, anyway, that's all water under the bridge now.

A convoy we took down through the Mediterranean, the navy was with us—I remember this so well. This morning we were on deck and you could see for miles ahead. The water, you could see your face in it, it was that calm. Up ahead there must have been thirty men in life jackets and a lifeboat full of men, all dead. The navy came up alongside the lifeboat at quite a clip and sideswiped it and turned the lifeboat over to let the bodies go in the water. Then we could see the navy hookin' some of the bodies up and cuttin' their life jackets off and lettin' them sink. Oh yeah, it was quite a lookin' mess.

We were gettin' $128 a month, seven days a week. We thought we were makin' a fortune. Today, if somebody came to me and says, "There's a ship in Halifax Harbour. Ten thousand dollars to take it to England, but there's submarines out there," I'd say, "It can stay there." But them days you just didn't care.

I'd never join the service. I tried when I was fourteen or so, when I didn't realize what I was doin'. I never had no time for the service. I seen guys that were a used car salesman, make 'em a sergeant, give you a hard time. I wasn't cut out to take orders. If I had been in the service I wouldn't have lasted no time, but in the merchant navy it was a different thing. Everybody was pretty well equal and we all got along great. I'd go back to the merchant navy again, go tomorrow. If there was a war broke out and they needed a few old fellas, I'd go, I'd be right there—enjoyed it, enjoyed it.

They never had to recognize me as a war veteran. My first trip across the

North Atlantic I figured I was as much a veteran as any man wore twenty-five medals on their chest. I always considered myself a veteran. That [not being recognized] was kind of a disgrace. A lot of old fellas are gone now and really went through hell. I remember one old fella over in Halifax, used to call him Shaky Taylor. He was an old Newfoundlander torpedoed three times in World War I and torpedoed four times in World War II, and torpedoed twice in one convoy. Now how do you like them apples? At the last of it, I heard older fellas speakin', if they were on a ship and they seen Shaky Taylor comin' aboard, they'd go and sign off. They'd say, "She's goin' to get it." He was jinxed. Torpedoed seven times in both wars, that's why he was a little shaky. There's a poor old fella went around. Those old fellas are all dead now. Great men, I have the highest respect for them.

John Samson

I wanted to get in the air force but at the beginning of the war, of course, in Newfoundland they weren't recruiting very much for the air force. Newfoundland you must remember at that time was a colony of Britain and Britain didn't have many airplanes. I decided to join the merchant navy and get over on the other side and see if I could get in the air force over there. We took the train to St. John's, came to Port-aux-Basques, came across the Gulf, took the train to North Sydney and went south to Alabama and picked up a ship. Everything was paid for.

Brave Coeur, an old 1917 merchant ship, had been mothballed during peacetime from World War I; she was an American but bought by the British. An interesting part about it, the last trip she made in 1918 the wireless operator went berserk and shot all the navigating officers, cleaned the whole works out, then finally shot himself. There was only the bosun left to bring the ship back to New York. They were down off Africa; they had left Port Elizabeth and headed out to the Atlantic. The bosun had savvy enough about him to shut everything down and let her drift, then start learning navigation with the navigation books that were on board. Finally, after about a week or something like that, two weeks, he had some idea of what he was doing and brought her home to New York.

I signed on as ordinary seaman although I'd been sailing master of a small schooner before. Unfortunately the fellow that was doing the examinations in St. John's, there was a bit of trouble between his family and my family back years before, so it reflected on me. We came to Halifax, joined a convoy and went across the Atlantic. Our first load was pig steel and pig iron. When we left Halifax we had one passenger ship that was supposed to be the escort, and on our own ship we had a bit of a cone-type apex upward, welded onto the poopdeck back aft, and one sailor with a Lewis gun. That was our defence. The cone-type thing was so that he could hide behind it while he was watching for aircraft coming in. That was it, but we made it across no problem.

We went to Newport in Wales; that was still a part of England then. I got off the ship there and went down to Bristol, was accepted in the air force and got far ahead enough that I was sent to my barracks and issued a uniform. As a matter of fact, I just got dressed in the uniform when I was called into the C.O.'s office. He started questioning me about how I got across the Atlantic and I said I worked my way across, which of course to some extent was true. He said, "But you were a member of the crew weren't you?"

"Yes."

"How come you didn't tell us that before?"

I said, "Nobody really asked me." So then he pointed out that because of the loss of ships at sea and the small amount of air force that they had at that time, where I was an experienced seaman, my services were better used at sea than they would be going into the air force. He immediately dismissed me and sent me back to the ships.

I just did the one trip as ordinary seaman, then I went sailor, which is just the same as A.B. The first wages I got was $30.31 a month, that was war bonus and everything. I sent home the $30 and kept the thirty-one cents and hoped I would get overtime enough to carry myself along. When I left England—I was there until 1947 still tied up with the occupying forces—my regular job was second mate and at that time the second mate was getting the same money in British ships as an A.B. was getting here. It worked out to about $98 a month at war's end.

I decided if I'm going to have to spend my time on ships, I may as well start to learn something about navigation. I bought myself some books and started studying. I got time off and went to school there. In those days if you started out as ordinary seaman, then you're supposed to do four years sea time. My schooner time that I'd spent around Newfoundland couldn't be used to my advantage. We didn't have any discharge books; there was no signing on or signing off. You just went and got a job and worked till the end of the season and that was it, so I had no record of that time. I had to work out all that time. Nevertheless, because of the shortage of men on the bridge and so on, they needed people, so they allowed me to go for a certificate with three years sea time rather than doing the four years. I got the certificate all right, used it and all that sort of thing, but I couldn't get it verified until the fourth year.

You just got your pay and that was it, period, nothing whatsoever. The ships were generally seaworthy; British ships always had a fairly good name. There were certain companies of course you tried to keep away from, that was known. They developed names in the Hungry Thirties. Ropener, for example, an old company in England, was known as "two of fat and one of lean." It meant that two ships were fairly good and the other was bound to be poor. But such things as Bibby Line and Funnel Line, they were all fine ships, well kept.

Food was not all that good. British merchant seamen fared very poorly as far as food was concerned. There was sometimes maybe an agreement between the steward and the captain back in those days when they would preserve the food and when they got on the other side they'd get rid of [sell] it. It was a common type of thing. During the war you didn't get the best of cooks. I remember one ship I was on, the bread was so hard that the crew on deck used to play football with the loaves. They'd hit up against a corner of a hatch or something and barely dent it. There was a shipping federation [to lodge complaints with] and if you didn't get satisfaction there you could go to the Ministry of War Transport, but that was your ultimate.

As a matter of fact we held a ship up one time [the *Brave Coeur*]; that was our first trip. We loaded the food in Mobile, Alabama. We knew what was coming on board; there was all kinds of good food. Our first meals in Alabama were very good, but it deteriorated to the morning that we arrived in Halifax we had boiled tripe and potatoes for breakfast—sheep's belly, the inside that's cut in strips like macaroni and just boiled. Here in Bedford Basin we demanded better food. Finally the navy came on board because we didn't sail on the convoy we should have sailed in. The lieutenant commander with his crew [from Naval Control of Shipping] came on board and had a look at the meals and what was on. Matter of fact, he arrived at dinnertime and we didn't have a very good meal; I don't think that anybody knew that they were coming. He investigated and found out what food was on board the ship and told the Old Man to feed his crew and get her out of port. That was about it. The meals really improved, there was no doubt about it. There were nine Newfoundlanders on board there at the time and we weren't going to sail without food. If we hadn't known what was aboard the vessel, we probably wouldn't have done it. If we'd have gone down and just walked aboard of her like you do on some of the vessels, then we would probably have thought, well she was being provisioned in England where things are short and we'd have gone along with it. But we put the food on board ourselves, so we knew what was coming aboard and we knew we weren't getting it.

In the first ships, as far as seamen were concerned, they were all in one big room—the A.B.s on one side of the after part of the ship or the forward part, whatever it might be, and the firemen, oilers and so on on the other side. Later on, as the years went by, you got down to four men in a room. Officers' conditions were a lot better. There was definitely a gulf between the crew and the officers on British ships. This was one of the things I began to get when I went on Canadian ships: I'd say I served seven years on British ships, people would say, "Boy, some strict there, eh?" But it wasn't really. They had a system that was carried from ship to ship. It didn't matter what company you were in, you pretty well knew what you were supposed to be doing, where the Canadian ships reflected the master's character quite a lot. You could have one ship, and a change of master could be just as big a change as if you'd gone on another ship. That was one of the things that really surprised me when I came on Canadian ships, I expected the same sort of thing.

The first two and a half years, '40 and '41, I spent on the North Atlantic. We'd search for weather sometimes. The plan was to get bad weather because submarines couldn't operate too well. We'd leave here in Halifax with a convoy and go up the Labrador coast; a couple of times I saw Cape Farewell, the southern cape of Greenland. That was the idea, to go up, sweep along by Iceland and then back down into Britain. We never stopped. There was no such thing as holidays. As far as I was concerned, up until after the war, the word vacation belonged in schools, nowhere else. You get off a ship, that was the only vacation you got, if you want to call it a vacation, was if you signed off. You had the privilege after six months on board of a ship of signing off if you wished it. At the beginning you had to stay a year, but then somewhere around about 1941 they brought it down to six months. It was more to give a break to men.

I sailed on cargo ships that went anywhere and everywhere. Tankers, colliers, they were all British ships. The *Fireglow*, *Afterglow* and *Sir David* [all ships on which I sailed] were colliers. London was running short of coal and the weather was bad and some of the older men that were on board those collier ships were probably much more cautious than younger men would be. When they were preparing for the Normandy invasion all the young officers that were on ships were asked to volunteer for the invasion and you got a V stamped on your identification card. So when they changed the crews on board them [colliers] and put younger men on board as master, mate and so on, we ran in all kinds of weather, we never stopped. This was from the north of England to the Thames to some of the gas works, and there were dozens of them at the time. We were carrying the coal to supply these gas works.

There was a lot of coastal work. The North Sea was a very active place during the war. The whole northeast coast of England was a minefield. You had to know where you were going, your navigation had to be accurate. You had tides that were sweeping, going around 360 degrees from any angle every twelve and a half hours, and sometimes strong tides. The information we were given about the tides was always very good, well documented. We didn't know where the mines were, but we knew where we weren't supposed to go. There were a lot of ships lost in our own minefields. You don't hear very much about it. And they were lost right up until just before I left there in November 1947.

One time we heard motor torpedo boats; we suspected that they were Jerrys. They were around and we knew they were around but we weren't sure. We shut down our engines and at the time there was dense fog. To keep noise down we were drifting with the tide, [but] the result was you couldn't be shut down very long. But we managed to get away from it and nothing happened.

I think it was the *Brave Coeur*, when we first went over to England, they took this conical thing off and put a four-inch gun on. We made a trip back across the Atlantic, [then] back to England. They decided to take off the four-inch and put a five-inch gun on. This was a British gun, quite a large gun. We went out in the Bristol Channel and fired two or three shots. All the steel bunks came down in the crew's quarters, shook the old ship just about to pieces. Went back in port, took it off, put the old four-inch back on again.

I joined the *Camp Debert* here in Halifax. She was a small Park ship built here in Pictou, I guess. The crew we had had been out around the Indian coast for two years and they were now on their way home after losing a ship. None of them had been home for two years and I think some of them had lost as much as three ships.

The *British Endurance* was an oil tanker. We were halfway across the Atlantic, heading for the Gulf of Mexico when the Japanese bombed Pearl Harbor. We got orders to go to Aruba, clean tanks and load on aviation spirits, diesel and all kinds of different cargoes. The idea was to supply the Yankee fleet in the Pacific. We spent a year at that over in Australia, New Zealand.

A number of devices were used to ward off enemy fighters when sailing in coastal convoys. One was the barrage balloon which was towed in hopes the steel mooring cables would shear off an attacker's wings or prop.

We had a load of, I don't know what it was we had on board now, but I remember it was an oily evaporation-type fuel. It was used for topping off aviation spirits, giving more humph to the Spitfires. They were saying it was the first time it had been loaded. I know we had trouble getting through the Panama Canal. This was the *British Endurance*; I believe we loaded it in San Diego. The reason this ship was loaded was that she had pressure gauges to each tank. I think there were twenty-eight or twenty-nine tanks on the ship. They [the pressure gauges] were all in the centre castle, a whole big bank of them. I believe it was seven pounds we used to allow it to build up to on the deck—that would be pressure underneath the deck, lifting the deck up, you might say. Then we would let the pressure off by allowing the gas to escape into the atmosphere through a couple of pipes that went up the mast. That was a continual watch all the way along. That of course was why they didn't want to let us go through [the Panama Canal]. For awhile we thought we were going to have to go around the Cape Horn to get back to Britain. If we'd have had to take that trip, we'd never had much left by the time we got to Britain.

I don't know where we were, probably a couple of days away from land as we came down through the Straits of Florida, sailing on our own, when we ran into this bad storm. It [lightning] managed to hit the mast and it caught so we had a couple of flame throwers for the rest of the trip. We couldn't get it shut off, because if we closed the valves to shut it, before we could get all the gas burned out of the line, the gas would build up on the deck so much that we'd have to open it again. We lost quite a lot through it. We thought sure that was going to be the end of everything; however, we made it across.

We left San Diego one time and we had two strange orders. Our orders were to go to Vladivostok, the Russian port up inside of Japan. This was when Japan was moving down the Asian coastline but hadn't yet got to Singapore in the early part of the Japanese-American war. Of course we knew very well there was no bloody way we were ever going to get into Vladivostok, but nevertheless we headed out in that direction. The next thing, we got orders to go to Singapore, so changed all the way across the Pacific and we were heading up towards Singapore when it fell. At that point I suppose we were just outside of the Japanese range; we got attacked but only briefly. They didn't do much damage, although it could have been bad. We got a bomb down one of the cargo tanks. It just blew a hole through and that was it, no fire took place or anything at all—a charmed existence. We finally got orders to go to New Zealand.

I'm not sure which one it was now that we got hit with a torpedo. We left North Sydney in a convoy and started off across the Atlantic. There were around twenty-eight or twenty-nine ships. We ran into a wolf pack, and three American destroyers came in on the scene. I remember that particular night I thought it was the most stupid thing that I ever saw. They started putting up fairy lights, big lights on parachutes, to light the place up. Of course I wasn't aware they were looking for submarines in the convoy. There were three nights there we lost quite a number of ships. Our captain said we got hit with a torpedo but it didn't explode. We begin to wonder if he was going a little screwy or not. But after awhile we begin to get water in the port bunker coming down on the coal. When we got to England and got the vessel in dry dock, we found out, sure enough, she had been hit. It hit somewhere around eight or nine feet below the water's edge and actually cracked the plate. They used torpedo nets a lot on the Canadian coast and some British ships had them as well, but I never sailed with them.

We had one, the *Empire Gull*, had a catapult and a plane on it. Empire was pretty well similar to a Park ship. I remember we were up here about '41 in the Bedford Basin. The pilot we had, I suppose there had to be something wrong upstairs, what a queer duck that fellow was. Tall, lanky fellow, must have been about six foot three. He decided that it was about time that we found out whether this thing would take off or not, because up to this point it hadn't flown. The idea was to counteract the German attack planes that would interfere with convoys coming into England. You had a fighter that would go up and attack the bombers and then once he ran out of fuel, well, he just simply ditched his plane and waited for somebody to come pick him up. It was almost a suicide thing. But anyway we decided we'd get this going.

The catapult was only eighty feet long and the plane was supposed to be going at eighty miles an hour when she left the catapult. There were two rockets set into the catapult that started it off. We got everything set up. I was on the rocket triggers in a little cabin, so I got the signal from the pilot to let go, pulled the trigger, and away the plane went. She dropped down, almost went down to the water, picked up and away he went. Of course he would land down to Shearwater when he finished playing around, bring it back on a barge and pick it up with the crane.

We were up on the bridge watching him doing his loops and one thing and the other. There was no doubt about it, he could handle a plane. All of a sudden he came towards the ship. There's a triadic stay that goes from one mast to the other, and all the halyards for hoisting the signal flags and that sort of thing hangs from the top foremast to the mainmast. So you got these two things there in the way as far as a plane is concerned. But he managed to get that thing through between the foremast and the bridge underneath that. Everybody ducked on the bridge because it looked as if he was goin' to tear the bridge off. We never put ours into [combat], not while I was on the ship.

My first introduction to war, I suppose the grisly side of war, was in

A catapult
merchant ship.

Swansea. My buddy and myself, another Newfoundlander, got in with a group that was looking after bombed-out air raid shelters. You'd be on a street somewhere or another and the crowd would be coming along in a lorry wanting to know what you were doing and if you could help, you jumped in with them. My introduction was an air raid shelter that had been built on the surface out of brick and sandbags all around the perimeter of it. It held about 250 people, mostly older women, older men and children. And it got a direct hit. It was grisly, there's no doubt about it, especially with the children. The dead wasn't so bad, it would be the ones who were crippled, lame for life, legs off, trying to get tourniquets on to stop blood and get them out of there. Sandbags would break open; you got all kinds of a mess; nighttime, dark, couldn't see much. That was my first introduction to the grisly side of war and it was grisly. As a result of that I went in an air raid shelter once after that and I just couldn't stay there, I had to get out.

A couple of ships I was on, the *Novelist,* for example, she was taken over by the navy and put into the invasion of North Africa. She would be somewhere around 11,000 gross tons, all kinds of guns—I don't remember exactly how many were on board of her now, something like 175. We had a load of all kinds of things—submarine warheads, torpedo heads and our number one hold was filled with kerosene, I think it was all in four-gallon, square cans. It wasn't stowed properly, so the result was the bottom cans crushed and all the kerosene went out into the hold. That was some job now to get that out of there.

We went into Bone, North Africa, the day of the invasion or the day after. Before the war it was a pleasure resort. Water Street was something like 250 feet above the docks and that was a sheer cliff because the Atlas Mountains came right out to the sea at that point. The harbour was manmade. Our purpose—the reason why so many anti-aircraft guns were on board the ship—was that we were floating batteries until establishments had been set up ashore. There were two ships of our nature there. Just a number— T214X—that's all they were. They were used by the navy with merchant navy crews on them. We had I think six navy gunners, all the rest was handled by [merchant seamen]. I know in my case I had a double machine gun. Every time you got ashore you were doing a certain amount of training all the time using different types of guns.

We got torpedoed. It was sort of a peculiar thing. We were there from the eighth or ninth of November [1942] until New Year's. The *Ajax*, a cruiser, was tied up alongside of us. Jerry by this time was getting bottled up in Tunisia, Tripoli and around there; he was getting desperate. They had these Focke Wulfs, a fighter plane. I saw one of them afterwards, there was nothing at all left in it, only the compass. Almost everything was stripped out of the plane to carry a torpedo. This particular day, New Year's Day, about one o'clock in the afternoon, this plane came in just over the water straight from the sea towards the port with this torpedo. I'm sure what he was after was the *Ajax*. The alarm went and we all rushed to the gun platforms. Just one plane. As he came in everybody started firing at him, but low, no one hit him.

He started to drop this torpedo and the front end of it let go but the back end of it hung. So now it's a stabilizer because the plane couldn't bank very well with this thing. Right ahead of him there's nothing at all, only the Atlas Mountains, so he's got to turn fairly quickly to get clear. He's trying to swing the plane, bank it one way or the other, to get rid of this blessed torpedo he's got hanging off there. I know it sounds as if it's a long time, but of course it's probably only a couple of seconds. Nevertheless it looked to be a long time because you could see this thing hanging down from the plane.

There was one section just forward of the funnel of the *Ajax* that was not reinforced the way the rest of the ship was, and as it happened to be— fortunate for the fellow that was flying the plane I suppose, he probably felt pretty good about it—the thing let go eventually and where should it hit but on the port side of the *Ajax*, right in the weaker section. Went right through and blew out two port engine rooms. I don't know how many men were killed on the *Ajax*; we had three. Blew a hole right through the side of her and in through the side of us, a hole about the size of the door, area-wise. Of course the *Ajax* could close watertight doors very quickly and all that flooded on her were the two port engine rooms. She took a list to port and touched bottom, but she could get away. We sank and rested on the bottom. Our decks were just covered with water and some of the rooms had water in them where we were down to deck level.

We would be getting an aircraft warning about every half to an hour, for twenty-four hours, mostly by Italian aircraft. We'd get the sirens and of course action stations right away. A lot of times nothing happened, but when the Germans came they always attacked. It was very nerve-wracking. You lost sleep; a lot of people got dysentery. We got our stores all messed up, water got into it. We were down to bully beef and a pound of tea and about enough water to keep ninety men.

I would say probably somewhere around the end of February we got her afloat, then we moved from where we were, out to a holding position. That was worse than anything, because as soon as the ack-ack guns would start going from the other ships, we were in such a position we'd get all the junk falling down on us. It would pour down, rain down steel, just showers of it. You didn't dare stick your head out. We were the only one because we were disabled and couldn't do anything. We were trying to work between air raids. We finally got the ship shored up on the inside and took off back to England. Came up to Gibraltar and we spent a couple of days doing some extra work on the hole and sailed in the evening in a convoy.

We got out to about maybe seven or eight miles from the anchorage, and two ships ahead of us got torpedoed. That was one of the points in my life I remember, sailing through men with their little lights on their [life jackets] and we couldn't stop. Once we got outside we got broken away somehow or other from the convoy. I can't remember now what happened to the other ships, but we crossed the Bay of Biscay. Usually it's rough weather or always something there, but we had an [uneventful] trip across, all the way up the coast of France and up in the [St.] George's Channel. We got about halfway up the George Channel and we began to run into a head swell and she began to leak through the cement that we shored up. By the time we got into Liverpool we had to shut down the fires. Tugs came, hooked onto us and dragged us right into the dry dock.

The amount of action that we were in, and to come out of it without too much loss of life—lost a few of our men, there's no doubt about that—[but] my experience is we didn't lose the average, shall we say. I hope it never happens again. At the time, being young, you didn't seem to worry too much about it. I see it on TV now and it's more frightening than it was actually being in it at the time. There were times of course when you had to be some sort of a crazy if you weren't scared to death, but all in all I fared pretty well with it, I guess.

Bill Roos

The *Bintang* was a 6,500-ton [Dutch] freighter. They had made a diesel ship out of her. It was rotten, an old crock, but they couldn't care, they just sent you out to sea. If they can push you out, good enough. We were on our way from Java around the Cape Horn to New York. As a matter of fact they towed us out; they were afraid of the Japanese war fleet coming in. It didn't take us more than I would say half a day to a day to put a new cooler in and be on our way.

We passed Cape Town no problem at all, and I would say that two days before coming in around Cuba, six o'clock at night, we saw a lifeboat sail. The captain thought maybe he could do something to help, but as soon as we turned half around her, he found out it was a submarine and the damn thing went down. It was a submarine with a lifeboat sail on the periscope; that's what they used to do. We went as fast as we could in a zigzag to see if we couldn't shake him. The end result was, at quarter to five—I had the twelve to four watch, dog watch, and I was already asleep, bare-naked because it was warm there in the tropics—she got two torpedoes.

It wakes you up in a hurry. I grabbed my lifebelt. We had four lifeboats. Two on the other side, port side, were destroyed; they came down in little splinters from high up in the sky. The starboard side, the motor boat had lowered with an engineer aboard; and the one in front too, the captain and the chief was in there, and they went with the ship. It was all over in about five minutes. Four rafts came off. I would say there was forty saved at the most out of, I would say, sixty. I had to swim. One raft with six men on was picked up in a week by a Spanish boat. One raft was picked up by seventeen days, one of them I think after nine days and we had it eighteen days.

We had quite a few, you couldn't call them bad storms, but monsoon time you have quite a lot of lightning coming down. We had one tin [of water]. We had a piece of canvas I found and, lucky enough, every night—it was monsoon weather, you know, in November—and we filled the can up as much as we could. These round flashlight batteries? I cleaned one out with my knife and each one got one in the morning and one in the night. And if it rained you could open your mouth and get as much. Not a hell of a lot [of food], a couple of tins of bully beef.

You could practically pet them [sharks]. You could hit them with poles. We tried it once but forgot about it; they were just swimming around. We saw ships in the daytime that passed us and you could see the people smoking cigarettes on the deck but they couldn't see you. You were grey and you're in a swell. In the nighttime you couldn't see anything. To tell you the honest truth there were eight men on that raft—I was in charge because I was the only officer [third engineer]—and I did not hear a bad word or cursing, nothing. You get used to it. We thought we were going anyhow, so what the hell? What's the chance in a big ocean like that on a raft?

Our eighteenth day, suddenly one of the fellas said, "Look! Look!" A big ship, you know. By Jesus, yes, it was, a big warship and he came dead at us; maybe he thought it was the top of a submarine. How they saw us, it was six o'clock in the morning and two fellows were playing on deck with the gunsight. When they saw something grey they put the alarm on. He was goin' away from us. He saw us all right, but they didn't know yet what we were. He circled around us and then headed straight for us because, again, it could have been a submarine top, you know. In ten minutes we were on the ship, an American sub chaser.

We came into Trinidad at midnight. I didn't know they [those on the other rafts] were safe because we had all split up. The chief engineer and the second mate were on one raft and they had picked them up the day before us. The girl in the house—there were so many torpedoed that came ashore—she said, "Sorry, we only have one more room left and we have a chief engineer and second mate in there. Would you mind having to sleep with three in there?" I said, "Yeah, sure." She opened the door and put the light on. I saw two stark white faces coming out of bed—one was the chief engineer and one was the second mate. Sure, I thought they got it, and they thought I was gone and that it was a ghost walking in there.

Yeah, we were cut in half [another time]. This was a nice ship [the *Java*, Dutch]. It was a fast diesel ship, 10,000-ton, with German machinery on it. Since she was a fast ship, they wanted to use her for the convoys to Normandy. The idea was that we were a smoke ship so if there is an alarm we had to steam around the whole convoy and draw the smoke screen so they cannot see you, and fall in again. We had the position of right behind the commodore. Now comes this signal, turn starboard, which would bring us right up to the Normandy beach; we go to the North Sea and, right, you hit the French coast. Full starboard. Our wheelsman made the mistake of port, full port. It's all dark. I think three ships missed him and the last ship hit him, well, before the propellor shaft. Lucky that our bulkheads held, the watertight bulkheads in the ass end. We asked for assistance and some tugboats picked us up from England and they brought us to Swansea. They did a beautiful job repairing her.

We had three cats on the boat and the captain didn't like cats. He said to the boatsman's mate [bosun], "Throw those cats over the side." He wouldn't do it because we had a hell of a lot of Javanese sailors, and a cat, it's Allah to them as far as I know. So the boatsman's mate didn't want to throw them over the side, so the boatsman threw them over. Right away the Javanese boys started to pray to Allah, "The one who throws the cats over the side is going to be killed and the one that saves the cats will be saved." Of course you shouldn't laugh about it. So that was the time we were hit by the other god-damn ship. Now we come to the people that were killed and there were quite a few. The boatsman's mate and the boatsman were both in the same cabin, you know, in the ass end of the ship. The ship that hit us, he hit us at a very good speed, maybe fifteen knots. He cut us in half and more because he stopped at our propellor shafts, so you can imagine how deep he was and he had an icebreaker bow. Looking in the back there was a hell of a mess. The boatsman's laying over there, all pieces, you know; he was dead. And the boatsman's mate, where was he? The bunks was one above the other and the bunk of the boatsman was nothing but blood and bones. The one on the top [that of the boatsman's mate] even the mahogany wasn't touched! Now that was amazing. It took him six hours to get rid [free] of it because he was really tied up. That's right, boy. Whatever I tell you is true. I was never going to say anything against them.

Adrian (Joe) Blinn

I was seventeen when I joined the merchant navy. My parents died at an early age and I thought that I would be a lumberjack. However, the axe got the better part of my left foot and therefore I couldn't join the military service. So I went up to Halifax lookin' for a job aboard ships. I went to a shipping company called Pickford & Black and the Belgium captain was looking for a messman. I got a job aboard a Belgium freighter, the *Prince de Liege*, a small freighter, 4,000 tons. There was another chap from Guysborough County that joined the ship with me, a fellow by the name of Clarence Howard Richardson. We were room-mates and the only two Canadians aboard that ship. Half of the crew were speaking French and half were speaking Flemish. I can speak French, but my French was quite different from theirs in those days. I joined that ship on August 14, 1941.

The invasion of North Africa was in November 1942. We left either Cardiff or Swansea, I'm not too sure where. We didn't know where we were goin'; we never knew where we were goin'. It was a very large convoy. We went through the Straits of Gibraltar and landed in Algiers. There was no great difficulty with the landing, the place was well secured. Unfortunately we were tied up very close to the electric power station; that was a main target for the German bombers, to put that out of commission. We had a load of octane, aviation gas, loaded in five-gallon cans. It seems to me it was eight of these jerry-cans in a cardboard box. They were in cardboard boxes because they didn't want any sparks at all. The ship had been fitted out with extractors, blowers that would suck the fumes out. No smoking aboard the ship. Galley fires, we had special meshes on the galley funnel. The ship was a diesel job; course in those days the galley stove was a coal-burner so we had to be very [careful].

During our stay there, we were bombed just about every night. Actually we could set our clock by the time the air raid sirens used to go off. Seven o'clock in the evening the sirens would go and the Germans would be over; I say the Germans, the enemy. I must say the Germans were very brave men. They'd fly over and come down and machine-gun us afterwards. If we had low-flying attacks we knew that Jerry was up there. If the planes used to come over, drop their bombs and take off, we knew the Italians were there. That's the way it went.

That ship lived a very charmed life and so did we. In those days most of the fellas stayed one trip, especially that one with the cargoes we were carrying. I was aboard that ship a little over two years and eight months. There was one instance we were unloading [in Algiers] and an incendiary bomb hit about three to four feet from a pile of octane on the dock. Its nose imbedded in the concrete, it was sticking out probably about two feet above the dock, and it never went off.

We used to keep the hatches open, it was a four-hatch job, to let the fumes escape at night so it would be fit to do down there. An incendiary bomb fell in one of the open hatches in between these cardboard containers full of octane. No spark; it didn't go off. If it had, I wouldn't be here. We didn't know what had taken place. These things are dropping all over the place, you're not really thinking about where it's hitting. When the soldiers came aboard next morning to continue discharging, they went down, it seems to me, number two hold just before the bridge, and they came out of there like a bat out of hell. We wondered what had put extra life into them. So they got the bomb squad to come aboard and they removed the bomb. We sort of went ashore just in case. We lived a charmed life, no problem.

In the invasion of Sicily, there was a 10,000-ton Liberty ship that got a direct hit. She was loaded with more or less the same as we had—ammunition, bombs and whatever. The ship was hit, an explosion, everything went up. When the junk came down there was nothing there. Nobody had a chance aboard that ship. There was always near misses. It was only actual hits we didn't want.

William Falconer

The thing to do during the war years, if you were too young to go into the military you went to the merchant service. I sailed under the American flag and the Canadian, that was it. There was three of us took a day off school for this. We were all basically the same age, just gone fifteen, I guess. My dad was a seafarer and I listened when he was speaking so I found the ins and outs on how about doing things. I guess I give 'em the right answers, I had a few words, the terminology, and I got hired; the others didn't. Unfortunately the other two went into the army and never came back. I went on merchant ships and came home.

I started off as a stoker. The only thing I ever fired or ever put coal into was the old woman's cookstove. It bloody near killed me shovelling coal and ashes and what have we. This was on what they refer to as a canal barge. You had two sizes of lakers at that time. You had the Great Lakes, the upper lakers, and you had the canal barges or canal boats. They were actual ships, self-propelled, flat-nosed to fit into the lock and that. They were the small ones that brought the cargo down to Montreal. When war was declared they started sailing the coast as far as the West Indies. Slow? Any slower we'd have been stopped. The least little bit of draft you knew about it, you could hear the engines throbbin' to go. Course the ships were pretty old.

I spent about a year on the *New York News*. It was owned by the Ontario Pulp and Paper which was a subsidiary to the *Chicago Tribune*. I signed on as a fireman and later on we were referred to as stokers. We used to run into

"I started off as a stoker. The only thing I ever fired or ever put coal into was the old woman's cookstove. It bloody near killed me shovelling coal and ashes and what have we."

Baie Comeau and a few ports in the Gulf picking up either newsprint or pulp for the mills. They had a big mill in Thoreau, Ontario, where they manufactured paper. During the winter months when the ships tied up we stayed there all winter in the ice and prepared the ship—painted out the cargo holds, cleaned up, painted the living accommodations—and then loaded cargo so all ships were deep into the ice and all ready. As soon as the ice breaks up we sailed. I forget exactly where we discharged our cargo, it was newsprint, and then we went to Trinidad and British Guiana, picked up bauxite for Port Alfred because they had an aluminum plant there.

Then I went into the manning pool in Montreal and got my first Park ship, the *Westmount Park*. I started off as a fireman and ended up on the upper deck as a seaman. I made one trip across the Atlantic as a fireman. That put the kibosh to that stupidity. I come out of the stokehold as black as the ace of spades and there's a sailor sitting there, nice white shirt on and clean. I said somethin's wrong, so I changed from stoker to upper deck. I can't recall the exact dollars, but I'll tell you it was bloody low. It'd be in around $60 a month and we used to get a dollar a day danger pay, providing we were at sea at a certain latitude and longitude. This is Canadian. Later on, I believe sometime in either late '43 or early '44, the war risk bonus was $44.50 and you got that regardless if you were in a Canadian port or whether you were in England or wherever. When the war finished I was making $105 so that was $60 wages, $44.50 war risk bonus and then overtime came in to play. Normally you worked eight hours a day, four on, eight off, four on, eight off. But then there were times that you worked extra and you never got compensated for it. Then overtime came in. An ordinary seaman got ten cents an hour and an able seaman got fifteen cents an hour overtime in 1944.

On the [American] Liberty ships, food and living conditions were better and money was far better, double what I was getting in Canada—$90 a month plus 100 percent war bonus on top of that again. There was a latitude and longitude change, so probably halfway across the Atlantic or somewhere in that line you would get an increase of $5 a day danger pay. And each attack or alert you got compensated for another $5 or somethin' and all the time you were in England you could get this until you come back to Canada or the States. Then it would be cut off again because they classed them as safe waters and safe country.

I got aboard of this American ship through the Montreal manning pool. Our Canadian way of life was you got a $10 draw or advance. You hadn't worked or anything but you got ten bucks and that was deducted from your pay of course later. I'd been aboard a week or ten days and I put in for ten bucks. The guy looked at me. "There's somethin' wrong. You can have

$100." I said, "Hold on there, buster boy. Give me my ten bucks." I knew about the $90, but I didn't know anything about this war risk bonus. "Ten bucks will do me." We made the trip over to England and back to New York City, so I'm leaving the ship there and coming back to Montreal. There again you signed on articles and you signed off articles. This guy is counting away and counting away. Holy Christ, I never seen so much money in my god-damn life. It looked like a bloody mountain of money. I don't think my hand left my pocket from New York to Montreal. I had a roll on there to choke a horse, all this extra war risk bonus, that 100 percent I didn't know anything about. This all accumulated and I've been drawing, under Canadian wages, $10; I may have got careless one draw and got $20. I didn't have a clue, there was nothing mentioned when I signed on articles about this. It was my first American ship. I made a bloody mistake of gettin' off it, I should have stayed put. Every now and again I think about it and I get quite a chuckle out of that.

On Park ships you lived aft and the officers lived midships. On the Liberty ships everybody lived midships. Cafeterias were on one deck, officers and so on on the other decks, and your bridge. They were the same size ship as the Park ship, only the superstructure changed. And of course they were oil-burners, that made quite a lot of difference. It took us a hell of a lot longer to build a Park ship than it did a Liberty ship. When do you want the goods, today or tomorrow? They were puttin' those Liberty ships out in four days; we were puttin' a Park ship out in a year or so. The Liberty ship was their first venture, then came the Victory ship which was bigger and faster, it had diesel engines. You had the knot ships, they'd be named after some knots—reef knot, bowline; they were like our 4700s. Then they had T-2 tankers, they had a lot of them, and they had three classes of freighter.

The first Park ship I went to sea in, they didn't have insulation on them, just plain steel and cork and had it painted. But later on they started to box them in, so you had plywood and then you had a ledge because of your degaussing gear. If you laid a knife or anything on the degaussing gear it was magnetized. The only ones you see with it on the outside [around the decks] would be passenger ships. The *Queen Mary* and *Queen Elizabeth*, it was fitted to the outside; too costly to put it inside. But the Park ships and wartime-built ships all had it built in.

I was on one Park ship, a 4,700 [ton], it was built for a tropical climate and the country wouldn't take it. It didn't meet their standards. We had [small] electric heaters for dampness; in the tropics it's very damp. And we're poundin' the North Atlantic with this son of a bitch. The ice would be about that thick in your wash basin. We couldn't shower, it was too god-damn cold. So we were about a month without having a shower and no heat to boot. Plain steel, you could look at the nice beautiful sparkle with the frost, so we'd string a blanket down there to keep the cold off you.

There was one [Park ship] we had a lot of trouble on. It was operated, as all these ships were, by the government, [then] by independent shipping companies. This particular one we had a Kipper [British] skipper, there were a lot of them Kipper bastards. The ship was registered in Montreal, at least it was when we boarded it. Of course we didn't have the Canadian flag in those days, we had that god-damn Kipper thing with the Canadian crest in it. Christ, the next thing we know, we got a flag and there's no crest on it, so we said to hell with this, if it's not a Canadian ship, we're not sailin'. This lieutenant commander of the Canadian navy come up and wanted to know what the problem was on this particular ship because we come under naval jurisdiction. We told him and down to the ship he went. Sure enough, he seen what we were complaining about. We went back aboard the ship and this god-damn Kipper bastard, he was from the Cunard West Star Lines, he says, "I'm not over here because I want to be, I'm over here"–British accent–"to help you Canadians." You know what our reply was. Needless to say, it was a very short trip to England and back to Canada and off. They're still a pain in the arse, they haven't changed any.

Of course we had to go and take gunnery courses. I can still remember in Montreal, we had the manning pool and we had this gunnery school in a big dome right in the city. These little aircraft would fly across on a piece of wire and you had to shoot them with bee-bees. They'd be slidin' down this wire sort of thing and as they come down you were to shoot them with these weapons. You had a couple of days of that stupidity and then they sent us up to Cornwall, Ontario, and we were firin' live ammunition. This was in the winter and, believe this or not, you could see the projectile when it hit the ice slidin' along and goin' right into this little village on the other side. Why nobody got hurt I don't know.

As things progressed we had a twelve-pounder forward which at one time was aft and then we had a four-inch gun aft. We had Oerlikons, twin-mount 0.5s, then for awhile we had a blimp we used to release on a wire to keep the fighter planes at a level away from merchant ships. They'd get tied up in these bloody blimps and wires and what have we. I was on one ship in the North Atlantic that had one. We had two banks of rockets, twenty-four I think to a bank. We were in a convoy, minding our own business and– WHAM!–our rockets take off. Lit the convoy up just like broad daylight. That was funny. The navy was fit to be tied. They were whoop, whoop, whoop, whoop, all over the place.

Another time things were getting a little rough. We always sailed with our lifeboats outboard, so we had to bring them inboard. This one lifeboat broke loose on us. We had a big canister there, we were never sure exactly what was in it because it belonged to the bloody navy. But we found out. Lord Jesus Christ, the boat hit that thing and away it went, zoom. It's lucky nobody got hurt. When it got to its destination a parachute opened up and this god-damn great flare, you could count every ship in the convoy. Oh boy, we caught hell for that, but for the rockets the navy caught hell because it was the navy that manned them.

A group of merchant seamen recruits, still in civvies, receive training on the four-inch gun at a base in England.

I remember a little incident that's funny now, but it wasn't funny when it happened. We were up in Bedford Basin here and we came in in ballast. They were unloading the ballast, just dump it in Bedford Basin, and nobody's payin' attention—the officers, nobody—to the rise of the bloody ship and the anchor cable. So the next thing we started to drift and we slid right down the side of a British ship, right over the top because they were down and we were up; we damaged a couple of their lifeboats, that's how close. They were runnin' around with their heads cut off, unaware to us they were loaded with ammunition. No wonder they were a little up in arms; no sense of humour I guess.

[Another time] we were layin' at anchor waiting to form a convoy. This happened in New York City. This was dense fog and I mean dense. It was either the *Queen Mary* or the *Queen Elizabeth* passed our stern that close you could have pissed on it. They were two of the largest ships in the world at that time and of course travelled by themselves. I think my eyeballs fell right out of their sockets to see this great massive wall going.

During the war we were into the Far East–Calcutta, Bombay–the Mediterranean, we took ammunition into Egypt, a full load of oranges from Valencia, Spain, to England and another trip we took a full load of bananas from the West Indies to England. Coming back from India to Canada if I recollect right we were bringing in mainly tea. I never seen so much god-damn tea in my life. You probably heard about those tea chests, they were about this square and about that high [three feet by two feet] and they'd get them packed in there I'll tell you.

We dropped a few landing craft for Italy. That was an escapade. We went in, dropped these landing barges off, the navy came over, took them and away they went. Outside of us, battlewagons were sendin' that iron confetti over our head. They're huge [the projectiles], it didn't look like the things were moving; you could sort of follow them, keep goin' boy, and then the bang ashore. We were in pretty close, but we weren't in close enough to see what colour the guy's eyes were. We went on to Port Said to unload the ammunition we had on board. The Old Man figured, well, we've been in Italy, we'll get the Italian Star. A letter came back, we were only there coming onto seven hours and we had to be there eight hours, so needless to say we didn't get it. I got quite a kick out of that.

Pillaging, we always had a ways and means department. On this trip to India, the stevedores in Saint John, New Brunswick, informed us that we had forty cases of Canadian Club whiskey on board. Wartime and we're carrying forty cases? What's the name of the game? He told us where it was and they had already started to get the thing ready for pillaging. They took a top lift wire down and put it around two bars that were in the ventilator, dropped the boom and of course the two bars snapped. That was our in, to get into the whiskey.

We had a British captain and a retired admiral as the first mate. He knew what was going on, the Old Man didn't, because we had a deck cargo as well so we could manoeuvre around the cargo holds and entrance to it without being seen from the bridge. He [the first mate] said, "I drink too." That was the mistake of his life 'cause every time we went by we dropped two forties onto his bed. He said, "You got to stop that. It's far too many, far too many." A hell of a good guy.

We were bringing it out fast and furious. You daresn't take a drink of water, it was whiskey. If you went to the vinegar jar it was whiskey. We had plenty of it stashed away so we had a hell of a good time with it. Then it comes time to unload the stuff in Calcutta. There was a little shortage, evaporation problems or something; bottles, boxes and everything evaporated. The Old Man sent the chief mate back. He couldn't find a god-damn thing. "I don't understand this. I don't understand this. Where did it go? Must have been the stevedores." They couldn't say too much because it was for somebody high up in government or something, so there wasn't too much said about it. We were takin' this booze ashore that we lifted. We couldn't get along with the Canadians in the Canada House so we got in with the Yanks. And what have they got? A huge bloody U.S.O. club and they invite us in so we bring the booze. They had a Coca-Cola factory, manufactured Coca-Cola right on the base.

Oh yeah, there was some fun to be had, it wasn't all work and no play. When you went ashore in England it didn't matter where the hell you went, you had to take a helmet and [gas] masks with a big brown bag. It was more for smuggling cigarettes and nylons. Christ knows how many we lost; get pissed and forget about them. You could get more for a pair of silks in those days than you could handle. Hold one up—you never held two up—"What am I offered?" They were complaining that some we were bringing over were too low, they wanted them high. I used to buy a good supply of them in Saint John, New Brunswick, in this one particular store. This doll was well put together. I can still remember her throwin' her leg up on the counter and she said, "Do you think this is high enough?" If they'd been any higher they'd been panty hose.

We had our territory in Halifax—this circle is our's, don't come in. Used to have joints that merchant seamen hung around. That was down around the Scotian Hotel. I don't think it got to an extreme, it was just one of these unwritten sort of things—this is our hangout and that was that. Then of course the navy had the North End Canteen which was up close to the shipyards. We'd associate, there'd be navy and merchant men in the Green Lantern; that was quite a hangout in the war years which is gone now. There were no bars. Allied Merchant Seamen's Club was where we could get beer. We had the Mission to Seamen for merchants. It was a club on Barrington Street. Montreal had a big one, but the one here in Halifax wasn't that big. Mainly entertainment, dancing, shooting the breeze with women. And I mean shooting the breeze because they were escorted home. It was like a hall and you got coffee and pop; there was no booze. It was for a foreigner, like maybe a sailor from Halifax stranded in Montreal, doesn't know anybody, he could go to the seamen's mission and do whatever was going on. They used to hand out ditty bags, I guess they called them, you'd probably get toothpaste, a couple packs of cigarettes, cards, writing paper, probably a pair of woolly mitts, socks, a scarf or a balaclava. They were put together by the various auxiliaries. That was given to you, no charge. At the end of the evening you went your way and the girls were all escorted back home to their domiciles. If you met later to party, that was up to you.

I had as much fun in Saint John, New Brunswick, as I did here and of course Montreal was my hometown so I had no problems there. You had places you went and places you didn't go, that was common dog. I was never in the manning pool in Halifax. I was in the pool in Saint John overnight and I was in the Montreal one a couple of times. That was quite a place, a retired Canadian Pacific hotel, it looked like an elaborate castle on the outside. Now it's government offices for the city of Montreal. It held a lot of people and it created lots of problems because we also had Kipper merchant seamen there too—no love lost. Canadians and Kippers never did get along, whether it was merchant or not. They were the only one of the sea, they were it. The only time we got along is if there was some other foreigner interfering with us, then we'd side with the British or the British would side with us.

I'm not sure which place it was, but I remember it was in Quebec, they used to have a sign in this particular restaurant, "No Sailors and Dogs Allowed," or something to this effect. It just said "Sailors," anything that floated or went to sea, I guess. One of the deadliest places to go was Bermuda. There's another place: sailors and dogs out. They didn't want you. It's sort of changed now, but during the war they didn't care too much for us merchant seamen. They knew we were foreigners the way we dressed, the same as we stood out like sore thumbs here in Halifax because we dressed to the Montreal styles, the latest of latest. Down here they were still wearing bell-bottoms. Ours were the other way around. Then of course you had the days of the zoot suit, and there was friction. The zoots, you could be that wide [narrow], but your shoulders would be this wide. The coats were kind of long and your pants really narrowed in. Then you had a big brim hat and a long chain that went down for no reason at all, decorative.

They had this dance hall in Verdun. A bunch of them [zoots] come in and there was a bunch of merchant seamen and a bunch of navy and it was a free-for-all, I'll tell you. That was the last of the dance hall, it never did reopen. This was one time the navy and the merchant navy got together and we got after the zoots. It was one hell of a battle, I'll tell you. [They were] either civilians or draft dodgers or somethin' we didn't like anyway. We had various scrapes with these bastards. They were probably working in munition factories and making big dollars. When we were in the manning pool, we made big dollars, five of them a week, that was our pay, five bucks a week and room and board. So how far did you go on five bucks? When you stayed in the Allied Seamen's Club, anything you did there you paid for, nobody reimbursed you, you paid out of your own pocket.

Now in the American naval hospital in Norfolk, Virginia, we had organizations front, right and centre coming in every day to visit you, entertainment every day. I met Bing Crosby and Bob Hope and a number of them while I was there. The nurses were fantastic. They'd work a hell of a day, come in at night and move us around so that we could see the entertainment, then move us back and go home. An hour, two hours sleep and back on the job again. It was unbelievable the time those girls put in. A lot of them in there, it was their final stop, like one of my partners, an American chap, lost both legs so he was finished with overseas service. There were people beyond repair, vegs, sympathetical things.

Durban [South Africa], I think it was, they had a seamen's club down there. You never seen anything like it in your life. Every room in there was done of a different wood so every time you changed from one room to the other, it was a different aroma. Port Elizabeth, East London, they all had [seamen's clubs] because they're British. England is loaded with seamen's clubs and they had marriage accommodations and single accommodations. These would be run by missions. They get their money through a percentage of cargoes or something to this effect and they get donations, rent rooms and sell meals. This is what keeps them operational. They were well organized. At one time there was so bloody many merchant seamen. You take today, you got a 500,000-ton ship with eleven men aboard. In those days we had a 10,000-ton ship with nearly fifty. There's a hell of a difference today. The prestige is disappearing.

We were in Calcutta when war finished and we stayed there for over two weeks waiting for orders. During those two weeks we picked up torpedo nets from other merchant ships and loaded them [on] our upper deck; they cut their nets then and there. Then they said all Canadian ships return to Canada. On the way back to Canada we dumped these things at sea. And a bunch of stupid, idiot sailors, we had never seen lights at sea before 'cause we were all wartime sailors. Every time you opened a door at night the lights went out, you had a fixture on the door. You closed the door, the light come on and you went through the blackout screen. No sir, a lit cigarette, that thing could be spotted I think it was a distance of five miles through a submarine periscope. Here we are, anything that would hold a light bulb we had a light bulb in it and we had it lit. This was great, sittin' on the upper deck at night smokin', no worries in the world, lights all over the place.

There's one thing I must say, the Canadian government really looked after us merchant seamen. The day the ship disappeared our wages stopped and that's what we were paid. The time in hospital we weren't paid for, then we got $75 allowance to reimburse you for your clothes you lost and that was it. Goodbye and just get on with it. They broke their heart to give us five bucks a week when we were in the manning pool.

I'll give you a good instance. We had DEMS gunners on board, Canadian navy. When problems happened they would be sent ashore, they'd get their rehab leave, they'd get their full kit—all their uniforms—given to them, then they'd get their survivors' leave, all on pay. We didn't get that; we got shit and abuse.[14]

Then after the war was over we got more shit and abuse with the Liberal government of the day bringing in this Hal C. Banks. Now they brought him into this country to break our union and allowed him to carry side arms, body guards, all kinds of good stuff, all done for us by the Canadian government. He had an elaborate house not too far from where my parents lived and he run a whore house to boot. He got caught smuggling cigarettes and booze across the border; a phone call, everything was straightened out. And that was done by our government. Our union had been branded as Communist; we had to get rid of those people. If you turned sideways in those days, if you think back, you were a Commie. There were actors and everything else lost their careers through being affiliated with some Communist party. In our union there were two or three of the heads of the union were Communist ticket carriers or whatever the hell they were called and that was it. The rest of us had nothing to do with the Communist party.

The life itself was enjoyable. During the war I didn't give two hoots to a holler where we went, but in peacetime you got a little choosy. I was in both the merchant service and the Canadian navy too [after the war]. If it hadn't been for the government screwin' us around, I would probably never have gone into the Canadian navy; I would have carried on as a merchant seaman. To me it was a good life. All told, wartime and peacetime, I had thirteen years [in the merchant navy and left the merchant service as a bosun and the navy as a chief petty officer]. But they screwed us around, wouldn't give us this, wouldn't give us that, they brought this goon in from the States, then the fleet disappeared; that was the end of the sea life.

After the war was over, a good percentage of us wanted education 'cause a lot of us quit school to go to sea. And when we come back we weren't qualified, yet my stepbrother [who served in the army] went through McGill University and came out as an engineer. When the war was over they never said good-bye or thanks or anything, that was it. Now they made the big ado over this DVA shit. What's it costing them? Peanuts to nothing.

Arthur Rockwell

The air force wouldn't accept me, I applied to the navy and they wouldn't accept me; I didn't apply to the army. I had varicose veins and they weren't too happy with them. So at that time I went to work with the naval dockyard in Halifax in the electrical field. I worked on naval vessels from '39 to '43. I put an application in Canadian National Steamships and they accepted me as second electrician.

My first voyage was on the *Lady Nelson* and we went down to the Mediterranean, to Gibraltar, picked up the army personnel that were wounded, took them to England and then we picked up the ones that were in England that were fit to come home and brought them back to Canada. This particular ship, the *Lady Nelson*, was the hospital ship. The *Lady Nelson* was torpedoed, raised [on March 22, 1942] and, when she was refitted, they converted her to a hospital ship. It was painted white with red crosses on the side of the funnel. We had lights all the way around the ship. It was lit up at sea—convoys went in the dark. See, a hospital ship was not allowed to be protected, it had to be on an individual basis.

This is where we had our problems, to keep all

CNS passenger ship *Lady Nelson* was torpedoed and raised on March 22, 1942, and subsequently converted to a hospital ship.

these lights going, all the way around the deck and on the side of the ship there was a big cross with lights all around it. Kept us quite busy just keeping the lights going. I made two trips, as far as I remember, then I went on the *Lady Rodney* and it was a troop carrier. I was only on the one voyage and we took troops to Newfoundland. I was only relieving personnel that were going on leave. We went back to Halifax and I put an application into Imperial Oil and they had a place for me on the *Nipiwan Park* as an electrician; I stayed with the ship for a year. Went to Montreal and we discharged our cargo and they wanted us to East Chicago, I think it was, to pick up what they call casing head. We wanted to move ship up to the locks. There was only one engineer aboard the ship and myself, and I had been with the ship long enough to operate one of the engines. In the process of getting the engines ready, the scavenger door on the side of the engine came down across my foot. The next day the ship sailed for Chicago, but I had to go to the hospital because my leg was in real bad shape. They put a cast on it and gave me some crutches. I grabbed a train in Montreal, went to Cornwall, Ontario, and I got there before the ship. I was disabled enough that I really couldn't work, but I did go aboard the ship for the fact that I had nothing to eat and no clothes. So I went to East Chicago and I think it probably took us ten days, two weeks, by the time we went, loaded the casing head and came back. When I got to Montreal the shipping master wouldn't let me go to sea. I wasn't able to do too much work, I was getting around but that was about all. They got a replacement for me and the ship went out and got torpedoed. So some things have got a good side to them.

Everywhere I went, I was an electrician. You were on call anytime. Routine maintenance in a lot of cases; it didn't matter what it was, everything had motors, pumps involved, especially in the engine room. Then of course there was stuff on the bridge. We used to have engine problems quite frequently so we'd be down to three or four knots sometimes. The convoy kept whatever its set speed was; if we disappeared they wouldn't bother huntin' us out. A lot of our troubles were we had twin engines and one engine would break down, then we'd lose so much time that we'd run out of food. We ran out lots of times and had to eat the rations out of the lifeboats. There was a time we were off the coast of France, it was quite a dirty area, we were in a storm and we were having engine trouble. So one day we were off this lighthouse and we were going up and down, we only had the one engine. The next day we were still off that lighthouse. We spent nearly twenty-four hours off the one area; didn't gain a thing.

I know you'd get an awful feel in your stomach when you're goin' along and all of a sudden the engine would stop. If you were sleepin' you'd wake right up. You were in a cabin and couldn't see what was goin' on. When the noise stopped, you were in trouble, that is what you figured. That was something you always had in your mind. We didn't seem to worry that much. You'd say, well look, may as well have fun tonight because we don't know what's goin' to happen tomorrow. If you only had two or three nights [in port], you were going to have a good time while you were there. Could be banged off anytime.

Harold Sperry

Another fella and I, a buddy from Toronto, decided that tanker life got a little humdrum—it was dangerous carryin' all this high octane and all this stuff—so we wanted to do more things, get across the other side a bit. So we decided we'd join the union. We paid off the old *Talaralite*, went up and joined the Canadian Seamen's Union. We got on a freighter right away going Halifax to Newfoundland. It was an English skipper and, boy, nobody liked him. We got all smashed up in a storm, a lot of damage to the ship, so we had to come back to Halifax and they put her in dry dock. Both my buddy and I, we could see the handwriting on the wall with this old English skipper. We said, no way, we had to get off this thing. They wouldn't pay us off; you couldn't break the articles unless they had a reason. My buddy was pretty smart about that and he found out that they already paid one man off and the articles were broken. Then we could get paid off, which we did. I think he got discouraged and went back to Ontario; that's the last I ever heard of him anyway.

I went down to the union hall. I was pretty green about that stuff, I didn't know too much how to ship out in the unions as such. A couple of days I was sitting there and I noticed when dinnertime came everybody left and went out to get their dinner. I couldn't get shipped out because I was a junior member, I didn't have the seniority a lot of them had; you had to go down the list and I was down the bottom. So I said I'm goin' to try a little strategy. I went out and had a bite to eat and I came back just before twelve o'clock. When everybody went out, I was the only one in the union hall. A rush order came, they wanted a seaman on an American ship goin' out of the harbour in convoy and wanted to know if I'd take it. That was the *Amos G. Throop*; she was a freighter, a Liberty ship.

I was registered as an able seaman at that time in the union hall and they wanted to know if I'd go on as ordinary seaman. The money didn't mean too much difference because the danger money is what counted at that time and the Americans were well organized. Accordin' to what zone, that's where you got all the extra money, you know, the big money. So anyway, I went on ordinary seaman. I said what's the difference, because I figured when I did get on it, if I didn't act stupid they'd know right away I was a seaman. I know what Americans are, I saw them before, they didn't know one thing or another about sailin' a ship or anything. I tried not to look too smart. I wanted to make myself a little stupid on account of the other fellas but they didn't know one thing or another, how to splice wire and all that kind of stuff like that. They didn't know too much about seamanship at all. As soon as I got on, they promoted me right away up to able seaman anyway.

I thought I was in a hotel when I went aboard that. Time I got aboard of her it was around ten, eleven o'clock at night. The union delegate came down and wanted to know what I wanted or how everything was. I wasn't used to havin' stuff like that. He got one of the cooks out and made me a big feed. I remember I had steak and ice cream; couldn't believe it, you know, right off the bat. Everything was so organized. They got a strong union, American unions. I got along very well with that bunch.

We went right over to Southampton. We had general cargo, but what we were goin' over for was the invasion. We didn't know it at that time. They discharged our cargo and we went to Cardiff and they said we were going to be there quite awhile. We happened to be layin' right in the danger zone and we got so much danger money a day. I don't know how many months we laid at the dock. We had twenty navy gunners on her and they had a ball team, and the crew made up a ball team so we used to go ashore and play ball. Oh, we had a hell of a time 'cause nobody worked. We knew we were there for somethin' big. We'd go ashore; we weren't allowed to go too far, but there were bars enough around to keep us from gettin' too dry.

We laid there until D-Day. They came aboard and started puttin' bunks in the holds, fixin' up for troops, so we figured it was somethin' brewin' pretty quick. I'll never forget, we heard the bands playin' as they were bringin' the troops aboard. We carried the tanks and all their jeeps. When we left that night to go across, it was quite an interesting experience. They never told us anything. We were destined to go to Omaha, that's the beach they almost lost. The heavy warships was outside of us. You could hear their shells screamin' over top of us and see them landin' in the town. There was a church steeple in the centre of it and when they was finished, all you could see was the church steeple standin' there.

We'd dump the equipment and troops off in landing barges and then we'd drive 'er back to get another load to Southampton and different places. We never battened hatches down or anything, just went right back. A lot of the airmen that had to parachute out, we picked them up and then we'd take 'em back to England next trip. We shot [Allied] planes down I'm sure; there were American Mae West jackets floatin' in the muck and stuff around. You can imagine what kind of night it was. We never got hit; all we had was a couple of bullets where the airplanes strafed us. It's wonderful how we got away with it, there was things goin' down around us everywhere. Yeah, she was pretty interesting stuff, boy. When you're into something like that you can't believe how matter-of-factly it is. So many things goin' on at one time, boy, I'm tellin' ya, it's somethin' I'll never forget. You don't think of your own personal safety too much at all, it don't seem to come into it. I don't know why; too busy, I guess. You often think about these brave heros and stuff like that [who] get all these medals. They don't do it [because] they're brave, they're just in the right place at the right time and you got to do what's to be done and that's all that's to it. There's not much thought behind it or anything like that. I'm sure we must have made ten trips back and forth carryin' troops and their equipment.

We had our stint done, we come back to New York and paid off. I couldn't send any of my pay home [while on board] and the American boys could send allotments home. I was Canadian and they had laws at that time that I couldn't send money home. Of course when we paid off in New York, it wasn't the best place in the world to be walkin' around. After comin' back off a trip like that, it was an awful lot of money floatin' around. A bunch of us got together and we decided we'd all hang around. They advised us to take the middle of the street and go, and that's what we did until we got up where it was more people around. They figured there'd be a lot of gangsters just layin' there waitin' for us. New York's a bad spot. I can see us goin' yet. Course I had a lot of money on me, it was a lot at that time, somewhere around eleven or twelve thousand. It was a lot of money for that one trip. I wanted to get right to a bank and get my money put in traveller's cheques; I had a money belt layin' around me. Then we decided we had to have a party in Boston. We got on a train, a whole bunch of us. The Beacon Club in Boston, I'll never forget that, we reserved a whole front section. Everybody was loaded. Americans spend their money, they didn't keep it. I had to be on my toes 'cause I had all this money on me and I didn't want to get in any trouble, so I didn't have that good a time that night I don't think.

I went and got on the train the next day and come home. I didn't hang around the States. I figured I was goin' to go back again on another ship. But the American government someway quashed that. They wouldn't allow us to go back on American ships anymore because they were short of men on Canadian boats. I turned around, quit the union and went back to Imperial Oil again. The war was just about over then. I stayed there until 1960, then I come home. It was quite a life, I guess, when you look back over it. It had a lot of good points, but you miss lots when you went to sea all your life. What you learn doesn't do you any good ashore.

That's one of the bad things [not being recognized as veterans] I still can't get over. The flak got so heavy they had to do somethin' to keep everybody quiet. That's my honest opinion, I might as well tell you. But it's a great thing, not in my case so much 'cause I can manage I guess. It's way overdue. It's so far overdue it hurts really to think they had to go that long.

Doug Bell

I really started off early. I went fishin' when I was eleven years old with a next-door neighbour and eventually I went for wages, if you could call it wages, went on shares; I used to get fifty cents a day. Then in 1942 the boys were makin' a dollar goin' to sea, which a dollar a day looked much better than fifty cents a day so I thought I'd try my luck at that [the merchant marine]. A gentleman down the road here was second mate on the old *Liverpool Rover* which was owned at that time by the Mersey Paper Company–Markland Shipping–so I got a job as galley boy. That was in April 1942; I was fourteen then. There's where I got my feet wet in steamboats. We had some interesting times around the coast when I was in her, but I guess she was too small to torpedo.

We used to go into Halifax a lot because, the way coastal convoys were set up, to the minor ports you went alone by night and to the major ports you went in small coastal convoys. When I was in Halifax my brother had a job in the shipyard and he was tellin' me about all the big money they were makin' up there. I said, "If you get me a chance up in the shipyard, well, good enough." So next trip we were in there, sometime in the fall of '42, I got a job as a loftsman's helper, that's where you make all the patterns and the moulds for various components of ship construction. They were building them tribal class destroyers in the shipyard at that time. We used to lay out all the frames on the floor upstairs over the plate shop. I got a job there at thirty-five cents an hour and I had the world by the tail because here I was working an eight-hour day, three nights mandatory overtime, and any other night voluntary overtime.

I had a rooming house up on Gottingen Street and I bought a bicycle. That didn't last too long. You could see down over the Narrows opposite the shipyard and every convoy and every ship that come in, I could just about see them and I couldn't stand the strain. The good money, the novelty, wore off. Boarding house mentality is what it amounted to; you were working and sleeping. I spent my fifteenth birthday working in the shipyard. "To hell with this," I said, "I'm gettin' out of here. I can't stand this anymore." They brought this ship in one day in the fall of '43 and she was a wreck. This was the *Robert E. Perry*. She had been in a collision; another ship had rammed her in the engine room. They tied her up over at the Windmill Pier and the crew was all off her. She laid there waiting for her turn to come into dry dock.

There's more that makes this yarn interesting, [which] is the vessel herself. She was built in Oakland, California. Her first voyage to sea was in the Pacific and then she come through the Panama Canal, I guess, and out on the coast. She was the fastest-built of all ships during the war. [Reading from a book:] "This vessel established a world shipbuilding record, being launched on the twelfth of November 1942, only four days, fifteen and a half hours after her keel was laid. She spent only another three days fitting out before putting to sea." They built her, fitted her out and loaded her in a week.

I had heard a rumour that she was goin' to sign on a crew of local men. So one day I got up courage. The North End ferry used to run across to Dartmouth just between the shipyard and the dock yard so I went down and went across and I went up aboard. There was only a few people aboard—the skipper, chief engineer, chief mate and a few of the navy personnel. I went in to see the mate and he confirmed that if he had his way, to quote him, he'd be hiring a crew of Nova Scotians and for me to keep in touch with him. They were having some problem with the American War Shipping Administration and the American consul in Halifax concerning hiring foreign nationals on this vessel; she was American flagged.

The old mate was from Clark's Harbour [Nova Scotia] originally; he had moved down to the States years before. He was an old man then; he was past sixty-five, smart though. He had joined Majestic Steamship Company there in Boston as a young man and he eventually rose up to master and a coast pilot. He had been retired and living just outside of Boston and he had been recruited because of the war and scarcity of people. Over in the States at the time—they had a similar situation here—where they had schools established to train young fellas for seamen; we used to call them "Ninety-Day Wonders." He didn't want to have anything to do with them in the North Atlantic. He figured it was bad enough in the North Atlantic in the wintertime with a good crew, much less with a bunch of Ninety-Day Wonders right out of these schools. He was almost certain that he was goin' to get it. He convinced the captain who was a gentleman from San Francisco to try and convince the American consulate that they hire a local crew. Subsequently they got the approval to do that.

Every once in awhile I'd go across on the ferry and keep in touch what was goin' on. Sure enough, I went over one day and he said he had a job for me. "Yeah, whenever you can come aboard, you can start to work." I was quite pleased with this. So I went back and I didn't say anything to my boss, Mr. Jones, who was the charge hand of the mould loft, until that evening. I told him I was going to quit. Well, he didn't think I could, it was wartime. I thought I could because I said, "I'm quittin' whether I can or I can't. That's it." He'd have to see the boss, I forget what his name was, it seems to me his name was Jones too, Hugh Jones; he had come out from Scotland. Anyway when it come five o'clock I punched my time card in and I never went down next morning; I went aboard the *Robert E. Perry* bag and baggage. I told my boardin' house lady that I'd be finishin' up there at the end of the week. I had a few tidying up things to do and I went down to the shipyard that weekend to get my pay that was coming due to me. As it turned out, I guess they considered at my age they couldn't force me to stay there—I don't know, but I assume that. Anyway they had everything straightened out and I got my pay. I disposed of my bicycle and I went on stand-by on the *Robert Perry*.

"I was going to go in one of the Imperial Oil tankers and changed my mind because I had never been in tankers before and heard a lot of bad stories—torpedoing and guys frying and cooking up and so on. I figured if I was goin' to go to hell, I didn't want to go to hell in hot oil."

We weren't signed on articles, we were on stand-by crew, so were doing maintenance work on board there in preparation for going into dry dock. I was seaman on deck. Everything had to be gone over, there was a lot of work. When the time come, it was after New Year's in '44, we put her in the graving dock and they rebuilt the hull where she had been damaged. She was cut right from the main deck down to her bilge keel. The hull work wasn't the big job; the big job was to rejuvenate the engine gear, generators and so on from salt water damage where she was flooded. Subsequently they got her shell plating done and then they took us out of the dock to make room for another ship; they were lined up, literally, on the docks. There was a floating dock there and a graving dock. We moved back over to Windmill Pier again and that's when we got up steam and we had shipyard people working straight time. They had to lift all the bottom end bearings and the auxiliaries, the steam generators had to be all torn down and new generators installed, but the steam engines overhauled.

As time went by, the word kept getting around the waterfront because there was a considerable number of men not involved with the manning pool that looked for jobs themselves. You went where they [the manning pool] sent you and the ideal situation was to pick your own vessel. I can remember at a later date when I got off that vessel I was going to go in one of the Imperial Oil tankers and changed my mind because I had never been in tankers before and heard a lot of bad stories–torpedoing and guys frying and cooking up and so on. I figured if I was goin' to go to hell, I didn't want to go to hell in hot oil, so I didn't go with Imperial Oil. There were quite a few fellas that floated around and got their jobs by going aboard vessels and presenting their credentials and hiring out. I learned quick. If you could find a vessel flying the Panama flag, ten chances to one she was American-owned and paid American wages. One of the first flags of convenience in the world was the Panama flag. If you could find a vessel that flew the American flag, she paid American wages. Now I was a sailor on deck. I was gettin' $100 a month, plus once you passed nine degrees west longitude you got an extra $90, I think it was. Then every aircraft attack you had, you got another bonus if you survived it. So you can see it was in one's interest to get in a vessel American-owned or flying the Panama flag as long as she paid American wages. You must remember that early in the war, Canadians weren't paid war bonus. Eventually they paid $44.50 a month and it commenced once you dropped the pilot whereas the American bonuses were controlled by war zones–like the North Atlantic bonus only applied once you passed nine degrees west longitude, once you come within range of German aircraft. Zero longitude is Greenwich, which is London, so it's roughly 540 miles west of London.

As time went along we kept getting new faces on deck and down in the engine room and we subsequently had quite a collection of Nova Scotians and a couple of Newfoundlanders. Out of the whole damn gang I guess the only Americans that was still on board was what was required by law and that was the officers–the master, the second mate, chief mate and the third mate. Anyway, we eventually got her that she was seaworthy, that she was able to get steam and everything was working, so we shifted her down to Pier 2 and started loading. It was a Liberty ship–general cargo, war materials, and we had twenty-eight Sherman tanks on deck when we left Halifax.

We signed articles on February 28, 1944, and I was on stand-by on her for a month before that, I guess. I don't remember if I actually told the truth about my age. I don't know if that question was ever raised, but then on the other hand he wanted fellas that had been in dories before or knew port from starboard, that's for damn sure. I was a fairly big boy for my age, handy six feet. It seems to me the mate was knowledgeable of my age but I wouldn't bet on it. The total gang was in excess of seventy because we had quite a big gun crew, naval gunners. We had eight 20mm, they were Oerlikons. We had a 3.55, which was a new type anti-aircraft gun, on the bow which was a high angle gun; you could shoot 180 degrees straight up. Then we had a big old surface gun aft, four-and-a-half-inch. Oh yeah, we were well heeled for armament and lots of slugs to go with them.

In any event, we left some time around the first week of April, I would guess. We was goin' out in bad weather and I damn near got washed overboard goin' out of Halifax, I almost never made the trip. The ships went every five minutes and you had to pass the old *Alfred & Emily* vessel that was stationed up there in the Narrows, a three-masted schooner built for the navy up in Meteghan for training purposes. She was anchored there as a control vessel so that there was nobody coming down and somebody

Sixteen-year-old Doug Bell (centre) aboard the Liberty ship *Robert E. Perry*.

comin' up at the same time. You got your orders from her when to heave up and get underway and so on and so forth. We still had the pilot aboard just outside Maughers Beach around Meaghers Rock and Neverfail Buoy. We were forward underneath the forward gun putting the lines down the forepeak. It wasn't fine at all and she was heavy-loaded right to her marks. You couldn't slow her down, her speed was set. And damned if she didn't pick a good green sea coming over the stem head. It drove me back over the windlass, oh, I was sore for a week after that. A couple of the gang went back over the deck. The gang was going hell, west and crooked; could have got washed overboard right there in the harbour. In any event we survived that initial ordeal.

Being the first Nova Scotian aboard of her, I was privy to some of the rumours before we gathered up any more crew. The story was that we was goin' to the U.K. on a six-week trip, which made sense taking into account steaming time and loading. Of course as time went on the rumour persisted, didn't change all that much. But that wasn't to be, the six-week trip didn't turn into a six-week trip. On the way across [it was] the usual thing. Eventually south of Iceland we got in some bad weather, a real gall buster, and broke the convoy all up. When the weather moderated we didn't have a ship in sight. Anyway we kept steaming and finally a navy ship come up alongside of us and identified us as being part of that particular convoy and they told us to proceed at full speed on our own, which we did. God-damn, we got to Liverpool in one piece! Even fully loaded we could make ten and a half or eleven [knots], which wasn't a big speed but it was good for them times.

We started to discharge. It was something that couldn't be helped but noticed that there was a lot of comings and goings of military people—American with a minority of British—on the bridge to the Old Man's room. At one point in time some people from the British Ministry of War Transport came on board and we was all mustered up in the saloon, the reason being they wanted to take us off that ship where we were British subjects. The captain refused, that as long as we were under the American flag that was a ball game that the British Ministry of War Transport or whatever they called themselves had no jurisdiction, so that argument was settled ashore and the result was we were left on board the ship.

Getting back to these people coming and going. The fact that they tried to take us off that ship bred all kinds of rumours. What in the hell's going on here? So cripes, when we got the last sling of cargo out of her, tugs come alongside. We thought we were bound out to anchor to wait for a convoy to go home. This didn't happen. Tugs come alongside, we got fast, and we made a shift to an oddball berth quite removed and the next morning we were swamped with shore people—shipyard workers—with all kinds of gear. We didn't know what the hell was goin' on. Then on top of that a bunch of us had to go up to the saloon. There was somethin' goin' on. This turned out to be to advise us that so and so would go this afternoon and so and so and so and so would go the day after tomorrow, go ashore for some training which they didn't elaborate too much on.

I was in the bunch that went ashore that afternoon and it turned out to be gas training, familiarizing us with gas-filled projectiles and how to wear these gas masks and how to deal with this stuff in confined spaces and on deck. Well, that only added more fuel to the rumours. Then of course we had to take more gunnery training, most everybody from the cook on down, because your gunners were all naval and your loaders were all of the civilian crew. That didn't fuel any particular rumour because that was a routine thing over here and over in the U.K.; you was forever updating on new types of guns or whatever.

When I came back that night with the boys that was on this afternoon gas session, down in between decks of number four and five holds they had started to build bunks. It seems to me they were five high. That settled everything, then we knew what was what. You didn't have to be too smart to figure out what was goin' on now. Along with the other changes, they were building latrines on deck. I can't remember how many troops we were rigged for, but it seems to me it was somewhere between five and seven hundred, but the number I can't remember. So they fitted us out, we had gas training, we had our gunnery training and the pilot came aboard one day and the tugboats come alongside and we went out. No convoy, we went alone. Left late in the evening and later we arrived in Loch Oban up in Scotland. When we arrived there it was obvious what was goin' on, it was a collection point for ships. There was quite a collection of vessels in there when we arrived and they kept coming days after that. Every once in awhile a German aircraft at considerable height would fly over, but we weren't allowed to fire at him. That was standing orders. They weren't attacking, they were just flying over on observation, I guess, and they let them go.

We were there quite awhile, I can't recall how long, but I would guess the better part of a month, just layin' at anchor, not allowed to move. During this time you could only speculate among yourselves what was in the works, so we figured it would probably be somewhere in southern France, either on the Atlantic side in the Bay of Biscay or in the Mediterranean, because when we were in Liverpool they put extra fuel in us in tanks that normally we carried water ballast and piped them so that we could transfer it from the deep tanks in the double bottoms into the other fuel tanks. That increased our range tremendously, not only our range but our stayability, if you want to use that term. In other words we could go on a certain operation and not have to worry about refueling, so that made us think that it was not somewhere close. But we wasn't right.

Eventually we got our orders; the navy come alongside. The ships didn't leave en masse, they left in dribs and drabs and I would suggest there was a reason behind that which is fairly obvious. In any event we arrived in Cardiff and we started loading under strict security. The only people allowed on the dock was the third mate to take the draft; nobody allowed ashore. We loaded all the goodies that goes with a military operation–ammunition, gasoline in five-gallon jerry-cans, and half-tracks, trucks, jeeps, all armed and fully equipped with ammunition. Then they topped it off with

Sherman tanks again; I just forget how many we had. We had the tanks on the foredeck, and on the hatches and aft we had half-tracks and trucks.

Of course the last to come aboard were the poor turkeys that was goin' in them. These boys come down, all Americans, I can't remember the outfit anymore. Seems to me they had an eagle on their shoulder, I think they were airborne. We got these people aboard, young fellas, and the last to come aboard was a battalion of coloured gentlemen and these were to be the stevedores and eventually I'll come back to that. So when hands were tallied aboard and accounted for, we turned to, brought the gangway up and secured her for sea.

We left Cardiff in the night and when we left we done something that we only done under certain conditions and it didn't go unnoticed by us fellas. We took good note of that, but the soldiers we had aboard didn't clue in at all. We uncovered all the guns and ammunition boxes and had everything ready to go. No, that wasn't standard. The only time we done that was during air attack or when the navy, during convoy, would put up a long black pennant, then we'd all go to our stations, wherever they may be. I was loader on number five 20mm up on the starboard wing of the bridge. We uncovered everything and even had the covers off the ammunition boxes, which was against normal regulations under a normal sea passage.

We come out of the Bristol Channel and we hauled south. Well, that made sense, goin' south, goin' to the south of France somewhere. But we got down there and come around Land's End and the weather was bad. Then the navy come and give us some signals; hard over and back we come into the Bristol Channel and anchored. You've probably read about how the weather delayed the opening of festivities. The weather turned fine, but the wind didn't drop out. We hauled out of there again, same courses, only more activity. Boys, when we come around Land's End we hauled her up to the eastard and we knew then what was goin' on, it had to be in the English Channel somewhere. When it got daylight, boy, here was all kinds of navy vessels and one thing or another and we knew the end was near. Somethin' was goin' to take place and we were close to it. It was amazing how so much activity could take place and the opponents, in this case the Germans, not know what was going on. Nobody could comprehend that this was possible, but there was a considerable degree of surprise there.

That night was the night of June fifth and I went on watch at four o'clock in the morning. I was on the four to eight watch, the mate's watch, and all hell was breakin' loose up ahead of us. There was all this racket and you knew you wasn't far from shore. It was startin' to crack daylight and we was just makin' Omaha Beach then and they had sunk a couple of ships around us there. We didn't go into Omaha, we turned and went down. The minesweepers through the night had swept a channel down the shore and we hauled down along the coast to Utah Beach at the base of the Cherbourg Peninsula. Our anchor, we were just a nice gunshot off the beach. In yards I don't know, but there was one vessel that blew up just alongside of us and the story says he was in thirty-three feet of water and we was drawin' thirty-one, so you know how close we was in. We was in as far as in goes.

We were topping derricks and getting everything organized and then the big barges come alongside. These gentlemen from the American military, these coloured gentlemen which were stevedores, they were to do discharging, but that didn't pan out. Unfortunately these gentlemen were again trained on shore with a post and a derrick onto it and so on and so forth and basically this was their first attempt to do such an operation under fire and they started smashin' up gear. There was a little roll on, a swell in the water, and she was rollin' a little bit. Quite a tide there and she was swingin' with the tide and sometimes she would beam onto the swell. These men never worked under those conditions and they started partin' gear and we couldn't keep the gear spliced and workin'.

Course you can understand what's goin' on, D-Day plus a few hours, and you got to get the gear off and get these men ashore. Yeah, it was [under fire]. The objective was to get our men off and their equipment and get out of there for another load. We was splicin' and workin' and finally push come to shove. The commanders, people in charge, had a conference with the mate and the captain and they put them [stevedores] in the hold hookin' on and strapping, and on deck hookin' on and strapping, and we ran the winches and the gear. Not to belittle these men, we done the job. I was running the winch on number two on the heavy lift [at sixteen years old]; had a 50-ton derrick there for heisting out their tanks. It took some hours to unravel this mess and by dinnertime we were doin' the job. It worked good and eventually got her discharged.

There was all these hundreds of ships to be discharged and the logistics was just monumental. You had these big barges propelled with outboard motors, and landing craft, and certain barges were assigned to a certain vessel. We had numbers; our number was MT216, Military Transport 216. The name of the vessel never appeared in any orders or directions, just the number. Well, they run ashore on the beach and maybe they'd get fast—the tide falling—and they'd be stranded and they couldn't get back to us. Well, that meant a delay. I can't remember, to tell you the truth, but it seems to me we worked all that day and finished her up some time that night. Anyway, we were many, many more hours unloading her than the stevedores in Cardiff were loading her.

When we got her discharged, then we booted her up the shore to Omaha

Beach, up the swept channel and out to open water clear of the shore, and from there there was a corridor that we travelled off of Plymouth and then from there down to Falmouth. We loaded another gang of troops plus their equipment and back again. That time we had a welcoming committee there that we didn't anticipate. It was the tenth of June. We figured that if we survived the first trip, the next trip the odds was in our favour by a considerable number. But that wasn't to be. We damn near met our Maker that next trip. The German air force was pretty well shot, but they still had some aircraft available. By God, that night of the tenth they raided the beaches with dive bombers. When all this took place we didn't get much warning. We no more than put the cylinders on the breeches—our shells were in the round drum—when they were there. All hell broke loose. The *Charles Morgan* was right alongside of us. We were close enough that we could yell to one another. We got up on deck there and all started firin' and goin' to hell, an awful racket. One of them dropped a stick of bombs, six, and they straddled us. Talk about luck. I've had a lot of luck, the gang that was on the ship, all of us had a lot of luck, I guess. Christ, three of them— if you picture this—the plane wasn't goin' fore and aft, he was goin' kind of from the port quarter to the starboard bow, sort of an angle. Three of them bombs landed on the port quarter and three of 'em landed on the starboard bow, in the water. Nonetheless the *Charles Morgan* got hit that night. It appears the bomb hit her aft in the ammunition locker. She was just like us, fairly well armed and carried quite a lot of ammunition. It peeled the deck off of her and showered us with shrapnel and junks of ship, it come across there and landed on our deck just like a snowstorm. Luckily nobody was injured seriously other than routine stuff on ours. Killed a lot of men aboard there and the next mornin' all that was left of her was her nose, the forepart of her, her fore topmast and her bow gun stickin' out and that was it. She was sittin' on bottom; she was only in thirty-odd feet of water. We considered ourselves some lucky.

After that we never had much problem. There was sporadic air attacks, but that petered out as their aircraft got cleaned up. What was a nuisance and it took awhile for them to solve the problem was E-boats. It took the armies awhile to get up towards Belgium and the Germans still had use of some small ports. The problem was there was a couple of renegade submarines in the Channel coming in from the south end and then these torpedo boats, E-boats, from the south end opposite Dover and those places. They done their dirty work in the night. In the daytime, Allied air power had control and they couldn't stick their neck out. This was all in transit; they'd never come near us at anchor. Most of this activity took place in that corridor from Southampton or Plymouth to the beaches because the ships from London and the ones based in them ports come down close under the Dover cliffs as far as Southampton and then went across. Our port was Falmouth, so we took the same route. We had a couple of close calls with these turkeys in the night. You put down a blanket of fire, but you couldn't see 'em, you could only go by the sound of 'em 'cause they ran with no lights or anything. So that was a nuisance and kept you on your toes and you lost sleep settin' around behind the gun barrel.

These explosive boats were actually E-boats with a big explosive charge in the nose of them which was detonated similar to that of a bomb. They were suicide boats of a type, the only thing is the men didn't blow up with the boat. They pointed her at the target and at a safe distance they jumped overboard, the boat kept on going, rammed the target and blew her up. They used them for conventional purposes until they ran out of ammunition and then that was their final shot, to take a ship with them.

We made one trip into Plymouth. That was where we seen a couple of these buzz bombs in the night. We were ashore one night and one of them came over and lit not too far from us. Man, them shakes you up; there's a lot of power there, I want to tell ya. Oh yeah, it kind of ruins your day. You get back aboard pretty quick. We figured we stood a better chance at anchor.

We was successful until some time in August, I can't remember the date. It was almost pleasant then. The biggest problem was mines. Good Lord, we were comin' down from Utah to Omaha and we met our Waterloo there, not by enemy action but by mother nature. What happened on D-Day and then subsequently after that, there was ships sunk from enemy action, mines and what have you. There was a [ship], I think she was British, sunk right off Omaha Beach and they had put a buoy on her. When the tide was dead low, or just before a dead low water or a full ebb, or on a full flood after low water, she would make a tide rip so you know there wasn't much water over top of her at low tide. They had a storm and by glory it must have shifted that buoy. Nobody paid much attention to it, I guess.

We was comin' down there and we hit this god-damn wreck doin' full speed, eleven knots. I want to tell you, it shook things up when she fetched up on that. It was just the same as hittin' a cement wall, you know, she went right up on top of it. That wasn't the bad part, the bad part was she started to break in two. She was full of fuel. She cracked at the base of number three hatch across to the bulwarks and she started down the side. Well, the Old Man figured out what time the low water was goin' to be to see if she was goin' to break off and they figured that she wouldn't. The navy come then and wanted to take us off and all this business. We had a gatherin' of the troops there and the general opinion was that we'd stick with her. We stuck with her that long and survived, we'd stick with her either in two pieces or one. So the Old Man said, "Thank you but no thank you. We're goin' to stick her out." They were almost goin' to take us by force. There was a lot of bullhorn negotiations back and forth, witnessed by all hands. The Old Man stood his ground. He said that he wasn't leavin' nor was his men and that we'd refloat her ourselves on the rising tide and if she went apart we'd abandon her.

By the chain lightnin', when the tide started to raise, the crack started goin' together, and when the time come we wound her up astern, backed her off and she come clear. We started across the English Channel and so help me you could take a piece of dunnage, which is usually an inch thick, usually hardwood, and she'd open up–there was a little swell on–and you could stick [that] down in the crack on deck and when she come together she'd bite it off just the same as if a pair of wire cutters. Any oh how we got back. They wouldn't let us inside the torpedo nets because she was leakin' oil so bad; we had to anchor outside off of Southampton. The navy come aboard and they had a big conference up there and we got the anchor up and we went to Swansea. We stayed together. It was beautiful, it stayed smooth, even out Land's End. You couldn't have been luckier, that's what I say, we were dogged with good luck. We took a shortcut in through there somewhere and got up in Swansea. They had the dock ready and we went right in. They reinforced her and plated her up and we went from there to Milford Haven to await a convoy and subsequently we got orders to proceed for Belfast. We waited there and picked up a convoy for New York. We arrived in New York, I can't remember the exact date, but my seventeenth birthday was October 9 and we signed off October 10; this was the fall of '44. I signed off of her, all hands did–we were Canadians of course, aliens–and we all came home.

We were invited back because the voyage went well and I had heard we got an excellent report for our effort in discharging with dispatch and no injuries or loss of life. I'm tellin' you, safety regulations and stuff like that went by the board. Under them circumstances, get the gear overboard so them men had their gear in fightin' order, not with a wheel tore off or bent out of shape or whatever you know what I mean. I came home for awhile, a week or so, and got goin' again. I went into Halifax and met up with a couple of my shipmates there, oh, there was a bunch of us on deck. See, the sailors kind of stuck together and the black gang–firemen and oilers–they would stick together. It was a natural thing, the deck gang was the deck gang. We left as a group for New York and they stopped us at the border. Unknowingly a directive had come down from Ottawa prohibiting Canadian seamen from sailing on foreign vessels, effective such and such a date.

God, they stopped us at the border and give us the sad news. Well, the nearest port was Saint John, so that's where we wound up. By the time we got to Saint John and got a boarding house and stuff, finances were gettin' kind of shy. Push come to shove and we had to join the manning pool. They paid you so much a day, it was in cents but you got four squares and a place to sleep. Eventually I got shipped to the *Rockcliffe Park*, one of them coal-burning 4,700-tonners. She was a charter to Canadian National Steamships in the South American–West Indies trade.

It was a lot of luck, really a lot of luck, all the way through it. Some fellas weren't so lucky. You can sit here and laugh about it, there was lots of humorous things that transpired over the years. I remember when I was on that Liberty [the *Robert E. Perry*] we had what we called a Lyle gun that was for shooting lines in case of distress. It was invented by some gentleman by the name of Lyle in the States. Anyway, we had two of them. All the equipment was up on top by the funnel for this Lyle gun. So we went up there; us young fellas were still full of foolishness. There was a steel locker welded to the deck and in there was the coils of line–line boxes–and there was a thing you shoved down the barrel, like a plug on the end of it and the rod come out the barrel with an eye on it and the line was made fast to that. Before you done anything like that you shoved this bag of gunpowder down the barrel, like an old muzzle-loadin' cannon, and you touched her off through a touch hole in the breach, you see. So anyway we thought that we'd have a laugh among ourselves, so a bunch of us on deck stuffed a couple of bags of powder down the muzzle of this cannon and we stuffed her full of old shackles, nuts and bolts and newspapers, aw, you name it. Really it was too much. We had two bags of powder; you was only supposed to put one. Anyway we lashed her to the rail and touched her off. When she went she parted the ropes and the Lyle gun went across the deck and overboard on the other side, right out through the rail. Well we retreated from there in a hurry and nobody knew what went on. It was just this god-awful bang, here was this bent rail, one Lyle gun missing. Everybody kept quiet, scared to death. Never found out. There was a great inquisition went on. A lot of fellers had a hard job to keep a sober face, you know, but the penalties would have been such it wouldn't have paid really. I'll always remember that. The gun went as fast one way as the shackles and nuts and bolts went the other way.

Oh there was lots of funny things happened. Another time we was in Demerara and we had a gentleman from up here in Liverpool. He used to drink a lot and his nickname, we called him Popeye. The old *Rockcliffe Park* had two fifty-calibre machine guns up on the boat deck; the twelve-pounder was aft. Now we had all these coloured gentlemen, stevedores, aboard and of course you work pretty well around the clock in wartime. Popeye went ashore with the rest of the firemen. He was a coal fireman, and they were a rough bunch generally. He came back aboard, his big jib drawn and well under the weather. And what does he do? He goes up into this gun tub, undoes the canvas cover off this fifty-calibre machine gun and starts swingin' her around, makin' believe, I guess, I don't know. Well, I want to tell you, there was stevedores jumpin' overboard, they was goin' down the gangway, they cleaned her, there wasn't one left aboard. Scared them to death. Needless to say somebody called the police and the police come and arrested Popeye and put him in jail till we left. They brought him down sailin' day about an hour before we sailed and put him aboard. That was the end of that episode. That was funny.

Anthony Ross

The *Keila* was a tramp steamer. We sailed in convoy and got away from the British coast about a day's run, which at six or seven knots was less than two hundred miles. There was a Focke Wulf Condor showed up one morning shadowing the convoy, just flying around the outside, barely visible. This was a deep-sea convoy, about seventy ships. He didn't seem to be making any effort to attack us and later we realized he was calling up a brother. And the brother was much more ambitious and aggressive. He had a go at one ship, missed her, and the next thing we knew he was flying down our fore and aft line from astern at only about two hundred feet. He let go a whole stick on us, five bombs. What a bloody mess. They weren't very large bombs, they probably weren't any more than two hundred pounds if that, each. Unless there was something in the way or unless it went right through the deck or something it didn't do all that much damage. But the superficial damage around the ship was very considerable.

The steering gear was rod and chain, and this was absolutely wrecked. It jammed hard over and the engine room was seriously damaged, a lot of water got in, and they couldn't shut the main engine off. She was a coal-fired steamship. The throttle spindle was so badly bent that they couldn't do anything with it. The Old Man ordered abandon ship, so we did and that wasn't so easy because she was going around in a tight circle at about six knots. It was a hairy proceeding. A corvette came back to see what was going on and her skipper was yelling something about "Stop your bloody engines!" One of the engineers on our deck said, "You come and f—ing well stop it yourself if you can!"

Anyhow, we got two boats away. There were some injuries. The engine

A Focke Wulf FW200K Condor shadows a typical old, heavily laden tramp in convoy. These long-range German reconnaissance aircraft were used to locate Allied shipping and radio their position, enabling the wolf packs to form up. With the advent of the catapult merchant ships and the merchant aircraft carriers, enemy pilots were not so bold as to come this close to the convoy.

room bunch, there were some bad scalds, steam scalds and that sort of thing, and a couple of people with splinters in them. The Old Man was in a pretty bad way too. I don't think he was hit by anything, but he was thrown into something and he had some internal injuries. The corvette stopped alongside the boats, gave us some food and said he would see that word was sent to the U.K. giving our position as soon as it was safe to do this. Now, the convoy's a long way off, so he took off at thirteen, fourteen knots, whatever they could do, and left us. We sat there and the ship was still going around in a bloody circle. Eventually, of course, since nobody was feeding any coal to the boilers, all the pressure went back and she came to a stop and was sitting there rolling in the swell.

That's another thing: the weather, we were very lucky. There was just a big oily swell, no sea, and very little wind. After a little while there was a bit of discussion in our boat. "We better get back aboard and see if we can get this old bucket under way." Some of the crew weren't happy with this at all, but the mate, who was a very robust individual, he said, "Well, it's a bloody sight better on board the ship than it is sitting in a boat here in the North Atlantic." And the bosun, who was a great huge Swede, he bunched his fists, which were like a bunch of bananas anyhow, and he said, "You no go back, I break your fucking head!" There wasn't any argument.

So we paddled alongside the ship and all the falls were hanging down. I don't know if you've ever been aboard an absolutely empty ship, but everything that can move does move. Everything has its own rattle or squeak or whatever, a real cacophony—a lovely word that—basically a racket, that sort of thing. We got alongside and the mate airily said to me, "Scramble up the falls, third mate. See if you think we can get this old bugger under way again." And the third engineer was given the same instruction. Again I don't know if you know anything about this but to climb a boat fall that's just swinging free and a ship that's rolling perhaps fifteen, twenty degrees is a bit of a circus act I'm telling you. I scrambled up first, I was a bit younger than the third engineer, and got onto the deck. I had realized that there would be a lot of mess and I'm looking around at all this god-awful shambles, and then something rubbed across the back of my leg. I'm not kidding, I was almost in orbit until I looked down and saw it was the little ship's cat. She was so pleased to see somebody.

The engineer came aboard by this time and his comment was, "Jesus!" So I said, "You go and Jesus your way down in the engine room and see what you can see down there while I deal with this lot and see if we can repair this steering gear. I think that is going to be our biggest problem." I had a look around. Meantime everybody else is setting in the boats. I came to the conclusion that the only way we could steer the ship would be by means of the docking winch on the poop. The steering gear was too badly damaged for any repair on board the ship; you'd need a machine shop to do anything with it.

Eventually the third engineer came up and he said, "I think we can get her under way again, but there's a fair amount of water down there, and we got to get that pumped out before we can do very much. She's got a bit of a list, so the boiler on the high side is dry. Maybe we can get that one going. That'll give us enough steam to start the pumps." I said, "Okay, you tell the chief that and I'll tell the chief officer that I think we can do something with the steering gear in time, but it is going to take time." Cut a long story short, we did get the pumps going and pumped the water out and she began to come upright and eventually got the other two boilers going. But there was steam escaping from everywhere; practically every joint was leaking. Had to take the throttle thing completely apart and rig an emergency one, which I thought was a remarkable job. How they did it, I'm damned if I know. [The steering gear and rudder were jury-rigged as well.]

Of course, in the bombing raid, the bridge compass had been ruined, so all we had was a little lifeboat compass, and trying to steer using a thing like this and having it close to the docking winch anyway didn't do its magnetic properties a hell of a lot of good, so we had quite a time getting this old bugger going. We didn't know if anybody had got a message through about us, so we backtracked towards the north coast of Ireland. When we were about, I can't remember the exact position, but we must have been about the crown of the north coast of Ireland, and a big salvage tug showed up together with an armed trawler escort.

We were only doing about four knots, that's the best she could do because of all this steam weeping from every joint in the engine room. It must have been bloody awful working down there. The trawler steamed around us slowly and had a good look at us. In fact, half the ship's company seemed to be staring at us with binoculars. We noticed an aldis lamp flashing and it was a two-word message—"Holy Cow!"—that's all. The salvage tug took us in tow then and took us to Glasgow and they paid us off. I was only in the ship for eight days at the most and they were eventful, I can tell you.

They actually managed to repair this ship and long after that towards the end of the war I was in Sydney, Cape Breton, and I saw a ship across the dock that looked familiar. I got the glasses out and had a look and damn if it wasn't the *Keila*. I went aboard to see how they'd fixed her up and she was in great shape. The skipper was a young fella and he said, "Oh, you were on her when she was bombed?" I said, "Yeah." He said, "She's a tough old bugger isn't she?" She was built in 1905 and we're now talking about 1943—shows how old she was. A great old ship.

I joined the *Ramsey*. She was owned by a small company on the northeast coast of England: Bolton Steamship Company. They only owned about a half-dozen ships, but they were well operated and they paid decent wages. I joined this ship as third mate. We made one trip to Montreal for grain, discharged that in Manchester and then we had to go down to London, and up the east coast eventually to Hull. Coastal convoys were not like ocean convoys. They were usually only two columns and they were very long columns, sometimes three, four miles long. The escorts had an almost impossible job protecting them. The reason for this was the relatively confined waters of the North Sea plus the fact, of course, that huge areas of the North Sea were mined.

Anyhow, one day we were plodding along going up the east coast and there was a signal from the commodore that they were expecting an air attack. We were looking around like this for planes up there. No bloody way, they were down there, wave-hopping, two of them. I'm on the starboard wing of the bridge and we had a single-mounted Oerlikon 20mm. I couldn't get it depressed enough because she [the *Ramsey*] was high out of the water. I'm trying to follow him around with the Oerlikon and no stops on this damned thing, you could have taken it right around the mounting. All I succeeded in doing was shooting out the foremast light, a nice brass and copper gadget; made a hell of a mess of it. The Old Man's temper wasn't exactly the best in the world for the rest of the day.

She paid off in Hull, so I reported to the merchant manning pool. At that time they had just brought in this sort of set-up that people in the merchant service stayed in the merchant service; there was no way they could go anywhere else. I think it was the latter part of 1940. I went to the pool and the girl said, "Have you ever been in a tanker?"

I said, "No, and I'm not all that fussy about going in one now, but if it's to be, it's to be."

She said, "There's a tanker called the *Inverarder* looking for a third mate, but I'll have to tell them you have no tanker experience."

"That's fine by me. If they turn me down, I'm delighted." But, however, I did join the *Inverarder*. I was sent from Hull to Southampton to join this ship. She was quite small in terms of tankers, only about 8,000 tons.

We went in convoy to the Caribbean for a cargo of bunker C and we picked that up in Trinidad. She survived the trip home no trouble at all and for a time we were used for fueling corvettes and that sort of thing at anchor in Londonderry Bay. Then we set out again, supposedly to go to the same place for more bunker C. We did some refueling trials with the escort of the convoy. Refueling at sea was pretty much in its infancy in those days, but we did quite a lot of work on it. We were somewhere around two-thirds of the way across the Atlantic. I had just come off watch and I was in my bunk; this was about one o'clock in the morning. There was a hell of a crash and I got thrown out of my bunk right across the other side of the cabin to the bulkhead. I thought we'd hit something and it wouldn't have been difficult because sailing in convoy close together, often in visibility not very good, it was remarkable there wasn't far more collisions than there were. That's what I thought it was. The next thing I heard a lot of shouting going on, so I pulled on my pants and she capsized before I had time to go out of the door. She'd been torpedoed and she went down rather quickly.

She just rolled over. My cabin was close to the deckhouse door. It was only a matter of going out one door and then immediately out another door before she actually went down. By the time I was getting out of the deckhouse door she was lying on her side, so all I had to do was walk along the side that was up and jump into the water. It must have been the first week of March 1941. I didn't have time to put a life jacket on, but I had always been a very good swimmer. I got some oil down my throat.

There was no time to launch boats or anything like that. There was lots of debris around. This submarine got several ships that night. In fact, I think we lost about 20 percent of that convoy. We had a crew of about forty, forty-two, and they picked up about two-thirds of them. This convoy was one of the first to have a rescue ship assigned to it. There were too many ships being sunk and too many men being lost, so they decided it might be an idea to supply a ship with each convoy whose sole purpose was to pick up survivors. So they commandeered a whole bunch of small passenger ships, ships about 2,000 tons, that kind of thing, with accommodations for anything up to a hundred passengers. They fitted them out with all sorts of gear for rescue and so on. It was a damn good idea and long overdue. So it was one of these things that picked us up.

There were several other attacks on the convoy before we actually got to Halifax and the rescue ship was jammed full of people. She had been employed on a regular passenger service up and down the west coast of Scotland, based out of Glasgow. She still had the coast-wise crew and these people were out on their feet, I mean they had been so hard-worked for the whole passage plus the fact they were not used to convoy work, they'd never been in a convoy before. Not only that, but they weren't used to North Atlantic weather. The skipper asked any deck officers who felt reasonably fit to assist on the bridge and take some of the load, so I went up and I said, "Sure, I'll have a try."

He said, "Have you got convoy experience?"

"Yes."

"Well," he said, "go up on the bridge and help the guy that's up there." When I got up there the second mate, his [Scottish] accent was so thick I could hardly understand what he was talking about.

There was no telephone to the engine room, just a voice pipe. Their idea of keeping station was so funny I wish I could write it up. If he thought he was coming up fast on the ship ahead he'd blow the whistle in the engine room by just puffing into the tube. You could hear the engineer down below saying "Aye." And he'd say, "Down a big one, Charlie" in order to avoid colliding with the next one ahead. Then when he thought he was just in position he'd blow the thing again and he'd say, "Up a wee one, Charlie." And that's how they kept station. I used to be hysterical with laughter all the time, [but] if it works why mess about with it?

We eventually arrived in Halifax on Sunday, pissing down with rain; terrible bloody weather. They put us at Pier 21 and up in the customs area of the upper floor of that shed there were big tables all over the place with tablecloths on them. Food? I never seen so much food. Great big urns of tea and coffee. Before you got to those tables you were given a little bag which contained toilet gear, shaving gear, toothbrush and so on. Those of us whose clothes were in poor condition were given something extra to wear because it was still cold even in March. This was all being done by a group of women from a church group in Halifax; they really were something else.

Then as many as could be accommodated in hotels were so dealt with and then when the hotel rooms were all filled—the ship was carrying four hundred survivors—various families opened their homes. Myself and our radio operator were accommodated in a place on Spring Garden Road. I can't remember the address or people's names, but they were really kind people. Of course up to now we hadn't really felt much reaction to all of this. In fact I didn't really feel it until we'd been ashore for two or three days and then I felt so damn sick, I didn't know how to hold my head up.

We were told to report as soon as possible to the merchant navy manning pool, so I did this with the radio man. The girl said, "Oh, you were off the *Inverarder*. You're due two weeks survivor leave so we'll be sending you back to the U.K. as passengers." I looked at Sparks and he looked at me and I said, "Well, what the hell's the good of that? We could be bumped out of another bloody ship. I'd rather have another ship. If I'm going to be bumped, I'd rather be working." So she looked a bit mystified and turned and spoke to a man and he said, "Well, if they want another ship, give them another ship." The girl looked down her list and she said, "You were third mate?" "Yes." She said, "The only job I've got is a fourth mate's job in a cable ship and they also want a radio operator so the two of you could go together if you wish. It sounds like a demotion but I understand it's not. The fourth mate on that ship does in fact the third mate's job and the first mate doesn't keep a watch, so work it out for yourselves."

She told us to go down to the Commercial Cable Wharf right next to Pier 2, so down we went in a cab paid for by the manning pool. We went aboard this ship, the *John W. MacKay*. I had never seen a cable ship before, I didn't know what the hell they were. This was considerably smaller than the *Inverarder*; she was only about half the size. She had the typical cable ship's bow with the bow sheaves. Some people think they're ugly, but I don't.

Bear in mind that the east coast of Canada at that time was a terminal for God knows how many telegraph cables. There were four cable ships based out of Halifax. The *John W.* was a much bigger ship than most of them. The average cable ship in those days was only about 2,000 gross tons, but this ship is 4,069 gross tons. At the time I joined her, she was the largest cable ship afloat. The other three were the *Lord Kelvin*, the *Cyrus Field*—both owned by Western Union—and the fourth one was a French one and she used to be based over on the Dartmouth side. Over the years there were quite a number of French ones based there. There wasn't much come and go between the three cable companies.

The *John W.* was responsible for repairs for the western half of the Atlantic, for all the commercial cable, and at that time there were six of them. The two Western Union ships were responsible for all the Western Union's cable; I think there were eight. And there were some French ones as well. The *Lord Kelvin* was the bigger of the two Western Union ships; she did all the deep-water work for the company.

I joined the *John W. MacKay* with the radio operator. She was big enough to lay cable, so she had just been taken over by the British government and was going to be used for all sorts of work, which is a story in itself. Telegraph

Commercial Cable Company's ship *John W. MacKay*.

cables are about that size, about an inch-and-a-quarter diameter. The core is in the centre of the cable and the strength member is steel wires on the outside. Cables are not made that way now, they're quite different. Its own weight is enough to sink it and also with cables of that size you could lay anything up to 7 percent slack, so every hundred miles there's seven miles of slack. That's to take care of bottom contours and also to allow sufficient slack to get it to the surface if there's something wrong and you want to repair it.

You got to hook it. You use a grapnel and there's a whole repertoire of grapnels used by cable ships, all developed on the ship. Some of them are works of art, they really are. A Lucas cutting grapnel is something to see, a beautifully designed thing. Lucas was a chief officer on the ship and he designed this thing. What it does, if you're doing a repair in a cable way and it's been laid a bit tight and you're not going to be able to get a whole bite of it up to the surface, you've got to cut it and a Lucas cutting and holding grapnel does that.

The cable ship *Faraday* had been the largest afloat and she was going to do the work that we did but she was sunk by bombing, and a considerable loss of life too. So rather hurriedly they had to put together a new expedition. We eventually sailed from Halifax. We still didn't know what we were going to do; it was a very well-kept secret. We went out into the South Atlantic and there was a German cable running from St. Vincent to a place well down towards Brazil called Fernando de Noronha. This had been laid in 1926 so it was in terms of a cable life fairly new. There was a real problem because pure copper which is required for the conductor was in damn short supply anywhere, so we needed some D-type cable in a big way. D-type is the deep-water stuff. It was our function to hook this German cable and cut it, pick up most of it and just disappear into the night.

It was all over in about a month. What we did, we cut it with a Lucas grapnel, sealed the end and dumped it over the side again. Then we went five hundred miles away and cut it again and picked up towards the original cut end. That's what fooled the Germans. Don't worry, the Jerrys knew it was going to happen and they tried their best to find us. At one point after we left Halifax, we were hunted for weeks on end; they didn't know where we were. We had a corvette escort all the time while this was going on. In fact the same corvette [*Fritillary*] stayed with us for the best part of a year and we became very good friends with the crew. [The *John W. MacKay* was also involved in laying cable for the D-Day landings.] We got close to five hundred miles of D-type, which was pure gold in terms of real value. She could carry close onto a thousand miles of cable. A cable ship, let's put it this way, it's worth as much as a whole division of troops if not more to the country that owns it.

I was more than ten years on that ship altogether with some gaps for leave. I loved the ship, she was just fantastic. I joined her in 1942 in March, went to Montreal and got married in April 1942 and I didn't see her again for two years.

Robert Bradstock

I was twelve years old when the war broke out. In 1941 I went on the Canadian government ship *Esteven* which was a lighthouse tender on the west coast. I went on as a cabin boy as the captain's ward; I was under the captain's protection. That's how I started out and then once you got your book and you got one ship behind you, then you're in, sort of. She was the lighthouse and buoy tender for Vancouver Island, up as far as the northern end of the island and down as far as the American waters. Much like the lighthouse tenders here, she was a single-well deck ship and you used to bring the big hooter buoys aboard and then service the lighthouses with food and coal and coal oil for the big rotating lights. She wasn't considered to be in a war zone, not in that particular area at that time, until Esteven Point got shelled. The night Esteven Point was shelled [by a Japanese submarine] they said, "Away you go and have a look for this thing." Can you imagine? We had an old twelve-pound gun [and] DEMS gunners on board. [They never found the submarine.] I've never known why they shelled the lighthouse. It wasn't lighted. What significance is a lighthouse?

Ten months [on the *Esteven*] and then I went to the *Restorer* which was an American cable ship but it was berthed in Victoria; *John MacKay* was a sister ship. There was a cable wharf in Victoria and she actually sailed out of Victoria all the time. I was just fifteen years old then. The Americans had a series of armed emplacements throughout the Aleutian Islands and they communicated by cable because radio was blacked out and when the Japanese cut the cables they cut the communications. They were attempting to take the Aleutian Island chain, but they didn't get them because the Americans successfully defended them. They'd go under the cables. They had ice-cutting [equipment] like a paravane wire running from the bow of the submarine up the conning tower, and they could actually get under the cables and they damaged a lot of them. We were up there re-laying them. We were up four months on this particular trip that I was with her; that was November and December of '41 and January, February of '42. The Japanese were hunting for us because we were the only cable ship.

There used to be three crack passenger liners on the west coast belonged to the CN fleet— the *Prince Robert*, *Prince Henry* and *Prince David*. They made two of them, I believe, into like a light cruiser; all navy on them. The *David* was an asdic ship, which nowadays they call sonar, and she did patrols around us twenty-four hours a day. She had depth charges and guns on her; [we had] no armament at all. And we had two deep-sea tugs going astern of us when we were laying cable—you lay it over your bow, of course—and they had an anti-torpedo net because you're a sittin' duck when you're a cable ship.

In November, December, January, February, it's not very nice in the Gulf of Alaska and it was a bitterly cold trip too because there was no insulation inside of this ship. She was built for the China station, down in the tropics. They put a string of radiators around through the cabins. The cable winches on the modern ships, you see them on the upper deck, but this one here was down on the first deck inside. We were layin' cable pretty well twenty-four hours a day so your port hatches are open and the nice cool Arctic breeze is runnin' down into the ship and of course all the radiators froze up. The cabins are down each side around the cable deck for the crew and then aft for the officers; it's a little better aft for them but forward it was just like in your cabin, there was ice on the inside from the humidity and freezing on the bulkhead of the ship. Right off the open winch there's the mess hall on the port side and you kept the door closed, but I mean when it's that cold it don't matter, it penetrates. But it was one of those things you accepted; you signed on and that was life.

Fifteen-year-old Robert Bradstock at Esquimalt, British Columbia.

The winch is quite large because you can't bend that cable sharp, otherwise you'll crack the cable. Then you figure the cable engineer's out there splicing cable in this, in the middle of winter, it wasn't a nice life. Talk about your fishermen having a hard life. They're quite a ship to sail on because they have four big cable tanks in them and the cable has to be immersed in salt water to keep it from drying out and cracking in the air. So you got like a big bollard in the middle of the cable tank—this is where you wind the cable around—and they fill them about four-fifths full of salt water. It's a great big free surface tank. They have tall masts on them; the *Restorer,* I think the communication wireless masts were 110 feet or somethin'. When you roll over in heavy sea and you go as far as a normal ship you're fine, but then all this water in the four cable tanks rushes over and you take that lurch and you meet the sea coming the other way. It's an experience you never get in another ship. It's almost constant gales up there and it's weather you wouldn't normally lay cable in peacetime, you wouldn't even think of laying cable.

We never knew anything [about enemy submarines], we were just there.

We went in once in the four months in Dutch Harbor [Unalaska Island]. There was a small [American] base at Sitka and Juneau and the large one was at Dutch Harbor. They had the harbour barred off with anti-submarine nets, much like they had out here. They thought there was a submarine came in under them when we came in, so they spent the next couple of days pattern depth-charging the harbour. You're in a steel-hulled ship and they're going off in shallow water constantly around the clock; you never heard so much racket in all your life.

Just the four months and then we came back and paid off in Seattle. My next ship was the *Mount Douglas Park*. I was second steward on her, sixteen years old. They were running ammunition out to Australia. No convoys out there—eight thousand miles of ocean to cross—everybody went their own way. What you did, I forget now whether it was clockwise or counterclockwise, but when you came up over the horizon and seen another ship, you went one way around the horizon and he went the other way, so you never met. If he came across towards you, you knew he was the enemy; if he kept on the other side he was a friend. That's how they told the difference and that would give you a fourteen-mile or so headstart.

Our coal hold forward of the boiler room caught fire and burned for a couple of weeks. You burned slack coal in those days; it's not hard-break coal, it's like coal dust, eh, and spontaneous combustion, it caught fire. We had planks on the main deck, the deck was so hot you couldn't walk on it. And right forward of that hold was a hold full of warheads for torpedoes. You didn't dare open [the hatches]. Let's face it, if you open the hold and WUFF, then you really got problems. So you just steam, smother, steam, smother, steam, smother until finally whatever combustible oxygen was in there burned up. And you had to fire out of the same thing, the bottom ends of them, because that's all you had for fuel. It was exciting for a couple of days, then it got kind of boring.

When I was waiting for the *Mount Douglas Park,* I went in the manning pool out there [in Vancouver] and it was horror city. Guys worked in the breweries and everything else all over town to make money, because your money ashore was almost nil. You got enough to get your meals in the manning pool, and there was constant fighting in the manning pool out there; I don't know what it was like down here—probably the same. When I was waiting down there I was washing bottles in the brewery to make side money. Oh yes, everybody was working. Coal trucks, a lot of merchant seamen hauling sack coal and stuff like that.

I made two trips out to Australia on her [the *Mount Douglas Park*] and I went ashore the second trip out there and I joined the *Nicholas J. Sinnot,* which was an American Victory ship, one of the two. They used to call them

Liberty ships, Victory ships. Liberty was built in the first part of the war and Victory in the second part. She was running ammunition up to New Guinea. That would be '43, '44, I guess. I was oiler, I went below. I don't know, I was always mechanically inclined and they wanted an oiler on this particular ship. You oil the main engine on a constant basis, lubrication on the system. We used to have some excitement there because there was the odd ship got blown up on the way. When you were running from Australia to New Guinea, you were in convoy, Americans with us. There was only one opening in the Great Barrier Reef and the Japanese kind of used to sit around there and pick ships off for fun, sometimes come up and shoot at them, sometimes torpedo them.

They had snipers and problems in Aitape and one run before we went in with the ammunition ships they went in with a destroyer and a light cruiser and they made a fast swing right around the harbour and just cut the jungle down–ZZZZZZ. What we used to do, go into Aitape harbour and unload in amphibious ducks with cargo slings all day long and then before sunset you had to get the hell out of the harbour because all they had for perimeter defence were 20mm Oerlikons. The Japanese had two engine bombers called Bettys and they used to come along, cut their engines and glide in over the jungle, drop in the bay and turn their landing lights on and if you were in the harbour you got it. They'd be running away from the Oerlikons, so they never hit the damn things. So you'd go out and travel up and down Torpedo Alley all night and then come back in the next day. You'd just go up and down the coast and that's where the submarines used to lay and wait.

An interesting thing there was a lot of sharks in the water down around there and we used to put the anti-torpedo nets, the big booms, out and we used to swim in there [between the ship and net] and put a guy with a .303 at each end. There's no forced air ventilation into the engine room, so when you're down there you could only stay about twenty minutes and you threw up. We swam for something to do. I mean, it was so bloody hot down there. When you were in there [unloading] during the day until evening you were allowed ashore in these ducks. When you're off watch we used to go and they'd throw a rope over the stern of these things and we'd get towed into the beach and back.

The way we washed our clothes in the engine room–there's no laundry as such on board–was with a forty-five-gallon drum with a cylinder head off a fuel pump, and a cable and a pulley up here and a pulley over there. Then there's a vacuum pump on the back of the engine. You know, you got the three pistons going up and down and there's cross arms go up and down on the back that run this great big air pump and a crossbar on that. We'd have this meat hook and just hook it on there. We had a steam line running into it and a water line above it and we'd fill it up, throw some soap in, clothes, and instead of having an agitator you had the cylinder head–kerjung, kerjung. A lot of people threw their clothes over the stern, but you threw a pair of dungarees over the stern and in twenty minutes the bottom of the legs turn to shreds from beatin' along on the top of the ocean in the wake of the ship.

Not in New Guinea but in the other island group, I think it was in Finch Haven in the New Hebrides group, they used to call it "Iron Bottom Bay." We stopped there on the way up or back. Ships would get torpedoed outside and make a run for it and sink coming into the harbour. They'd blow the masts and part of the superstructure off of them so they wouldn't interfere with ships coming in. You could look down and see all those ships sitting right flat on the bottom. Crystal clear water, you could see them beautifully. There was one ship sitting right alongside one of the docks there [on the bottom]. What happened they had just unloaded it and the Japanese dropped a bomb down through number four hold and blew it open. The ship just, blub, blub, down.

The only time I remember really being scared was on the *Nicholas J. Sinnot*. The engine room was more or less amidships. You got that long shaft tunnel, steel tunnel, that runs through the holds and the main shaft goes back through it. There's a light spotted here and there and you're checkin' the bearings. There's water dripping in. For some unknown reason when you went out of that engine room and closed the door and you were all alone in that tunnel and you got that long walk back there, all of a sudden it didn't feel so safe anymore as it did in the warm, lighted engine room. You were the oiler and you wouldn't dare say, "No, I'm not goin'." I'll never forget walkin' back down there. You were going to go just as far if there was a bang, but it's kind of comforting to be in the company of somebody else.

I just made the one trip up there and back [on the *Sinnot*] and then she come back to San Francisco for refit. One of the fellas had a car there and he was goin' across to New York and he said, "If any of you want to come along, we'll pay so much for gasoline; if anybody wants to get off along the way and take a train back or whatever." It was a bit of a skylark. I had about $800, $900, which was a vast amount of money then. We were coming up through the foothills of the Rockies and we thought it was a small earthquake. What happened, there's a place out there, a bay, I think it's called Port Chicago, north of San Francisco, and an ammunition ship blew up in the harbour. I think it was 1944. Tremendous bang; there was a lot of people got hurt and killed ashore, I think. It was almost empty when it blew up. We heard a lot of it on the car radio when they interviewed this guy. Anyhow, the funny thing about [it], the oiler was on watch down below. I could equate with this. He said, "I was sitting there with my feet on the bottom of the ladder, sitting on a butter box. One minute I was sittin' there, the next thing I was in the water. The bloody ship blew away and there I was in the dark, in the water, all by myself." Nice warm, brightly lighted engine room and all of a sudden you're in the bloody harbour. People listening to it, if they hadn't been in an engine room, couldn't relate but I thought that was the funniest thing I ever heard. You could picture it.

Joseph Noade

I was only fifteen at the time and all my buddies, fellas that were sixteen, seventeen, eighteen years of age, had joined the merchant marine. One particular fella made a couple of trips before I did and when he came back to Halifax on the *Vancolite* he said, "There's an opening for a utility boy in the galley. Why don't you try for it?" So I did. Those days they'd take anybody. I never told anybody, I skipped school, the whole bit. It was the greatest thing really. It didn't take long to grow up. My mother tried to stop the *Vancolite*; she found out I was on it, I'd been gone a couple of days. She went to the Mounted Police. She said, "He's only a little boy; he's only fifteen." The Mounted Police said, "Mrs. Noade, not even Hitler could stop that ship now."

Utility boy. Isn't that a nice name? I said to myself, this is goin' to be all right. First time I'd ever heard the word; I was doing the washing. Whenever the mess boys would bring in the dishes or the pots and pans they would throw them in the sink for me. Pearl diver, that's what they called 'em, you're in the water all the time. I had to do the officers' cabins—change the beds, do their floors. In the evening I had to pump a couple of tanks back aft with fresh water for washing and drinking. Every day. There was plenty to do. A hundred and two bucks a month, which wasn't much. The lowly utility boy, he's the one that had the most work. I would never look for another galley boy's job. The hours were anywhere from ten to twelve to fourteen a day.

My duties first thing in the morning was to bring a cup of tea to the bridge to the captain. He used to go to the bridge around five o'clock, so I had to be up at 5:30. Well, one particular morning I had overslept and he himself came down and was quite furious about it. I told him I was sorry. "This won't happen again, Captain." He said, "No it won't because you'll be awake at 4:30 from now on," so I never overslept after that. He was a very nice guy; Captain Sarty was his name. He logged me; I guess he figured he'd teach me a lesson. I think it was $8, which was quite a lot of money. He logged me two days for one. When we paid off, it was a Wednesday morning, January 5, 1944, over in Dartmouth. When it was my time to collect my pay off, he said, "What do you intend doing with your money, Noade?" I think I only had four hundred bucks. I said, "Well, I'm goin' to present that to my mother." I used to send her ninety bucks a month for years when I was on the American ships. He said, "That's very noble," so he gave me my $8 back.

My mother worried a lot about me and she never dreamed that I'd go right back out. I was only home three days and got an American ship. They had a union hall on Hollis Street where merchant seamen congregated; I don't think it was a union per se at that time. You could go down to see if there were any ships in. The dispatcher would call "An A.B. wanted for such and such a ship, a wiper or trimmer for such and such a ship." I met a friend of mine. He said to me, "You know, there's an American Liberty ship in and they're lookin' for a couple of fellas. Why don't you try it?" I had just turned sixteen; I had my age down as seventeen and a half. They couldn't care less as long as you had the experience.

I went over to the WSA, that's the War Shipping Administration. It was located in the Bank of Nova Scotia on Hollis Street. They took care of the American ships that were coming in here. It was open seven days a week. The lady there, her name was Mrs. MacKay, asked me if she could help me. I said, "I'm applying for a job aboard an American Liberty ship." I never saw an American Liberty ship before in my life. She asked me if I had any discharges and I showed her. She said okay, that's fine, so she sent me down. A galley boy again, only this time it was a world of difference because I was used to livin' back aft on the tankers. On the American Liberty ship everything is forward, midships—your work, living quarters, the galley, everything. You never have to go on deck if you don't want to. The only time I went aft was to dump the garbage.

You don't dump any garbage during the day. They have a barrel back aft. The reason they didn't dump it during the day of course was because of submarines. If they see any garbage—ashes, same thing—they could follow that. They waited till the very early morning hours and the A.B. or ordinary seaman went back aft, let the line go and the drum would automatically empty.

There was a little joke about them mass-producing [Liberty ships]. That's when they were welding them, prefabricating them. They were completed in four or five days, no problem. One of the dignitaries asked the mayor's wife to perform the christening, so they gave her a bottle of champagne. As I say, they were building the Liberty ships pretty quick. She said, "There isn't any Liberty ship there." He said, "By the time you swing that bottle we'll have one there."[15]

They were a nice ship, very comfortable. I sailed on quite a few of them. The *Ethelbert Nevin* was my first. We left here and went to Cardiff. She was loaded right down—ammunition—and the deck cargo we had army trucks. When I went aboard they told me the wages was $187.50 a month, which was quite a jump from $102 plus a 100 percent bonus because you were in a war zone. I may be only two days outside of Halifax, that constituted a war zone. If you were attacked, I think we got $500 but we were never attacked. Oh, they paid fabulous.

We lost two that particular trip and my next trip—another Liberty ship, the *Abel Stearns*—we lost three, three tankers. We weren't too far from Dover. The trip was uneventful, a marvellous crossing, and it was around noon. My golly, I heard the boom and we all looked over. Sure enough—BOOM, BOOM, BOOM—three of the ships. And you know after the war I sailed with three guys that were in that convoy and were survivors off two of the tankers. This was 1946. We were all back on number four hatch getting acquainted. One fella said to me, "Where you from, Joe?" I said, "I'm from a little place that none of you guys ever heard tell of: Halifax, Nova Scotia." One guy did a double flip. He said, "Man, I left there in a convoy and was torpedoed," and he showed me his body where he had jumped overboard and was burnt from here right up. Oh what a mess he was. Two Norwegians were on that ship and were in the same convoy and were torpedoed. We had quite a chat about that.

The *Comol Cuba* was a tanker. Little did I know what I was getting on. They said there was a tanker over in Jersey, a place called Sea Warren, a tanker port. It took me a day or so to find the place. The bosun was a great guy, he was from Peru and could hardly speak English. I was ordinary seaman, the first time I ever went on deck in my life. It was under the Panamanian flag, although they did pay American wages; no complaint there. They put them under that flag to avoid paying high taxes. Food was great, all holidays were paid for, any overtime was paid for. I said, "Where are we runnin' to?" I thought maybe we were goin' overseas. He said, "Cooba." "Cuba?" A place called Hookero; I don't think anybody else has been there to be truthful. Now, you won't believe this. I said, "What are we haulin?" He said, "Molasses." Well, if a torpedo ever hit that it wouldn't do nothin', just stick there.

The *Mount Orford Park*, a Canadian ship, we hit a storm three days outside of Halifax and it ripped two or three of our lifeboats off plus the storm doors; had a lot of damage done to that ship. The carpenter on board was from Newfoundland—Chippy; hardly knew anybody by their names. He had enough work on there to last him two years. He said, "I don't think I'll live long enough to repair this ship." Funny thing about that particular trip, we had three trimmers: I was one; Leo MacDonald, a good guy; and another fella from Cape Breton. As soon as we left port, the fella from Cape Breton was seasick and he was seasick all the way over and all the way back. Leo and I had to do what they call six and six—six on and six off—which is horrendous. You really work when you're trimmin' coal. By the time those six hours were up, you were full of coal dust from head right down to the bottom of your feet. No way you could worry about getting cleaned up. As soon as you got off that shift, right into the sack, you were completely exhausted.

I fell down the bunker hole about thirty feet, just slid right down. It was just lucky. If it had been lumps of coal and it wasn't—was quite a lot of slack—I would have been buried alive; it would have followed me down. In the side pockets there's ladders. I never knew there was, but I groped around and found the ladder. The next time I went in there I went with a line around my waist tied to a pad eye welded to the deck of the ship.

The very last trip I made was on the *Mount Orford Park*. I guess there were two tankers torpedoed in that convoy. That particular day, I'll never forget it as long as I live, it was April 12, 1945, the day President Roosevelt died. This was at high noon. I was just going back aft to go down into number four hold when BOOM! You could hear it all over. I don't care how far back you are in any of those convoys, you can hear the report of it. I looked over I think it was the port side and a tanker gone. Another one! Two of them. There was really no need of any more sinkings because for the Germans the war was actually over. That was April 12 and the war was over May 8 in that area, less than a month away.

I sailed in seven different capacities aboard ship—galley boy, trimmer, ordinary seaman, A.B., wiper, oiler and fireman. A wiper has duties to perform in the engine room wipin' down any oils that may accumulate on the floor or deck, on the engines, dynamos, painting, it's more or less a maintenance job—jack-of-all-jobs. It's a learning process is what it is if you don't have any experience. If you have any ability at all you will eventually be promoted to fireman and oiler. I'm glad I had that experience and I met some marvellous people and I had a great, great time.

There's a lot of people under the impression that some of these merchant seamen only made one trip overseas. Even if they did, they made the one, that's enough. But most of us made four, five, six and seven trips over. And a lot are not aware that we joined American ships. It was great money, sure, but it wasn't enough really, not for the dangers that were involved. That's a lot of baloney [that merchant seamen were mercenaries who hired out for the most money]. The thing is they [the armed forces] would have taken advantage of that situation too had they not been in the navy or army. Yeah, they'd have jumped at it. It was the shipping companies that were paying that, not the government. Those shipping companies were making billions; we were making peanuts compared to what they were makin'. They were under charter. How can you put a dollar sign on a man's life? You just can't do it. But the money didn't last either—easy come, easy go. When you're young and carefree, devil-may-care, you said, oh, there's always another ship.

It was a shame they never maintained the merchant fleet in Canada. I guess it must have put thousands and thousands of men out of work and I don't know how many families. We had a lot of ships, a lot of Park boats; they were great ships too, well put together. God, you know you could look out in the [Halifax] Harbour and as far as the eye could see—ships. You're lucky to see a trawler out there now. It's a shame.

Clarence (Bud) Purcell

My father died when I was eight and at that time there was no widow's allowance. We never owned our own home; we had no income. When your father died and was a railroad man, your pension died with him; therefore my mother had to go to work to support us. I left school in Grade 7; I was livin' in Musquodoboit. We had very little; what you got is what you sow, like snarin' rabbits or come in town sellin' eggs to people in Dartmouth. Rabbits you got for ten cents a pair and sold them for fifteen cents a pair. You wouldn't make any more than three or four dollars peddlin' eggs, so you see what you could make sellin'.

We moved to town here [Dartmouth]. I got a job on a fishin' boat as a cookee over at the National Fish [in Halifax]. That was in 1942: I was thirteen. I made two trips on her; near died, seasick, eh? I got off of her and a feller that was livin' upstairs said, "You want a job? I got a job for you on the *Ocean Eagle*." The *Ocean Eagle* was a tugboat out of the Department of Transport. It was workin' for the boom defence layin' a torpedo net. We took the nets, the cement blocks to hold the net and everything into Bay Bulls, Newfoundland. That was a winter convoy port for St. John's when she was blocked with ice.

I come back from there, so one day I said, I must go back to sea. I went over to Halifax and because of my age I was havin' a hard time, they wouldn't even talk to me. They'd look and tell me to go home. A feller by the name of Ross Cranton from Dartmouth, I seen him in the street. He said, "You got a job?" "No." He said, "Go in the Norwegian consulate there, they got a lot of jobs on Norwegian ships." So I walked in. He said, "Yeah, lookin' for seamen, deck boys. How old are you?"

I said, "Sixteen."

"Are you sure?"

"Yeah."

"Well, you'll have to get your mother's consent to go." So I went out and made one up and brought it back. They gave me a ship called the *James Hawsom*, a tanker. When I came home I said to my mother, "I got a job." She says, "Where?"

"A tanker runnin' down the coast."

"How long will you be gone?"

"Oh, a couple of weeks."

A U.S. navy blimp spots for U-boats above a coastal convoy.

So I got on her and we went to Texas: Halifax to Boston, out through the Cape Cod Canal, get another convoy to New York and go south. You used to have these blimps to escort them goin' down spottin' for subs. It was gettin' pretty wild down that way then. We loaded in Port Arthur, go to Galveston, pick your convoy up and head her back up again to Halifax and leave in another convoy to go across to Europe. You go to the big Manchester refineries. They used to have to take the smokestack off that thing goin' up, it was too high for the bridges. They used to take it down and take it with a tug. A lot of ships used to have to drop their masts; most masts on ships years ago were telescopic.

You should have seen some of the guns they had. On the *James Hawsom* you opened the breech and shoved an armour-piercing shell up, take fifteen pounds of cordite, run that in there, close the breech. There was another little firing mechanism on the back. Take a primer, put that in, and then you close that. You were all right for elevation, but you had to get a guy on the end of the barrel and point it, push it around. You had a lanyard, and the gunlayer would say fire. That was built for the Japanese navy after 1914.

March 1943 was the first time I'd been across. We lost two ships in the Bay of Biscay. We left Manchester and come back and the ship went in dry dock in New York 'cause she was carryin' gasoline before and her plates were all gone. I guess a ship can only carry gasoline so long 'cause it rots the tanks. You change either to a crude, or a light or heavy cycle. You don't carry the same cargo every trip. They had to do a lot of work on her. So I got off there in New York and I got on another Norwegian ship called the *Tercero* as an ordinary seaman. She was carryin' half cargo, half ammunition. See, they'd load 'em half with half, then they wouldn't have to pay the bonus. You got to be carryin' a full load of ammunition before you get paid the extra money, danger pay. That's what they done. We took that ship and done the same run, Halifax across the western and went into Southampton, England, unloaded there and come back to New York. She had to go in the slips so I asked them to go home. I'd been away nine months while I'd told my mother I'd be back in a couple of weeks, but I was late gettin' there.

I sailed on the Norwegian ships from March 1943 till the war was over. I come home and I had to go back, but I never had the money to go [to New York] and I missed it [the *Tercero*]. After awhile I got back on her in New York again so I didn't desert her. I turned around and went over to Halifax and they called out a ship, the *Acasta*, a midship tanker. That means all your engine room was midships; most tankers it's always on the aft part of the ship. She was on the Chinese coast in the First World War so she was an oldy. You had hard lairs. You had to go to a pump and draw your water and then you heat it with a steam jet. You were issued a bucket; that's to do your wash and your clothes in, to wash your face and shower in. All you had was a cubicle where you put your bucket in a hole, soak yourself around, then you rinse yourself by dumpin' a bucket over your head.

We had a French Canadian aboard that ship who deserted the Canadian navy in Halifax so he could go to sea. That's not a word of a lie. He got sick of layin' at the dockyard in Halifax. He got on the ship, got a job, didn't ask no questions. The Shore Patrol come out to try and take him off the ship. I was right there when they were talkin' to him. They said they wanted to take this man because he deserted the Canadian navy. He [the captain] said, "Well, listen, we're sailin' day after tomorrow. I got to have that man for the ship." He was an ordinary seaman too. "Well, we want him." He says, "You're not gettin' him. I'm the master of this ship!" And they didn't take him. He was still on that ship when I got off it.

There were fourteen Canadians on her. We signed on for one trip and she never came back here. We were on the coast of England shuttling and that was one of the worst god-damn places you could be. You had to cope with E-boats—motor torpedo boats—and they were the terror of the sea. All the English coast, all the approaches to the harbours, were mined. When you sailed in convoy there you went in two lines, you weren't too wide. You'd steer so long in this field and then you'd change course to the next one and that's the way you'd go to get clear of the mines. I seen an old coal carrier hit a mine one day. Matter of fact she was an old Lake ship from up on the [Great] Lakes which they had sent over there, an old flat-bottomed tub. All you could see was coal dust, we even got some onto us. Bottom went right out of her and down she went.

You had to do extra watches for aircraft and mines and you never got paid for that. After a storm that's all you seen was floatin' mines on the coast; they'd break the moorings and come up. Then we had to fire at them on the 20mm. You fire a spray pattern and you have an arc of fire. The one ahead would fire and if they miss it, you get it. After a certain degree of arc you couldn't fire on account of the ship astern of you. Lots of times nobody got it and the escort would turn around and they'd have to go. They were magnetic mines triggered by a release. Another one was a vibration mine, it was let go by the vibration of your propellers. That's the ones they put out the last goin' off. Same as what they call the acoustic torpedo. They'd fire it in a pattern and it run in circles and closed in and nailed you. Mostly blow the ass end off 'cause that's what was drawin' it, the propeller.

All the supplies were comin' into England. Southampton, Portsmouth, Plymouth and all them were the main convoy ports for unloading. And that's where all your troop concentrations left to go into France. We used to run to Scapa Flow and take bunker A for the navy ships and then we were in Invergordon, Scotland. We used to run to Belfast and up to Londonderry, that's where all the escorts used to round up.

They turned around and pulled us off that run and put us in Bangor Bay, Ireland, about fifteen miles outside of Belfast. We had to supply the American fleet. Being over there we never qualified for ration cards for clothing so we looked like a bunch of bandits. You'd just get somebody's castaway or something like that. We got nothing. We weren't allowed ashore. The Norwegians used to get letters from home with the big swastika stamp on them. Them Yankees used to buy them like hot cakes; used to trade them for dungarees and stuff like that. One fella we had on the ship, a Cockney from London, his mother died; he went home and he brought back a piece of flying bomb. We cut it all up in small pieces and sold that for cigarettes and clothing.

Norwegians had priority to us. Norwegians done their six months and then they automatically go ashore and get a rest. Not us; we never got holidays, no rest, nothin'. You were stuck on, they had you where they wanted you. My mother used to write the captain to find out if I was still on the ship. I never used to write home, which you don't realize when you're young. He said, "I'll pay you off when I get somebody to take your place, but I don't know what's wrong with you. I hadn't been home for two years before the war and I'm still here and I can't get home." I wanted to get back this side because you worked a lot of hours and you never got compensation for it. And you get kind of sick of the ship after a little while, it was an old ship, hard lairs on it.

The only reason I got off it, they were flyin' Norwegians back that escaped into Sweden. This guy came on the ship, he was only about sixteen years old. Matter of fact, he skied across the mountains three days and

Bud Purcell holding a four-inch shell on board the *Vive*, a Norwegian tanker that was involved in a tragic accident in New York Harbor in February 1945.

escaped that way. There were five of them. I paid off in Glasgow, Scotland, and I went to Liverpool and I had to join the manning pool. They wanted to put me on a British ship goin' to the Far East. I said there's no way I'm goin' on a British ship. I wouldn't sail on English ships if they give me one to captain. They were one of the dirtiest ships afloat. They said, "What do you do?" Me being a smart aleck, eh, I said, "I can't do nothin', useless." I showed them my pay book. It was Norwegian, they wouldn't know what it was. I said, "Don't worry about me, I'll get a ship. I'll get out of here." They stamped my pay book that I was no longer a member of the British manning pool.

I went up to the Norwegian consul where I had been before. "Yeah, we'll get you a ship out. We got no jobs for ordinary seamen, but we got a mess boy's job." I said, "I'll take her." I picked up the *Vive* in England. We had about seven different nationalities aboard her. We had Australians, Finlanders, Danes, Swedes, Canadians, British, Chinamen and Arabs plus the Norwegians. I was the only Canadian. They got along pretty good. You get somewhere, a guy gets sick, pays off and they sign on a person there. They can't send back to Norway 'cause she's occupied, so you have to fill the position.

The day I was joining that ship there was a Chinaman chasing [an Arab] up the catwalk with a cleaver. He was from Haifa, Palestine. I said, this is goin' to be a nice ship. I asked what happened. They had a Norwegian cook on there and he didn't do nothin', the Chinese done all the cookin', they done everything. He [the Arab] was the captain's steward and he wanted to get some butter. The Chinaman had a block of butter where the stores were and he said, "Butter, you take it." The butter was soft, he wanted firm butter. "No, you take it." So he went in, grabbed a pound of hard butter and he hit the Chinaman between the two eyes with the pound of soft butter. That's why he was chasin' him up the deck. The captain had to get them separated.

We went in and loaded in New Jersey just off Staten Island. That's where one of the biggest oil refineries in the world is. That was in February 1945. We had bad weather comin' in, that's why they brought us through the Cape Cod Canal and in New York. We were stuck going in two days in ice, we had to break 'er to get us up through into the East River goin' down to New Jersey to load. We loaded and went right back out stream; a tanker, you're in and out.

We went out to our anchorage; captain went ashore. The *Panclio*, a Panamanian I think, was comin' through the wrong anchorage and somethin' pulled out in front. Instead of goin' full astern, he went full ahead, give it the wrong rudder, and she rammed the *Springhill* midships and she blew–an American tanker, she just loaded up and come out ahead of us. She had 120,000 barrels of aviation gas. She was right within swinging distance of us, right across from us. Ended up there were five ships involved. There was quite a loss of life. We got the worst of it because we were layin' beside her. When you swing anchor there and come around, the stern of the ship would be right up to your bow.

The concussion blew out two tanks and as soon as she hit she ignited. She [the *Panclio*] got away, just backed off and got out of there. It's pretty light ends, aviation gas, the vapours saturated everything. When she [the *Springhill*] went, she buried us in octane and we went with her. They bailed over the side of her because, I mean, it's just run for your life. Sprayed everything, the water was all afire.

I was down below in my cabin when it hit. I seen this fella runnin'. He said, "She's all afire, get your jacket and get on deck!" So I grabbed my life jacket; it's a good job I did because I can't swim. I got the surprise of my life when I come on deck. She was all afire then, practically to the stern. You couldn't see nothin' forward of number eight tank, that was all just blackened flames goin'. She had all wooden superstructure on her too, teakwood; geez, did that thing ever go. We were loaded with kerosene oil. She burnt right to the water's edge. And every time one of them small ammunition lockers go off, that'd make it a little more hair-raising; thought she was goin' to blow good. When I come on deck the mate was standin' by the well deck and the ammunition locker for the 20mm let go in her. It killed him. Well that panicked everybody then.

We tried to get a lifeboat down. My job was to get the plug in the bottom. Somebody knocked the life raft overboard and jumped. Our propellors were startin' to turn 'cause they thought they were goin' to heave anchor, I don't know what the hell for, but that made it worse because that just brought the ship running around in a circle on the end of the anchor chain. Ah, Jesus, everybody was panickin' because there was no way you could fight it with the fire hoses. The flame was terrifying.

There was three guys in the engine room trapped but they got out of her. The pump man lost both eyes and was burnt pretty bad. The fourth engineer, nobody called him. He was, I guess, in his bunk and didn't know what was goin' on because there was no bang or nothin', just a fire. She was roarin' on deck but you wouldn't hear it maybe if you were sleepin' down below. All the guys I joined the ship with—the bosun, the carpenter, electrician, chief mate, chief steward—there was nine we lost altogether. We lost the three Chinese fellers. But the other ship, *Springhill*, oh geez, I don't know how many was lost. I guess altogether maybe twenty-seven or somethin' like that. The American ships had half a crew of gunners and they lost a lot of them fellers. Here's a sad thing. The chief cook, Peterson, was on the same ship twice and survived [attacks]—they got her in both times—and the third time he lost his life.

You couldn't reeve [the lines] through the bits, they were all froze up.

Chinaman trying to cut them with a knife. That's when I jumped. The propellors were goin' and there was a vacant spot [which wasn't on fire] so I tried for that. I never had my [life] jacket tied up. I figured the wash would take me clear of it anyway because I was goin' to burn up here if I stayed. I said here goes and I jumped about twenty-five feet into the water to get that life raft. There was a British gunner standin' on the life raft screamin' at the top of his lungs for help, and us in the water. I could never figure that one out. Panicking to come and get him. The propellors drove me clear and the fire only got the back of my head singed.

I was terrified because when I hit the water I thought somethin' took my insides out. I hit ice cakes in the harbour; on February 5 [it was] all ice cakes. I'll tell you, you hit that water it's just like somebody took and whacked you right in the stomach. I didn't know what I hit because [it was] everybody for yourself; you had to panic, there was no way. You didn't know what to do and there was nobody there to help you or guide you, so you're on your own.

One English gunner saved one of the Norwegian gunner's lives. He had no jacket on. When he jumped he hit an ice cake right in the groin. He kept his head up with him till he got out of the water. A great big fella too, he was about six-foot-two and this English gunner was a little fella.

There were a lot of guys in the water with no jackets on and that was a problem for me because I never had mine laced and they'd grab a hold of you. It's every man for yourself, you have to nail 'em, fight 'em off, because it wouldn't support the two of us, you're taken under water. It's an awful thing to do but he'd drown the both of us.

A tug seen us in the water and they shot a rope. It was [like] fishing, they hauled us in. Geez, there was an awful gang on it. The people that had jackets on had to stay in the water to get the people out that had none because they were slippin' away. You were a hell of a mess when you come out of that too, especially in New York. Your clothes were all full of gasoline from the water. They stripped you, took all your clothes and wrapped you in blankets and gave you a shot of brandy or somethin', I don't know what the hell it was. They took me to Staten Island Marine Hospital. I was never in the hospital in my life and they drove me in the operatin' room and I seen all those lights. I said, "There's nothin' wrong with me." The guy said, "We'll have to have a look at you anyway." I was there for I think it was eight days but just [hypothermia] from the water; kind of strung my back a little bit the way I hit the water.

It's a good experience. If I had to do it over, I think I would. Ah, you get the knocks. What the hell, that's life.

Norman Rees-Potter

At the outbreak of war I was the junior third officer of the *Queen Mary*. My first ship in Cunard Line was the *Britannic* and I went home on leave from West Indies cruising and back to the *Queen Mary* and war broke out. We crossed the Atlantic in blackout halfway across. It was a regular voyage, but it was apparent that war was going to break out while we were en route. That was my first experience with blacking out the *Queen Mary*, of all ships. What a job. Imagine the number of portholes and exits where light could appear across the water in a ship like that; you can imagine the number of lights there are to cover up.

We got stuck in New York for months and months because the ship had to be manned of course and everyday the [Royal] Navy were calling up their reserves and the Cunard Line flew the blue ensign, which meant they were Royal Navy Reserve and which meant they had a certain percentage of their crews as Royal Navy Reserve ratings and officers. They were being called up by the navy in half a dozen at a time or so and the ship was being stripped of her crew. Originally there was 1,120 or something like that, it varied a bit with the number of passengers; it could be up to 1,200 of a crew.... It came to the point where we were just like a ghost ship. I would do my rounds at nighttime to make sure everything was fine and I wouldn't see a soul, she was just deserted or seemed to be so, even though there were several hundred of a crew still aboard. Gradually the ship was painted grey all over, it was shocking to see. She was the Cunard colours [before] with black hull and the white deck work and the red bands on the funnel. Everything was grey, every darn thing top to bottom to the waterline.

Then I went on the *Britannic* and we were trooping out to India. When she was built she was the world's largest motor ship. She and the *Georgic* were managed by the White Star Line and when the merger came between White Star and Cunard, Cunard took them over–the only two ships in the Cunard fleet that still carried the White Star flag, inferior to the Cunard flag, and ended their names with *ic* rather than *ia*. We were crammed, we had a hell of a big load, probably around two thousand. I did one trip to India in that ship as I remember, and maybe one or two across the Atlantic to New York and from there I went to the *Queen Elizabeth* as senior first officer. In those days we had captain, staff captain and a chief officer, then the next was the senior first. There were twelve officers in peacetime, all with master's tickets. That was a Cunard boast, but of course they couldn't do that in wartime. I had my master's ticket in March 1938. I did one voyage in the *Elizabeth* as chief officer, that's third in command. I still had to keep a watch because we were short-handed, so I kept the four to eight watch, morning and afternoon, as the senior officer in charge, which meant looking after the navigation during those four hours, of course, and many other things.

I was on the *Queen Elizabeth* for quite some time, about eight months back and forth from New York to Gourock on the River Clyde, carrying troops. We started building these bunks, they had a name for them—standees—five high in some parts of the ship. I think we carried a whole division at a time, fifteen thousand was the maximum. There wasn't enough room even with the standees to sleep them all below decks so I don't know how many

Her Majesty's transport *Queen Mary*, loaded with troops, makes her way eastward at speed. Sailing as an independent, relying on speed and zigzagging for protection, she usually operated without escort until close to the Western Approaches. Her very prominent degaussing girdle for neutralizing mines can be seen around the hull.

thousands were sleeping on the promenade deck side-by-side with the whole promenade deck blacked out. Normally that was open to the weather, but it was boarded up. They would alternate, they'd sleep one night on deck and then they'd go down below. Same with the feeding. No man had more than two meals a day. They'd go all day long from five o'clock in the morning until eight o'clock at night. They were all allotted their time for first meal and second meal and there was always a long, long line waiting for food.[16]

Sickening, sickening—beautiful ships, such gorgeous ships—just to see the way they were treated. A lot of the treasures in the ships were covered up, the interior decorations for instance, so they wouldn't be destroyed or damaged in any way during the war. The wooden handrails around the ship they would carve their initials in them. At the end of the war great pieces of these rails were cut out and they were replaced by new ones. They were cut up into sections and sold as souvenirs. I don't know who sold them or where they were sold, but I know that they were sold. It was teak, you know, and it was hard to carve too, but they'd spend their time doing that. They weren't deliberately destructive of things, no, not at all.

We had all kinds of guns when the war ended. We were gradually adding more and more all the time and every kind of defence mechanism that you could come across, rockets and balloons, ah gee. Not the kind [of balloon] they flew around London, but smaller balloons. You shot these darn things

Aerial view of the *Queen Mary* plowing through the North Atlantic. "You didn't give way to the sea.... It was a miserable situation down below decks."

off and the balloons opened up and dropped a lot of fine chains down slowly. Supposed to come in front of an oncoming airplane and get tangled in his propellors. It was a fantastic idea; I don't know of any airplane that ever hit one. We had all kinds of funny things like that.

In wartime, [it took] five to six days [to cross] because there was zigzags in the coastal areas or if there were any of these armed merchant cruisers around. In the open spaces on the Atlantic, if as far as the Admiralty knew, there were no enemy around, you certainly went straight. They were such huge ships [80,000 tons] that when they rolled they took about half an hour to get from one side to the other and you wondered if they were ever going to come back; that was in a bad sea. You didn't give way to the sea. I cannot ever remember heaving to, as the expression has it. When she will not steer or where the weather is so bad that you're afraid you might fall off the sea, you heave to and just keep enough speed to stay head onto the sea so that you don't roll excessively. I never knew any instance where we had to do that in the Queens. It was a miserable situation down below decks. Young fellows from the Middle West hadn't ever seen the sea before and there was a lot of sickness. I guess some of those poor lads didn't eat anything all the way over in spite of the good meals they were provided. They suffered, there's no question about that.

I remember one guy. They were American troops and they were leaning over the side up on the boat deck and I was doing the rounds with the chief master at arms. One of these guys was facing inboard. He was watching me coming down. As I got abreast of him, he sort of stepped forward and he said, "Hey mister. How would you Limeys like to own a ship like this?" Typical guy from the Middle West somewhere. Sure, everybody thought the ship was American; full of American troops, must be American. Everything's got to be American if it's big, you know.

In 1944 I got a letter from the Cunard Line offering me command. What they say is I could remain as first officer of the *Queen Elizabeth,* but if I was interested in command of a cargo ship built by the Americans and the British management, they might have something to offer me in the near future. Who could refuse? I was only thirty-three years of age then and I was a fairly senior officer in Cunard thanks to the Royal Navy taking away the RNR [Royal Navy Reserve] boys; they took such a lot of them that promotion was pretty rapid. To get command at the age of thirty-three. It was a United States Liberty ship built in Brunswick, Georgia, the *Samfoyle.* I was in that ship right up to the end of the war and that's where I ran into one piece of trouble that had nothing to do with the enemy, although I suppose indirectly it had a great deal to do with the enemy.

The armed forces were very anxious to get landing craft out to the East. Of course these things had very limited engines so they didn't want to drive them out there under their own power, they'd be no good when they got there—if they got there. So the idea was to tow them out through the Suez Canal, which was available at that time. They were all assembled on the east coast of Ireland in a harbour there and they were to be towed out by certain ships in a certain convoy as far as, I think it was to be Malta or Suez, I'm not sure, and they were to go under their own power through the canal, I know that much, to be picked up again at the southern end of the canal and again towed out to where they were needed in the East for the Japanese war.

I had two of these, that was the tragedy. There were seven ships chosen out of a big convoy, each of which was told to tow two LCT. Each LCT was manned by fourteen young naval ratings with a sub-lieutenant in command.

And they had been up on the Scottish coast training for six months or so on these things, but they'd never been out on the open sea. We took these two LCTs in tow [from] Rothesay Bay on the east coast of Ireland. Once we anchored, they were made fast by the towlines, which were very lengthy, heavy wires, one on the port quarter and one on the starboard quarter. We lay there until everybody was ready and the navy told us to proceed. Off we went out of the harbour and down south through the Irish Sea into the western end of the English Channel toward the Bay of Biscay, bound for Suez.

Well, in all my years at sea—I was fifteen years at sea—I never, ever seen weather like that, what developed a few days after we left Ireland. As I say there were seven ships, each with two tows. I don't know how many ships were in the convoy, probably about thirty or so. We were rear ships in each case in seven columns, because we had the tows, so that there was no fouling up. It's not a good place to be in the rear end of a convoy normally, but then by that time the war had developed that we had more or less command of the oceans again. The submarines were just about finished at that time— fourteenth of the tenth month of 1944—they were on the way out.

I had made some objections to the navy about taking these things. We were asked to give our opinions so I said, "Well look, I'm not fully loaded, so my propellor will be out of the water partly in good weather and in bad weather it'll probably cause a lot of pounding which isn't good; I have two tow wires hanging over the stern." Furthermore I had, I think it was, two locomotives across my number one hatch, and they extended over the side of the ship, wasn't good to me. In general I said this month of the year too is one of the two worst months in the North Atlantic for weather and I realize the urgency of this, but I'd like to put it on record that I consider that the weather will not be suitable for this kind of job.

It's a sad story of my life. The weather got simply terrible. I was reduced to practically no speed at all, just steerage way; all I could do was keep enough speed on my ship so that she wouldn't go off on the wind and beam onto the sea and roll over. That's what I was fearful of because she was light. So I had to keep enough speed on to keep her head to the sea and I figured that this was probably too much speed for these poor fellows behind because they were going up and down. And every time they went down they'd slack the wire and when they went up they'd pull the wire taut. It must have been hell for them! It was, it was hell for them! They were all lost.

A destroyer came alongside and he sent me a signal which I had to take. I had a mate and a second mate and a third mate and none of them were any damn good at signalling. That was the state of affairs at that time of the war, you'd take anybody who had a certificate. They were giving certificates for people who didn't really deserve them, they couldn't use an aldis lamp. My master mariner's certificate here says, and fortunate it was for me, that I'm certified to having passed the board of trade examination in signalling, special signalling. I answered this destroyer and he said, "I have a signalman on board for you, but I cannot land him because of weather. Can you manage?" I said, "Yes." Then it was up to me to signal whenever I could see one of these LCTs. He'd come up over the top of a wave, get a signal quick—maybe half a signal—and he'd go down out of sight, come back, and finish the signal. "Are you all right?" "Yes, but leaking forward," and so on.

Another indication of the weather was a series of messages, marconigrams, from a ship in the convoy which was in distress. They bring tears to your eyes. They sent a message in clear; we were supposed to use code, of course, but he sent a message in clear. Obviously he figured he hadn't got much time anyway. And he said, "Anyone in near vicinity can help? Have lost bridge. No lifeboats. No compasses." And so on. The message is here [in my files]. I don't think he was [a] towing ship, but he was a big, very big, first class [ship]. I believe he was a PSNC cargo ship—Pacific Steam Navigation Company. The point was, he asked for help, nobody could help him, so he sent out an SOS and the next thing we knew it was dead silence. He was gone, all hands. That's the kind of weather it was. It was a very shocking situation.

Both of my tows broke away, pulled the mooring posts out of the foredeck. Aw, it's indescribable. Tremendous strain. These were thirty-five, forty-foot seas, wicked. It was all I could do to keep my ship afloat and head onto the seas. I knew there was a [British] submarine in the vicinity—I don't know how I knew, I haven't got any record of it here—but I feel that the submarine tried to help the crew of one of these LCTs and hopefully he did take some off. I don't know, I don't know. Of the seven ships which were towing, one completely disobeyed all his instructions from the navy and he headed into Milford Haven which is a beautiful harbour on the southwest coast of England. He saved his two tows, he got them in there out of the weather, and the rest of them were all lost.

My ship would have turned over [had we tried to go back to help]. No way I could do anything and that's the sickening part about it. You see, all my life I've lived with this. What could I have done? What should I have done? I know I did the right thing, there's no other, I had forty people on my ship. You risk the lives of forty to save fourteen? I should maybe, I don't know. But it wasn't a risk, to me it was a pretty obvious disaster.

Garfield Chinn

I was born in Newfoundland and came over here to join the navy, but my eyesight failed me. I went to see if I could get a Canadian [merchant] ship; there was no ships to get. I'm walkin' down Brunswick Street and I met this old fella, captain he was of a Dutch ship, and he told me he was lookin' for seamen. I said, "Okay, you have one." I joined on the *Kelbergen* as ordinary seaman in '40 and we was going to Holland loaded with iron ore from Newfoundland. When we got down just about to Holland in the English Channel, an English destroyer came up and said "Follow me into England; Holland is invaded." So we went to Cardiff and they put guns on her, unloaded and we left for West Africa and came back with a load of palm kernel; that's what they grease the bullets with, palm oil.

When I joined here in Halifax and went to Newfoundland, I was goin' to run away there. I was seventeen. They couldn't speak English on the ship and here was me, just a dope. You sit down to a table like this, you couldn't say pass me the bread or pass me a potato, you had to get up and walk around, go take it and come set down again. Oh, it was terrible. Got to Newfoundland, I said to myself, I got it made. There was a Dominion Coal ship in there loadin' iron ore, so I told one of the guys–what a fool I was– I said, "I'm goin' to stow away on this one and go to Sydney. I'm not goin' across on that." A Newfoundland guy too, he went and told the mate and the mate told the Rangers. They had Rangers in Newfoundland, like Mounties. Come over to the gangway and put one right there. One evening I'm goin' ashore. He said, "Where you goin'?" "Ashore." "No," he said, "you don't. Back." So I had to go back. Oh boy, she was really somethin'.

When you went on that ship–I didn't know–there was a bond put on you, and you could not sign off in no other port but the port you sign on. I signed on in Halifax. That was it; we never came back no more. This bond was the killer; I think it was $50,000. If they hadn't had that, I'd been gone in England. I'd go to the Swedish office; I tried there three or four times. The Swede was the most money of all, paid £80 for an ordinary seaman and that time the pound was $4.40. What about me? Seventy-five dollars a month and livin' on old goats and raw herring. But one place to the other, they had "That feller's under bond, you can't take him." I wasn't so smart, I didn't understand. Like now, I wouldn't be on no five years, I'll tell you that. I'd be out of it so quick; I'd be back in the woods. All that while on a Dutch ship!

They was good seamen, that's somethin' I must say. There was one guy there, a young fella, I said, "How about you teachin' me how to speak Dutch? I'll teach you how to speak English." "Yes," he said. So this kept on, kept on, after a year it was comin', two years it was gettin' better. Just before I left there I could have a conversation just like with you, speakin' Dutch. But at first it was terrible, man, oh man, oh man.

You had to get used to the food; the food was very fat. When you have beef and potatoes for dinner, we'd have no gravy to put over it, just the bare fat. And salt herring, they eat them raw. Bacon, same thing, just cut it in pieces, raw. I couldn't go it. I got used to it after awhile; I was there the whole war. The rations, they give you one tin of milk, fourteen days, and a piece of cheese like that [three-inch square], fourteen days. I'll tell you boy. We went down to Sierra Leone in Africa and we ran out of meat comin' back. They sent over some goats [on board] and the cook went down with the big cleaver. Cut the head right off, cleaned it, put it in the pot and cooked it.

I sailed on Dutch ships the whole war—*Kelbergen, Stad Arnhem, Katwijk, Trompenberg, Jaarstroom, Keilehaven*. The most of the sailin' that I done was in Africa and South America. Never got torpedoed but was machine-gunned once in the English Channel. I stayed on the coast over there for about six months to Glasgow, Edinburgh, London, Liverpool. We was goin' down the coast to London and the old feller—he was a fireman—was back on the stern of her. He had saved all his money, "When I get home," he said, "when the war is finished, goin' to buy this and buy that." A Focke Wulf came down, machine guns goin' and that was all of it. Hit him and away he went, right over the stern. That comes to mind a lot.

I never had nothing about guns. They had these Lewis guns. One night this Focke Wulf was comin' over. I grabbed the gun like this. You're supposed to put them under your arm, but I didn't do that, I put it up here [shoulder]. When I pulled the trigger, man oh man, I went belly up, and still holdin' on the trigger, see. I was sprayin' bullets through the top of monkey island. If some of our men had been there I'd 'ave cut the legs right off them. After that they sent me to a gunnery school in Liverpool for six weeks.

One night I went on a leave in London. They had places for seamen over there just like a big hotel. I went to this place and signed in, had a nice room, bath, shower, everything. I can remember I had two suits of clothes. My bed was there like that and I hung my suit up on a nail like that. I went up in the west end and I never come back all that night. The Germans came over and when the bomb came she took half the room. I can see it, the bed was hung up like this next morning and here was my suit still hung up. I was some lucky. If I'd been there, that'd been all of it.

We went to West Africa and took another load of this palm kernel. Geez, comin' back, we got off North Africa and we got hit. A convoy comin' this way and we was goin' that way in the fog, hit a Yugoslav ship. She was crossin' like that and we struck her right in number two hatch. It didn't do

too much to us, right in our bow, but the other one, cut her almost in two. The next morning it cleared up and man oh man. German planes started comin' off from Dakar and they sunk a big, big English ship loaded with meat from Australia—Blue Funnel Line, I can see her now, a big ship about 14,000 tons. She went to Freetown for a convoy and they must have hit her in the night sometime; she slowed down anyhow and was right alongside of us. It was some pitiful. When the torpedo hit her and then the planes bombed her, she opened up and all that meat, the blood comin' out—the sharks started to come. The guys jumped over the side and the sharks would get 'em. An English destroyer came and picked as many as she could up. She sunk right there. Terrible. You could hear them hollerin' and screechin'.

Less than 50 percent of merchant crew members survived the sinking of their ships during World War II. Pictured here are a group awaiting rescue, a rescue that many times never came.

We were just dead in the water. They came after us too with machine guns, but mostly they were tryin' to get this other one. An American destroyer got the [Yugoslav ship] in and then they came for us and we went into North Africa. The Americans had just invaded Casablanca and that's where we went. Seventeen weeks in Casablanca and from there we went to Gibraltar for seven weeks. Spain was neutral and the Germans was in there. The Germans paid [civilians] to do this stuff. They'd take their dogs, tie a little [magnetic] bomb on the neck of the dog and take her off in the boat. When they got alongside the ship they just throw the dog over the side. The dog would swim close to the ship like that, the ship would draw the dog and all, see, and whenever she hit—whack—just like that, she'd explode. They don't make a big hole, but you have to run your ship on the beach, you couldn't fix it. I seen Liberty ships, English ships, nobody aboard 'em, just left them there. There was quite a lot of water to the stern of them; I guess maybe after they got 'em off.

They put them sticky mines on [ships' bottoms]. There's your ship, eh? They have a wire goin' from the bow to the stern [port to starboard] and you take here and I take up there. You'd come this way and I'd go that way, keep the wire tight, and once you get up there, then the next hour somebody else would take it. Every hour, scrapin' our bottom with wire, it would knock it [the mine] off.

There was a Greek ship. They told all of us, don't take nothin'. They'd go off in a little boat askin' you for cigarettes and all that kind of stuff. But this Greek ship gave them a loaf of bread or some cigarettes and they give them [the Greeks] a bottle of rum—they thought it was rum. They went down in the fo'c'sle to have a drink, takes the cork off like that—that's all of her. Blew the whole, killed most all of 'em. They used everything.

When the war was finished they were some bad, I'll tell you. We was goin' to Iceland and about three o'clock in the mornin' the news said the war was finished. The next day, nice and fine, this ship was comin', nothin' into it. Up comes a submarine—BANG!—sinks her. The Germans on their way home sink ships. Young guys, eh? Terrible, you know, some bad. It was not nice.

I went through it but never got a scratch. Lucky? I was real lucky. After I came back I forgot all about it. I was only a kid when I went over there. It was really terrible, I'll tell you that. It was a long time I couldn't talk about it. Not too bad now, but it was years I couldn't.

Roland Gaudet

My brother joined the army and I wanted to join the same time he did. I couldn't on account of I have a foot that I split with an axe as a young fella workin' on a farm. I mulled around and I went to the American consul in Halifax and they told me how to get on the ships, so I kept on from there. They were tellin' me there was better pay and accommodations [on American ships], which was true and there wasn't that many Canadian ships to get on. I had a lot of help from a big Scotch fireman because the way I fired—shovellin' coal and I do mean shovel coal—I put the fires out; we couldn't have got anywhere because there's a knack to it. He knew his work and was very good to me. He did my work too for awhile till I learnt.

I was just a little green; that was my first time I ever went to sea. Seasick, you want to believe it, and then of course my shipmates were teasin' me. When you're kind of seasick and you get sweet soup—peaches, apples and all the fruit mixed together—and pickled herring for breakfast, it doesn't go very good. I went on one ship, the *Bestun*, that was Norwegian but under Eastern Steamship Lines. The Germans had Norway, so these ships that got out before war started, the Americans chartered them. I was the only Canadian on board. The Norwegians were the best crew of people I ever sailed with, because they were good to me. When I'd go in the mess they would stop talkin' Norwegian, speak English, and after I left, the Norwegian would start all over again. It's hard to understand but that stuck in my mind.

A Murmansk-bound convoy and battleship escort at anchor in Reykjavik, Iceland.

I always stayed up on the North Atlantic. Most of the time that I sailed with the American ships we delivered ammunition to Iceland and ammunition plus tanks and, believe it or not, gas shovels to Murmansk. I didn't know any better. When you're young and just from the country, it doesn't dawn on you. Going up to Murmansk sticks in my mind because it was so damn cold. I wouldn't like to do it again. Go twenty-four hours without sleep, day after day. We had to turn back to Reykjavik because there were too many ships sunk. The *Edinburgh*, a British cruiser, was with us for protection and she got hit and had to limp for port. That left us pretty well on our own. We had to come back and wait for another convoy because we didn't have enough protection.

In this convoy goin' up there was a lot of tankers and we ran for hours and you still see the tankers burning in the background, just a glow. When they first got torpedoed we could see the men on the ships and then all of a sudden there was just flames. Even if you jump in the water there you're dead because the water's burnin' with all this benzene, oil, gas and so on.

We had an icebreaker by the name of the *Montcalm* they had lent to the Russians. The ice was heavy. They were dive-bombin' that ship and at times you couldn't see on account of the bombs hittin' around her. Then after we could see the ship and she was rollin' like that, but after all that bombing she was still going good. Two of the ammunition ships blew up. Of course I was on the ammunition ship too, so that doesn't help the nerves any. It would blow the plates right out of the ship and the debris, we'd make a leap for underneath the overhang on the bridge when we'd see that metal flyin' because we were at battle stations of course. Every time we'd sit down to eat—I think they kind of knew when we were ready to eat—the alarm bells would ring on the side of the bulkhead and up to our battle stations. We spent a lot of time up there sometimes. These ships were gettin' picked off because there wasn't much protection at that time, around '41, when the wolf pack was bad.

I've got to tell you something that sticks in my mind. On the Murmansk run we had a ship's cat for a mascot and she took liberty somewhere because she had a batch of kittens. Every time the alarm would go off, she'd have the kittens by the neck and put them underneath the lifeboat so nobody would step on them. Then after the all clear sounded she would take the cats back out to where it was warm. Now that was something.

At times there was a mist a little over mast high and we could hear the German planes overhead lookin' for us. Now you got to remember that we're goin' back to when they didn't have the radar, it was all visual. So they couldn't see us and we wouldn't get bombed. When this mist would come over the top of the ships we were all very happy. That saved us because it was mostly all daylight and they could get us at any time. When you hear those planes overhead tryin' to get at you and there's only the mist between the ship and the bombs, now that sticks in the memory. It was quite an adventure; it's hard on the nerves. You have to be through it.

We took another convoy and went to Murmansk. We had tanks on the deck and they were unloaded by women. Our ship's derricks wouldn't lift a tank, so what they did, they'd wait for the tide. They'd keep unloadin' in the hold and when the tide was just up and down, they'd drive two or three tanks from one side, turn the ship around and drive the tanks off the jetty that way. The women would drive them to the front to the other tankmen. It was all women. The Russians were strict at that time. Some of us made lunches for the women workin' the winches and they weren't allowed to eat it. It would freeze solid right there. If they had to go to the bathroom they had to ask permission. For ballast they had the railroad cars along the side, and the women were there with shovels, shovelling that in buckets and putting it in our hold to get back.

On the way back from Murmansk to Reykjavik we hit a German minefield. We got the alarm and battle stations of course. I can remember there was one ship, a Russian, turned right around in the convoy and sailed back out. There was about ten or so ships that got sunk. The captain of the ship ahead of us flashed he wanted to change places with us in the convoy because he had a slower ship than we were. Our captain said no. About half an hour after that–BANG!–a mine came up and hit the ship. We were watching the ship after she got hit in the bow and the seamen lowered the life raft. A torpedo hit in the middle of the lifeboats and they just disappeared. It goes to show you how life is. That could have been us.

I got to tell you this one; this was quite an experience. I was on this British ship and we were deliverin' ammunition all around Iceland. These British seamen decided they'd mutiny, so they did, off Iceland. They wanted better food and they wanted better this and better that. They wanted me to go in with them. I said, "To heck with you fellas. I'm not goin' to spend the rest of my life in that prison in Iceland." So the captain and the mate put the flag upside down on the mast, [which signals] mutiny. The British soldiers came aboard in the launch with their rifles and bayonets and herded all the seamen over in a prison. The next morning they released them and they were some glad to get out of there. They needed all the men they could get. They didn't mutiny anymore after that.

There was one convoy I was in that went [from Halifax] to England and there was twenty-three ships. Seven of us made it. They picked off our escort which was a couple of mine sweepers and then they had a field day with us. After they ran out of torpedoes they used their deck guns. You could see the submarine, we were looking at the conning tower right there going by us. Course we had deck guns but we couldn't fire on account of the other ships; they come right between the ships. Our anti-aircraft guns were no good because they were made to fire up.

The captain had orders to keep goin' because they wouldn't jeopardize a load of ammunition or cargo just to pick up men. I don't mean the men weren't valuable. It's a hard job to get a cargo, but you can get more men; no doubt that's the way they look at it. There were wooden ships–on account of mines—that would follow a convoy and pick up the men in the water. We had to keep sailin'.

They got all those ships in one night, not too far away from England. I never took so long to go down in an engine room in my life. After standing up on the deck and watching these ships for the last four hours gettin' sunk, it took quite awhile to get down to relieve the other fellow down below. At that time we had ammunition and a deck cargo of trucks. I didn't run down like I used to. When a ship would get sunk, when you're down below, the floor plates lift up under your feet; you're waiting and then you hear the bang and the floor plates lift. Four hours watch is more like twelve or a day or two. The ship was sunk over there and you're waitin' when it's your turn. And you know in ammunition ships you don't have a chance. You don't have a chance down below anyway.

That was a British ship. I didn't like the ship and I got off in Sydney, Nova Scotia, and the ship was torpedoed and everybody drowned. And I got off!

Another kill, witnessed from the conning tower of a U-boat. "After they ran out of torpedoes, they used their deck guns."

George Evans

I was born in St. John's, Newfoundland. I was fifteen when I left on my first ship. I always loved the sea. I was brought up in a big fishing family and we were all mostly seafaring people. I was in the naval cadets, what we called the CLB, the Church Lads' Brigade. When war broke out in 1939 we were all so anxious, especially young people, to get in on the action and have some adventure. Of course when I seen all the barracks being built and the American troops landing in Newfoundland—it was Lend–Lease bases—and the British and Canadian bases going up, this was exciting times for me, not quite fifteen then. I went down and tried to join the Royal Navy. They asked me how old I was; I said sixteen. They said come back next year when you're seventeen. I said, you won't see me, I want to go now.

I was fishing with my dad and we were coming in one morning and there were a lot of ships in the harbour, some with holes as big as you could put a Volkswagen in from being torpedoed. This chap was on the deck and he was waving us over to the ship, so we pulled alongside the gangway and he wanted to purchase some of our fish. This was the *Einvik*, a Norwegian ship. While he was doing business with the chief steward, I went aboard and went back aft talking to some of the crew. They were a mixed crew—Norwegian, British, Canadian. After I'd eaten—it was around noontime—I cleaned up the dishes and everything and took the pots and pans back to the galley. I just done that for gratitude for giving me my dinner.

In the galley was a man dressed in civilian clothes and he asked me, "You clean the dishes?" I said, "Yes sir."

He said, "How would you like to sign on?"

"Bye, this is great, this is wonderful! When do you want me to start?"

"No, not yet," he said. "First of all I want you to get your birth certificate and a letter from your parents and also a police report."

I said, "That's no problem," but I was wondering about my birth certificate. I tried to erase it and the more I attempted, the worse it was, so I tore it up and threw it away.

I went to work on the ship [next] morning about seven o'clock. I was the cabin boy, mess boy, same thing, helpin' the cook peelin' potatoes, cleanin' up in the galley and settin' the table for the captain and the officers. I used to stay at home while the ship was in dock for repairs. She tried to make three or four trips across the Atlantic, but it broke down on account of poor coal, and the engines weren't so good; it was an old ship. Every time the captain would ask me for my certificate I used to dodge him. "Oh, I left it home in my trousers when I was changing. I'll bring it aboard. You'll be sure you get it anyway." He tried to corner me at times and when he did I always had an excuse.

George Evans, 15, served aboard the SS *Einvik* as a mess boy. U-501 torpedoed the ship on September 5, 1941, sending the crew into lifeboats for eight days.

A few days later we're sailing and my dad came on board and wished me goodbye. We're leaving, goin' out the harbour, and all these ships are blowin' their horns and dippin' their flags. We were goin' out to meet the convoy from Sydney; there were three or four of us; two ships from Belle Isle. We were carrying pulpwood, I think, to make paper. I had my own cabin midships just above the engine room. The engineers would be workin' like old heck tryin' to keep the steam up. When we got about three or four hundred miles out, we broke down and we couldn't catch up with the convoy. The convoy would only be about five or six knots and we were doin' about three or four knots. A Canadian corvette come alongside and told us where the convoy was, but we couldn't keep up.

So anyway about two or half-past two the next morning—it was on the fifth of September 1941—one of the fellas come back and said [there] was somethin' dark on the water. They said no smokin' on deck or no lights showin' and tighten all the portholes and so on. I goes up back aft and I've been talkin' about different things—torpedoing, you know, and life in the lifeboat and everything else. They said, "Go up you little f–. You go talkin' about torpedoing, you're sure to get it." So I went and I didn't take off my clothes, I just laid down in my bunk. I'd just fallen off asleep when I heard this BRUMP!, this bang in the side of the ship. I jumped up, grabbed my life jacket and ran out on deck and this time another torpedo hit.

I was goin' along the deck and I fell down or tripped up and a couple of A.B.s picked me up and I ended up in the wrong lifeboat. You had port and starboard lifeboats and I was assigned to the starboard one, which was the captain's lifeboat, and I ended up in the chief officer's lifeboat, the port one. When we were away from the ship, the two lifeboats come together, the captain mustered all the crew and there was one missin'—the wireless operator, he was about eighteen. When he give out the message, then the submarine started firin' shells at the ship and blew up the after lifeboat. They fired shells at the radio room, but the wireless operator was out then on deck. He lowered a little jolly boat and got away from the ship.

We were goin' back for him in our boat before the boats got together and, when we were rowin' to the ship, one of the chaps said, "It's better to lose one man than losin' a whole boat full." The chief officer said, "Well, we'll have to take that chance." The shells were whizzin' over our heads. When the captain mustered the crew, then we seen the little jolly boat on the horizon, so we rowed over to where he was and got him on board.

It started to get cold and it was blowin' and snowin'. Three or four days later my feet started to get numb and [we'd] rub one another's legs to keep the circulation goin' because you were cramped up in a small boat—eleven of us in one boat and twelve in the other. We started to get mountains of sea then and we put out a sea anchor and that'd keep you from goin' back. The other boat was a motor boat and had towed us, [but] it got rough, it broke clear and they went on one way and we went another way. We had a sail and put the sail up. It was about 450 miles south of Iceland.

When we got a couple of days out from Vestmann [Vestmannaeyar] Island, Iceland, fishermen were out and came alongside, took our tow line and towed us in to Vestmann after eight and a half days. That was my home for eight and a half days, out in a lifeboat. We had to ration. We were only allowed about an ounce or two of water, two or three times a day. We had hard biscuits and meatballs and gravy, that's all we had. Then we got to the Icelandic fishermen and they gave us their lunch—coffee, hot chocolate and their grub. I'll tell you, it was some great to have hot chocolate and food, it was really wonderful.

When we were goin' in, the cliffs were high and people were wavin' to us; they had the Norwegian flag back aft of the lifeboat. There were about fifty British soldiers on that island at the time. An army truck came down to the dock and a big pot of tea. I was the last one out of the lifeboat. They had to lift me out; I couldn't walk because my feet were so swollen. I was in the hospital about a week, I guess, on Vestmann Island and then we were interrogated by the British soldiers—where we were born, what happened—

see, I suppose, that we're not enemy. I had oversize rubbers on. I couldn't wear shoes because my feet were swollen; I had a cane too.

They put us on a small boat then to Reykjavik, and in Reykjavik we went to the Norwegian barracks and the Norwegian doctors examined us and then they put us out in the country in a rest home for a few days. Then they put me on a troop ship to Gourock, Scotland as [a] distressed British seaman. After a few days ashore and rest, I went and joined the British manning pool. My next ship was the *Daytonian*, a big [British] freighter. I was fireman and trimmer.

The first thing when you go down on your watch, you clean the ash pits and then helped the fireman clean the fires. When you had that done you went in the bunkers and dumped ashes overboard. You wheeled the clunkers and ashes forward to a chute and it'd go up—hydraulic-operated by steam—and then tip overboard. Oh, it was really dirty [work], sweat, you only had a singlet on, a sweat rag and dungarees. When you had that done you went in the bunkers on the starboard and port side. You're talkin' about sixteen feet wide and about fifty feet long on each side. You got to keep the ship on an even stability, so you'd take so much coal on one side and then you go over and take coal from the other side into the chutes that go down to the stokehold to the fireman. You were burnin' I would say about 35 ton a day, that's twenty-four hours. The trimmer'd be there alone, all on your own, four [hours] on, eight off. When that's all used up on the pockets, what we call the pockets starboard and port side, then you get down to the main bunker. You have sledgehammers; when you get the big knobs, you have to start breakin' 'em up so the fireman wouldn't have to do it. After that you had an hour to load the galley up with coal.

When we left Gourock we went to Norfolk, Virginia. We had ammunition and two big sixteen-inch barrels on the deck for the battleship HMS *King George V*. We left there, went to South Charleston, South Carolina, loaded up general cargo and went to Sydney, Cape Breton, and convoyed then to Liverpool. I paid off in Liverpool. A few days later I went to the British manning pool and they sent me on a Dutch ship, the *Aurora*. That was in the Channel ports and on the coast, whatever cargo they had to carry—ammunition, guns, dry cargo. I stayed on her for awhile, then I happened to be in the Dutch shipping office in London and a phone call came. They wanted a fireman and trimmer for the SS *Pieter de Hoogh*, a Dutch ship. They said, "You ready to go now?" I said, "Yes, my seabag and everything is all ready. I'll just go and pick it up." They give me a taxi to go and pick up my seabag and everything and a train ticket and a letter. When I got off the train in Hull, England, I held the letter up like that and this big Dutchman come up—uniform on, chief officer of the ship—and he said, "You the new member?" "Yes." He had a taxi and we went down [to the docks].

When I seen this great big camouflaged ship there tied up alongside and the guns on her and all the deck cargo, I said, "Jeepers, where's she goin'?" They didn't tell me. She was a big ship, about 10,000 tonner; there were about fifty-eight crew members. The ones goin' to Russia or to the Middle East were quite heavily armed. She had four 35mm and she had Browning and Hotchkiss on the bridge besides rockets with about five hundred feet of piano wire tied to a rocket. When a plane came over and it hit, it'd take the wing off. Then we had a four-inch gun and a twelve-pounder.

We got up in the pub havin' a few drinks and some said we're goin' to the Far East and some said Russia. I said, "I heard a lot about ships goin' up to Russia and gettin' torpedoed, bombed and everything, and the storms, the gales and the snow." I said, what the heck, I might as well go, I couldn't get out now anyway because I was signed on. They'd offer you three ships. I always took whatever it was, I just went. It didn't bother me that much. Some used to try to choose their ships and find out where they're goin', but I didn't give a damn; I was on my own anyway.

It was the 20 of March 1942, I think, when we left Hull and went to Loch Ewe in Scotland. It's one of the convoy ports; all the ships assembled there for the convoy to Iceland. In Iceland we seen all the battleships, cruisers, destroyers, submarines and aircraft carriers coming in. Oh, it was just a wonderful sight to behold; just in awe when we seen all this sea power.

We weren't allowed shore leave because we were on twenty-four hours notice. A man and his son, I guess, were comin' across the harbour and I called them alongside, put down a rope on the back and shimmed down. I give them a carton of cigarettes; I wanted to go ashore to say I'd been in Iceland. I went to the British canteen there, went in, had a beer and that, come out and they never asked me where I was from. He brought me back to the ship. That evening the skipper called me up and there was the admiral of the place there and immigration and the shipping master all around the table. They give me old heck for goin' ashore. They said, "We could have you shot for that, desertin' your ship." I said, "I'm not desertin' your ship. That's my home. You think I'm goin' to leave my home? I just wanted to say I'd been ashore in Iceland, that's all." Anyway, I was fined about five or ten pound.

The 21 of May 1942, we left about four o'clock in the evening, thirty-five ships. We were issued like Arctic explorers with the duffel coats and leather boots and rubber boots. It was not that cold but the water was really cold. We were right up to the edge of the Arctic ice. The reason for going up as far as the ice was to keep away from the enemy air bases in Norway. We got in the Denmark Straits and that evening it started to blow and then it got thick with fog. The next day you couldn't see your hand before you, what they call the Arctic fog. Ships would start goin' astray, breakin' off, you'd hear the whistles blowin'. No radar. They had a lookout at the bow and stern and the sides. That was about a day and a half. The amazing part about it, there were no collisions.

George Evans joined the SS *Pieter de Hoogh*, Dutch flag, on March 16, 1942, in Hull, England; sailed from Iceland on May 21 in Murmansk-bound convoy PQ-16, losing several ships to enemy dive bombers, torpedo-carrying aircraft and U-boats; arrived back in London on July 8, 1942, and made several voyages to Canadian, U.S. and South American ports before returning to Murmansk in convoy JW-53 on February 15, 1943, arriving safely once again in England on December 13, 1943.

When we got up so far the British cruisers and escorts left us, they said they went back to fight the German surface craft. Some of the escorts were there, but the bigger ones left. That put a chill right down our back because we lost half our power. I think the reason was that they had no aircraft carrier and they didn't want to take any chances losing their ships in the air raids. There were dive bombers and torpedo planes and they couldn't cope with them, there'd be too many because you'd get thirty, forty and probably a hundred planes coming out at times.

We were under attack for six days on that trip and we lost seven ships of that convoy, PQ-16; six were bombed and one was torpedoed by a U-boat. It was perpetual daylight, there was no dark at all. We couldn't sleep. You'd go down below and do your duty, then when you're off you'd be passin' the ammunition or on one of the guns. I was on the starboard gun with the bosun and the bosun was loadin' the boxes of ammunition; you clip it on the side of the 35mm. The planes were comin' over and you couldn't see 'em because the sun was to their backs out from Norway and shinin' in your eyes. You could hear the noises of the planes, and when the bombs dropped, the side of the ship would go up like a jack-in-the-box, the propellors would come right out of the water. Oh yeah, very close. The shrapnel and water come up over the side of the ship because we were down deep in the water with a load of tanks, guns, ammunition and planes in crates. We got kind of scared and who wouldn't be? We dropped the gun and run down off the boat deck to the weather deck. When I was goin' down, a piece of shrapnel hit me right there on the wrist and I bled quite a bit. We fought our way through, we didn't scatter.

When we got to Murmansk, outside of the harbour, a British warship hove to and the Russian [harbour] pilots come aboard in their big gray uniforms from the naval base there at Pol'arnyj. We went ashore to the Artica Hotel and while we were there part of the building was blown [up] so we got out and went right back to the ship. We thought we'd be more safe aboard the ship. There were over three thousand merchant and Royal Navy survivors from the convoys waiting to go home in Murmansk and a lot of them at the Artica Hotel.

We were still under constant attack. They were comin' over bombin' and droppin' a lot of mines in the harbour and we had to get out pretty quick. They bombed hell out of it. When we were alongside, the bow of the ship got bombed but there wasn't too much damage done to it. We had to pull away because the piers were on fire. When we were out in the harbour you'd see the whole dock ablaze and—BOOM!—all the black smoke, and everything goin' up in flames, the cargoes we had discharged had been blown up. The Russians used to haul in a load of timber and rebuild them again after the bombing for the ships to come alongside and discharge. Oh yeah, a daily routine. They used to load [cargoes] onto trains to take down to Leningrad and then the train to come back with a load of timber from Leningrad or around that area to rebuild the docks.

You could see the railroads with all the cars loaded up with ammunition, tanks, guns, planes and everything and it would be mostly women unloading them. They were White Russians who refused to fight for Russia during the war. You'd see a soldier with a machine gun guarding all the prisoners. When they were discharging, they'd be hungry and you'd give them a slice of peanut butter or jam bread and the guard would come and take it away from her. They tried to keep us away from the civilian population as much as possible. They wouldn't let us go out with any girls there or associate with us. If any were caught with foreigners they were taken and sent to Siberia or somewhere. Or they'd say they're crazy or somethin' like that and they'd end up in the asylum. Use any excuse in the book that they can in order to teach others–if you go out with any foreigners, it's goin' to happen to you.

They said they had to move all the ships out of Murmansk soon as possible because of the bombing takin' place. We kept right to the ice comin' back; it was on the 27 of June. When we were comin' back, the convoy PQ-17 was goin'; it left Iceland the same time we left Murmansk and of course we crossed paths. There were submarines in the area, but they were after the loaded ships goin', they didn't bother us at all. They passed us on the fourth of July and out of thirty-five ships, then, twenty-four were sunk.[17]

In London all the crew were decorated by the Dutch queen. I didn't get one, they told me that was only for Dutch seamen. Since then I wrote to the Dutch ambassador and a letter from the Dutch government [came back] thanking me for serving the Dutch government on their merchant ships, which they appreciated, but they said there were no exceptions made, they couldn't give me the Dutch Cross.[18]

Anyway we made several trips then to the United States [on the] *Pieter de Hoogh* and down to San Juan, Puerto Rico. This was 1943. We went to New York and then back to England and we started loadin', gettin' ready [to go] up to Russia again. The two apprentices on board from England, they were officers, they said, "You goin' up there again?" I said, "Yeah, this is my home, I been at her so long now"–over two years– "I wouldn't want to leave her. The only way I'm goin' to leave her, she's goin' to get sunk under me."

We were carryin' ammunition, tanks, planes, same thing. That was on the 27 of February 1943. Instead of goin' to Iceland we went right to Russia. Convoy JW-53, it was supposedly called after Joseph Stalin and Winston Churchill; it was about twenty-three ships I think. Three or four broke down because of weather and one of the warships lost the top part of a gun turret or something and she had to go back to Scapa Flow.

It was snowing and was dark this time of the year too. I was goin' up off watch to make a pot of coffee for the boys and when I was comin' back a big wave come–the ship was rollin'–and hit the pot. That water was darned cold, I'm tellin' you. I managed to get down below and the fellers said, "Where's the coffee?" I said, "It's gone overboard." So I got dried and I went through the propellor shaft and come right up aft. I got the coffee and come back this way again.

We discharged our cargo in Murmansk and then we loaded up cargo to take back to England. We were still under attack, but we didn't get hit, didn't come close. Quite a few planes were out, but they were driven off by the gunners. Then it was dark too and we were covered during the daytime by fog or snow or storms, so there wouldn't be submarines or planes come out in that weather. After Murmansk we went to the White

Sea area in Russia to a place called Molotov. Alongside there were American ships and British. Nearly eleven months we were tied up there, or eight months anyway, nothing to do. They took the fast convoys first and then the convoys were stopped on account of the German fleet that was out to get the convoys.

We ran out of food, we were starvin' to death there. We were gettin' brown bread, what the Russians could give. One of the DEMS gunners and myself asked permission to go ashore and go up to the British naval commander in Archangel. They give us a pass and we went on the train. We went to see the naval commander and told him our story, that we were hungry, that we had no food or anything on board and our clothes were gone, been there so long. He told us, in a few days I'll be down and the trawler HMS *Lady Magdalene* will be down with a load of supplies and you'll soon be goin' home because the British army and the Americans are going right across Europe and the war will soon be coming to an end. That was 1943! He was tellin' us all this stuff, even before D-Day! We didn't know the difference because every time you'd get a letter and there's anything in it, it's censored. Every time we'd write a letter we'd say something in it and the Russians wouldn't let it go. I never heard from my parents for quite awhile and they must have thought I was lost at sea. My mother wrote the Admiralty and they traced all over and they said, "As far as we know he must be lost at sea, we don't know where he's at."

We left [the White Sea] on November, but it was 13 December when we got back to Loch Ewe. When we got to London they come aboard and give us chits to go up and get some clothes; fitted us right out from top to bottom. After that I got paid off and from there I went to a British ship, the *Fort Charnisay*. On her we went to Gibraltar with army jeeps and ammunition for the Rock.

The British, it all depends, sometimes you had a hard bunch especially from Liverpool, they were the hard nuts, always fighting and things like that. The food wasn't that good. You had your mess room and your bunks all into one, like a pig sty, so to speak. Although, every Sunday, this skipper would be down with white gloves on and goin' through it seeing if there was any dirt and everything. If there was you'd be logged so many shillings. Welsh captains were pretty hard; I was on a couple, they couldn't care less about your health, they only cared about theirselves and the company and didn't care about the average person on board. There were some that were pretty good, but there were some that were very nasty. Some of those like Harrison Line in Liverpool tried to run 'em as lean as they possibly could. On the Dutch ships they were always kept clean and the Norwegians were clean and the food was pretty good.

In the English Channel between France and Dover going into the Irish Sea there were air raids. You couldn't wear life jackets because you couldn't work with a life jacket down below. The ones down below had a very slim chance of survival once you got hit with a torpedo, especially midships. That's why it was hard to get people below. You could get a lot of people on deck but very seldom to go below. I was scared many times, but that's the chances you take. I liked the work that I was doin'; it was hard work, you sweat and come up black as the ace of spades from the bunkers and coal dust. You talk about workin' in a mine, it was just the same. It was hot as anything between decks, no ventilation [or] very, very little, and the coal dust comin' down, you could hardly see; goin' down your lungs. It was pretty tough, but I guess it's just what you get used to. It's an experience that I'll never forget, it'll live with me forever.

The Russian run was the hardest of all that I participated in because of the Arctic weather, U-boats, dive bombers and torpedo planes. An Arctic storm, everything was rolling and you're trying to keep your feet and get a shovelful of coal to put in the fires. Mountains of sea, oh, it was terrific. Then when it got calm a bit, you got the submarines and then the planes. The torpedo planes come and spread out, then make an attack on the ship. We'd be on the deck of the ship with binoculars and we'd shout out to the bridge, "Torpedo comin'!" Then the skipper would turn the ship ninety degrees and the torpedo would perhaps pass. We had that happen several times.

If I had my life livin' over again, I can say now, because I'm alive, I wouldn't mind goin' through the same thing for my country, although it was tough. I wouldn't mind it one bit. I get a pension because I lost my kidney in the lifeboat. I know we went through hell but nevertheless we're here. It was a great life. I'm not sorry about it, not one bit. The thing is, we think about our shipmates, it makes no difference what ship we served on, they're still our shipmates and we think about them lost at sea. We try to remember them and give thanks for those of us who survived it. What more can a fella say?

CHAPTER 4

Prisoners of War

"You are in the power of the enemy. You owe your life to his humanity, and your daily bread to his compassion. You must obey his orders, go where he tells you, stay where you are bid, await his pleasures, possess your soul in patience."
—Winston Churchill, commenting upon his experience as a prisoner of war while a correspondent covering the Boer War in South Africa

One estimate puts the number of POWs held by both sides in World War II—including all nationalities, civilian as well as military—at fifteen million. Although no one will ever know for certain, at least six million are estimated to have died, possibly as many as ten million.[1]

Prisoners have been a by-product of war since the days of Cain and Abel. In the beginning, prisoners were simply killed where they stood. Later on it was found more profitable to sell them as slaves or hold them for ransom. As mankind became more "civilized," prisoner exchanges were arranged— if the prisoners first promised not to fight again—but this often proved unsatisfactory when they simply forgot their vows and returned to combat, drawing out the affair. The only sensible solution appeared to be to hold prisoners until the cessation of hostilities, leading to the establishment of prison camps in the mid-nineteenth century.

The earliest camps were far from humanitarian, giving rise in 1864 to the first of four Geneva conventions out of which was born the international Red Cross movement. General in nature at the beginning, the Geneva Convention of 1929 dealt specifically with the rights of POWs. It laid down rules for what was acceptable in lodging, hygiene, food, discipline, physical exercise, work duties, compensation for work and who could be made to work. Perhaps best known of all its articles was the one that stipulated what information a prisoner could be forced to give—name, rank and serial or regimental number.

In theory, safeguards were in place to protect POWs and it was up to the warring nations to ensure they were honoured. However, Russia, for example, had been excluded from Geneva meetings in the 1920s and thereby felt no compulsion to follow its directives while operating some three thousand prisoner-of-war camps.[2] For the most part, POWs held by the Allies were well treated, although history written by victors tends to dwell on the sins of the vanquished. By war's end, Britain operated 86 camps, the United States 666 and Canada 21.[3]

Japan maintained 176 camps on her home islands with 500 more scattered throughout her Asian holdings. Germany had 90, and by 1943 had taken over the 21 camps run by Italy.[4] The Germans took a paradoxical approach in their handling of POWs. They basically adhered to the convention on the western front when dealing with French, U.S. and British prisoners, but ignored it in the east against the Russians. Japan, although signing the 1929 Geneva Convention, never ratified it, but announced in 1942 that she would nevertheless follow its directives, with "necessary changes having been made." For all intents and purposes this spelled doom for POWs. "The reason for this was bushido, the centuries-old code of conduct espoused by the military.... Bushido, among other things, equated compassion with weakness. To the Japanese mind at that time, a soldier's greatest calling was to die on the battlefield. Surrender was unthinkable. The Japanese soldier, if captured, was required to commit hara-kiri or face disgrace in the eyes of his family and his emperor. And the Japanese expected this not only of their own troops but of enemy soldiers as well, so it is not surprising that the Japanese viewed prisoners of war with utter disdain. Without the Geneva Convention to protect them, Allied servicemen who fell into Japanese hands were treated in the most callous, cruel and contemptible manner."[5] Statistics bear this out. Of the 95,000 British, American, Canadian, Australian and New Zealand POWs held by the Japanese, more than 28 percent died while imprisoned. By comparison, only 4 percent of the 260,000 British, Canadians and Americans interned by the Germans died.[6]

Canadians made up less than one-half of 1 percent of the estimated 15 million POWs, numbering fewer than ten thousand. Of these, 6,791 were in the army, 2,475 in the air force and 98 in the navy.[7] A group not included among these numbers are the 198 merchant seamen, 23 of whom spent more than three years in Japanese camps.[8] On average, Canadian service personnel were interned for thirty months, much less than the fifty months endured by Canadian merchant seamen.[9] This chapter contains five of their accounts—one held by the Vichy French, one by the Japanese and three by the Germans. It has been said that war is hell. This book has so far told the stories of merchant seaman who daily faced death by fire, explosion, exposure and drowning; these five sailed into a corner of hell that only those who have been there can truly appreciate.

Roy Thorne

I'm different than a lot of other seamen, I was known as a freelance seaman. I didn't belong to the manning pool. I couldn't get in the Canadian navy because I had a punctured eardrum. I heard they were lookin' for seamen down around the docks, so I went to join the manning pool and they said I was too young. Even though I lied about my age, they still wouldn't believe me.

This Dutch ship, the *Olaf Fostnoss*, was down in the dockyard gettin' repairs done to her. Some guy I knew that worked in the shipyard told me they were lookin' for a galley boy. I joined her and I didn't stay too long because they were scarin' me to death. The Dutchmen were tellin' me how good it would be to have German and all this stuff. They were pro-Nazi, I guess. I worked on her eight or ten days while she was in dry dock. I had some job to get off her.

I used to hang around with a gang and some of the guys said they managed to get a Norwegian trooper. She was a passenger ship in peacetime. They got on her; I didn't because they had their quota. The Norwegian consul had established an office then in the old bank building down at the corner of Hollis and Barrington [Prince]. When Norway was invaded, a lot of their ships were at sea, so headed for here, especially some of their whalers and tankers. I found out through other guys if you wanted to join a Norwegian ship you just go down, put your name [in], and a ship comes in lookin' for Canadian seamen, they'd take you. But they had nothin' to do with the pool. The manning pool dealt mostly with British and Canadian ships, not too many foreign ships. Even the Swedes and Danes operated through their own consuls in Halifax. They liked Canadians but couldn't stand Englishmen.

We did not have a discharge book, at least I didn't. I don't recall any Canadian or foreign seaman to the Norwegians had a regular discharge book. A Canadian or British one is a book form with block pages in it and as you joined a ship and when you paid off, it would be stamped just like a passport book. But when I went with the Norwegians there was a pay book, you'd sign that, and I had to get an ID card from the shipping office down on Hollis Street. That's just a little piece of card showing your picture, thumb print and particulars—your hair [colour] and eyes. These are issued by the Canadians. Then you sign a sheet of paper just like articles. You signed on for so long, to stay on a ship for either a month, three months, six months, a trip, whatever. That was the difference between me and guys who sailed through the manning pool. When they signed articles they used to sign either I think a year or two-year articles, which meant once they joined a British or Canadian ship they couldn't pay off until that ship came back here. Now if that ship took twenty-eight months you couldn't pay off until it got back to Halifax.

I sailed out of Liverpool, England, for about a year and a half, two years, I guess. I was on the beach two or three times. "On the beach" is an expression, you're out of work. The problem was trying to get one that was coming home. You'd go to the consul, they'd say, "Yeah, we got one that's goin' to New York, might go to Philadelphia, and it's goin' to call in Halifax for convoy." Geez, when I joined her it might be six months or a year before I'd ever get near here. The scuttlebutt around the deck would be, hey, we're goin' here or we're goin' there, and all the time they don't know their ass from a hole in the ground. The Old Man knows and nobody else but him, his chief mate and chief engineer; there's only three of them involved as to the actual destination that ship was goin'.

Money would be one factor [for sailing with Norwegians] because as a young feller the more money you would get, the more you would want, and they paid more. As a mess boy in those days I could make, I figure, about $80 a month which would be about double of what I would get on a British or Canadian ship. When I became a deck hand on one of them I made nearly double again. They paid good money. A deck hand is a day worker, from eight o'clock in the morning until five o'clock at night. You'd be chippin', you could be workin' in lifeboats, you'd be paintin', scrapin', anything, but that's all you would be doing, you wouldn't be on the wheel. I moved up to ordinary seaman and you'd do your stint at the wheel; could be a half hour, could be an hour. Then the next wheelsman come up, takes over, then you'd go below and have coffee, tea or whatever. You'd just lay around until your watch was pretty well up; couldn't do chippin' or paintin' in the dark, eh. But in the daytime now as wheelsman, those on relief would be working with the deck hands.

I used to do lookout in the crow's nest. That used to be a son of a bitch, especially in the wintertime. You'd be up in the forward mast in the open with nothin' around but your duffel coat on. You couldn't see nothin'. It was only later on in the years that they put the enclosed crow's nest in which gave them heat and a telephone to the bridge. But in the older ships it was just a tin can hung on the side of a mast. You'd be up there and you're tryin' to look in all different directions and there was no way of communicating with down below unless you rang a bell. Then they'd look up and say, well, he must've seen somethin', and they'd all start lookin'. You can say again it'd get a little cold.

One Norwegian ship I was goin' on was scheduled for the Murmansk run but she ended up being sent to the shipyard; somebody put sand down in her propellor shaft. I don't know if it was sabotage or what, but we couldn't make it. I would have loved to have gone there just to see. Maybe I might n'have come back, but everybody was talkin' about Murmansk, Murmansk. We were all in the mess room and the Old Man come down. "Canada, how do you feel about Murmansk?" I says, "What's the difference? Money's money." You'd double the war bonus. A lot of ships during the war, you were given a war bonus for different trips. Murmansk was a real dandy. I'm awful sorry I missed that run.

I was about fifteen when I first went out. I think it was late '40 or early '41 when I took a Norwegian tanker, the *Madrono*. I just made the one trip on her overseas. She had been to Aruba and was on her way to Scotland. Then there was the *Tugre, Heimgard, Harpefjell, Askot, Germa* and *Malmanger*. All were Norwegian and one Swede– the *Tisnargn*. I was hit twice in 1942– the *Tisnargn* and the *Malmanger*–and held as a POW by the Vichy government for six months.

That Swedish ship the *Tisnargn* had one hold loaded with liquor, two holds loaded with general cargo which consisted mostly of clothing, and a half a dozen cars goin' to Buenos Aires with six passengers. Now this is wartime but that didn't bother Jerry, he sunk us anyway, it was cargo. We had Swedish flags painted on her, port and starboard. He said he didn't give a shit what flag it flew or anything else.

We took convoy from Liverpool, England, headin' for South America. We were hit off the West Indies off Trinidad. We were in convoy till we got a couple of days off there, then we left the convoy, and as far as we could diagnose we were followed because of the way we were hit. We weren't hit by a U-boat, we weren't mined; she was hit by an AMC, an armed merchant cruiser. Germany had a lot of AMCs patrolling. Submarines and AMCs were increased in the South Atlantic in 1942, an awful lot of sinkings in 1942 in the South Atlantic.[10]

We were away from the convoy for about a day and we had lights on at night 'cause we were travellin' alone. The thing wasn't lit up full glare but there was lights. That night I'd just come off a watch; I was a wheelsman on her, an ordinary seaman. I was sittin' in the wireless operator's cabin amidships on the upper deck. All of a sudden, BANG! She just rolled and come back, then the lights started flickin'. Then a couple more bangs. The wireless operator said to me, "Go!" So we got out the door and when we got out we could see where the fire was comin' from. It was on the starboard side, we could see the flashes. Then all of a sudden, BANG! She'd rock again. What they were doin' was shelling us; quite a few of them hit.

First thing I heard was the bridge go. The stern of the bridge where we were sittin' in the wireless cabin got it just after we got out. We were on our hands and knees crawlin' along the deck alongside the hatch coamings where the hatch comes above the deck. I wanted to get back aft because that's where my lifebelt and stuff was. When I went down below, all the lights were out and the guys were jumpin' all over the place, pushin' and shovin' guys. What a panic it would be, everybody wakin' up. All of a sudden another one came through the mess back aft; how that missed us is beyond me. It passed right through the bulkhead, went right down where your steps were to go to the upper deck from down below, landed in through and all of a sudden that cabin just disintegrated. It hit the bulkhead and exploded.

I had a little dog, a little pup about that big, I never seen him anymore. I remember gettin' to my cabin and all the lights were out then. I knew right where my lifebelt was. I always kept all my papers in a bread paper bag, then I put them in a canvas bag and sewed it. That was always hooked on with my life jacket hangin' on my bunk. I managed to grab that and come out. They were all yellin' in Swede; I was the only Englishman on board other than the passengers—two women and four men—business people goin' to South America. I was runnin' around with one of these little hand lanterns.

She was startin' to burn then, you could see the flames comin' up because she had a hold full of booze. Like throwin' a match in a gasoline tank. I remember them yellin' "Bow board, leeboatin; bow board, leeboatin," which meant the port lifeboat. Some of them were there and they were all pushin' one another. I'm tellin' you, the panic is out of this world. We got the boats down and all the Old Man was worried about was the six passengers, so we got them in. A woman got hurt, the side of her neck was cut; a piece of shrapnel hit her, I guess. We got two boats away. Five guys had jumped in the water; we fished them out. In the meantime then they started machine-gunnin' because you could see the tracers comin' over. The moon was out but it was cloudy, all you could see was flashes.

Now she was hit at eight o'clock in the evening and she didn't sink till one o'clock that afternoon next day. Now if she'd been torpedoed she'd have gone down faster than that. Two holds were on fire. We laid off about a mile and you could still see them poundin' hell out of her. Then all of a sudden we could see lights on board of her, so they must have sent a boarding party to see what they could find on the bridge. What they would be looking for would be convoy information, log books, what kind of manifest you had, what kind of cargo she was carrying and what not. We seen their lights for maybe a couple of hours, then the Old Man said we were goin' to row further away from her. She really started to throw flames, but in the morning she was still afloat. They didn't throw no more shells at her, they just left her because they knew she was on fire anyway.

The Old Man said we're goin' to go back on board and see what we can salvage such as food and stuff. So he said to me, "Canada, you"—the Swedes nicknamed me Canada—"you, and you and you and you." I was cowering over in the bow. The chief mate's boat came alongside; all together there was about thirty-eight people includin' the passengers. I switched to the chief mate's boat and three seamen, myself and the chief mate went back aboard. We still had Jacob ladders over the side and you stick your foot on deck, boy, talk about fry. But we managed to get to the store room on the other side of the galleys. We had a dingy boat on board which was used for painting, so we managed to get that over the side, then we started to throw the supplies down. We had enough supplies in that dingy to do us about another year on the Atlantic Ocean, and booze.

The smoke was comin' up through the hatch coamings then and up through the deck covers, then the covers all of a sudden burst. A lot of it was light flame but heavy smoke. The mate said, "You, Canada, you, you, and you go to the bridge and throw the box over." I didn't know what he meant. There was a big steel box and it had holes in it and was locked. Now they didn't bother goin' for that, it was still there. The Old Man hardly kept anything in his cabin. Manifests of what the cargo was and all this stuff would be kept in this thing on the bridge, so we just heaved it over the side. Then he yelled about gettin' back because she was startin' to go down bow first. We managed to get in the boats and started to pull away and up she went. She was only a brand-new ship built in the late thirties; might have been a 6,000-tonner. The Old Man and a few more of them stood up and give it the big salute, you know, goodbye dear.

We got sort of straightened around, pulled the dingy between the two lifeboats and started sharin' water and food from the one to the other. The Old Man and the second mate sort of figured out where we were. "It's good for three or four days sailing, or faster if we get picked up." All of a sudden a woman yelled, "Oh my, look a' there. Over there, over there!" We could see smoke on the horizon, but you could see him zigzaggin' too. Within a matter of about two hours this big 10,000-tonner came alongside. An American cargo ship, she worked for the Black Diamond coal people in the United States. She had already picked up four other crews from sunken ships.

Boy, it was rough, the swells got heavy. Course guys were tryin' to save stuff they'd taken in the lifeboat. No way, boy, them Yanks weren't waitin' for nothin'. They said, "Don't grab anything, leave it." They threw nets over, besides Jacob ladders. The women we had to hoist aboard. Just cut the lifeboats loose and let them go with all that food and booze. Geez, when we got up there here's a bunch of Hindus, a bunch of Indians, Britishers, some

Canadians off other ships that were hit. The Americans landed us in Port of Spain in Trinidad.

We were on the beach there, and then they distributed us to the merchant navy clubs and whatnot. I met a Canadian family and they found out I was from Halifax. He was the bank manager of the Royal Bank in Port of Spain and his wife and I went to the same school in Halifax. So he said, "You ain't stayin' here at the merchant navy club, you're movin' in with me." So I moved in with him, his wife and two daughters and I stayed there for three weeks, I guess. We had a board of inquiry in Port of Spain and different guys were asked different questions. You had to be very careful what you said because she was a neutral ship and what was she doin' in a convoy and all this stuff.

Then I got my offer to join this Norwegian tanker, the *Malmanger*, [which] was supposed to be goin' to New York and then Halifax. You don't know nothin' till you join, till the thing gets there; I joined her to get home. Instead of goin' to Halifax or New York we were goin' back and forth across the Atlantic. Two trips to Gibraltar carryin' crude oil for the British navy. Gibraltar was quite a busy port and they were pretty well poundin' hell out of there too.

If that thing done nine knots she'd tremble all over. First trip we went over in a convoy and then the commodore of the convoy must have got mad and said, "You ain't comin' with me anymore." The next trip we went alone. We got hit about a thousand miles off the coast of Africa.

I was a peggy on her, a mess boy. I was sittin' down havin' a cup of tea or somethin' in the mess room and all of a sudden–WHAM-O!–she got one forward first and then one aft. Torpedoes, both of them, one up in the fo'c'sle and one back aft. In a tanker your engine room is back aft and your sleeping quarters for the deck crew. Up forward you had some cabins for some of the crew. She got one between the fo'c'sle and number one hold, and back aft she got it between the mess and the engine room. We lost three men in the engine room–the donkey man, a fireman and an oiler.

This was at night, pitch black, when she got it. I'd say roughly she took about five minutes to go down. I guess we was scramblin'! You had one [lifeboat] port and starboard on your stern; amidships had one on port and starboard sides, those had already been let go so they were gettin' into them. The one that the bosun and I were headin' for on the back aft, the god-damn block was rusted that it wouldn't drop, she wouldn't let go. All of a sudden he said, "Jump!" and before I knew, a big arm was around my neck, and him and I went overboard. The other boat got off. I guess there might have been a dozen or so of us in the water.

He [the bosun] was a big Norwegian boy; he was strong and his head was shaved as smooth as the top of that stove. He was sort of a lookout for me. I sailed with a lot of Norwegians and if they take a likin' to you, they'll do anything in the world for you. They liked Canadians [but] couldn't stand Englishmen. Him and I got along good.

Just before he was made bosun, we had lost a bosun overboard. In fact it was a couple of days before we were sunk. Him [the former bosun] and I, I'm in the bow of the lifeboat and he's in the stern and we're checkin' the supplies, the water and canned goods and stuff that are encased in metal containers. The boats are slung over the side over the port and starboard. She just rolls, heavy swells, and I happen to look back aft and he's gone. Geez, I could see him in the water. He grabbed a life jacket when he fell, it was layin' on a seat in the lifeboat, but he couldn't get it on. As each swell went up, you could see him. I yelled, "Man overboard! Man overboard!" Now a tanker doin' eight, even nine knots, you're goin' to go quite a distance before you stop. She was a 10,000-tonner I think. By the time we got around he was gone. We stayed till dark. The Old Man said, "We'll even put the lights on till we find him," but you couldn't.

Anyway this big guy that took over from him, if he hadn't have grabbed me I'd 'ave gone down with her, I guess. We were in the water maybe a couple of hours swimming around before you got picked up. They couldn't see who was in the water because of the oil. Crude oil stays at the top like molasses and if you go under that without a belt or somethin' that will bring you back up you got some fight to try and come up out of that oil. We had these little battery-activated lights [on the life jackets], they blinked red. That's the first thing you had to do was try and get that oil off that bulb. Jesus, you're black, full of oil. So they managed to get us anyway. Him and I got in the chief mate's boat.

So while we're in the lifeboat we see this big black thing come up out of the water, then the moon started to come out. The guy started in English, "How many men are in these lifeboats?" The chief mate answered him. At first I thought it was an English submarine, there wasn't a flaw in his English. "Pull alongside." You could see the flurry then, the Jerrys were mannin' their small gun on the bow and they were also standin' by the conning tower with machine guns—two officers and I'd say about six seamen. "Pull the other one alongside. Which one has your captain in it?" Captain stands up and they help him on board. "Is your chief engineer a survivor?" "Yes." "Pull alongside." He was in my boat. They just took the captain and chief engineer, then they said you're *x* number of miles from Freetown, South Africa. He give us the directions and told us with good weather we should make it in six days. "Have you got enough provisions?" The mate answered yes. Nobody argued, we didn't know what the hell to do. After they got them aboard he said, "Pull off!" He was the last one to go down. It looked like a petty officer by his rank, you could see all these stripes on his uniform and a little German cap. He's in the conning tower and he's yellin' at us. He didn't say they were goin' astern or they were goin' forward, but she came back and we right behind her. We thought she was goin' to ram us so we all went back in the water again but they didn't. It was just the way they were comin' astern to go down. The captain and the engineer, I never ever found out what happened to them guys.

The next morning I could just about see; my eyes were burning [from the oil]. The bosun didn't need a haircut but I did. They took a pair of little scissors out of a Red Cross box and cut all my god-damn hair off with all the junk and oil. And then washed your eyes out with salt water. Now, can you imagine? Then after the salt water they turned around and said, well, I guess we can afford to give him some fresh water.

Startin' into the second day it was decided to see what we had. First of all everybody wanted a cigarette. When I went over I grabbed a bag that had a can of tobacco in; I thought it was a carton of cigarettes. The second mate he had a couple of tins of tobacco. Couple of guys pulled out a carton. See, somebody always kept stuff like that 'cause there was always the chance that you could grab it and take off. I'd say we had smokes for maybe a week but, boy, you smoked pretty careful. You had one cigarette and passed that around, four or five guys on that one. Then when all the tailor-mades were gone, we had Prince Albert pipe tobacco; that's what the second engineer used to smoke. But we didn't have no papers. In the containers of food there were little pieces of solid chocolate about an inch square and they were wrapped in wax paper. The first thing the mate said, save the paper off them chocolates because it was thin and all wax. You imagine, lightin' one of those full of Prince Albert tobacco and holdin' that thing together, passin' it around, about four or five guys to get a drag off it. The mate was all right, he had his pipe with him, the ol' frigger. He'd be layin' up there puffin' away with this ol' thing hangin' out. He wouldn't pass that god-damn pipe around, no way. We used to be down there, "You son of a bitch." We were lucky to get his cans of tobacco.

Then it came to the food situation. There were metal containers with a cap on top to waterproof it. In that container would be pemmican, which looked like peanut butter but solidified. That would be cut into about one-inch squares and the mate, boy, when he cut them he made sure that they were cut [precisely]. There was hardtack and they must have been in there from the First World War 'cause, man, they were hard. You couldn't even soak them in salt water. Used to take and pound them and hold your hand underneath to get the crumbs. There was another tank underneath the seat which had a cap on it and I think that held somethin' like five or eight gallons of water. It had a long cylinder with a chain on it that fit down inside and that would hold maybe a cup of water.

We had three DEMS army gunners in our boat, three Irishmen from Belfast. I was the only Canadian, the rest were all Norwegians. There were eighteen men in the lifeboat and somethin' like sixteen in the other one. It was decided to split the lifeboats; whichever one made contact with anybody would say, "Hey, we got a boat we left here" so that they would go there. [The other lifeboat made it safely to Freetown.]

The first few days we lived pretty high on the hog, but then it started to rain and thunder and lightning. All I had on was a pair of shorts and a singlet, nothing on my feet. A couple of others, that's about all they had on too. But the army guys had their fatigues and boots on because they were goin' on watch when she was hit. The mate said, "We're goin' to start doin' watches," so each guy was given a watch. I done my share, four on, eight off; the other guys would do the same, it was split up between eighteen men. Being as I was the smallest, I was the only guy that could fit into the rope locker in the bow of the lifeboat, so they'd take the rope out and when I'd want to get sleep I'd squeeze into that and have my little sleep until she rolled over.

First we started rowing for awhile, then we'd get tired and throw up a sail. Catch rainwater by sail. We hit some heavy swells and all of a sudden everybody yelled, "She's goin'!" Girrrch, right over. Never lost a thing 'cause everything is made fast in a lifeboat. You want to see eighteen men scramble to turn a boat back up. They were heavy boats, and I mean heavy. They could hold twenty-eight men, so you're lookin' at, could be thirty-foot length; they might be fifteen feet wide and they draw five feet at the water.

We turned over about twice. You'd see the sharks followin' us all the time. We used to throw the empty cans at them to scare them off, but it didn't. The fear of being turned over was sharks. You could see the fin, but then they'd only circle and follow but they wouldn't come any closer. I think the smell of oil, because the boats were covered too, that's what sort of kept them off.

I'm tellin' you, I can remember to have the odd crap it'd be three or four days because you had nothin' in there. The rolling and the bumping and the swells of the water comin' up sometimes would make you urinate more often.

We passed two or three ships, or they passed us, rather. Lit up, so they could have been either Spanish or Portuguese in that part of the country 'cause they were neutral too. We shot flares and everything, but nobody; then all the flares were gone. After the eleventh day we sighted land. You could see it off on the horizon. We got close to it, but it was so rough we're kind of scared we could have been smashed to pieces on the rocks. So anyway the chief mate spied an opening like a river coming down towards the ocean. We managed to row to get to that and then we rowed up. What a job goin' up and the current comin' back. We could see a bunch of natives on the shore and a lot of guys wearin' red fez hats. They were what they call Singhalese soldiers, they were in the French army. We landed in French West Africa, [but] we didn't know at that time where we were.

We went up the river and there was a little wharf juttin' out; there was a village and a big mud brick building. We were so glad to get ashore, we just beached her and got onto the beach. We must have all dozed off maybe three or four hours on the beach and finally we came to and all the natives were around there lookin' at us. The French soldiers would jab us with sticks; thought we were dead, I guess. Finally we got enough sense and we seen a white guy there all dressed up in a French uniform and we thought, oh boy, we're in the Cameroons, which was Free French islands off the coast of Africa in those days. But it wasn't; they were the Vichy French.

You're just like a lot of other guys, a lot of Canadians. "Were we really at war with the French?" Well, who the hell did they think they were fightin' besides the Germans when they invaded North Africa, if it wasn't the French? The Vichy government took over when the Germans invaded France in 1940. Marshal Pétain, who was the general, somethin' like De Gaulle in those days, he and Laval took over the French government under German control. They had colonies throughout Africa which were still under the French but at that time became under the Vichy French before the invasion of North Africa in 1942. But we didn't realize who they were until about eight or ten days later. The Cameroons were Free French islands off the coast of Africa. These were De Gaulle's people, Free French who managed to get through to be there with the knowledge that some time the invasion would come off. Some of them were from these colonies in West Africa, or from Oran, Algiers or Morocco.

Some of us had been burnt bad with oil. The oil caused boils and blisters to come out on the skin. My ears, all the backs down here were burnt and all around my neck. My head, aw Jesus, it was a horrible lookin' mess. They managed to help us up to this big building. They got us in there and more white people started comin' in to see who these guys were. This French officer took over control and he spoke fair English. He said somethin' about these people were goin' to take so many and take them home with them to look after them. Still nobody realized where they were.

Some were four at one place, some five, with the different plantation owners. This woman, her husband and her sister took three of us in and she looked after me. They had a big peanut plantation and quite a few native

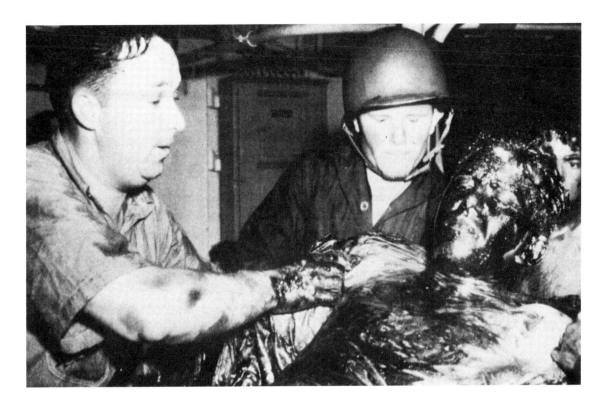

workers. She used to come in in the mornings to check on me to make sure that this native done his chores that night such as washin' me, seen that my head was always clean and bathin' the sores and boils that I had on my body. There were quite a few people we met that were sympathetic [towards the Allies]; they were to a certain extent.

Oil could inflict terrible suffering. "The oil caused boils and blisters to come out on the skin. My ears, all the backs down here were burnt and all around my neck. My head, aw Jesus, it was a horrible lookin' mess."

We were there a week or ten days, then all of a sudden she came to me this morning and said to us—the cook and I and one of the younger seamen—we have to go down to the village and meet with this French officer, and there's another commandant there and a couple more people from Dakar and all this bullshit. Dakar was only about five hundred miles from where we were on the coast. We got down to the building and we go inside. All of a sudden we see the doors are locked and guards are posted at ten-foot intervals and they're heavily armed this time. Then we happened to look up on the wall and the mate says, "Oh my!" There was a great big picture of Marshall Pétain and Laval was alongside of him. Then we knew where we were.

We seen a boat down at the dock when we came down the road, like a little tugboat, and that was heavily guarded. So they said, "You're goin' home, we're goin' to send you south," which would be about nine hundred miles to Freetown, or the nearest British port. We had landed about two hundred miles north of the British border. We all marched down with what clothes they gave us. I'm still in my bare feet. We got down to the boat and they made us go down in the hold. When they put the hatch covers on and put guards over it, we knew god-damn well we weren't goin' home. I think it might have been a four- or five-hour boat ride and we landed in a place called Conakry. It's an island off the coast of French West Africa and it's attached to the mainland by a causeway.

There were quite a few people on the dock, Frenchmen and natives. We're being marched up and I'm touched on the shoulder and told to move over there. Another feller is touched on the shoulder and told to move over. There were about four of us and we were being taken to a hospital because of the burns and boils. The rest of our crew was led up to another big building in the heart of town which was an empty school. I was in the hospital for about five days, so when we got out we were taken to the school with the rest of our buddies. And in that school were about another half a dozen ships' crews, mostly British, that had been picked up and put ashore there. There were three Americans and a couple of Aussies off of some ship.

We were distributed and put in one big room like a dormitory. You were given a poly ass [paillasse]—an old straw mattress—a couple of sheets and a frame bed. Then they give us a mess kit—a can and a mug with a little handle on it. That mug would be about a half a cup. You got three containers of coffee a day and a French stick of bread and then whatever their meal might be, could be rice and vegetables, could be potatoes, could be yams. Some meals they used to kill right in the yard if it was a sheep or a small animal—they'd do him right in the yard. Red Cross packages were very few and far between but they came. Now that family [from the plantation] used to come and see me every two weeks. They used to bring me cigarettes and fruit, but they couldn't come in, they'd have to hand it to me through the gate. So what we'd do is split it up between four or five guys.

We were there maybe from August until about October. We used to get out in the morning and wave sheets at the British reconnaissance planes [which] came over taking pictures. They knew we were there; you don't see a bunch of guys out wavin' sheets and flags for nothin'. The soldiers used to yell at us, but they never had a loaded weapon. Their guns were never loaded, but they could use those bayonets though. They had the old-fashioned First World War French rifle with a star-shaped bayonet. It started big at the stem where it went into the attachment on the barrel and it narrowed out that it looked like a little star. Boy, they knew how to use 'em.

One Sunday everybody was ordered down in the square; we were there a couple of hours. There were two French officers, one was a lieutenant, the other was a captain. A little police inspector was in charge with these two. We still had our three DEMS gunners with us and that's the first thing, they took them three from us. There were two German officers and as far as we knew they were Gestapo because of the old sign—the black leather coats and the black hats right off of TV. When I see that on TV, that reminds me so much of them two bitches. We could only surmise they took them to Dakar, of which there were a lot of British prisoners taken there.

We knew we couldn't get off the island. We had one guy they found in the jungle; he was gone for five days. He tried to make it on his own but he couldn't. The stories were gettin' around that there were lots of piranhas that swam where the causeway joined and that nobody, even these prisoners just doin' time, ever escaped. So what we used to do was go in town through the sewer and we'd hide behind the buildings and see the French officers and French people sittin' over in their open cafés with their women, drinkin', havin' a ball.

The school had washrooms outside for the kids. In each washroom you had a square of tile that would be about three by three, just a hole in the middle and two footprints—no seats. There was a flush box in the wall but it was hidden so only the chain would come out. When you'd pull on the chain you could watch it go and the sewer was big, you could crawl through it. The way the sewer was built was on a slant and you could come up through a manhole anywhere in the middle of the little village or go right through to the harbour. I wouldn't say it was spotless, you knew there was stuff in there, but it wasn't that bad that you couldn't go through it and come back. All we had done was put old pants on and stuff, and me being a youngster and in my bare feet, it didn't make much difference anyway. Two or three of us went through it, I don't know how many times. But the last time we went out we didn't get the chance to come back, we got caught. Then I got food taken from me and I was rationed and all this stuff, but the guys would never see you do without; they all got together and they'd share.

I had the hot house for four days. The hot house was a big shed with ten-foot sheets of corrugated metal formed into a box with no roof in an open end of the compound. The guys used to come by and be throwin' their bread over. Some guys would have bottles they could put their coffee into and they'd throw it over. I was eatin' good, but boy, that sun used to be some hot in the daytime. But the nighttime you'd near freeze to death; all I had on was a pair of shorts.

One thing you got to hand the British, I don't care what you say about them, they were pretty smart. They had what they call their prison committee. You knew some guy was stealin' your goods or you had problems or any information was brought to us by people who were pro-British or pro-American, you went to one of them guys. The word came to us that the invasion [of North Africa] was coming and that we were goin' to be moved. We got this from a guy who was in contact with Britishers in Freetown, I guess, or Cape Town. Everybody got all excited, we're all goin' home now, but we didn't go home. We were shipped another fourteen hundred miles inland to another big camp, a big tobacco plantation, in a place called Kankan.

In total it'd be around two hundred prisoners; that's the different crews. We were put into cattle cars and it took us, I think it was, a day and a half to travel it. You had two [French guards] in each car and this time their weapons were loaded. The stops we used to come to, the people in the villages knew there were prisoners being brought up and they would be there cursin' us, spittin' at us, throwin' stones, callin' us names and everything. These are French people now! We'd just ignore them. We weren't allowed out of the cars anyway unless you went to a washroom. To get out and crap you had about five guards on your back. Then the orders came: anybody that tried to run or escape would be shot.

We were interned in this big camp with another bunch of British seamen, also Frenchmen, Lebanese, a bunch of Syrians. They had been plantation owners and business people who worked in the different towns and picked up because of their sympathies towards the British and the Americans. They were there when we got there. In that camp there might have been around five hundred, that's all the different crews plus the civilians. The civilians, their people used to come every weekend in carloads with food and booze and cigarettes and everything, so they'd let us have it. Outside of our compound was a big native village. Those people used to bring us fruit and barter with us for cigarettes and stuff we used to get from the Red Cross. Sometimes they'd bring their French cigarettes and, geez, smokin' one of them, you'd be smokin' ol' tar paper.

We were in barracks-type buildings, maybe a dozen or so of these tobacco-curing buildings. The stockade fence must've been fifteen, twenty feet high, all pointed. You couldn't go to the outhouse unless you had a guard with you. We didn't do any work. All we done was sleep, eat and get fat and play cards. The guys were doin' all right except I was the only guy in that whole camp that still didn't have anything on my feet because my feet were only takin' a six and a half and all the boots the Red Cross used to send were army boots, size nine up. Now can you imagine running around? When I come back from overseas my feet were so hard in the soles that I could stand out there on a hot coal and it wouldn't bother me. The only way

I got a pair of shoes, there was a Red Cross nurse used to come to see us, mostly for guys who had malaria or dysentery, and she noticed me running around in my bare feet. I was as black as [the natives] were there anyways, so she didn't know if I was white or black. Anyway, when I started talking to her, she said, "There's two other Canadians in here too." These are two guys that were in school with us and I said, "Yeah, I know them." She said, "You've got nothing on your feet." "I can't wear any. What can I wear?" The next time she come up she had taken a pair of sandals with Cuban heels and cut them so I got a good pair of leather sandals 'cause she only had a small foot. After about three months runnin' around in my bare feet, I finally got somethin' on my feet.

The funniest thing was being in an outhouse and about a fifteen-foot snake keepin' you company. Their outhouses were built on mounds, they'd dig a big hole and put a straw hut over it. There was maybe a half a dozen built. I was into one and didn't realize until the next morning when these natives were all excited, running around the back between the outhouse and this big stockade fence, it was in the shithouse that I had been in the night before. We all gathered around, about a dozen of us, and here they had pulled him around and lopped his head plus maybe a couple of feet and that thing was still wigglin'. This great big, god-damn snake, it looked to me about thirty feet long; he was one big sucker, boy.

Well, then the fun started. I said, "I want him." A feller come over and said, "What makes you think you should get him?" I said, "Because I got more money than you got." We had been playin' cards. I got the skin for two thousand francs; a hundred and fifty francs to five dollars at that time, so you're lookin' at sixty bucks. They done it for me, stretched it and dried it. So in gettin' the skin for me they split 'im and they found three or four rabbits in him whole and I don't know how many yams they got out of him. That's how they caught him; he went to sleep after he ate. The natives said to me, "He old. He old. He old." That's why he was big, I guess. After about a week or so, the thing was all ready to cut into sections for me. I forget how many wallets and pairs of shoes and purses the guy told me he could make out of the skin. I had that until we were released and somebody stole it on me comin' back on the trooper, stole my whole kit bag.

The invasion started in October, and the Yanks and them swept right through Africa, cleaned them right out, didn't fool around. We were actually released in December of 1942. We had three weeks of freedom before the French would let us out because of transportation [problems]. We were demanding that they let us out because we were classed as political prisoners of war because we were civilians and all political prisoners of war were to be released immediately, which we weren't. That's when the

Britishers went berserk. We burned everything that reminded us of that camp. We burnt all the beds and about half of those sheds and we even had half the stockade down before we left. There were bonfires every night. All we'd do is sit around drinkin' hot cocoa. They [the guards] were there but they wouldn't interfere, just let us go.

Then it came time, they said so many could go in town, maybe fifty, where the canteens were. They would be taken in by an escort and then brought home. Jesus, when them Englishmen got in town, they cleaned everything. They raided their bars and there wasn't a woman safe on the streets. Some of them guys had been there since the war [started], a good couple of years. They come down from Timbuktu [Tombouctou], which was another big French prison camp during the war. You've heard the expression [Timbuktu], that's where it comes from. There was a big French prison camp in the French Sudan and up there they used to work, make them load sand, filling sand bags for battle placements and what not. How some of them got to the camp that I was in is because they were ill; a lot of guys had malaria, dysentery, beriberi and what have you.

Then it came word that we were goin' to be sent back to Conakry and from there to Freetown. On the way down there wasn't nothin' the Frenchmen could [not] do for us. Their homes were wide open, all kinds of booze, women, anything you wanted. Could have even slept with the mayor's wife. All the cigarettes, clothes, they were throwin' the stuff at us. That was comin' out. Goin' up was another story. When we got to Conakry we had five or six black guys from the West Indies, they were lookin' for the police inspector, the instigator of this whole shootin' match. If they'd 'ave found him they'd 'ave strung him up, [but] they didn't.

In the morning we were ordered to meet at the school, the same school that we had left, and we had to walk from there through the jungle maybe four miles or so. We were carryin' a few guys on stretchers that were sick. When we got to the opening it was clear on both sides; the road was about sixty feet wide, all gravel. They took us to the line, then the French officers with us met with their officers. The press were there with their cameras and a lot of bullshit, you know. One side was lined up with army trucks and soldiers and the other side was lined up with ATS girls, Wrens, army personnel, Red Cross nurses and tables. Each table had a different item of clothing–a battle jacket, battle pants, boots, socks, underclothes, caps. The next line of tables was food. Jesus, when the guys seen the food they went right berserk. And the next table down was kegs of beer. There was an Australian regiment there called the Springbucks and they were stationed in Cape Town and they were allotted to look after the POWs comin' down. We were all checked out by doctors right there.

Crews that sailed with different companies, representatives of their companies were in Freetown. I went to the Norwegian consul and they seen that I got passage aboard a troop ship, a Dutch trooper takin' back Italian prisoners and also a few Germans. I got back to Glasgow, Scotland, to the Norwegian consul, so instead of comin' home I got them to pay my passage to Liverpool, England. Once they paid my passage, I'm paid off, then I got to look for another job. When I got paid off, I was given six quid too, that's six English pounds. That was a pound a month for each month I was interned, and in those days a pound was worth four dollars and forty-some cents.

Within about eight months I was sunk twice and a POW. Both times I was torpedoed I was classed as DBS, that's a distressed British seaman, because we were still a British subject. The Canadian consul was supposed to look after me, but I couldn't go to the Canadian consul because I was with the Norwegians, so they would give me the extra quids to pay my board and meals. I was on the beach there [in Liverpool] for a couple of months workin' as a bartender. Then the next job I got was in a shipyard because I was waitin' for a ship home. I sailed with the Norwegians up until 1945. The *Germa* was the last one I think I was on. I was at sea when war ended in Europe. I paid off in Sydney [Nova Scotia] just after the day Halifax was rioted. The detectives picked me up the next day [in Halifax] 'cause I used to hang around with a gang of guys and we used to live down in that area. I had a brand new leather jacket that I bought in Sydney. These cops knew me 'cause I lived down in the slums, I was born there. Jesus, I'm walkin' along Barrington Street and all of a sudden, Wrrr! Two guys got out and grabbed me. I said, "Hey, what's goin' on here?"

One guy, Detective Spears, I went to school with him, said, "Get in this car, Thorne! Where'd you get that jacket?"

"What are you talkin' about, where'd I get the jacket?" I'm diggin' in my pocket. It just happened I had the receipt for a leather jacket that I bought at a men's store in Sydney. I said, "Why?"

"You see the mess around here?"

"Yeah. So what?"

He said, "And you weren't involved with any of these racketeers?"

"Not me, boy, not me." Son of a bitch.

Since I been home I fought both governments for forty some years, Norwegian and Canadian. When I first started fightin' this outfit, the Canadian government said, well, I didn't sail under a Canadian flag and I didn't pay income tax so I'm therefore not entitled to any benefits or anything from the Canadian government. And the Norwegian government would say the same thing because I was not a Norwegian national. So I had no claim to any benefits or anything from them. I even had to join their [Norwegian] union and pay dues, but yet when I applied for benefits I couldn't claim them because I wasn't a Norwegian even though I was to get what Norwegian seamen got regardless of what happened, but it didn't pan out that way. When I was torpedoed on their ship and held as a POW, they were compensated for the time that they were POWs, but I wasn't by their government after the war.

About every five years I'd write to the Canadian government and also the Norwegian government and I was still gettin' the same answers till one day I seen that Norway recognized Canadian merchant seamen and you will be decorated as such. Then the Canadian government recognized Canadian seamen in 1956, but all they would send us would be the medals, nothing else. Now that was another big fight, qualifications and all that garbage. Aw Jesus, I'm tellin' you, it's been pathetic.

Preston Ross

German-held prisoners of war were for the most part the responsibility of the various German military branches. Army POWs fell under the Wehrmacht, air force under the Luftwaffe, and navy, which included merchant navy, under the Kriegsmarine. Camps, or stalags, were built for each respective group. While many stalags were built in Germany to house army and air force prisoners, one main camp was established for navy personnel. This was Marlag und Milag Nord. Known by the Germans as "Siberia," it was located fourteen miles from Bremen near Westertimke–Tarmstedt.

I joined the merchant navy in 1939, right at the start of the war. I joined an English ship in Halifax called the *San Demetrio* for the Eagle Oil Company of London. They had quite a few ships, oil tankers, called the San boats. She was a new ship, just out a year. Diesel, sixteen knots, she was a big ship in 1939, 16,000-ton; same as a supertanker would be now. I was on her almost a year and she was commodore ship of every convoy that I made.

We run from South America to Scotland and London. We convoyed mostly from Bermuda, but we'd come to Halifax in the wintertime to convoy. I signed on for two years, but when we came back to Halifax the next fall I paid off sick; I hurt my back. That same ship, when she left, she got sunk four days out of Halifax, shelled, I guess, caught fire and broke in two. She burnt for two days. One half sunk, and the other half the crew took back to England. I knew the crew quite well because most of them were on all the while I was there.[11]

It's a big story to that. The fella that took my place when I got off in Halifax was an American and I can't remember his name. When the ship was [attacked], the ones in lifeboats that went back to the ship and took her in, he was the one decided they should do this. The highest survivor in rank was the second mate, his name was Hawkins. I was on watch with him all the while I was there. He was the one that took the ship in as captain. When they got in London they had quite a big party and presented the flag to the fella that took my place. He was a big hero in England for awhile. He got missing; they never heard tell of him. They found his little satchel with the flag in it, but I guess probably they never found out what happened to him. They could never figure out why he changed his name. He was calling himself Ross Preston, my name backwards. I wouldn't have ever known anything about this but it came out in *True* magazine. They wanted to know if anybody knew anything about it to let them know. They were trying to find out what happened to this guy, why he changed his name. A fella that was on her wound up, after being sunk four or five times on other ships, in the same prison camp that I was in and that's how I know all about the story.

I was around about two months ashore before it [my back] got better and then I tried to get in the Fleet Arm, the marine department of the air force. They had these crash boats that went fifty miles an hour. I passed the medical and they had no place to put us so we were just supposed to wait around for a couple of months until they got this boat that was coming over from England. We weren't supposed to go away because we had signed on and everything. While we were waiting we come across a job on a ship, the *A.D. Huff*, that was in Halifax shipyard. We went to the air force office and they gave us permission to make one trip. That one trip was a long one; that's the one I was on when we were captured.

She was an old American ship, a freighter that was chartered by International Paper of Montreal. She was a hard-lookin' old thing. She had a bomb dropped on her on the trip comin' here to Canada. One wing of the bridge was gone completely. They dropped two bombs on her. One didn't explode; the head of the bomb was still in her. It was there all the while I was there. I signed on as ordinary seaman. We went to Sydney and loaded a part load of steel and from there we went to Dalhousie, New Brunswick, and finished up with a load of paper and come back to Halifax for convoy. From there we went to London. We were in London while the blitz was on. That was early in '41. They flattened Coventry and scooped everything up, brought it up with barges and loaded it into the ship for ballast.

We were sunk on the way back, five hundred miles off Cape Race,

Newfoundland, around noon. The convoy had just broken up and we knew they were sinkin' other ships around because they were pickin' up messages, the SOS. They sunk us from ten mile away. They claim it was ten mile, I don't know. It was a battleship [cruiser] called the *Gneisenau*. The other was the *Scharnhorst*; she's more famous. The two of them operated together. Each one had a supply ship and the four of them were always in touch with each other.

They fired warning shots first. The captain gave orders to fire on them. One 4.7, and this was a 26,000-ton battleship with eleven-inch guns and eleven hundred of a crew. That was curtains right there. We had a navy gunner but he refused to fire. You could just barely see something; you could see the masts. You don't see much at that distance. We did throw a smokescreen over the side but that didn't make any more smoke than a cigarette. They gave orders for us to heave to and stop, but we just had a new captain, a Scotsman, and he was determined he wasn't going to heave to. He called the engine room to change the burners to try and get an extra knot. We steamed eight knots and she steamed about thirty. They fired warning shots, lobbed them ahead. Big guns like that, you'd see the flash first and then you'd hear the report. Then you'd just wait to see where they're goin' to land. It's not a very good feeling. Everybody was out [on deck] by that time.

We still kept going. Shortly after, they fired again. I was out on the foredeck ahead of the wheelhouse, not too far from where the shell hit. Right on the bow there's a windlass that you use for hoisting the anchor. It's quite a big chunk of metal, big drums and chains. The first shell hit the windlass and that went up in the air, I don't know how far, and all these big plates and phalanges and chains came rattlin' down on the deck. I ducked behind a hatch coaming.

We knew we were on our way so they broke into the bonded stores and took all the cigarettes, liquor and whatever was there and put in the lifeboats. We only had two lifeboats. While they were doing that, a couple more shells hit by that time. What they try to do is hit the radio room so you can't send out messages. They probably aimed for it first but were a little high. The next one hit a little lower than the first. Instead of hittin' the radio room it went just below that and hit the engine room and there was two fellers lost—the fourth engineer and an oiler. They hit the main steam line, I guess, and it was just like fog, so thick you couldn't see a thing, only felt your way. First thing the ship started to list.

I went to the lifeboat I was supposed to go in and that was gone, they had hit it. So I went to the one on the other side and it was gone as well. It was still hanging on the blocks down in the water. I just jumped out to the falls and slid down the rope. The ship wasn't goin' down bow first. The battleship come right up close range and sunk her with small arms. They fired a pile of shells into her before she sunk. We had rowed quite a ways. We set a course for Newfoundland, that's where we were goin' to row towards, but she come alongside and picked us up.

They searched you and whatever you had they'd take. They put us five decks down, all in one big place [with] hammocks. They had sunk ships before, there were quite a few aboard then, mostly British. It was in the afternoon they sunk us and that night [at] nine o'clock they sunk another ship, British. You were jammed up so much you had no room. The air was so bad you couldn't light a match; before the brimstone would burn, it would go out. I can't remember getting anything much except bread. They let us on deck an hour a day for air and exercise. The navy were as good as they could be, I suppose, they weren't bad.

Then we transferred from that battleship to the supply ship. We got sunk the twenty-second day of February and that would be a week later. There were about 250 on each one [of the supply ships]. The ones from the *Scharnhorst* went to the *Ulchmark,* and the ones from the *Gneisenau* that I was on went to her supply ship which was the *Ernland.* That was a rush job, it had to be; we didn't know why. It was as rough as any day I've seen at sea. That was quite a feat to transfer five hundred men on a day like that at sea with these little motor launches. There wasn't one lost or hurt bad. They were really good seamen.

I have no idea what part of the Atlantic Ocean that was, but it was in fairly warm weather so it wasn't too far north. We were on the supply ship for about three weeks. They were big ships, had five hundred of a crew, and near as I could tell they'd alternate crews on the battleship; they were all navy. They were tankers that carried fuel to supply the submarines or whatever; they carried airplane parts, food supplies, everything. Disguised; in the morning that ship would be buff and maybe by night or the next day all her superstructure'd be white. We used to have to work—paint, change colour; we used to have to help fuel the German subs, put the big hose out.

We were again in hammocks, but we were right up in the bow, right to the very bottom. There's where they had their cordite all stored for supplying the battleship. We had to move all that first. The German navy was good; they paid us I think forty finnings a day or something like that for working, then they'd sell us cigarettes. I can remember one thing that I thought was awful strange was soup, sweet soup with strawberries in and that sort of thing, that's a dish they had.

We landed in a little place called La Rochelle in France, not too far from Bordeaux. The captain came and made a speech. He told us that we'd be goin' ashore and we'd be under the army and we probably wouldn't be treated as well as we were there while with the navy. They had a bunch of buses there. We went from La Rochelle to the outskirts of Bordeaux in an old Foreign Legion camp where they kept us waiting to get organized to go to Germany. We only stayed there for ten days, which was a long ten days. It wasn't very good goin'. The weather was cold and miserable. We never had anything much to eat, turnip water. Anyway, we survived.

We went from there to Germany by train, five hundred of us, but there was twenty missin' time we got there; twenty jumped out. There was two off our ship got back. A feller by the name Eddie Shackleton from Saskatchewan, he spoke German, and there was an oiler, I can't remember his name, he spoke French. They were almost a year before they got home. We were 105 hours in that train and we never got out. They were passenger cars, wooden slat seats. They hit a few soup kitchens along the way; I can remember one in France and one in Holland, maybe one in Belgium. We got in Germany on a Sunday morning. I'm not sure of the name, but I think it was a little place called Bremervorde. We had to march from there to the prison camp we were goin' to, probably ten miles. That was my first march; we weren't very good at marching. We were walking up through the village and people would be sittin' out in front of their house on a lovely Sunday morning. You could hear them saying "English swine." They weren't real keen on seeing us, no.

Anyway we got to the camp; it was called Sanbostel. That was a big camp, forty-five thousand in that one. It was all divided up into different compounds–French, Dutch, navy, there were some women there, everything. I had an old Foreign Legion army coat. It was so heavy I could just about lift it. Used it for a blanket at night to keep warm. I wasn't there too long before there was a hundred of us picked. We didn't know where we were goin', they just took us. That was my second march, to the train station. There were a couple of boxcars there that said fifty men or eight horses, so they loaded us on those. The German officer could speak a little bit of broken English. Someone got brave and asked him where we were goin'. He said in his broken English, "You're goin' to Berlin to see Hitler." We didn't know if we were or not, so we piled in.

We went to a place called Wilhelmshaven on the coast. That's where the big German naval base is. There were four big barracks, so they put us in one of those, away up in the attic, I suppose you would call it, just rough. Back in the hammocks again. In the middle of the night there was an air raid. There was an air raid siren, you can imagine what they sound like when it's right over the top of your head there on the roof. Everybody come down and out pretty fast. They had to rush you from there, way down to the basement. You might be there for an hour or two, however long it lasted, until the all clear went, and then you'd go back. You might just get up five or ten minutes or a half an hour and it'd go again. That might go on seven or eight times during the night. They'd come and go and they'd come back again—what they called nuisance raids.

We found out after a day or two that we were there for interrogation. They'd take one maybe in the morning and one in the afternoon, maybe just one all that day, some days maybe three, some days none. I was one of the last ones to be interrogated. Take you down in nice quarters, cigarettes on the table. A big admiral would come in and ask you a whole lot of questions—where you were born, when was your birthday, what ships you were on, what damage did you see, different countries you had been to, all that sort of thing. It went on for hours, just the same as I'm talkin' to you now. They were right nice. First thing they'd try to trip you up and jump back and say "Where were you on your last birthday?" or somethin' like that to see if you were tellin' them lies. I couldn't tell them anything; they could tell me more than I could tell them. They could pull out the ship's registry and tell you all the ships Britain had, what they was doin' and where they was goin' to and everything.

Some of the captains, I suppose, they gave them a bad time. For instance, the captain of the *Huff*, the one I was on that wanted to open fire on them and wouldn't heave to, they gave him a bad time. They kept him in solitary confinement for I guess a couple of years. I only saw him once after that; I can't even remember his name to tell you the truth. If you wanted trouble you wouldn't have to step out of line very far before you get all kinds of trouble.

We were I think a month or so in Wilhelmshaven before we went back to Sanbostel. A room not as big as this, there would be about twenty-odd three-tier bunks. I worked on a few different jobs. We worked in the peat fields from six o'clock in the morning until six o'clock at night. You got a little bit of soup once a day. That was long hard days cuttin' peat, stack it up, dry it for fuel. It wasn't too long before they moved us again to Stalag 10/B [Marlag und Milag Nord]; that's where we stayed for the rest of the war. We had a long march that time, must have been twenty miles or so.

I was on the job of building camps and stretching barbed wire for a few years; *Draht Kommando*, that was the wire gang. There were about twelve to fourteen of us. In fact we built the whole camp they kept the Dieppe prisoners. I believe there was two thousand, pretty well all Canadians. All the barbed wire work we did; somebody else built the barracks. That was outside [my camp] a few hundred yards. Then there was another one, that was air force. We built quite a bit of that one too. That was only a few hundred yards again from the Dieppe one. There were three right close together; we were the first one there. There were eight thousand in the merchant seamen one.

When there wasn't that much to do we were on different jobs. One winter I was puttin' in power poles, diggin' holes by hand, not like you do now with an auger. A foot of frost in the ground; hit that with a big iron bar, might be a chip come off as big as your fingernail. We had to put them [poles] up by hand. What wood we had to use [for fires] we had to cut ourselves and

POW Preston Ross (second row, third from right).

carry in on your back. Two fellers would tie pieces of wood together in a bundle and carry it for half a mile. I wasn't very good at that; I didn't like that job. Some worked on the farms, cleaning up around the camp. When we'd be marchin' out on work gangs, we used to pick up coke alongside of the road that they had built the roads of; the same as gravel alongside of our pavement. If there were eight or ten guys, everybody'd pick up a piece and shove it in their pocket; we'd have enough to cook supper.

There is some good in every country, good and bad. Our boss on this wire gang that I worked on for a long while was one of the good Germans. If he could get a chance for us to get something—a few potatoes or something in our socks, coat, cap or wherever you could hide them—he would go ahead of us. He could only do it certain times. He knew the guards on the gate that we had to go in and out. He would go and tell them–I don't know what– but he told them something and we'd march through. You find a few good ones everywhere.

The Germans were great for mass punishment. Say something happened in one barrack, if they couldn't find out who did something–they wouldn't try very hard–they'd just punish the whole works. Sometimes you didn't have to do very much. A feller on this wire gang that worked with me, a little Englishman, I can remember we had a new guard one time, I guess he just didn't like the looks of the fella. The fella never said a word to him or anything, but he just up with his rifle and clobbered him in the shoulder with his rifle a few times. When they [the Germans] were wounded in the front line and they had to come back and maybe go in the hospital, be fixed up and maybe they couldn't go back to the front line duties again, they would give them this job of guardin' prisoners. Some of them were a little bitter, I suppose, probably for that reason, I don't know.

When we first went to that merchant navy camp we had all navy personnel for guards and they were the best of all. But they wouldn't leave them there long enough for you to get familiar with, maybe six months to a year. They would go and there'd be a whole new bunch come in. Might be the air force. The air force would go, the marines would come and maybe back to the navy again; they'd keep changing. To my estimation the air force were the worst and the navy was the best, army in between. That's the way I found it and I know a lot more did.

At one point, probably in the middle, about two years there maybe, they had an exchange of prisoners. Called everybody out to the parade square and we were there for hours and hours. The old commander would be in the middle of the square with his book, a blue book, and they'd call out a number. A long while later they'd call out another number. Nobody ever knew what this was for. I think it was a hundred and some odd altogether names and they just took them. We still didn't know for sure what was happening but they were exchanged for German prisoners. That was the blue book affair. We always waited and waited for the next two years for that blue book to come out again but that was the only time.

There were a few escapes but they never got very far, they always got caught. In fact there was one fella escaped, I believe, three or four times and in the end they took him away to some other part of Germany. The last great escape I think there was a couple hundred got out, but they were all glad to come back. That was right on the last of it and it was more dangerous to be outside than it was to be inside so they sent out messages for them to come back in, which they did.

They used to tunnel from underneath the barracks right out under the fence and come up on the outside. A lot of those British seamen had worked in mines in England and they knew how to tunnel. It's all sandy soil. In order to find something to prop up they used the bunk boards that were crosswise in the bunk. You could take one or two from each bunk and you wouldn't miss it; just spread them out. After awhile they were gettin' so scarce there'd be one board here and one board there, you didn't have enough to sleep on.

The Germans were bound they were going to stop the tunneling. You have a double fence with all kinds of wire tangled up in between the two fences. Then maybe ten or twelve feet each side of that you have a trip wire just so high. There's a guard in every tower with a machine gun, a rifle and searchlight. If you're caught over that wire they can shoot you. The only aspect of the tunneling I was involved in, in one end of the camp between the trip wire and the main fence, we had to dig a trench maybe eight or ten feet deep down almost to a point. I could never figure out when we started what it was for, but in the end we figured it was so they couldn't tunnel out, they'd end up in this trench. We never did get the whole way around the camp, only the one end, and that was the end of the war.

We got back to London one day before the war ended. They were flyin' out at a rate of a thousand a day to Brussels, then from there to London. That's the best part of your life—sixteen, seventeen. Six years I never saw lights at night except the two months I changed ships when I was home the time I hurt my back. Everywhere I was was blacked out, even when we come back in June 1945, that troop ship maintained blackout right up to Halifax Harbour.

I have no regrets. I wouldn't want to go through it again, I can assure you that and no one else would. It [veteran's status] should have happened long ago. It's far too late for us now. They're all in their seventies or more and they're dyin' off at a pretty fast rate now. There isn't too many left and there won't be after a few years.

Clyde Getson

I had seven brothers and four of us sailed on merchant ships during the war. One got killed, Fred; he was on one of the Imperial Oil ships that nobody survived, the *Victolite*. I went to sea in December '39; I was seventeen. Jobs weren't very plentiful then. I tried to go in the navy but at that time it was hard to get in, so I decided to go in the merchant marine.

In December 1940 I joined the *Canadolite*; my uncle was bosun on the ship and he got me the job as ordinary seaman. I never had no experience, I was just on two other ships before that. One was called the *H.H. Rogers* and the other was called the *I.C. White*, both oil tankers. Imperial Oil had them chartered under the Panamanian flag. I didn't make too many trips on her [the *Canadolite*]. I joined her in December and I got captured on 25 March. We made two trips to West Africa and our second trip we got caught.

We travelled without convoy down there. We unloaded our oil at Freetown and got orders to proceed to the Caribbean to pick up some more but we never made it. I think it was six hundred miles out of Freetown we got captured. A German raider, *Kormoran* her name was. They followed us from five o'clock in the morning till daylight around seven o'clock or 7:30. They had a big searchlight on us all the time. We didn't know what it was first till it come daylight. They signalled for us to stop, but the Old Man wouldn't, he kept on goin'. First thing, BANG!, a salvo across the bow and we still wouldn't stop. Then another one come. So after they fired seven or eight, the Old Man said, "I think we better stop. It looks like they're gettin' closer every time." And they were, every shell was comin' a little bit closer. She done twenty-five knots and we only done nine; we couldn't outrun her. So he said, "To hell with it, we'll abandon ship." They were shellin' all around us. Took to the lifeboats and just left her.

We figured the longer we stayed aboard they was liable to blow us out of the water 'cause we weren't gas-free or anything. If one shell would have hit that ship, that would have been it, we probably would have exploded same as the *Victolite* did. That's what happened to her. They sent out a message. They torpedoed her first, but they couldn't sink her. A submarine surfaced and they shelled her. When they sent out their message they said, "We're being shelled and on fire." They give their position and that's all, the radio went dead; that's when she exploded.

I was in the same situation. We started to row away from the ship and we got a long way away from her. We thought they were goin' to let us go; we weren't that far from land, six hundred miles. There was two lifeboats and we had charts and everything and the mates knew their navigation so we headed for land. They decided they had other plans and they launched a big steel motor boat and come and towed us back to the ship. In the meantime, other Germans boarded the ship from another boat.

When we got aboard we had to line up on deck. They searched us all and had machine guns trained on us. We weren't allowed to go in our cabins till they had searched the ship all over for weapons. If we had any we had to give them up. There were a few small arms—.22 rifles and stuff—but nothing big. Any kind of a knife you had to surrender to them too. They could all speak perfect English. They were in uniform. You had to be escorted everywhere; you had no freedom aboard the boat. We wasn't locked up, but there was always somebody patrolling.

We stood watches, we steered and they kept a Canadian engineer on watch in the engine room with them. They put time bombs in the tanks and we had to help. They wasn't goin' to let the Allied forces take her back, they planned to blow her up. If they couldn't have her, they wasn't goin' to let anybody else have her. That was rigged up to the engine room; they could set it to ten minutes or five minutes. They told us everything what they were going to do. They were going to give us so many minutes to get off the ship and they told us which lifeboats we could take if they had to blow her up.

We went on our own. She [the *Kormoran*] took off; I don't know what route they took. It took us three weeks from the time they captured us until we landed in Bordeaux, France. We only had another couple of hours and we'd have run out of fuel, we just made it. They put a big swastika on the flying bridge up on monkey island, draped it all over the top on account of when we went into France the German planes came out to meet us, so they knew it was a German ship. They tied her up to the dock there and they left us aboard, I think, one day. The first night they bombed the dock; we heard all this bangin' but we wasn't allowed on deck. The next morning we got up, three parts of the dock was gone. There was quite a few people got killed there. We were just plain lucky we were farther down.[12]

The next day they took us to a prison camp in France; it was only a small camp. They didn't give us a whole lot to eat. They treated us kind of bad, I think. There was more than merchant seamen in that camp when we arrived; there was army, navy, air force, we were all mixed up together. They only kept us there about a week and then they transferred us into Germany. We weren't allowed to carry anything, they took most of our good stuff. When we got in there they give us old stuff to wear, army stuff, mostly off dead people. None of it fitted. We didn't have too much clothing. First when we got there it was cold as hell. The Red Cross saved our necks. They supplied us with some good clothing after awhile. There was another camp right alongside this one; they were dyin' there like flies from starvation, malnutrition, being worked hard. They were droppin' dead.

There was three-tier bunks and the guy in the top bunk was right up against the ceiling, he only had enough clearance to get in. Boy, they was so crowded, there was about twenty-five in one room. That's a lot of people in one small room; there wasn't much room to move around.

They didn't interrogate us [in France], but they did when they got us into Germany. They interrogated pretty near everybody on our ship, individually. They didn't get no information out of us, you'd just make believe you were dumb, you didn't know anything. They asked me where we were going and who we thought was going to win the war and all this kind of crap. What did we think of Hitler and what did we think of Churchill and all kinds of foolish stuff. Yeah, they wanted to know what we thought of Hitler. Well, you daresn't say that you thought he was a bastard, you know, you're liable to get your head blown off. At that time, my geez, they were doin' some bad things, especially that first camp we were in, geez, they were bad.

We only stayed there [Sanbostel], I think, a year or six months, then they decided they were goin' to have a merchant seamen camp; all merchant seamen were goin' to be put in one camp [Marlag und Milag Nord]. We built our own camp; there was hardly anything there, we built it from scratch. Everything was prefab, it was all in sections; they went up fast. All they done was pound posts in the ground and build it on posts. It didn't take very long, I think we had it up in a couple of months. But there were a lot of prisoners, I forget how many were workin' there, three or four hundred. Every couple of days there was some more merchant seamen comin' in because they sank a lot of ships. It was quite big; I think once around the compound was a mile. When they used to bomb Bremen, the old ground used to shake; even Hamburg you could see the sky lit up different times, you could see the searchlights.

We had every nationality in the world in that camp. We even had some Russians in there. The Canadians were all in one barracks. It was quite a big building, I imagine a hundred feet long. Two-tier [bunks], I think there was only ten in a room. There was a big hallway right through it and rooms on both sides. We weren't allowed out of our barracks in the night after dark. You had a big can in the hall you had to use; there was two or three of them and the next day you had to dump that. If you went out after dark you could get shot or killed by a dog. There was one guy got killed in our camp. He staggered out after dark, half asleep, forgot about it, and he got shot. He was only a young feller too. The guard that shot him, they only kept him there a day after that, and they moved him somewhere because they were scared, I guess, the prisoners would kill him. It probably would have happened too. Boy, I'm tellin' you, after dark that place was pretty quiet. And when an air raid was on, then you really had to be careful, that's when they used to bring the guard dogs in.

You just had to be careful what you were doin'. I could have been killed one day. I kicked a young fella, a young German, in the ass; he was only about eleven years old. He spit in my face as we were marchin' out to work one morning. I stepped out of line and, geez, I give him an awful boot in the ass. This German guard came back with a fixed bayonet as if he was going to ram it into me. He could speak good English. "What happened there?" I said, "That young bastard spit in my face." "Get back in line," he said. If that would have been another guard, I probably would have been dead. I was some lucky.

You had some good guards. The majority of them was bad, but you struck the odd good one. The last couple of years they wasn't bad at all after they got all the young guards out of that camp. When we first went there it was all young guards, eighteen, nineteen years of age, and they were really rough on you. I don't know why but they were. I guess they were Hitler youth guys, most of them, and they had no idea, they thought for sure that Germany was going to win the war. When they captured us they said, "You won't be a prisoner very long, two or three months you'll be out of Germany, because we plan to win and it ain't goin' to take long to do it." Oh yeah, they were pretty cocky. But then after awhile they got all these older guards, they were really good. They had all the young fellas up to the front.

We never had much heat in the wintertime. We had a little stove but everything was rationed. We never used to have any heat in the nighttime because we used it in the daytime to do our little bit of cooking and makin' tea. We had to go to bed early or otherwise you'd freeze. Nine o'clock everybody had to be in bed. You had windows but they had shutters on them and they had to be closed every night. We wasn't allowed [to have lights on]. We didn't have very much bedding. The bunks were all wood, there was no such thing as a spring. We had a straw- or shavin'-filled mattress, but that wasn't very soft. We had one blanket under us and one over us, that's all. One guy to a bed. Lots of times you slept with your clothes on in order to keep from freezing. I slept with my boots on different nights to keep my feet warm. You'd wake up lots of times and the water would be froze in the room a couple of inches. But, geez, we survived.

There must have been twenty-five or thirty barracks, I guess. Every barrack had a hut captain; he was elected by ourselves. His duties wasn't too much. It was just the idea, you had a hundred men there in one barrack, you need a little discipline. He'd wake everybody up to get you out on muster to be counted. Your day would start around seven-thirty in the morning. Every barrack had to line up separate and be counted. You had to line up five in a row. The guards would come along and count everybody, then go out in the middle of the parade square and tell how many prisoners there was, how many was sick, how many escaped and how many died. That went on every day. You had to be counted twice a day.

[The hut captain's] job was to look after the rations and make sure the barracks was kept clean. He was in charge of makin' sure everybody got their right share of bread 'cause that was very important. Seven men to a loaf of bread, boy, you daresn't go off very much or you'd hear some cries from the prisoners. Seven men to a loaf of bread, I'll never forget that—*sieben mann ein brot*. Everybody had that down pretty good. Black bread it was. There was sawdust in it too, they used to find balls of sawdust into it.

We kept our barracks good and clean; we were spotless. We had a wooden table that had to be scrubbed every day. We used to use sand and water to rub that. Our room was always mopped up every day; everybody looked after their own room. Some of them did [get lice] but I didn't. There were so many nationalities; there were Egyptians, Arabs, those guys didn't keep their barracks very clean. That's where most of the lice and stuff was in the camp, strictly to those kinds of barracks. We had to keep ourselves clean, otherwise you could get all kinds of diseases.

[There was] a hospital right in the camp, a barrack made into a hospital, but they had nothing there, nothing to work with. They had no drugs. At times that stuff was there but it was in short supply, drugs were very scarce. If you got really seriously ill, like cancer, you really suffered because you had nothin' to kill the pain. They had a burying ground there outside, special for prisoners. The prisoners used to dig the graves. They had a wooden box and a little cross. Your prisoner of war number went into the coffin.

We had a dentist too. If you had a tooth pulled, you had no freezing. I had teeth pulled over there. Lord God Almighty, I'm tellin' you, I never screamed so much in my life. One guy had a hold of you in the chair and the dentist pulled. That's cruel, you know, getting teeth pulled with no freezing. But it was better than a toothache. After the pain was gone, but boy. An awful lot of people had that done over there. I'll never forget that.

They separated the officers from the men but they were in the same camp. They had their own barracks. They wore their stripes. They didn't get no more than we got. The only trouble was we had to work and they didn't. They got the same food as we did and they didn't enjoy it anymore than we did. We never seen a cooked meal all the time we were there outside of our Red Cross parcel—we used to cook up something ourselves, get a few potatoes. When the Red Cross parcels wasn't there we just had to eat the soup and the bread. I remember a good many times spewing my guts out, you know, food that was spoiled you couldn't hold it down. You get some of that rotten sauerkraut and fish soup together, and everything was spoiled, geez, that was horrible stuff. Most of the soup was so thin it was unbelievable, and you never got any good meat into it. It was horse meat or an old cow that had died, it was always bad stuff.

They had a big mess hall there. When you got your soup at dinnertime you could eat in the mess room if you wanted to, but not many people did; you'd always bring it to your room. We got soup once a day, a ration of bread, and we got a little bit of fish cheese and boy that was putrid stuff. That used to stink from the high heavens; not many people could eat it. You'd try to eat it but you'd spew it right up, it was that bad. They used to make jam out of turnips. Man Jesus, it was horrible stuff.

You'd get used to it. You had to live on it or else. It'd weaken you down after awhile, then you conserved your energy. You rested a lot, go to bed early; you knew how much you could do. When you were gettin' the food you could see a big difference, but when food was scarce everybody's activity wasn't very much, you didn't see many people walkin' too much. I don't think the home guard got a hell of a lot, the guys that were lookin' after our camp; their rations didn't seem to be too strong.

The Red Cross saved our lives. There would have been a lot more people die there if it wouldn't been for the Red Cross. Most any prisoner will tell you that; I don't care where they were, they'll tell you the Red Cross saved their lives. If I ever win a lot of money I'll give them quite a bit. Every prisoner that was there got a Red Cross parcel, it didn't matter what nationality he was, but a lot of prisoners didn't have as much as we did. The American prisoners seemed to do very good because they seemed to be well organized.[13]

There was two different food parcels, the British Red Cross food parcel and the Canadian. The Canadian was really the best. You got a can of powdered milk, some of those big round biscuits, a package of processed cheese, a can of sardines, a can of salmon, a can of bully beef, a small package of prunes or raisins, a bar of soap, tea and a little bottle of decaffeinated coffee. You got them every two weeks if they were available. They [the Germans] used to keep a lot of them, but there were so many being sent, we still got quite a few of them.

Red Cross didn't send cigarettes, that's one thing they didn't, they sent strictly a food parcel and a clothing parcel. They [cigarettes] had to come from different organizations in Canada, and the Canadian Legion used to send some too. There was a clothing one that was only allowed to be sent every four months. You'd get socks, mittens, dungarees, chocolate bars. There was only so many pounds they were allowed to send. It wasn't a whole lot of stuff, but it was nice to get a pair of dungarees. We got [boots] from the Red Cross, but most of them didn't fit you. I wore a pair all the time I was there, but I never had a shoe to fit—too big.

Our parents could send a clothes parcel every four months [actually two months], but a lot of them didn't get through. I lost an awful lot of them but some did [arrive], which was a big help. They could send so many chocolate bars in the clothing parcel, but they wasn't allowed to send anything else. They were allowed to send towels and facecloths in the one from home. Not all the time we could get these things, but when they come in regular we were livin' pretty good. There was one time over there we never had any Red Cross stuff [for] six months. We had to live on the German rations and, boy, that was grim. Everything was rationed, a little bit of this and a little bit of that.

Soap was a precious thing over there. We used to get ours through the Red Cross and hoard it up. Boy, we used to get some good buys from the German [farmers] with the soap; that was a good tradin' thing. You could get a pretty good knife if you wanted it, a half a dozen eggs if you could get them in. Their soap over there was hard stuff; I don't know how the hell they ever washed with it. We tried different times. We couldn't get suds out of it, whatever the hell it was made out of. Chocolate bars were another thing, and cigarettes were lousy, terrible. You could even get a bottle of booze too if you had enough things to dicker with. We used to buy even from the guards, mind you.

They'd come around and get you to go to work. You were doin' all kinds of things. Harvest time you'd help get the crop in. Then we helped to build a rifle range. That was illegal, we wasn't supposed to do that. The Geneva Convention says you're not allowed to help the enemy, but we had no choice, we had to do it. They made us dig airplane ditches so British planes couldn't land. They were zigzagged, quite deep—three or four feet—and they'd be quite long. Not every field [had one], just some of them. Then we unloaded coal at the railway station. The village we were in was called Westertimke, it was only small. Most everybody around there farmed. I worked on a lot of farms.

I worked all the time I was over there. I went outside the camp every day pretty well. Anytime there was work I used to volunteer to go out. If they called for a hundred volunteers and nobody'd step out, they'd just start picking you. I stayed back one time, I wouldn't volunteer, and they picked me, so I said after that, well shit, when they call for volunteers I'm just goin' to step out 'cause they're goin' to take you regardless.

Sometimes you could get a couple of eggs in if you were lucky. They [the farmers] would give it to us. The majority of them were good, they didn't like the war. One guy was a Gestapo—one of the guards told us that—and you couldn't get anything from him, a bastard. You could always steal stuff and bring in. The guards that were with you might be good, they'd say help yourself, but when you got to the gate, you'd have other guards and some of them would be right strict, you wouldn't get anything in. But lots of times we'd get through. You had secret pockets everywhere or you thought you had secret pockets. You had them in the sleeves of your army great coat or your pants. Every time they'd search so many; some guys would get caught and other guys would get through. They didn't punish you, just dump the stuff out. Jesus, you used to get piles of potatoes that high.

In the summertime you worked about nine hours, but in the winter you wouldn't work that long. Sometimes you used to go out and bring in wood for the camp, but then they cut that out after awhile. I don't know why; I guess one time quite a few escaped. That was tried several times and some of them got out. It was a pretty hard place to escape from. The only way was through a tunnel. I don't think anybody ever made it back out of that camp, they'd get captured after a day or so. Some of them was loose one time, I think, for a week. They used to punish them a little bit but not too much. They'd put them in solitary confinement for awhile. They put them in a special punishment camp for that, then bring them back into camp afterwards.

There was one guy on our ship, Roy Shaw, was in there three months. He used to write a paper every week. They caught him with his typewriter and everything. I don't know where he got it from; somebody smuggled it in for him. He had some pretty nasty things wrote in his newspaper about the Germans. He was tellin' the truth but they said it was propaganda. He got away with it for quite awhile. They took him into court somewhere in Germany but he got clear somehow. He was really scared, he thought they were going to kill him but they didn't. They put him in solitary confinement. I'm tellin' you, when he come out of there he didn't look very good.

Every once in awhile, about every six months, every barrack would be searched and they'd find an awful lot of stuff. One day they searched for eight hours; we couldn't get into our barracks. And you wasn't allowed to roam around, you had to be lined up. You didn't have to stand at attention, but you had to stay in one spot. You weren't even allowed to sit down. That was in the summertime—good job. They couldn't find everything, they tried their damnedest, they'd find a lot of stuff but they couldn't get everything. You take when you got three or four thousand prisoners in one camp, boy, you got some smart people. They were looking for arms and stills. Oh God, yeah, there were a few of them. They used to find an awful lot of them because they were hard to hide.

There was one in our barracks. It wasn't hid, it was just in the room. They found that. The guy that had that was a Canadian from Alberta. Nobody would say whose it was. They didn't punish anybody for it, just smashed it up. We used to get prunes and raisins in the Red Cross parcels and a lot of people didn't like them, so they'd divide them up and get quite a bunch that way. Or you'd trade somethin' that the other guy didn't have for the raisins or prunes and that's how you'd make your booze. You'd use potatoes too. They used to make some pretty good stuff in there. The only trouble is, it's a wonder we didn't get poisoned from it because most of the stuff we were using was tin and it's not the best thing to make a still out of; it's supposed to be copper. I don't know where it used to come from. I guess out of the Red Cross cans and stuff. I don't know how they ever got it soldered together like they did, I could never figure that one out. I imagine there used to be fifteen or twenty of them. They would never tell you when they were goin' to make a search, just come in on you. Some of them [guards] caught 'em right in the act one night makin' it, but they wouldn't say a word. No, they wouldn't drink with us.

We didn't have too much entertainment; you had to make your own. You could visit any barracks that you wanted to. They had a canteen there but they never had anything in it. We got paid when we worked–it amounted to forty-five or fifty cents a day–but we could never spend our money because there was no place to spend it. We used to gamble with it, play poker in the evenings and Sundays. Everybody wasn't out working. There'd only probably be a hundred, maybe three hundred at the most, out at one time. [The rest] were just loafing around the camp doing nothing, just walking, playing rugby or football or baseball. They used to have boxing matches. We had a place where we used to play sports, a big field all barbed-wired in. That was right past the camp; there was a gate and at nighttime that was closed.

I used to play baseball; I was on a team. We played for about three years, I guess. Once the American prisoners started comin' in there they were the

"It was a good pastime, it took your mind off the camp and we had a lot of fun. Nobody took it real serious. The German guards used to watch; they enjoyed it."

Team Canada: (front row, L-R) Lawley, Arsenault, A.K. Spencer (Mgr.), Smokey Dennis, Gordon Olmstead; (back row, L-R) Tache, Morin, Legendre, Assaf, Clyde Getson, Bro. Lavallee.

ones started the baseball. They got organized and got all this stuff; we had baseball bats and uniforms. I'm tellin' you, the Americans were really organized. I don't know if it was through the Red Cross [it was the YMCA]; you had gloves, masks, you had everything that a baseball player needs. As soon as they got over there they wasn't long gettin' a baseball game goin'. We had leagues formed. We had New York; I used to play for Boston. I got a diploma for playing. I had three of them–runners up one year and the championship one year. One guy, he was an English fella, he made all these diplomas. They were well made too. It was a good pastime, it took your mind off the camp and we had a lot of fun. Nobody took it real serious. The German guards used to watch; they enjoyed it.

We used to get some [reading material]. You could write so many letters–little cards–a year. The letter was only one page; it folded up. The Germans had to censor all these letters before they left the camp. When my parents would write, sometimes you were a long time getting them. They were censored on both ends. On our end they used to black them out and the

Germans used to cut them out. My parents didn't know a thing about us for three months. They had a picture in the Halifax *Herald* about us—"Missing and Presumed Dead"—I got my name on the front page.

The last year went quick, especially after they made the invasion, because our hopes were really up then. But until that happened it was still touch and go. We knew when the invasion started that it wasn't goin' to last very long. We had radios in the camp; they weren't allowed but they couldn't find them all. We knew [about the invasion] even before they [the Germans] announced it. Then they really give us strict rules. Anybody tryin' to escape after the invasion was on would be shot on sight.

They liberated us in the middle of the night, just two weeks before the war ended. We were in a crossfire. The British were shelling one way and the Germans were shelling the other. We were all dug in. The Germans told us there'd be some fighting going on around there, they said you want to prepare yourself for safety. They give us a bunch of shovels and stuff so you could dig your little trenches if you wanted to, or you could stay in your barracks, it's up to you. Some of the shells dropped pretty short. There were no direct hits but there was a lot of shrapnel that come in.

We got liberated by the Scots and Welsh, the 51st and 52nd Welsh Guards I think they were called. They had wire cutters and come right through, they didn't come around in the gate. They were fierce. They were hollerin', "You're liberated! Get out of your trenches!" We couldn't believe it, we couldn't believe it. We slowed 'em up quite a bit. They could have fixed them off a long time before that if it wouldn't have been for the camp, but they didn't want to kill any of us. They [the German guards] were scared to death. They didn't have their rifles loaded. That night they knew what was goin' on. See, they were all pretty old guys compared to the guys that liberated us; they were all young men.

We was free, we could go outside the camp, but they told us where we could go because they were still fighting only a couple of miles from the camp. There were some snipers around, hid out in old barns and buildings. It was dangerous to go too far. We went out around the village, stole cars, motorcycles, bicycles, whatever we could get ahold of and drove around. Geez, it was wild around there for a couple of weeks. We had all kinds of movies right away, good food, drivin' around in tanks, we had a ball there for awhile, kept late hours, didn't get much sleep.

Those people [villagers] were all hollerin' and wavin', they were glad it was over. They couldn't believe it, they were really happy. They didn't harm any of those people. They wanted to know how we were treated and if the civilians treated us rough they wanted us to point them out, but most of them didn't so we couldn't tell them that.

They sent us home to England the day the war ended. Not everybody got home that day, but I did. I arrived in London three o'clock in the afternoon on 8 May. I weighed 100 pounds and I weighed 160 when I got captured, so I lost some. We went back with the clothes we had and when we got to England all that was burned and they outfitted us with new. We were in a convalescent place just outside of London and we stayed there quite awhile. We had to go to Liverpool to come back to Canada. I come back on a Dutch trooper, *Volendarn*, with a lot of prisoners, war brides, a lot of army, and landed in Halifax. All my family was there—my mother, father, sisters, some brothers, someone from Imperial Oil—we had quite a reception. Everybody was glad to be home. I got home in June, and in January I went back to sea on one of the Imperial Oil tankers.

I wouldn't want to do it over again but, you know, you learn a lot through it, you really do. You appreciate life more, I think. A lot of people have it so easy all their lives that they take everything for granted. For awhile we had some doubts, you always do, especially the first couple of years, you couldn't see where they were makin' much progress. At times, especially when the Red Cross parcels wasn't comin' in, it used to be kind of bleak, gloomy. You could see the difference on people's faces, I'll tell you that, they were a different people altogether. You really appreciate life more when you go through something like that. I certainly wouldn't want to go through it again; I don't think any of the rest would. It's part of your life. At certain times you can black it out, but then it'll always come back.

Ray Swinemar

Before the war I went as mess boy, then fireman, on Imperial Oil ships. War broke out and the *Canadolite* was the one I wanted to get on, that was deep-sea. Oh yeah, young and full of piss and vinegar. We were down in Africa I don't know how many months, from Aruba, Dutch West Indies, to different parts of Africa, back to Aruba, Venezuela, up the Caripito River, having a great time oiling up the different navy boats. The Germans wanted us bad, we were supplying the navy. We loaded into a Norwegian whaler they had for a supply tank so when the navy come in they'd fuel up from there. If it wouldn't be for us, how would the navy keep goin'? The navy couldn't do nothing without us. But we made one trip too many from Aruba to Africa. On our way back from Africa that's when the Germans got us.

It was an armed raider. We were goin' towards Aruba and they were goin' the opposite way. It was about daylight. She was all lit up like a Christmas tree when she went by us. We thought it could be anything, a neutral ship. Nobody every thought that, hell, that's a German raider all lit up. They fooled everybody. After they just about got out of sight they turned around and come back. They took our captain, chief engineer, wireless operator, and our gunner with them. They had their own captain, wireless operator, their own everything; they had seventeen men on her, they call it a prize crew. The crew was versed on what to do because that ship had German engines into it; it was built in Germany.

We took her into Bordeaux, France, and they bombed hell out of us in there that one night we stayed on her. The British were bombin' hell out of France then. Jesus, there was shrapnel all over the deck everywhere. You talk about bombs; boy, they were droppin' 'em, but they didn't get us. They put us in a camp there with a lot of other prisoners, just barbed wire all around us. They took us from there and put us on a train to Holland to Germany. I don't know how many days we were on that, four or five maybe. I remember when we were comin' through Holland the train stopped. There was water running out of like a mountain and a woman come with a bucket of water. The guard hit her with the butt of the gun and the bucket of water went flying. That wasn't good, that was cruel. By the God Almighty, that's the first startin' that I seen that was really bad, the way they treated them people in Holland.

They took us to a place [in Germany] called Sanbostel; it had another name. Nothin' there—a big barracks, no bedding. There were more prisoners—a lot of Yugoslavian army—oh God, there were hundreds of them. They give us something, I think it was water and sauerkraut in a bucket. Geez, nobody felt much like eatin' there, I'll tell you. As far as eating goes there was nothin' to eat. They made us take everything we had off; they were goin' to give us different clothes and delouse us and all that. They turned on a sprinkler system, oh boy was that cold, and when we come out they just threw clothes out to you. They were old army clothes, could have been Yugoslavian, Czechoslovakian or Dutch or whatever countries that they took. And they were full of lice. In all the seams of the legs, in the crotch, you could see little white eggs and lice. A pair of riding britches is what I had. Then I traded with another guy who had a god-damn big pair, too big for me, but you just kept trading until you find something that fit you. They give us a new pair of shoes, British army shoes, and whether they fit you or not, it didn't matter.

From that one camp, Sanbostel, we marched into this other camp, Marlag und Milag Nord. There were thousands of prisoners in there. That's where I spent the rest of my time, roughly four years. We marched all day. We had changes of guards, there wasn't one bunch that took us right through; they got tired. There was lots [of prisoners] that didn't quite make it, they fell out, and you never heard of them no more. Whatever the hell happened to them,

I don't know. We all made it, every one of us got there.

You were in this big campground, all barracks, I don't know how many, probably seventy-five anyway. They had an awful lot of Englishmen. That's where they captured a pile of prisoners, on the English merchant boats. The only bedding we got would be something from the Red Cross, a blanket, or whatever the hell you could get. Red Cross did send us battle dress—pants and jackets. A lot of us had army coats.

When I went in I weighed around 132 pounds, I remember that pretty well, but when I come out I was a skeleton; yeah, pretty thin. We got three slices of bread a day, hard bread. That's what you'd get a day, that's it. Now and then they had what they call a meal; it was only soup. But Lord God, it was nothin', just water and some potatoes into it! Oh geez, I don't know how you could ever describe it. Nobody ever bothered with it very much. They never had enough for their own, never mind givin' it to the enemy. I would say you were classed as a different person than the army or the navy. They knew you weren't fightin' men, you weren't out to fight and kill.

The only thing that saved us was the Red Cross sending parcels into us. Wouldn't 'a' been for the Red Cross, we'd never made it, no possible way. There'd be a little package of tea, enough to make maybe eight or ten cups, sometimes there'd be a little can of cheese, a bar of soap, cookies, crackers or somethin' like that. Sometimes there'd be a chocolate bar if you were lucky enough to get it, if they didn't open it and take it. We don't know how much they took but they got some of it. There was times they'd even take your soap and take their dagger and smash the soap all to pieces to see if there was anything into it. Well, what the hell could be in it? But they done it anyway. There'd be a can of Kam, meat, powdered milk, sometimes a little sugar—a little bit of everything like that. Tobacco, now that came through the Canadian Legion.

You'd hear there's some Red Cross parcels comin' and there's cigarettes comin'—we'd get the wire somehow or another—then we'd hear there was a bomb and it blew everything all to hell. Then we'd say, aw, that one was gone. See, there was steady bombin' all the time. When a bomb dropped, it shook everything. We could tell they were close [but] nothing came in the camp. They knew where we were, I guess, pretty well. The British come over and bombed day and night, night and day right over our heads. God!

I didn't, but a lot of them used to play football or baseball or some damn thing. There was lots of little things goin' on for those who felt like doin' somethin' like that on a weekend, but I never enjoyed anything like that. There was a lot of us that didn't. Sit around and do nothin'. There was a lot of it, just sit around thinkin' you ever goin' to get out of this place? Or you goin' to live tomorrow or the next day? Or is a bomb goin' to land? There's lots of things went through your mind. I'll tell you, there was a lot didn't make it. A lot of them went crazier than me. I'm not goin' to say no more.

Yep, they had doctors in the camp. I had my appendix taken out right in that camp and there was no anesthetic. I was cut open here, took my appendix out through the hole, put them in a little bottle and give 'em to me. I still got them. I was lookin' at them about two months ago. How do you like that for apples? But I forget that, I ain't goin' to tell you about it. I couldn't sleep last night thinking about things.

Daylight in the morning they'd get you out on parade and count everybody. You didn't have a name, just a number. They'd just call out your number. Do I remember? 93610. Good God, I can't forget it. Every day you had your farm work to go to. Everybody didn't work because everybody couldn't, people were too sick or too tired or hurt or old. They'd call your number and you'd fall out. They'd name different farms, if you're goin' plantin' or harvesting or making hay. No problem to learn the language, you had to learn as much as you could if you were out workin'. Some people were stubborn and wouldn't learn, didn't want to learn, but a lot of us, every word we heard we never used that word hardly at all in English then. When you learn to say work—*Arbeit*—and you learn to say farmer—*Bauer*—and you learn to say potato pickin' or potato diggin'—*Kartoffel wählen*—you didn't forget it. You had your Saturdays and Sundays off as a rule, not always, but you never worked on Sundays.

Go out from early in the morning until late at night, whatever time you come back home. Walk [to the farm] with a guard, maybe sometimes two guards. You got the guard standin' back there watchin' you [work], maybe one that end and one the other end with the gun. There was no point in escapin'. Where the hell would you escape to? There was no point in goin' unless you were a German or you speak German fluently and you had a German uniform because everybody had a uniform, everybody was in the service. You just couldn't go walkin' around.

Out working on the farms, sometimes you could steal a few potatoes or whatever if you were lucky. With a farmer you could trade if the guard wasn't watching; you had cigarettes or some soap. If you were on a good farm they'd give you a slice of bread and maybe a bowl of bean soup, if you had a good farmer. Some of them were no good. I mean you're just a pig and that's it, you're the enemy. Maybe you get on a bad one and maybe his son was shot and his house was blew up or his father or mother or sister was killed, why you are not very popular. You English pig. You're the enemy, why give you somethin'? You killed my mother and father and blew my cousin up. We were all English pigs; we weren't Canadians or whatever, you were just an English pig. *Engländer Schweinehund*, that's what they called it.

They [the German guards] couldn't be friendly, they might wanted to be but if they.... There was some of them we know could speak English but they wouldn't, they weren't allowed. They didn't put their arm around you and say it's too bad or this and that, you know. They were scared of one another more or less, they didn't know who was Gestapo—you couldn't tell—so they wouldn't take chances. You could see the older fellers in uniform, we'll say forty-five, fifty, sixty years old, they knew the score, but the younger god-damn saucy things—I got a smack in the mouth, knocked my teeth out, split my lip, with the butt of a gun. We were out diggin' potatoes, wasn't diggin' fast enough and just looked at him the wrong way and bang-o. Didn't take very much, you had to be careful. I could have took him and I could have tore the arms right off of him but you daresn't. Bang, that's the end of you. When you catch on, you just don't do those things. A few of them got bayonets stuck into 'em, not kill 'em, but into your arse, make the blood come.

Two or three times in the wintertime we had what they call a wood gang; you go out in the woods and pick up pieces of wood to bring in to make a fire in your stove. They had like a little square stove, nothing heated it. You never had nothing to burn really. The clothes you had on, that was your heat. You don't take your pants off there and hang 'em up or somebody'll have 'em right quick.

[The toilets] were in a great big place maybe fifty feet long and twenty-five or thirty feet wide. There was holes in the concrete floor; some of them had like a stall in between and you just squat. It had a place underneath, like a tank under the whole length of the building and that had to be cleaned out. That was another good job—Smelly Nelly. That had to be hauled by hand; oh boy, that was a good one. I never had to. Certain ones were picked and they called it the *Strafe Bande*, a punishment gang. If you happened to step out of line one way or the other, okay, that was your job and they made sure you got it too. You had to take that and haul it out over the farmers' fields; that was the very best of manure that was. They'd pull a lever as you're goin' with it and it used to spray like. A great big, big tank, same as you would use here for cleaning the septic tanks. Just four wheels and you pull it like a wagon. They had no gas to do that with, that was manpower. Oh, that was punishment. By God, everybody hoped they'd never get on that, down underneath in there, right inside, uuugh.

It was a holiday camp the last goin' off; we'll say at least the last six or eight months, you were just a prisoner, it got fairly good. When they took France and Holland, they knew damn well their goose was cooked, that they were on the losin' end of it. It was hard goin' but they weren't so cruel, there was nobody givin' us big orders, there wasn't too much goin' on.

When the army released us, the war was still on, it went for about three weeks after. The Germans didn't quit, they fought right in their backyard. We were about three days before they got us. We could hear them comin' and we could even see them way off through a big field, you could see the tanks. The Germans were firin' that way and we were right in the middle of the battlefield. Well, you just dig a little hole and get into it, you had to lay low. In the morning they made their big drive and come right down through and mowed down the fences and barbed wire and freed us. Well, they kept right on going. There was some of us went right along with them, about nine of us.

I went right into Bremen. Four of us got a car; no trouble to get gas from the boys. I think I was the only one could drive. We had a lot of fun then, we were getting fat, we had a lot to eat then. Take whatever you want. We were young, you know, had a great time. There was a lot of that goin' on. We loaded up with kegs of schnappes, whiskey and stuff and come back to our camp again. We didn't bother with a bottle, we had kegs. Oh man, everything you wanted.

They said, "Now stay right here in your barracks and when we get around to it we're goin' to take you back to the airport and fly you back home." Well, a few of us got all drunked up and we missed our airplane and never made Scotland. She was an old bomber or somethin' or other, she was full of holes and everything else. She landed somewhere in the English Channel, we heard. Them boys didn't make it. I said we were lucky we didn't get that one. So then there were a few of us got a ride, and we landed in Scotland. We stayed there for three or four days, then they took us from there on a boat and train and we landed in Liverpool, England. We were in Liverpool for a couple of weeks, eatin' good then all that time, then we got a troop ship—one of those big liners—in Liverpool and landed here in Halifax.

I don't know, I'll tell you right now, I think I'd be a big coward if I had it all over to do again. It was too risky. It still bothers me today. The only thing that did save me and a few was being young; I was twenty years old, strong and able. Look at the pile that didn't make it, my God.

Edison Yeadon

I was walkin' along Water Street [in Halifax] and some fella come along to me and he said, "How would you like a job?" I said, "Sure." I was just seventeen. I joined the ship in October [1941], the SS *Aust*, Norwegian. She was a tramp freighter and was loaded with pig iron from India going to the

British Isles. I got on her and the next day we took off for Sydney for coal and from there went across to England just as if there was no war at all. Five-knot convoy, we could probably walk as fast as the convoy went because we were just old tramps.

We went to Newcastle-on-Tyne to put a new gun on her and new cabins, so I was there for about two months in Newcastle in dry dock. We left there, it must have been in January, February, and we sailed to Loch Ewe in Scotland. We were comin' across the Atlantic and off of Newfoundland we ran into submarines at night. This big flare went up for the convoy to disperse so that they couldn't get us all and that's what we did. We got hit by somethin', it must have been a dud torpedo, that loosened up a few plates of the ship and we had to go in dry dock in New York when we got there. We loaded up with tanks and army trucks, oil and all that stuff—a general cargo of war supplies. Sometime in March '42 it was, we left for India. No convoy, travelled all alone from New York, no escort.

We were supposed to go in St. Lucia, but there were submarines in the St. Lucia Harbor so we went to the American port of St. Thomas, Virgin Islands, picked up our coal there, went to Parnaiba, Brazil, and we bunkered there again. Ten days out of Parnaiba, just south of the equator—Good Friday, April 3, 1942, around noon—this sea plane dove down and took our aerial so the wireless operator couldn't do anything. Then the raider [the *Thor*] in the distance started shellin' us and the sea plane machine-gunned the decks. The gunners tried to get to the gun; the big gun[s] was put away 'cause they didn't figure there was anything down there.

She was shellin' us, but I don't think any of the shells hit the boat, but they were landin' around. We just gave up because there was nothin' we could do against an armed raider. The captain said, "Abandon ship," so we abandoned ship. There was four lifeboats, I believe. Everybody got off, about forty; there was no casualties whatsoever. When they saw us abandon ship, they ceased fire. The only person left on board was this radio operator [Ozzie Collett] and he couldn't swim. He was up on deck and he jumped in the water with a lifebelt on and managed to get to the lifeboat I was in. He kind of says I saved him, but he was scared to death because he couldn't swim. I pulled him aboard the lifeboat. He still mentions that in his letters.

We were rowin'. Our lifeboat went down just below the water line [from bullet holes]; it didn't completely sink. We climbed into another lifeboat and we rowed and rowed. I guess we were in the lifeboat about an hour and this big ship [the *Thor*] comes up. We climbed up aboard that and they stripped us off and made us shower before we went below decks. They gave us hammocks, and every time they went into action they'd lock us up. They come up on this British ship goin' from Cape Town, I think, to somewhere in South America at night and turned the searchlights on her and blew her out of the water. The reason for that was they used their radio. I guess quite a few [were] lost there. They went and picked them up. They already had two or threw crews on board; I think that was the last ship they picked up.

We went from there and headed south. It was rough wherever we were goin'. They'd allow us on deck for thirty minutes a day for fresh air, machine guns pointing at us so we wouldn't try to do anything. The Germans weren't too bad. I mean they didn't give you anything in excess because they didn't have that much themselves, I guess, but most of the food we were eating was off our own ship anyway. I was on the raider a month. Then we went up into the Indian Ocean and they transferred us at night, just at dusk, in these rubber rafts to the German supply ship.

We laid around there in the Indian Ocean for a good month or two, I guess. The raider went off and captured this passenger ship, the SS *Nankin*, from Australia. She had all kinds of food; I guess she was taking mutton to India. She carried around a hundred passengers, I guess. They transferred all those people to the supply ship, women and children; I think a baby was born on the raider. After laying around the Indian Ocean, we took off for Japan. I remember going through the East Indies and Java and those places, but we weren't allowed on deck going through there. Oh yeah, steaming hot. We got into Japan and they transferred us from that supply ship to another supply ship, still a German, and we were on that one for about three weeks, I think, before the Japs decided to take us or had a place for us, I don't know what it was.

It's been bothering me. The international law states that civilians are not supposed to work. We're supposed to be civilians and the Germans turned us over to the Japs for slave labour. They lined us all up on the dock at Yokohama and we had to bow to this Japanese colonel or whatever he was, some kind of officer. That was our first experience of bowing. There must have been some kind of a speech, but I can't remember that part of it. The Japs could speak English, some of them. The Japs said they were not at war with the Norwegians, so they didn't take them. There were some American ships that they had captured and put on that supply ship that was at the dock. There was one American ship could do eighteen knots, but she stood and fought [and was captured]. There was a British ship that nearly brought down the seaplane. The British, Canadians, Australians [the Japanese kept as prisoners]. They put us in lorry trucks and took us to the Japanese prison camp at Kawasaki, maybe ten or fifteen miles. Kawasaki's in between Tokyo and Yokohama.

I guess there was around two hundred [prisoners], a mixture of merchant men, Americans, Chinese, Indians, Hong Kong fellas. There was only two of us [Canadians] in my camp. When the Italians gave up in Singapore, the Japs brought them to the mainland and brought them in our camp [Kawasaki Camp 1.B] and they beat them for givin' up. See, the Japs never took any prisoners; with them, they weren't supposed to be a prisoner of war, suicide was their motto. We were just the same as the army fellas, there was no difference. I walked by a Jap one time in the hallway

Kawasaki Prison Camp 1.B, Honshu Island, Japan. Pictured is the central hallway with bunking areas down both sides.

and I didn't bow to him. He laid off and let me have it with his fist. We didn't have too much dealings with civilians, only with the ones we worked with on the railroad and they didn't seem too bad. Women used to spit at us and throw rocks.

There was eight of us in a room. Bedbugs, geez, still smell 'em. They'd drop from the bunk above you. You'd be sittin' down eatin' your meal and little bedbugs crawl up your legs. Bedbug-infested mats [to sleep on], a canvas round pillow with sawdust in it. The last six months there was only one person that slept inside and I guess he had no feelings and the bugs were all over him, but we couldn't. I had lice and they took my clothes and put them in the steamin' barrel outside. My head was always shaved. The Japs used to bathe just about every day. I think it [the bathtub] was about four feet wide and about eight feet long. After the Japs had already bathed that was the bathtub for two hundred people. It was the Japs, then the [POW] officers and then us. The way it is, you wash yourself down first with a little wooden bucket of water and then you crawl into this tub.

There was no medicine whatsoever. We had army doctors, but the doctors had nothin'. They set a guy's leg, one fellow got a broken leg, and you could hear his scream from one end of the hall to the other. There was seven of us got sick all at once and they put us in a separate room. Some of them weren't as bad as I was. I know I messed myself and all that stuff; kind of horrible. The yard was just full of human waste [from dysentery], you had to hopscotch the yard. I still got scars from open sores up my arms from malnutrition.

I stole a pair of gloves and got beat up for it. The Japanese all wore white army gloves when they dressed up; I guess the things were only worth five cents. They come in straw bags. I don't know why I wanted to steal them, I don't know, I had no reason; I couldn't wear them. First thing you know, the soldiers come after me and pounded the living lights out of me. I got sick after that and was sick for about a month, spewing up worms and stuff like that. Some of the guys said they didn't think I'd make it. Two of these British friends of mine that worked on the railroad stole some tangerines and gave them to me. That's what brought up the worms so I got better.

Food? Well, it wasn't very good, just enough to exist on. First went in there, thought they were giving us a real treat, a hot dog bun was our meal with watery soup. One time they had pumpkin vines [in the soup] but they'd put those great big horseradishes in there. Rice, curry and rice, and one time they gave us soya beans but they were only half cooked. We got meals three times a day; course, we were working men. Somebody's pig got loose and they [the Japanese]

"There was eight of us in a room. Bed bugs, geez, still smell 'em. They'd drop from the bunk above you."

captured that and killed it and they sent the bones over to us in the camp. But there was nothin' on the bones at all [so they ate the marrow]. There was supposed to be fish for the prisoners, but they'd eat off it till it got bad then it'd go in our soup. The water was good.

I worked for one Chinaman [in the kitchen]. He killed a chicken for the Japs and kept the blood and cooked the blood up. He was smart wasn't he? Sure, blood pudding. Everything there came in these little straw bags and all you had to do was put your hand in. The only egg I ever had was a stolen egg. This Scotch friend of mine was working on a cargo of eggs. He called me up and he says, "Get down in the corner, I got an egg for you." He punched a couple of holes in it and I sucked the egg out of it. The name of the game was you steal everything you could get your hands on as far as eating. We had some engineers in there, American engineers, and they got to making these electric hot plates. The fellas used to wear two pair of pants when they went to the railroad and they'd tie the inside pair of pants. They'd put their flour or rice down inside these pants, then at night we'd bring it back in and make dough boys or somethin'. The Japs couldn't figure out why all the fuses were being blown. They caught them eventually. Stand outside all night with a bucket of water over your head; if you let it down they'd bat you. Punishment like that. This didn't happen to me, but it happened to different ones.

Before breakfast they'd roll call us. The American officer, Commander Newman, came around with the Japanese officer and we'd have to number off in Japanese. I can still do that [his number was 138]. At 8:30 they came around and counted you again at night. I don't know how many guards we had, maybe ten of them, I guess. We weren't goin' anywhere; we didn't look like them. They rotated them off and on. We had some of them that were in the China war and got wounded. When a shipment of candy came into the railroad station, they'd have this guy up there, he had one arm, one leg and I guess one eye, he was really beat up in the Chinese war. He was guardin' the candy.

You'd work two weeks and get one day off and that was to wash your clothes, clean up. I worked on the railroad carrying bags of rice, bags of charcoal, shovellin' coal, cement. This was just a local [spur] for Kawasaki, the one that goes from Tokyo to Yokohama. We'd march, I'd think it would be, about two miles there and back every day. They had us down to the shipyards a couple of times. [Others worked in factories or the mountain tin mines.] We'd at least put in eight hours or more, maybe ten hours. No breaks; lunch, that's all. A little cup of rice, that's all. When we first went into that place there was a guy there loadin' up these buckets to clean out the septic thing. Holes in the floor and you just squat. They had big steel bowls and every once in awhile they had to dip 'em out with ladles and put them in buckets. They use it for gardening, human waste. One time there they made all the officers clean them out; just being mean. They weren't supposed to do any work at all, but most of them worked.

I learned how to sew. I'm pretty good with a sewin' needle patchin' up my pants and stuff life that. You take a dishcloth and put a string on the end of it and tie it around your belly; that's all there was for underwear. And for clothes it was army clothes from Hong Kong. They used to give us grass raincoats, straw hats; looked like a bunch of monkeys. Worked in the rain, come home soakin' wet and laid down in your wet clothes.

We got five Red Cross parcels the whole time we were there [three years]. Got one a year the first couple of years, at Christmas time, which was a blessing. Most of them came after the war eased off when the Japs started to surrender here and there. Very little mail. The first couple of years we didn't write any letters, weren't allowed, but the first of the third year maybe we were allowed to write a few; only allowed to put twenty-five words on it. [It was] a year after I was captured [before my parents found out what had happened]. You get to the point where you didn't care one way or the other. There was a fella that died of melancholy in there at the first of the war, a very young fella too.

Greetings from home written on the reverse side of a postcard could be no longer than twenty-five words.

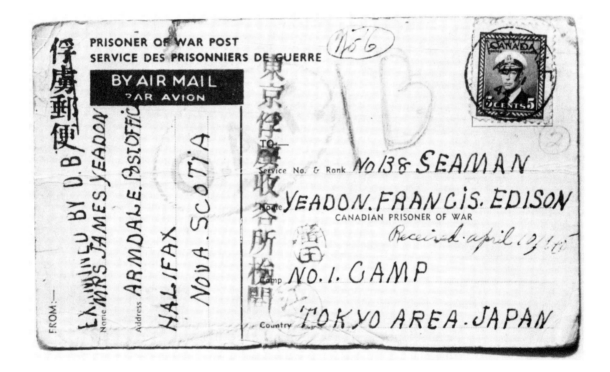

I guess the biggest fire in the world was Tokyo and Yokohama when they fire-bombed it. They sent us out to the paddy fields. You could see them droppin' incendiaries not too far away but they seemed to stay clear of the camp. It was just like small tornadoes; you would see the houses going up. Their houses over there were quarter-inch wood and dry so they were just like matchboxes. That was some fire. Next mornin' you could look as far as you could see and you wouldn't see a house. A little bit later, I guess, they dropped the atomic bomb.

The only reason I'm here is because of the atomic bomb, I'm sure of that. Killed a lot of people, but it saved a lot of people too. They'd have killed us, because they were always out there with those damned swords practicing, bamboo swords. They were to execute all prisoners of war if the Americans invaded. That was in the war documents.

Kawasaki, Prison Camp 1.B, Honshu Island, Japan. At war's end, prisoners painted PW on the rooftop so Allied planes would drop food.

When the war ended, the airplanes off the aircraft carriers came over. There were some of the pilots in there from Guam and those places in our camp and they got up on the roof and started flaggin' 'em down and they come down with their wheels down about thirty or forty feet off the top of the camp. They put PW [prisoner of war] on the roof so the airplanes would drop food and stuff.

What's his name [MacArthur] said, "Send all prisoners of war to the beaches," so they put us in a truck and took us down to the wharves. The Americans sent in landing barges and took us out to a destroyer. They gave us ice cream and hot dogs. The first white nurse on the hospital ship, you'd be surprised what that does to a person. I don't know what kind of a feelin' comes over you, but you haven't seen a white woman in almost four years;

it's not a feelin' that you want to touch her or anything. It just gives you such a lift it's unbelievable. We left Yokohama when they were signing the peace treaty. They took us down to the Philippines and we had to fill out whatever happened in the prison camp and stuff like that. We had new clothes, but the bombers dropped those. I did get a hundred dollars for a suit and I got a dollar a day for being in a prison camp, compensation. And my wages were cut off as soon as the boat was missing.

I had my twenty-first birthday on an American troop ship. I spent my teenage years [as a POW], five months with the Germans and three years with the Japanese. You know, the merchant seamen were at war as soon as they left the Halifax Harbour. All these army fellows, they come back and they got good jobs. I think they were jealous of the merchant seamen because they went over on these big passenger ships that travelled thirty knots and the submarines couldn't catch them. They saw the merchant men on them and they figured, oh, they're havin' a good time and they can do what they like and all this and that. But when you get on one of those tramps you're just a target for the submarines. They didn't realize if it hadn't been for the merchant navy there wouldn't be any England now. I don't think there would be.

"Few knew the colossal tasks these unsung heroes achieved. They were overshadowed by the epics of fighting men who had done no more and probably less. Only their families really knew. If they came home—which thousands failed to do—they soon had to go out again and face the same conditions. We navy men did not go through the torments they did, nor did the other fighting services. A merchant seaman could fortify himself with nothing but hope and courage. Most of them must have been very afraid, not for days and nights but for months and years. Who is the greater hero, the man who performs great deeds by swift action against odds he hardly has time to recognize, or the man who lives for long periods in constant, nagging fear of death, yet carries on?"

— Alan Easton (*50 North: An Atlantic Battleground*)

Two merchant survivors from a torpedoed ship who were picked up by HMCS *Ottawa*. A few hours after this photo was taken, the *Ottawa* was torpedoed with a loss of 114 men. What was their fate?

PHOTO CREDITS

INTRODUCTION

p-3   Neg #13365, Maritime Museum of the Atlantic, Halifax, N.S.
p-11   Royal Canadian Legion Somme Branch, Dartmouth, N.S.
p-12   Neg #14258, Maritime Museum of the Atlantic, Halifax, N.S.
p-17   Neg #19912, D.N.D. photo: courtesy Maritime Museum of the Atlantic, Halifax, N.S.
p-18   U.S. Navy photo: taken from *Canadians at War 1939-45.*

CHAPTER 1

p-24   PA 134327, National Archives of Canada.
p-25   PA 105297, National Archives of Canada.
p-27   Beaton Institute, Eachdraidh Archives, University College of Cape Breton.
p-32   #602-B, E.A. Bollinger Collection, Public Archives of N.S., Halifax, N.S.
p-34   PA 105675, National Archives of Canada.
p-53   D.N.D. photo: courtesy Captain Jack Matthews.
p-58   D.N.D. photo: from *Canadians at War 1939-45.*

CHAPTER 2

p-63   Neg #15634, Maritime Museum of the Atlantic, Halifax, N.S.
p-66   Courtesy Captain Jack Matthews.
p-72   D.N.D. photo: from *Canadians at War 1939-45.*
p-78   N-7466, H.B. Jefferson Collection, Public Archives of N.S., Halifax, N.S.
p-82   Neg #8956, Captain Mike Harrity Collection, Maritime Museum of the Atlantic, Halifax, N.S.
p-89   80-G-405291, U.S. Navy National Archives, Courtesy George Evans.
p-98   From *Victory in the St. Lawrence: Canada's Unknown War.*
p-104   Courtesy Roland Pickering.
p-108   Courtesy Gordon Hardy.
p-112   Courtesy Gordon Hardy.
p-116   Courtesy Gordon Hardy.
p-120   Royal Canadian Legion Somme Branch, Dartmouth, N.S.
p-125   Courtesy Eugene Wilkie.
p-130   Neg #18528, Maritime Museum of the Atlantic, Halifax, N.S.
p-134   Neg #9479, Mike Harrity Collection, Maritime Museum of the Atlantic, Halifax, N.S.
p-137   N-19911, Canadian National Steamship Photo, Courtesy Maritime Museum of the Atlantic, Halifax, N.S.
p-147   Courtesy Aubrey Jeffries.
p-153   D.N.D photo: from *Canadians at War 1939-45.*

CHAPTER 3

p-169   Courtesy Michael Ness.
p-180   Neg #8532, Maritime Museum of the Atlantic, Halifax, N.S.
p-187   Radio Times Hulton Picture Library (from Time/Life Books).

p-190   PA 105943, National Archives of Canada.

p-197   From *Victory in the St. Lawrence: Canada's Unknown War*.

p-201   Fox Photos Ltd., London (from Time/Life Books).

p-207   Courtesy Aubrey Jeffries.

p-214   U.S. Navy Dept. National Archives (from Time/Life Books).

p-216   Courtesy Doug Bell.

p-226   Neg #15745, Maritime Museum of the Atlantic, Halifax, N.S.

p-232   Neg #11554, Maritime Museum of the Atlantic, Halifax, N.S.

p-235   Courtesy Robert Bradstock.

p-244   80-G-450625, U.S. Navy Dept. Naval Archives, Courtesy George Evans.

p-247   Courtesy Bud Purcell.

p-252   Neg #13382, Maritime Museum of the Atlantic, Halifax, N.S.

p-253   Courtesy Norman Rees-Potter.

p-259   D.N.D. photo: from *Canadians at War 1939-45*.

p-261   Courtesy George Evans.

p-264   Imperial War Museum photo (from *Victory in the St. Lawrence: Canada's Unknown War*).

p-266   Courtesy George Evans.

p-270   Courtesy George Evans.

CHAPTER 4

p-287   D.N.D. photo: from *Victory in the St. Lawrence: Canada's Unknown War*.

p-300   Courtesy Preston Ross.

p-311   Courtesy Clyde Getson.

p-312   Courtesy Clyde Getson.

p-322   Courtesy Edison Yeadon.

p-323   Courtesy Edison Yeadon.

p-325   Courtesy Edison Yeadon.

p-326   Courtesy Edison Yeadon.

EPILOGUE

p-328   PA 116455, National Archives of Canada.

END NOTES

INTRODUCTION

1. Allan Harvie, as told to C.V. Tench, *Star Weekly*, March 27, 1943.
2. Tony German, *The Sea is at Our Gates: The History of the Canadian Navy* (Toronto: McClelland & Stewart, 1990).
3. *The Canadians at War, 1939-45,* Vol. 1, Readers Digest Association (Canada), 1969.
4. Winston S. Churchill, *Closing the Ring* (Boston: Houghton Mifflin, 1951).
5. *Battle of the Atlantic: 50th Anniversary (1943-1993)* (Liverpool, England: Brodie, 1993).
6. Joseph Schull, *Far Distant Ships: An Official Account of Canadian Naval Operations in World War II* (Toronto: Stoddart, 1987).
7. Barrie Pitt, *The Battle of the Atlantic* (Alexandria, Virginia: Time–Life, 1978).
8. Tony German.
9. The Royal Navy designated various convoy routes with prefixes, i.e., Russian-bound were PQ, later changed to JW; outbound from Halifax to U.K. were HX; inbound from U.K. were ONS; Sydney convoys were prefixed SC, meaning Sydney–Clyde, but came to be called Slow Convoy for ships incapable of meeting minimum nine-knot speeds.
10. Joseph Schull.
11. *Battle of the Atlantic: 50th Anniversary (1943-1993).*
12. Ibid.
13. Winston S. Churchill, *The Hinge of Fate* (Boston: Houghton Mifflin, 1950).
14. Ministry of Information, *Merchantmen at War* (London: His Majesty's Stationery Office, 1944).
15. *The Tools of War, 1939-45* (Montreal: Reader's Digest [Canada], 1969).
16. Winston S. Churchill, *Closing the Ring.*
17. Joseph Schull.
18. *Battle of the Atlantic: 50th Anniversary (1943-1993).*
19. Ibid.
20. Winston S. Churchill, *Closing the Ring.*
21. Joseph Schull.
22. Tony German.
23. Gordon J. Brackett, *It Was Almost Too Late*, from the first report of the Standing Committee on National Defence, Ottawa.

24. The number forty-five comes from Tony German's book, *The Sea is at Our Gates: The History of the Canadian Navy.* By comparison, a considerably smaller figure of twenty-four is given by Captain Earle Wagner of Halifax. Captain Wagner conducted extensive research on Canada's wartime merchant losses for a memorial that was dedicated on November 11, 1993, at Halifax's Sackville Landing. Only ships positively identified through archival sources were included, a number that also omits those from Newfoundland, which during both world wars was a British colony and not a part of Canada. By his own admission, Captain Wagner recognizes that discrepancies exist, in large measure as a result of the lack and ambiguousness of records and that, over time, historians may well change his and other's findings, not only in relation to the number of ships lost but also the number of merchant seamen.

25. *Battle of the Atlantic: 50th Anniversary (1943-1993).*

26. S.C. Heal, *Conceived in War, Born in Peace: Canada's Deep Sea Merchant Marine* (Vancouver: Cordilleran, 1992).

27. Tony German.

28. *Canadians Serving Canadians* (Dartmouth, N.S.: Palm Communications, October/November 1992).

29. Ibid.

30. Tony German.

31. James B. Lamb, *On the Triangle Run* (Toronto: Totem Books, 1987).

32. David Howarth, *Sovereign of the Seas: The Story of Britain & the Sea* (New York: Atheneum, 1974).

CHAPTER 1

1. Paul Brick interview, Dartmouth, N.S., 1991.

2. Lionel Chevrier, *Canada's Merchant Seamen* (Ottawa: Edmond Cloutier, 1945).

3. Navy League of Canada, *Navy League Merchant Seamen's Club*, brochure.

4. Lionel Chevrier.

5. Eric W. Sager, *Ships & Memories* (Vancouver: U.B.C. Press, 1993).

6. *The Canadians at War, 1939-45,* Vol. 1 (Montreal: Reader's Digest Association [Canada], 1969).

7. *Esso Mariners: A History of Imperial Oil's Fleet Operations from 1899-1980* (Toronto: Imperial Oil, 1980).

8. Jack MacBeth, *Ready, Aye, Ready* (Toronto: Key Porter Books, 1989).

9. There was a training facility for Norwegian merchant and naval personnel in Lunenburg, Nova Scotia, during the war known as "Camp Norway"; the air force counterpart in Ontario was called "Little Norway." Chester provided R&R conveniences for the Norwegians.

10. The largest convoy of the war comprised 167 ships and sailed across the Atlantic on July 17, 1944, escorted by Canadian warships. It met no opposition.

11. An informative account of the Naval Control Service can be found in Frederick B. Watt, *In All Respects Ready* (Toronto: Totem, 1986).

12. War risk bonus was danger money added to the basic wage of merchant seamen. It could vary depending upon the country. Canada paid a war risk bonus of $13.12 in 1940 and had raised it to $44.50 by 1944.

13. After Captain Brick's interview in 1991, he and others conducted research while attending the Battle of the Atlantic 50th Anniversary celebrations in England during 1993, finding more names of Canadian merchant seamen lost during the conflict. A more recent estimate of losses would put it at approximately one in eight, higher still.

14. More than one thousand men went to the navy from merchant ships. Sixty-five came from Imperial Oil ships, twenty-four of whom were officers and engineers whose role it was to train naval personnel in engine room and deck procedures.

15. Another merchant seaman told of having to cut lines at night one time while standing guard when Arab intruders tried to scale the ship's sides.

16. More than 14,000 tons of bombs were dropped on Malta. During the first seven months of 1942, only ten of thirty merchant vessels broke through enemy blockades to reach the island. Submarines were used at one point to transport in 65,000 tons of goods, which were hurriedly unloaded by 15,000 dock workers. The most important convoy to sail the Mediterranean during the war was code-named Pedestal. During August 1942, fourteen merchant vessels carrying food, ammunition and gas–and escorted by two battleships, three carriers, seven cruisers, and twenty-four destroyers–fought through a German and Italian gauntlet of six hundred planes and twenty-one submarines. The mission was a "success," although nine merchant ships and four naval vessels were sunk.

17. Nicknamed "Chase Me Charlies," glider bombs were defeated by the electric razor. British scientists discovered that if electric razors were plugged in on board ships during attacks, the radio frequencies guiding the bombs were disrupted, causing loss of control. Throughout the war Allied scientists out-dueled their enemy counterparts, and the winning of the Battle of the Atlantic has been credited in large measure to this scientific victory.

18. In the Mediterranean, Italian navy special assault units were responsible for sinking or disabling 131,527 tons of merchant ships and 86,000 tons of Allied warships, a total of twenty-eight vessels.

19. Not all U-boats were lost to depth charges; most were "killed" from the air. Regardless of how, the numbers are sobering. The Kriegsmarine lost approximately 780 of 860 U-boats. Entombed with them were thirty thousand submariners out of a force of forty thousand. This 75 percent loss ratio was the highest by far for either side.

20. St. Margaret's was a temporary training facility to meet wartime needs for cadet officers for merchant ships. Attendance was not mandatory to become an officer. In fact many acquired their tickets or certificates by combining sea time with leaves for courses.

CHAPTER 2

1. Michael Gannon, *Operation Drumbeat* (New York: Harper & Row, 1990).

2. Winston S. Churchill, *The Hinge of Fate* (Boston: Houghton Mifflin, 1950).

3. Homer H. Hickam, Jr., *Torpedo Junction* (New York: Dell, 1989).

4. The issue of who was paid more has raged for years. Merchant seamen who sailed aboard American or Swedish-flagged vessels were without a doubt compensated much better than their counterparts sailing on other Allied ships when all bonuses are taken into account. Comparing the RCN and Canadian Merchant Marine, a report of the Subcommittee on Veterans Affairs of the Standing Senate Committee on Social Affairs, Science and Technology, entitled "It's Almost Too Late" (1991) states on page 7 that "no MN [Merchant Navy] officer under the rank of captain or chief engineer received as much pay as the RCN [Royal Canadian Navy] equivalent, even in 1944, and that the 1940 rates for all MN ratings were much lower than RCN rates until 1944."

5. Imperial Oil was one of the largest employers of merchant seamen during the war. In addition to their own fleet of ships and some American-owned, Panamanian-flagged tankers they managed during the early U.S. neutrality period, they also operated and manned thirteen of nineteen Canadian government-built Park tankers.

6. The article to which Mr. Duncan refers appeared in the *Daily News* on February 5, 1991 (page 3) and raised the ire of many merchant veterans. One particularly incensed veteran wrote a letter on February 23, 1991, to the Minister of Veterans Affairs in which he makes many references to the alleged remark, venting his anger in one passage by stating that the quoted defence department spokesman "apparently believes people like me (in the bowels of a ship off Iceland for instance) were worse than terrrorists, who believe in something; we were mercenaries—people who believe in nothing but money."

7. Merchant ships were indeed used as bait. By 1943 the Allies were willing to trade two merchant ships for every U-boat sunk. Heavily defended merchant convoys were intentionally sent into dangerous waters to lure the U-boats into attacking, thereby making themselves vulnerable to improved anti-submarine forces.

8. The incident to which Eric Publicover refers could quite possibly be that of the five Sullivan brothers, who were all lost when a Japanese submarine torpedoed the U.S. cruiser *Juneau* on November 13, 1942, during the Battle of Guadalcanal.

9. Graham Metson, *An East Coast Port: Halifax at War, 1939-45* (Toronto: McGraw-Hill Ryerson, 1981).

10. The *Trongate* crew was considered the "toughest, fightingest crew" to enter Halifax during the war. An example was one crew member who, on being ejected from a seamen's hostel, bit a policeman on the hand causing blood poisoning, then went to a dance where he had both jaws broken in a fight, only to return the next night ready to scrap again with his assailant. The crew of the *George Washington* were a close second to the *Trongate,* but the *Trongate* seamen were considered tougher in fighting circles because they used their fists only, whereas the *George Washington* battlers were nicknamed "the razor men."

11. Apparently not all the ammunition was recovered. The Halifax *Chronicle-Herald* dated Thursday, September 2, 1993, carried an article about a possible ban on diving and anchoring near the *Trongate* site when navy divers recovered forty-two large shells a week earlier, believed to be from the ill-fated British freighter.

12. Some parts of Pierre Simard's account have been taken from an article he wrote for the November 9, 1984, Maritime Command newspaper *Trident.*

13. Historical accounts show the belief that U-boats machine-gunned hapless merchant crews in the water or lifeboats to be for the most part untrue. On the contrary, many German submariners showed genuine concern for the safety of merchant survivors. At least one known exception was a U-boat which tried to murder the survivors from the Greek ship *Peleus.* Its senior officers were subsequently tried at Nuremburg and executed.

14. A number of luxury liners were requisitioned to transport troops. The *Queen Elizabeth, Queen Mary, Aquitania, Mauritania, Andes, Empress of Japan,* and *Empress of Canada* were a few of the better known. In 1942 the British turned her two Queens over to the United States to use in their best interests, with the British government picking up all operational costs. This was in some measure compensation for the U.S. Lend-Lease Act.

Each was capable of carrying, after alterations, fifteen thousand troops in summer and ten thousand in winter. By war's end these two alone had ferried a million and a half soldiers.

CHAPTER 3

1. Ronald Bailey, *The Home Front: U.S.A.* (Alexandria, Va.: Time-Life, 1978).

2. Barry Broadfoot, *Six War Years, 1939-1945: Memories of Canadians at Home and Abroad* (Don Mills, Ont.: Paperjacks, 1976).

3. J.L. Granatstein and Desmond Morton, *A Nation Forged in Fire: Canadians and the Second World War* (Toronto: Lester & Orpen Dennys, 1989).

4. Gordon J. Brackett, "It Was Almost Too Late," (First report of the Standing Committee on National Defence, Ottawa).

5. *Battle of the Atlantic: 50th Anniversary (1943-1993)* (Liverpool, England: Brodie, 1993).

6. George H. Evans, *Through the Gates of Hell* (Antigonish, N.S.: Formac, 1980).

7. Richard Collier, *The War in the Desert* (Alexandria, Va.: Time-Life, 1977).

8. Robert Wallace, *The Italian Campaign* (Alexandria, Va.: Time-Life, 1978).

9. Douglas Botting, *The Second Front* (Alexandria, Va.: Time-Life, 1978).

10. Joseph Schull, *Far Distant Ships: An Official Account of Canadian Naval Operations in World War II* (Toronto: Stoddart, 1987).

11. William Joyce, alias Lord Haw Haw, was an American-born "British turncoat" who broadcast German propaganda from Berlin during the war. He was captured, tried and executed in 1946.

12. The Swedish freighter *Stureholm*, after returning the survivors to Halifax, was torpedoed in mid-ocean on December 12 and went down with all hands.

13. Degaussing was the Allied counter to the German magnetic mine. It involved wrapping an electrically charged cable around a ship, which neutralized the magnetic attraction between mine and steel hull. When the Germans developed the acoustic mine, the Allies countered again with an electrically driven hammer fitted to a ship's bow that produced a noise that caused a mine to explode prematurely. The first mines, contact mines, were countered by towing paravanes on each side of the ship that hooked the moored mines, cut them loose and allowed them to float to the surface where they were destroyed by gunfire.

14. Sixteen hundred Canadians served as DEMS gunners during World

War II. Unlike the merchant seamen who also manned guns, they were afforded full veteran status following the war.

15. One of the main reasons for victory in the Battle of the Atlantic was that United States shipyards could build vessels faster than the Germans could sink them. The U.S. itself lost more than eight hundred merchant ships. By 1943, 1.5 million workers were producing 140 Liberty-class ships a month. The mastermind behind the program was American Henry J. Kaiser, whose prefab components allowed a Liberty ship to be built in ten days or less.

16. Ham-slicing machines ran twenty-four hours a day and breakfast required thirty thousand boiled eggs. Soldiers were given sandwiches when leaving the dining room to tide them over until the next meal, twelve hours later. Officers fared better, of course, receiving waiter-served, four-course meals in Cabin Class.

17. The story of Russian-bound convoy PQ-17 is a truly tragic one, recounted in many books. Another example of using merchant vessels as bait, the British Admiralty has been accused of botching this attempt to lure German battleships out of hiding in Norway by prematurely ordering the convoy to scatter, leaving it devoid of escort cover and at the mercy of German planes and submarines. It was slaughter, with twenty-three of thirty-seven ships going down, most of them American.

18. After waiting fifty years, George Evans finally received his medal in April 1993 when the Netherlands government sent the cross and two clasps to him in the mail with a note which read in part, "[While it is] formally no longer possible to award you the War Remembrance Cross...due to the fact that you rendered your service to the Netherlands Merchant Navy in the Second World War in an excellent way...I have decided to make an exception" (Halifax *Chronicle-Herald*, May 1, 1993).

CHAPTER 4

1. Ronald H. Bailey, *Prisoners of War* (Alexandria, Va.: Time-Life, 1981).
2. Ibid.
3. Ibid.
4. Ibid.
5. Daniel G. Dancocks, *In Enemy Hands* (Toronto: McClelland & Stewart, 1990).
6. Ronald H. Bailey.
7. Daniel G. Dancocks.
8. *Canadians Serving Canadians* (Dartmouth, N.S.: Palm Communications, October/November 1992).

9. *Impact of the Merchant Navy & Civilian War-Related Benefits Act*, Canadian Merchant Navy Prisoner of War Association, January 16, 1993.

10. Ten German armed merchant raiders sailed during the war, in the Atlantic, Pacific, Indian Ocean, Arctic and Antarctic. Heavily armed converted freighters disguised as friendly merchant ships, they sank 130 Allied or neutral vessels between 1940 and 1943, totalling more than 850,000 tons. *Atlantis* was the most successful, accounting for twenty-two ships. Other raiders were *Orion, Widder, Thor, Pinquin, Komet, Kormoran, Michel, Stier* and *Togo*. All but two were hunted down and sunk. Two others, the *Hansa* and *Coburg,* were outfitted as raiders but never sent to sea.

11. Mr. Ross has confused his San boats somewhat. According to an article in the *Toronto Star Weekly* of April 10, 1943, it was the *San Alberto* which broke in half after being torpedoed in December 1939. Some of her crew did indeed try to sail one-half of the ship back to England but gave up after a few days and were taken off by a destroyer. The *San Demetrio*, part of the infamous *Jervis Bay* convoy, was gutted by fire and explosion after being shelled by the *Admiral Sheer,* yet her crew did return aboard and bring her back to England.

12. *Canadolite* was renamed the *Sudetenland* and in 1944 was sunk by the RAF while bombing Brest; *Kormoran* was sunk by the Australian cruiser *Sydney* in November 1941 off western Australia.

13. The American Red Cross provided 28 million packages to almost 1.5 million Allied POWs. Of these, 115,000 were American. In fact the American Red Cross handled all but British [Commonwealth] POWs. In total, 200,000 tons of food, clothing and medicine were packaged. Each parcel weighed exactly eleven pounds and measured ten inches square by four and a half inches deep to meet German postal regulations. Each American and British POW was to receive one parcel a week; other Allied POWs were to get one a month. Russia refused to allow German POWs to receive Red Cross parcels, so the Germans reciprocated when dealing with Russian POWs. Very few Red Cross parcels made it into the hands of POWs held by the Japanese.

SOURCE REFERENCES

CHAPTER 1

1. Paul Brick, Dartmouth, Nova Scotia, p. 22
2. Charles Macauley, Nanaimo, British Columbia, p. 45
3 Arthur Curren, Halifax, Nova Scotia, p. 51

CHAPTER 2

1. Earle Wagner, Halifax, Nova Scotia, p. 62
2. Jack Matthews, Dartmouth, Nova Scotia, p. 66
3. Bruce Duncan, Dartmouth, Nova Scotia, p. 76
4. Jim Boutilier, Dartmouth, Nova Scotia, p. 81
5. Paul Fralic, West LaHave, Nova Scotia, p. 84
6. Doug Oxner, Lunenburg, Nova Scotia, p. 85
7. Henry Kohler, Lunenburg, Nova Scotia, p. 87
8. Eric Publicover, Windsor Junction, Nova Scotia, p. 92
9. Harold Sperry, Pleasantville, Nova Scotia, p. 96
10. Donald Mosher, Halifax, Nova Scotia, p. 97
11. Elbert Coldwell, Dartmouth, Nova Scotia, p. 100
12. Roland Pickering, Seaview, Prince Edward Island, p. 104
13. Ernest Pike, Summerside, Prince Edward Island, p. 106
14. Gordon Hardy, Ingonish, Nova Scotia, p. 108
15. Pierre Simard, Halifax, Nova Scotia, p. 113
16. Gordon Troke, North Sydney, Nova Scotia, p. 118
17. Doug Bauld, Dartmouth, Nova Scotia, p. 119
18. Ralph Kelly, Milton, Nova Scotia, p. 122
19. Eugene Wilkie, West LaHave, Nova Scotia, p. 124
20. John (Stan) McKenzie, Yarmouth, Nova Scotia, p. 129
21. Aubrey Jeffries, Dartmouth, Nova Scotia, p. 132

CHAPTER 3

1. Warren Stevens, Port Medway, Nova Scotia, p. 155
2. Michael Ness, Summerside, Prince Edward Island, p. 160
3. Angus Campbell, Halifax, Nova Scotia, p. 163
4. Percey Lambert, Halifax, Nova Scotia, p. 168
5. Leandre Boudreau, Porters Lake, Nova Scotia, p. 173
6. Anonymous, p. 175
7. Bernard McCluskey, Dartmouth, Nova Scotia, p. 179
8. John Samson, Halifax, Nova Scotia, p. 183

CHAPTER 4

SELECTED BIBLIOGRAPHY

Bailey, Ronald H. *Prisoners of War*. Alexandria, Va.: Time-Life, 1981.

Bailey, Ronald H. *The Home Front: U.S.A.* Alexandria, Va.: Time-Life, 1978.

Behren, C.B.A. *Merchant Shipping and the Demands of War*. London: HMSO & Longmans Green, 1955.

Bethell, Nicholas. *Russia Besieged*. Alexandria, Va.: Time-Life, 1977.

Blond, Georges. *Ordeal Below Zero*. London: Mayflower Books, 1965.

Botting, Douglas. *The Second Front*. Alexandria, Va.: Time-Life, 1978.

Broadfoot, Barry. *Six War Years, 1939-1945: Memories of Canadians at Home and Abroad*. Don Mills, Ont.: Paperjacks, 1976.

Brookes, Ewart. *The Gates of Hell: The Terrible Story of the Arctic Convoys of the Second World War*. London: Arrow, 1973.

Busch, Harald. *U-Boats at War: German Submarines in Action, 1939-45*. New York: Ballantine, 1965.

Carse, Robert. *A Cold Corner of Hell*. New York: Modern Literary Editions, 1969.

Churchill, Winston S. *Closing the Ring*. Boston: Houghton Mifflin, 1951.

Churchill, Winston S. *The Gathering Storm*. Boston: Houghton Mifflin, 1948.

Churchill, Winston S. *The Hinge of Fate*. Boston: Houghton Mifflin, 1950.

Collier, Richard. *The War in the Desert*. Alexandria, Va.: Time-Life, 1977.

Cremer, Peter. *U-333: The Story of a U-Boat Ace*. London: Bodley Head, 1982.

Curry, Frank. *War at Sea: A Canadian Seaman on the North Atlantic*. Toronto: Lugus, 1990.

Dancocks, Daniel G. *In Enemy Hands*. Toronto: McClelland & Stewart, 1990.

Detmers, Theodor. *The Raider Kormoran*. London: Tandem, 1975.

Eade, Charles. *The Dawn of Liberation: War Speeches by the Right Hon. Winston S. Churchill*. Toronto: McClelland & Stewart, 1945.

Easton, Alan. *50 North: An Atlantic Battleground*. Markham, Ont.: Paperjacks, 1980.

Edwards, Bernard. *They Sank the Red Dragon*. Cardiff, Wales: GPC Books, 1987.

Edwards, Peter. *Waterfront Warlord: The Life & Violent Times of Hal C. Banks*. Toronto: McClelland-Bantam (Seal Books), 1988.

Essex, James W. *Victory in the St. Lawrence: Canada's Unknown War*. Erin, Ont.: The Boston Mills, 1984.

Esso Mariners. A History of Imperial Oil's Fleet Operations from 1899-1980. Toronto: Imperial Oil, 1980.

Evans, George H. *Through the Gates of Hell*. Antigonish: Formac, 1980.

Gannon, Michael. *Operation Drumbeat*. New York: Harper & Row, 1990.

Gentile, Gary. *Track of the Gray Wolf: U-Boat Warfare on the U.S. Eastern Seaboard, 1942-1945*. New York: Avon, 1989.

German, Tony. *The Sea is at Our Gates: The History of the Canadian Navy.* Toronto: McClelland & Stewart, 1990.

Granatstein, J.L., and Desmond Morton. *A Nation Forged in Fire: Canadians and the Second World War.* Toronto: Lester & Orpen Dennys, 1989.

Hadley, Michael L. *U-Boats Against Canada: German Submarines in Canadian Waters.* Montreal: McGill-Queens University Press, 1985.

Hadley, Michael L., and Roger Sarty. *Tin-Pots & Pirate Ships: Canadian Navy Forces & German Sea Raiders, 1880-1918.* Montreal: McGill-Queens University Press, 1991.

Hanington, Felicity. *The Lady Boats: Life & Times of Canada's West Indies Merchant Fleet.* Halifax: Canadian Marine Transportation Centre, 1980.

Hansson, Per. *One in Ten Had to Die.* George Allen & Unwin, 1970.

Hay, Doddy. *War Under the Red Ensign: The Merchant Navy, 1939-45.* London: Jane's, 1982.

Heal, S.C. *Conceived in War, Born in Peace: Canada's Deep Sea Merchant Marine.* Vancouver, B.C.: Cordillera, 1992.

Hickam, Homer H. *Torpedo Junction: U-Boat War Off America's East Coast, 1942.* New York: Dell, 1989.

Hope, Ronald. *The Merchant Navy.* London: Stanford Maritime, 1980.

Horton, Edward. *The Illustrated History of the Submarine.* London: Sidgwick & Jackson, 1974.

Hough, Richard. *The Longest Battle: The War at Sea, 1939-45.* London: Weidenfeld & Nicolson, 1986.

How, Douglas. *Night of the Caribou.* Hantsport: Lancelot, 1988.

Howarth, David. *Sovereign of the Seas: The Story of Britain & the Sea.* New York: Atheneum, 1974.

Hoyt, Edwin P. *Raider 16.* New York: Avon, 1970.

Irving, David. *The Destruction of Convoy PQ 17.* London: Granada, 1985.

Jones, Geoffrey. *Defeat of the Wolf Packs.* London: William Kimber, 1986.

Kaplan, William. *Everything That Floats: Pat Sullivan, Hal Banks and the Seamen's Unions of Canada.* Toronto: University of Toronto Press, 1987.

Kemp, Paul. *The Russian Convoys, 1941-1945.* Dorset, England: Arms & Armour, 1987.

Konings, Chris. *Queen Elizabeth at War: His Majesty's Transport, 1939-1946.* Wellington: Patrick Stephens, 1985.

Lacey, Robert. *The Queens of the North Atlantic.* New York: Stein & Day, 1976.

Lamb, James B. *On the Triangle Run.* Toronto: Macmillan (Canada), 1986.

Lamb, James B. *The Corvette Navy.* Toronto: Macmillan (Canada), 1977.

Lawrence, Hal. *A Bloody War: One Man's Memories of the Canadian Navy, 1939-45.* Toronto: Macmillan (Canada), 1979.

Lawrence, Hal. *Tales of the North Atlantic.* Toronto: McClelland & Stewart, 1985.

Leacock, Stephen. *Canada and the Sea*. Vol. 1. Montreal: Alvah M. Beatty, 1944.

Lund, Paul, and Harry Ludlam. *Night of the U-Boats*. London: New English Library, 1974.

Lynch, Thomas G. *Canada's Flowers: History of the Corvettes of Canada, 1939-1945*. Halifax: Nimbus, 1981.

MacBeth, Jack. *Ready, Aye, Ready*. Toronto: Key Porter Books, 1989.

Macksey, Kenneth. *Military Errors of World War Two*. Toronto: Stoddard, 1987.

Macpherson, Ken. *Frigates of the Royal Canadian Navy, 1943-1974*. St. Catherines, Ont.: Vanwel, 1989.

Mason, John T., Jr. *The Atlantic War Remembered: An Oral History Collection*. Annapolis, Md.: Naval Institute, 1990.

McNeil, Bill. *Voices of a War Remembered: An Oral History of Canadians in World War II*. Toronto: Doubleday Canada, 1991.

Metson, Graham. *An East Coast Port: Halifax at War, 1939-1945*. Toronto: McGraw-Hill Ryerson, 1981.

Middlebrook, Martin. *Convoy: The Battle for Convoys SC 122 and HX 229*. New York: Penguin, 1978.

Milner, Marc. *North Atlantic Run: The Royal Canadian Navy & the Battle for the Convoys*. Toronto: University of Toronto Press, 1985.

Ministry of Information. *Merchantmen at War*. London: His Majesty's Stationery Office, 1944.

Mitchell, W.H., and L.A. Sawyer. *The Oceans, the Forts and the Parks: Wartime Standard Ships*. Vol. 2. Liverpool: Galleon, 1966.

Moore, Arthur. *A Careless Word...A Needless Sinking*. Kings Point, N.Y.: American Merchant Marine Museum, 1983.

Morison, Samuel E. *The Two-Ocean War*. Toronto: Little Brown, 1963.

Moser, Don. *China–Burma–India*. Alexandria, Va.: Time-Life, 1978.

Newman, Samuel. *How to Survive as a Prisoner Of War*. Philadelphia: Franklin.

Pitt, Barrie. *The Battle of the Atlantic*. Alexandria, Va.: Time-Life, 1978.

Raddall, Thomas H. *Halifax: Warden of the North*. (Revised edition.) Toronto: McClelland & Stewart, 1971.

Roberts, Leslie. *Canada and the War at Sea*. Vol. 2. Montreal: Alvah M. Beatty, 1944.

Roskill, S.W. *A Merchant Fleet in War, 1939-1945*. London: Collins, 1962.

Rugg, Bob, and Arnold Hague. *Convoys to Russia, 1941-45*. Kendal, England: World Ship.

Sager, Eric W. *Ships & Memories*. Vancouver: U.B.C. Press, 1993.

Sawyer, L.A., and W.H. Mitchell. *The Liberty Ships*. Second edition. London: Lloyd's of London, 1985.

Sawyer, L.A., and W.H. Mitchell. *Victory Ships & Tankers*. Newton Abbot, U.K.: David & Charles, 1974.

Schull, Joseph. *Far Distant Ships: An Official Account of Canadian Naval Operations in World War II*. Toronto: Stoddart, 1987.

Shaw, John. *Red Army Resurgent*. Alexandria, Va.: Time-Life, 1979.

Ships of the Esso Fleet in W.W. II. New Jersey: Standard Oil, 1946.

Showell, Jak P. Mallmann. *U-Boat Command & The Battle of the Atlantic*. London: Conway Maritime, 1989.

Smith, Marilyn Gurney. *The King's Yard: An Illustrated History of the Halifax Dockyard*. Halifax: Nimbus, 1985.

Stephens, Patrick. *British Vessels Lost at Sea: 1914-18 & 1939-45*. Wellingborough, U.K.: Thorsons, 1988.

Tarrant, V.E. *The U-Boat Offensive, 1914-1945*. Annapolis, Md.: Naval Institute, 1989.

The Canadians at War, 1939-45. Vol. 1. Montreal: Reader's Digest (Canada), 1969.

The Tools of War, 1939-45. Montreal: Reader's Digest (Canada), 1969.

Wallace, Robert. *The Italian Campaign*. Alexandria, Va.: Time-Life, 1978.

Waters, John M. *Bloody Winter*. Annapolis, Md.: Naval Institute, 1984.

Watt, Frederick B. *In All Respects Ready*. Toronto: Totem, 1986.

Whipple, A.B.C. *The Mediterannean*. Alexandria, Va.: Time-Life, 1981.

Wolf Packs. Alexandria, Va.: Time-Life, 1989.

Woodward, David. *The Secret Raiders*. London: Nel, 1975.

Young, Peter. *Decisive Battles of World War II*. New York: Gallery, 1989.